The Convoluted Universe

Book One

By
Dolores Cannon

comprehend. Thus they often use words that are not correct English. They will make words out of the nearest nouns and verbs they can find in the subject's mind. However it is done, it works, and we can understand what they are trying to convey.

Dolores Cannon

SECTION ONE

The Search For The Prodigy

CHAPTER ONE
LINDA AND BARTHOLOMEW COME INTO MY LIFE

I initially intended to include Linda's story in *The Custodians*, but that book grew to such a size that I had to remove this section. The predestination of meeting and eventual working with Linda had many strange and unusual overtones. Our initial encounter was at my first lecture in Little Rock, Arkansas, in the summer of 1989. The first volume of *Conversations With Nostradamus* had been printed, and I was beginning the promotions by lecturing and doing booksignings in my own backyard, so to speak. After my lecture Linda was one of many people who bought a book and stood in line to get an autograph. As I signed her copy she handed me her business card and said if I ever wanted someone to work with, she would be available. She seemed self conscious and did not say any more at that time. Other people also gave me their cards, or wrote their names and contact information on pieces of paper. Some of their comments indicated they thought they had had UFO encounters. I made notes on these cards vowing to get back with them first, because I was conducting UFO investigations with Lou Farish in Arkansas at the time. I soon realized that it would be impossible to meet with all the others.

In the past I always tried to work with anyone who wanted a hypnotic past life regression, because I didn't know what importance it might have for them. After my first book was published, the bombardment began, and I soon realized that things would no longer be that simple. My life would never return to that slower paced normal style. There was no way I could meet and talk with all these people, let alone regress them. I assumed the majority of them were just curiosity seekers, looking for the experience rather than answers to problems in their lives. Putting the cards and pieces of paper in my purse, I fully intended to make a serious effort to contact them if it were at all possible. Linda's card was among these. I soon became caught up in too many events to get back with Linda and the others. At that time she was not an individual, but a blurred face in a crowd, one of many.

A few months later I returned to Little Rock for another lecture, and had my first session with Janice. I made a special effort to see her because she suspected she had a UFO experience, and I soon discovered that her case warranted further investigation. I arranged to work with her each time I made that long four hour drive to Little Rock. (The story of the amazing things we discovered were reported in *The Custodians*, and the second section of this book.)

By coincidence, I discovered that Linda was a friend of Janice's, and she said Linda was disappointed that I had never gotten back with her. I explained the situation to Janice: that I was being flooded with requests, which were now coming in by phone and letters. I had become very selective in choosing those I would have time to work with. Because Janice said Linda wanted very much to meet with me, I reluctantly scheduled an appointment during my next trip to Little Rock in the winter of 1989. I was reluctant because I knew I would be very busy. I had scheduled several sessions in addition to a lecture, and I knew from past experience there would also be people wanting to stay up all night to visit. Though worried I would overload myself with too many curiosity seekers, out of respect for Janice I agreed to see Linda. I certainly was not expecting anything to come from the session, most certainly not an ongoing relationship.

Every time I traveled to Little Rock I stayed with my friend, Patsy, and she allowed me to set up appointments for regressions at her house. There was always privacy because Patsy was at work. When Linda arrived we sat in Patsy's living room and talked. She was an attractive woman, probably in her 40s. Nicely dressed, her hair attractively arranged, she seemed not to be the type (if there is such a thing as a type) to want to explore past life regression. She was a business woman operating her own pet store. Most of her children were grown and had left home to pursue their own lives. Quiet and soft spoken, not the type to encourage idle dreaming or fantasizing, she led a busy full life.

When she heard about my first lecture she felt an overpowering impulse to attend, even though she did not really have that much interest in Nostradamus. She said she was excited on the night of the lecture, having a great air of expectancy, although she could not understand why. As she sat in the audience during the talk she told her husband that she had an uncontrollable urge to speak with me. Even though the urge was almost overpowering she hesitated to approach me. After the lecture she stood in the line of people waiting for autographs, debating whether or not she should say anything. She was afraid of how it would sound. Her husband encouraged her; saying that if she felt that strongly about it she should go ahead. But when the moment came she could only hand me her card and say she would like to work with me. Of course, she was unaware at that moment how many times I had heard that request that day. Our conversation was very brief and when she left the auditorium I put her card with the others in my purse. I forgot the incident until fate brought us together in Patsy's living room.

When I questioned Linda about her reasons for wanting to have the hypnotic regression, she could not tell me. She was not looking for the answer to any problem, nor curious about past lives. It was a compulsion that would not leave her alone, and she felt there was something she had to give me, but had absolutely no idea what it was. Because my work concerned Nostradamus she vaguely thought it might have something to do with him. I was already working with several people on the completion of that project, which resulted in two more volumes of *Conversations With Nostradamus.* I really didn't need a newcomer, especially one that lived four hours away. She had no knowledge of the other projects I was involved in, so was at a complete loss as to why she was there.

I sighed, thinking the regression would probably turn out to be a simple, mundane past life with no importance other than to her. I had conducted many of these during the past few days, and I was really not in the mood to do another. I was recovering from a sore throat and my energy had been low during the entire trip. Though tired, I knew I had to do the session for her sake. As we began I was expecting absolutely nothing, and was soon pleasantly surprised and taken completely offguard. It was another example of going into something with no expectations and discovering the stage was being set by forces beyond my control.

I used my normal hypnotic induction method that would place Linda in a past life. When she entered the scene her voice was so relaxed and quiet it was difficult to hear. I knew from experience that her voice would become louder as we talked. She saw leaves on the ground and knew she was in a forest, but was surprised to see that her body was that of a man. She was wearing boots that came to her knees and a long sleeved shirt. Her description was of a young man in his twenties with long brown wavy hair and a beard and mustache. His eyes were piercing blue. He was busy chopping wood in the forest near where he lived. This seemed to puzzle Linda. "I'm getting the feeling I don't really need to be doing this. Other people would do it for me. But I like to do it, because I'm alone and I like the feeling and the exhilaration of the work."

I suggested she see the place where she lived. "It's a castle, with a drawbridge, and flags flying on the top of the walls. My father is the king."

D: *Then you really don't need to be chopping wood, do you?*
L: No, but it's fun. It makes me feel good. (Quietly) People think I'm crazy.
D: *Why do they think that?*
L: Because I like to work. I do not like the life of the court. It is so superficial. When you work with your hands you feel a

sense of accomplishment that nothing else can give you.

His name was Bartholomew and he lived in the castle with his family, and many, many other people including servants. "It's quite a large community. They all live within the walls."

> D: *At least you don't get lonely, do you?*
> L: Oh, yes. They do not care about me. They do not know my interest for learning. They care not for knowledge. I'm happy in my own way.

The situation in his country was not peaceful. There was danger, and they had to stay close to the castle walls.

> L: The peasants want to riot. They are not treated very well. And so you cannot go outside without an escort.
> D: *What does your father think of the way the people are behaving?*
> L: It is his fault. He is not very kind. He does not try to help them. He only uses them for his benefit.
> D: *You said you were interested in knowledge. Do you have a certain type of knowledge that you like to study?*
> L: Yes. I like to study the stars. The universe. And that is why people think I am mad.

Of course, I was assuming he was talking about astronomy or astrology.

> D: *How do others perceive the stars in your time period?*
> L: As just twinkling little pieces of the moon.
> D: *Aren't there other people in your time that like to study the stars?*
> L: Only one. He is my friend.
> D: *Is he the one that helped you to learn these things?*
> L: Yes. He knows. He is not from here. But he is very old, and soon he will leave me.
> D: *But maybe he can pass on his knowledge.*
> L: Yes, that is what he is doing at this time. And it is a very big responsibility that I must carry when he leaves. Then it will be mine. I have to learn and pass it forward, so that it will not die and be lost. It must not be lost.
> D: *What type of knowledge of the stars is it?*
> L: It is the knowledge of the universe. All of God's creation, not just of this Earth. But of many, many, many universes, and stars that are so far away that we humans cannot even

conceive of where they are. This man that I study with has been to many places, and he has come here to gift me with this knowledge in the hopes that my mind will give it forward for the future people to come, so they will not be afraid.

D: *You said the old man came from somewhere else?*

L: Yes, he came from the Pleiades.

D: *He did?*

Now my interest was captured. This was not a simple regression.

D: *Where is that?*

I knew it was a star constellation formation, but I wanted to see what he would say.

L: It is ... in the Milky Way. Very far from here.

D: *Doesn't that seem impossible?*

L: No. He came here on a beam of light ... (puzzled) which is very hard for me to understand.

D: *I think it would be. When you first met this man, did you find these ideas hard to believe?*

L: No. I knew they were so. There are many things that are created that we humans do not understand. We can only feel they are so, in our hearts.

D: *What does this man look like?*

L: He is very old. He is bent over, has white hair and wears a robe. A very plain old, old man.

D: *Where does he live?*

L: I don't know. He just comes to me. Wherever I happen to be, he just comes to me.

D: *How is he able to do that?*

L: I don't know. At first I thought he was magic, but I don't think that's right. I think he has powers I do not conceive of at this time, because my intellect is not advanced enough for me to understand.

D: *How is magic viewed by the average person in your time period?*

L: It is a way of life here. There are wizards, but they are fake. My father puts great store in these people. They are not who they say they are.

D: *It would seem he would be interested in your friend.*

L: No, because I cannot tell them of this man. His existence would be threatened.

D: *Have you been studying with this man for a long time?*

L: I have been studying for five years now. I was ... twenty.

D: *What did you think when he first came to you?*

L: Ah! I thought, "Why me? I need peace. I do not need this." (Reminiscing) I was sitting in the forest under a tree, contemplating my life. And when I opened my eyes, he was standing right in front of me. I asked him who he was. And he said to me, "I have come from a very far distance to teach you things you cannot conceive of being." So I said to him, "What makes you think I want to learn these things?" And he said to me, "Because it is destined to be. And because of this you *will* learn them."

D: *As if you had no choice.*

L: That's what I said to him. "I will do what I damn well please." And he said to me, "Yes, and you will please to learn."

D: *He sounds like an interesting man. (She chuckled.) Did it take very long to convince you?*

L: No. I knew in my heart that this was so.

D: *Even though it was strange. And he's been coming for about five years now, wherever you are?*

L: Yes. Most every day. He does not let me rest very often, because there is so much I must know. He told me when he leaves me I must find a prodigy who is much younger than me. And in this way the knowledge will live. I cannot write this material down.

D: *Why not?*

L: Because of the dangers of it being destroyed. It must be a living knowledge passed from one generation to another. And only chosen ones are allowed to have this knowledge. I feel very thankful and fortunate to be the chosen one in my time.

D: *It is a great responsibility.*

L: It is a great honor, yet I feel the weight of this honor presses very hard on my soul.

D: *Then you are to remember what he says and not write it down?*

L: No, I cannot write it down. It will be stored in my intellect, and when I find my prodigy it will all be recalled, as if by magic. It will come in the proper sequence, so that this prodigy will understand exactly the knowledge he needs to have. And then he will store it just as I have. It is not allowed to be written.

D: *Don't you think there's a danger of forgetting some of it?*

L: No. The intellect is very vast. People do not understand the intellect.

D: *Isn't there the danger, as it is passed from one generation to the next, that there could be distortion?*

L: No, because there is something that keeps it intact in the intellect.

D: *I'm thinking of how people are. They change information over long periods of time.*

L: But this is stored in a very special place, and can only be drawn upon at the proper moment. I cannot discuss this with anyone at will. It is only discussed in the proper time, and then that portion of the intellect is tapped for the information.

D: *But is it all right if you talk to me of these things? (Yes) Because I pose no threat to you?*

L: That's right.

D: *Did he come specifically to see you or has he been living on the Earth?*

L: He came for me only. I don't think others can see him. Others hear me talking to him, and that's why they consider me to be mad. They do not see him.

D: *That would be confusing, wouldn't it?*

L: Yes, but that's all right. I know I'm not mad. We are very isolated where I live. There are not many people in this area. We live very far away from most other kingdoms.

D: *Have you been taught any kind of religious belief?*

L: We believe .... Only magic. Fire. God of fire is very powerful.

D: *Is this part of what the wizards teach? (Yes) Is this why your father believes in these things?*

L: Yes. He's very misled.

D: *Then this information is not for him, is it?*

L: No. He could not conceive of these things. He could not accept them. I must travel very far.

D: *Have you been told this?*

L: Yes. When my teaching is finished I will have to travel very, very far away to find a prodigy to give this knowledge. I will never return to my forest. That's why I have to enjoy it now.

D: *Wouldn't you be able to find someone suitable where you live? (No) How do you feel about leaving?*

L: Very sad.

D: *Are you the heir to the kingdom?*

L: No, I am the youngest. If I were the heir I would not have been chosen to do this work.

D: *You would have other responsibilities.*

L: Yes. And since I have none, I can go.

D: *I am very interested in the information that you are being given. But let's leave that scene and I want you to move ahead in time to an important day. A day when something that you consider to be important happens.*

The foregoing was strange enough and had peaked my interest, but I was not prepared for what came next.

D: *(Long pause) What is it? What do you see?*
L: (Emphatic) I am in the universe. I am on a journey. I am on a sight seeing mission.
D: *How is this occurring?*
L: I was asked to go on this mission, that I might give my opinions to others in a land far away. I am traveling very fast, but it seems not so. It seems as if there is no movement.
D: *How are you traveling?*
L: I am in a ... capsule.
D: *What is that?*
L: It is a round affair.
D: *Is it very large?*
L: No. It's just a very small oval room. No, a small oval section of light. And there's no one in this place but me. I do not ... I'm not driving it. It just travels by itself.
D: *Are you seated inside?*
L: I am standing, but I could sit down if I wished.
D: *Then it's large enough for you to stand up in it?*
L: Yes. It has a window in it. An opening, but you can't put your hand through it.
D: *Why not?*
L: Because there is a covering of some kind that doesn't allow you to go outside of it. But it enables you to see what is around you on the other side.

This has occurred repeatedly when I have regressed someone to the time period of the Middle Ages. They do not know what glass is. It must have been uncommon during that time because this is a repeatable pattern. When such remarks are repeated they have validity because the subject does not know what the other people have reported. These are some of the little things I have learned to watch for.

D: *What are you seeing through the opening?*
L: I am seeing it's very dark out there. Very dark indeed, very black, very peaceful. And occasionally I will see things floating about me. There's not much color here, like on

Earth. Very black and gray. Not much color at all.

D: *What type of things do you see floating by?*

L: Oh, I see formations of ... black rock sometimes.

D: *How did you get in this little place?*

L: I was sleeping and I was awakened and asked if I would come. And I said, "Of course." And then I went to sleep again. And then I was aware I was in this little room. I don't know how I got here. All I know is I just consented to come and then I was here.

D: *Was it your friend that asked you?*

L: No. He said he knew my friend, but he was from another place in the universe. Not the Pleiades. On the other side of the Pleiades. He was from a planet called (Phonetic: My con) Micon. Micon? I never heard of that place.

D: *What did that person look like?*

L: He was little, very little. He had no hair. He had a very large round head.

D: *Could you see what his face looked like?*

L: I don't remember if he had a face. I only remember his head being very large and very round. And his body being very little. And I wondered at the time how he kept his balance, because of the largeness of his head.

D: *Of course, it was night, and it was difficult to see his features anyway. Would that be right?*

L: No. Because he was ... silver. Bright! Silver colored, and he was bright.

D: *(Surprised) You mean he was shining?*

L: Yes. That was why I couldn't see his face, because it was too bright. And I was sleepy, and I couldn't see. (Linda looked downward.) I am wearing a *big* belt. (Hand motions.) A big belt on my waist. It is very *thick* and very warm, and it is silver also. It has compartments around the front of me, like pouches. I am wondering why I am wearing this belt, and what purpose it is serving. It is not leather though. It is very soft, it is not hard. It doesn't feel like anything that I know. (Using hand motions, she also seemed to be examining it.) There is no beginning to this belt, no buckle. And I don't remember putting it on me. This distresses me a little.

D: *Is there anything in the pouches?*

L: They feel like they have things in them, but there is no opening, so I can't see in them. (The belt seemed to be bothering him.) I guess I'll be told soon why I have this belt on my body.

The voice throughout this portion sounded older and had a distinct enunciation not similar to Linda's normal one.

D: *It won't bother you. It's just a curiosity.*

L: Yes, it is. It is very strange, this feeling. I feel like my stomach is expanding underneath the belt.

D: *But it's not an uncomfortable feeling.*

L: No. It's very light, very light.

D: *Are you wearing your ordinary clothes underneath the belt?*

L: No, no, no. They made me leave them in my room. I am wearing .... (He seemed to be examining it.) It's shiny also. I don't know what this stuff is. The garment is very light, and it encompasses my whole body. I have these shoes on. They are not boots, they are shoes. And it is all together. It is all one. I'm encased in it. I do not have a hat on though.

D: *Is there anything on the walls, or is the room bare?*

L: Let me see. (Long pause) There is a huge window.

D: *This is different than the little opening?*

L: No, this is the opening. It's very long. (Pause) I'm wondering where the door is. I do not see one.

D: *It just gets curiouser and curiouser, doesn't it?*

L: Yes, it does. I wonder where I am going.

As soon as he wondered this, the answers began to come. They seemed to be coming from somewhere else, because it was as though he was repeating what he was hearing. It was new information to him.

L: They tell me it won't take long. I am going to visit a new place where people have gone to start a new life. And the reason that I am going there is to ... (Surprise) find my *prodigy*! (With delight) *I* am going to find my prodigy. I have been searching for such a long time.

D: *You haven't found him on Earth?*

L: Nooo! I have looked everywhere, and I am very old now. And I was so afraid I would not find him in time. (With delight and pleasure.) *That* is where I am going. I am going to this new place to find my prodigy.

I suddenly had an idea. This was too good an opportunity to pass up.

D: *Would you be willing to share the knowledge you have been taught, not only with your prodigy, but with me?*

L: I will have to ask first. I cannot do this unless I ask.

I checked the tape recorder and saw that our time was running out.

D: *All right. If I come again at another time and speak with you, would you have time to ask and get permission?*

L: Yes, I will ask.

D: *Maybe you can share it with two prodigies that way, because I am also very curious.*

L: (Delight) Oh, wouldn't that be wonderful? (Almost in ecstasy) Oh, that would be two fold. Wouldn't that be marvelous?

D: *So I would like it if you would ask permission and then I can come again and discuss it.*

L: That would be nice. I was very worried that this knowledge would be lost. And I felt so happy that I would be finding my prodigy. But it very much disturbed me that my knowledge would be lost to this Earth. And that would be a shame, because even though the people here are very primitive and do not care about such things, this knowledge should remain.

D: I agree. I'm going to ask you to continue on your journey. (Yes) I'm not going to interfere with Bartholomew's journey. But I want the other part of you that I am speaking to to leave that scene, and drift forward in time.

I then conditioned Linda with a keyword and brought her back to full consciousness. I was now disappointed that I had only put a 60 minute tape in my recorder when we began this session. But I had no way of knowing this type of information would come forth. I was expecting a dull, mundane past life, and that was the way it began. Normally I am able to go completely through a life in a 60 minute session, because nothing spectacular happens in the simple lives. When Bartholomew began talking about the strange visitor and the information he was gaining, I knew I could not complete the story in one session, so I didn't try. I knew this would be a new project that would take several weeks to complete if I were allowed to gain access to the hidden information. Apparently I was embarking on a new adventure, although our conversation beforehand had not indicated anything of this merit in Linda's subconscious.

When she awakened she seemed confused and was still a little groggy. She remarked, "I had a message to give to you. I remember that. And I feel a big responsibility. It's really important. I don't know what the message is. I just know that there's a lot of knowledge that we do not have. It was taken away from us, because of our primitive ways and our fears. And it's time now to return. And for some reason you are chosen and I am chosen to bring that back to this planet. And it is a very big responsibility. I feel that. It weighs very heavy on my soul. That's all I remember about the session."

It was obvious she was somnambulistic, because she had gone so deep in trance that she could not remember anything else that was said during the session.

I now was definitely interested in pursuing this story. To me it was like opening a Pandora's box. I love a mystery. And when somebody says they're going to tell me things that have been lost and that I need to know, that is too intriguing to ignore.

The only problem would be the distance I would have to travel to work with her. Thus I decided to come to Little Rock at least once a month, and try to work with both Linda and Janice on the same weekend.

* * *

I now had two separate projects developing between Janice and Linda. In order to work with them I felt I would have to make a special trip to Little Rock in January 1990, and do nothing but have sessions. I intended to devote the entire trip to working on the material coming from the two women. This should have been easy since I did not have a lecture planned. My friends said they wouldn't tell anyone that I was coming so we could keep the visitors away. Of course, it didn't work out the way we planned. An acquaintance of theirs found out I was coming and wanted a regression. I scheduled that for the Friday night that I arrived, even though I was tired from the long drive. That way I could devote the rest of the weekend to the two women.

At first I thought of alternating the sessions, but then decided it would be easier to follow the train of individual stories if I concentrated on one thread at a time. Also, if we alternated that meant that one woman would have to wait while I conducted a session with the other. We decided to work with each woman on separate days. I would try to have three sessions with Linda on Saturday, and three with Janice on Sunday. This was the first time I had ever attempted this and did not know how it would affect them. I expected they would be tired, but not as tired as I would be, because they would have the feeling of taking short naps all day. It was an experiment and we didn't know how it would work out. But if we could manage it I could get the equivalent of a month's work done in only one day.

* * *

My first session with Linda was to begin on Saturday morning. When she arrived for this series of sessions I saw that her lower right arm was in a cast. She had fallen on the ice before Christmas and broken it. I was a little concerned that it would be a distraction during our work because it would be awkward and uncomfortable. I thought she would be unable to rest properly and this might interfere with going into a deep trance. But she put a pillow across her stomach and rested the cast on that.

Before searching for the information Bartholomew was supposed to impart to me, I wanted to find out more about his background. If a book were to be written later this would be necessary to set the stage. I would have to uncover what happened in his life between our first meeting and his journey in the space craft to locate his prodigy. This was the first order of business. I used Linda's keyword and it worked immediately. The cast on her arm did not seem to cause any problem. She was able to ignore it when she entered a deep somnambulistic trance. I then counted her back to the time of Bartholomew and asked her what she was doing.

L: (She began slowly and softly again.) I am in the grounds. It is within the walls of the city. Like a marketplace. There is such activity. There are many things going on today. People with their goods to sell. People who are making things. Blacksmith is there. Children running. Dogs, animals. It is very busy today. I am here because it is the fall equinox celebration of the harvest. That is why there is so much activity. It is the time after the harvest is in and people are celebrating their good fortune. And also to give thanks to the gods for the favors they have given to them during the growing season. This celebration will last for three days and three nights, culminating in a huge celebration on the last night.

D: *What type of gods do you worship?*

L: There are many. There are the gods of the elements. The gods of the earth. The god of the Sun and the moon, and the wind and the rain.

D: *Would you have anything in your country called the "church"? (Pause, as though he did not understand.) Like the Catholic church?*

L: They came here many times to try to convert the countryside, but it was not accepted. Those that came were stoned. They now leave us alone.

D: *The people didn't like them trying to change their beliefs?*

L: No, because they called us pagans, and treated us poorly, as if we were not good enough.

D: *Your people still worship the old religion, is that right?*

L: That is correct.

D: *Have you had contact yet with your teacher? (Pause) Do you know what I mean?*

L: I have talked to someone recently, but he has not told me he is my teacher.

Apparently we had entered his life at an earlier time than when we spoke in our first session.

L: He is a very old man. He does not come from here. He came to visit me a while back when I was in the forest. He was walking along and I was sitting under a tree contemplating. And he just walked up to me. He had a knapsack, a bag, on his back, so I assumed he was journeying somewhere. And we just talked, that is all.

D: *Where did he say he came from?*

L: He didn't. He just said he came from a very far place. One that I did not know. He asked me what I was thinking so hard about. And I said that I was just contemplating my life. We got to talking about this and that, and about how people don't understand.

D: *Is that the way you feel? That people don't understand you?*

L: Yes. It is like they have a totally different concept of what is happening in their life. They don't live their life in the same manner that I would wish to live mine.

D: *Did this old man feel the same way you do?*

L: Oh, yes. He said it is the times. And that people do not realize.

D: *That was good that you found someone you could talk to.*

L: Yes. I was very sorry to see him go. But he said that he might be returning back this way soon. And that maybe we could talk again.

D: *That would be very good. Did he tell you a name?*

L: Yes. His name was very strange. His name was ... Christopher. I never heard that name before. I found it very odd in some way.

D: *Do you mean it is an odd name for your country?*

L: I have never heard this before. He was an old man, and it almost seemed like that name should be for a very young man. When I say it it gives me a very peaceful sense.

D: *But now you're enjoying yourself there at the festival, aren't you?*

L: Oh, yes. Lots of fresh food and all kinds of wares that were made by the peasants. Lots of singing and dancing.

D: *That's a good day. Let's leave that scene. Drift away from that scene. And I want you to move forward in time to when you are older in that life. What are you doing now? What do you see?*

L: I am in a city far away from my home. It has streets made of stone. It has a very dirty ... many people who are beggars. It is very dreary. I do not like it here.

D: *Does the city have a name?*

L: I had to go on a boat to get to this place. It is in the country of England, and the city's name is Liverpool. It is very awful here.

D: *What are you doing there?*

L: I have traveled very far to see how people live on this planet. To see how different they all are. Sometimes I stay a long time, and sometimes I leave very quickly. I will probably leave this place tomorrow. It is very sad. It distresses me to see the level to which people have sunk. They are very bad to one another.

D: *But you said you have visited other cities and other countries also?*

L: Oh, yes, many. For the last ten years or so I have traveled from one place to another.

D: *What are some of the countries you have visited?*

L: I have visited Gaul, and I have visited Rome. I have visited many places. I visited the east. Most people have never been there.

D: *What is in the east?*

L: Oh, it is a very large country. And their philosophy of life is very different from ours. They have different colored skin, and they do a thing called "meditation." In which they get in touch with their (had difficulty) ... inner knowledge. They are very wise.

D: *When you go to these other countries, how do you travel?*

L: I walk.

D: *It would be a long way, wouldn't it?*

L: Oh, yes. Sometimes if the water is there I must take a boat, but generally I walk.

D: *How do you know where to go?*

L: Oh, I just go wherever I feel I should go. In that direction, I just go.

D: *Do you have to worry about having money or food?*

L: Sometimes. Generally I meet someone along the way, and they are very kind to me. They take me in for a while, and so far I have not had to worry. I have been taken care of.

D: *Do you know now the name of the country that you came from? Where you lived when you were younger?*

L: Sometimes people call it different things. Some people call it ... (difficult) Seeton (phonetic). (Long pause) I can't remember. It has no name as such. It is a kingdom all its own, and they do not travel from there at all.

D: *Then it was very unusual for you to leave?*

L: Yes. No one ever leaves there.

D: *It was very brave of you to want to go away.*

L: I really didn't want to leave, but I was told that I must. I was told to see what life was all about in very many places. But not to worry, that I would be taken care of on my journeys. And I have been. And I am not lonely.

D: *That would be frightening to go out into the unknown countryside and not know anyone.*

L: It was at first. I was petrified.

D: *Who told you to do this?*

L: My friend who comes to me periodically. He said it was important to see what life was all about here. That my kingdom was so isolated that I could never fathom in a million years what other people were like, if I did not find out for myself.

D: *What have you learned about people?*

L: I have learned a great many things about cultures of people. And how they are different, because of their location and the way they live their life. How that has a bearing on how they look at life. How some are very good, and some are very bad. Some are very ignorant, and look no further than the end of their nose.

D: *Everyone speaks different languages, don't they?*

L: Yes, they do.

D: *Do you have difficulty communicating with them?*

L: No. My friend has taught me many things. One of which is to focus on the middle of one's forehead, and the communication can take place without speaking a word. It is from mind to mind. It is not like a conversation, but of information exchange.

D: *Do the other people you meet have to concentrate?*

L: No. They are amazed at first. They will start talking to me, and when I fix my gaze on them it is like a calm falls over them and we communicate. And after our communication is finished, they continue on, in a fashion, where we started. It's very strange.

D: *Do they remember afterwards?*

L: No. It is like a lapse of time that takes place. And they aren't even aware of it.

D: *Is there a reason for that?*

L: Yes. Because they would be very fearful if they knew and would probably put me to death because of their fear. They would think I was evil.

D: *This type of communication makes it easier for you, doesn't it?*

L: Oh, yes, very much so. I could not talk with them otherwise. That is very nice to do this. I speak to peasants. I speak to noblemen. I speak to kings. I speak to farmers. I speak to tradesmen. It has been quite educational.

D: *You have met important people, like kings?*

L: Yes, on my travels I have sometimes met kings, sometimes just the noblemen. I have met priests, high priests. Their philosophies are always interesting to me. But they always are very righteous. I find that sometimes laughable. I don't tell them that.

D: *Do they think their own philosophy is the only one?*

L: Yes, yes, this is what I find amusing.

D: *One time when I spoke to you, you said you were also searching for someone. Is that true?*

L: Yes, I am looking for a young man that I can teach what I have been taught before it is my time to leave, so that he might carry out my work. And so far I have not found him.

D: *How will you know him when you find him?*

L: I will know immediately. There will be a sign given to me, and I will know.

D: *Do you know what the sign will be?*

L: No, but I have been told that when we start our communication, it will be told to me.

D: *Would that be one reason why you are traveling? You don't think you would find the young man in your own kingdom?*

L: Yes. But also as I am traveling, I am learning many things. And I can tell this young man what I have seen.

D: *You have seen very many wonderful things, I suppose.*

L: Yes. And I have seen some very bad things also. But that is what life is all about. You have to take the good and the bad together.

D: *You can't make any judgments.*

L: No. That would serve no purpose. I cannot do anything to improve the status at this time. It is a gathering of information that is taking place at this time.

D: *Yes, it would be useless to try to help the people. There are just too many.*

L: They would not listen. They are not ready to make any changes in their outlook at this time.

D: *I suppose you're like an observer? (Yes) What did your family think when you decided to leave?*

L: They were sad. However they have always felt I was mad. So it was just something else.

D: *You were never the same as they were.*

L: That is correct. So they just let it go. I miss them sometimes.

D: *I imagine you would be lonely sometimes.*

L: Yes. Even though they do not know the things that I know, a family is a very comforting place to be.

D: *Yes, I can understand that. But now you are in a place called Liverpool?*

L: Yes. I am going to leave here tomorrow. I will probably go to Spain.

D: *Will you have to take a boat again? (Yes, yes.) Have you ever thought of journeying the other way, across the ocean?*

L: There has been some talk of this. However, I don't think at this time there has been a proven route. It is a very big ocean out there, and I am not ready to undertake that project at this time.

D: *You mean people have not been going in that direction?*

L: There is much discussion about that. There is a man named Columbo, who says the Earth is oval. And people laugh at him.

D: *Did you see the man called "Columbo"?*

L: No, I have not seen him. I only heard about him from the townspeople. They were talking about him and laughing. And I thought to myself, how sad. So I just stood there and listened for awhile. And for awhile I thought maybe I would help him out a little, but I was told not to. But he is right. He does not know how right he is.

D: *How do you know?*

L: I was told about these things from my friend. I could help this man, Columbo, in his journey. But I have been told to keep silent.

D: *What did your friend tell you was out there?*

L: He showed me pictures. They weren't drawings. They were what he called "photographs". I do not understand what that is. It is a picture, but it is not like anything I have ever seen. It is not drawn or painted. They are very beautiful. And he shows me unbelievable things about this Earth, that I could never ever have imagined.

D: *Can you share that with me?*

L: It was as if I was very far away in the night sky, looking down, down, very far away. And it was most beautiful. You could see the shape of the Earth and places in the ocean that I could never have known about. You know, people today only think of the existence of where they are. They do not ever consider there would be another place. And there are very many places that no one knows about, or could even imagine. Much larger places than where we live now. Much bigger masses of land, with forests and hills and mountains. Unbelievable places. Some where there are people, some where there are no people, just land waiting. (This was all said with a wistful tone of voice. Almost melancholy.)

D: *What are the people like in these places?*

L: I have not visited them all. I have only visited a very small segment in my area, because to walk to these places would be impossible. I am told however, that perhaps some day I might be able to visit these faraway places also.

D: *You said you were shown pictures.*

L: Yes, but they were not of people, just of the Earth and the land from a great distance away. I would really like to see those people there though. I wonder if they are like us.

D: *Do you think this is where this man, Columbo, is going?*

L: He thinks he is going to the east. I don't think he knows about those other places. He does not know they exist.

D: *And your friend doesn't want you to tell him.*

L: No. He said that would be very bad. He said he would not believe me anyway.

D: *That's true. He has to find out for himself, just like you have done. In your time, what do the average people believe is out there?*

L: They believe if you go way far on a ship, there are very many evil things there that will take you over. And you will be lost forever.

D: *Do the people of your time believe there are any other people over there?*

L: No, they don't believe there is anything beyond what they see.

D: *When he showed you the pictures of the Earth, what shape did it look like?*

L: It was kind of round, and there was lots of water. (Excitedly) And you know what? I think that the Earth turns around and around and around.

D: *Did it look like it did that?*

L: Yes, but very slowly. And there is water and land, big pieces of land. Everywhere more water.

D: *Do the people in your time believe the Earth looks like that?*

L: They don't know that I have seen these things. They think that Earth is only where they are. And beyond that there is nothing. Most people are very fearful, and they stay with what they know. They don't venture very far away from where they live.

D: *So you have been very brave to do these things.*

L: I had to be very trusting with my instructions that were given to me. It was very hard at first. But after a few years it was not hard at all.

D: *You were probably afraid too. You didn't know what was out there.*

L: I was very frightened. I was very fearful. When I figured out that I would not be hurt, that I would be taken care of, then it was very easy.

D: *Do you still see your friend?*

L: Yes, occasionally he will come and talk with me. He shows me very nice things sometimes. He tells me things that I need to know. He shows me about the Earth. And he tells me how things will be many years from now. And how people will progress in their thought patterns and in their lifestyles. And how much civilization will change. It is very interesting. It is very hard sometimes to think that these things will really happen.

D: *What are some of the unbelievable things he has told you will happen?*

L: (Excitedly) He told me once   and I find this very difficult to believe that there will be carriages that fly in the sky. Is that not silly?

D: *Oh, that does sound strange, doesn't it?*

L: And that people will travel in them all over this Earth. And that they will know of all these places that we don't know of now.

D: *That sounds very miraculous to think that someone could fly.*

L: That is very exciting. I cannot ... (Sigh) my mind cannot fathom such a thing. I asked him if the horses would have wings. And he said there would be no horses. Can you imagine that?

D: *No, I can't imagine how it would happen.*

L: I can't either. There will be many wonderful things. He said there will be machinery that will do the work of ten men. And that all they will have to do is push buttons and things will be made.

D: *That would save a lot of work, wouldn't it?*

L: Yes, it would. He said that people would communicate together better than they do now. They will have things to

speak through from one place to another, and
you could hear them for many miles away. He said this will
open the communications for the whole world, so that we can
all talk with one another. And not be ignorant anymore.

D: *These are all good things, aren't they?*

L: Yes. It would be so nice if some of these fears could be
taken away. And people would be kind to one another.

D: *Do you think that would happen if they had things like that
so they could speak to each other?*

L: Yes. Then they would not be so fearful. You see, people
are very isolated now. They live within their own families in
their own little cities. And they are very fearful of
anything beyond those boundaries. And because of
this fear they do not communicate very well. They could
learn much from one another if they would only allow it.
Ignorance would be abolished by these methods.

D: *So you think the answer is learning to communicate?*

L: Very definitely. Lack of communication is very bad, because
it allows fear to envelope one's being, and not see the reality
of what is before them. It cloaks everything in darkness.

D: *So he told you about things they could talk into or talk
through?*

L: Yes. And they could hear too. They were little machines.
I don't know what they look like. He just told me they were
little machines.

D: *And this would be good because then they could
communicate with each other.*

L: Yes. You see, then they could give their ideas on things, and
the other people could give their ideas. And maybe the best
idea could be used.

D: *That sounds very good to me. Did he tell you other things
that were hard to believe?*

L: Yes, very many things. He said there are other earths in the
universe. And that these people have progressed much faster
than we have. And they have more knowledge than
we do. But as our world grows and we have these machines
to help us become more educated, these people from the
other places might come and visit, and exchange their ideas
also.

D: *That all sounds very good.*

L: I think it would be wonderful.

D: *It's hard to think of people living on other earths, isn't it?*

L: Yes, it is. It is very hard, although I have always known this.
And for some reason that was easier for me to understand,
than thinking there were other places on this Earth that I did

not know about. I don't know why I had such a hard time with that.

D: *It was easier for you to understand there were people out there on other worlds?*

L: Yes, I could understand that much easier than that there were other places of land on Earth, and that the Earth was not just here.

D: *But isn't it difficult for other people in your time to think of other worlds?*

L: Oh, yes, they think of that as evil and bad, and they are very afraid to think of such things. It is their fear that keeps them back. Anything they do not understand they call evil and bad, and they try to get rid of it by killing it or burning it. They are just very afraid.

D: *When you went to Rome, isn't that where the Catholic church has its home?*

L: Yes, they have very many beautiful places there. They have many priests that teach that religion to the countryside. They too are steeped in fear.

D: *Do you think so?*

L: Oh, yes. I think so. They try to keep the peasants under control with their religious philosophy. But it is all a cover for the fear.

D: *Why would a religion have to be afraid?*

L: I don't know. Their God must not be very good. If He were good, why would they have such fear?

D: *You mean, the priests themselves are afraid?*

L: Yes, they have this system. It is like a kingdom. It is the same old thing, just a different name, to keep the peasants in line. A system of the higher ups against the little people. They believe that there is only their God, and that all the others are evil. That there is only one way to be good, and that is the way they teach. And if you do not follow their instructions you will be damned for eternity. This is incorrect. There are many, many avenues. This is a word I learned, you know? The word "avenue". Isn't that a strange word?

D: *That is a strange word. What do you think it means?*

L: Avenue means trail or pathway. I find that a very interesting word. Avenue.

D: *Yes. But you think it is wrong for them to think their religion is the only way?*

L: Very definitely. They tell them that they are very, very holy or very, very wise and that this is the way it is. It does not allow the individual person to examine his own inner truths. They teach that he is very limited. He must follow directions explicitly and only do it in one manner. And this is very bad. It does not allow a person to think for himself. (Sigh) But this is the times. You know, it is like that all over. It is not just Rome. It is not just with the religion. It is with the politics of the day. You are not allowed to think for yourself. You are told what to think and what to do. I was amazed that there was such a thread of consistency, a pattern throughout the world. They may have different customs and do things a little differently, but it is basically all the same. The fear is all the same. It may be over something different, but it basically is the same cloak that people wear. And they allow it to color their interpretation of life, and they allow it to hold them back. They are afraid they will be punished.

D: *They would rather stay with what they know. They're safe with that.*

L: That is correct. And then there is no danger of being stoned or hung or put in a box.

D: *What do you mean, put in a box?*

L: They have these things. They are very awful. They are wooden boxes. And people are put in these boxes and kept there for days without food or water. They sometimes die there. It is very awful.

D: *These things are done to people that don't believe the same way?*

L: Yes, or if they question. Oh, there are some bad people out there who deserve to be in those boxes. They steal or kill or that sort of thing. But to be put there just for believing differently is a very bad injustice, in my way of thinking. Who could it hurt if you think in your mind something different? It might be better, you know?

D: *What have you found about people's health, as you travel?*

L: Some places it is very good and they live a long time, especially if they live out in the open on the farms. If they live in the city it is very, very bad. As I said, cities tend to be very dirty, and there is much disease. People live not very long. There is much death in the city.

D: *Are there people you would call "physicians" to take care of these people?*

L: Yes, but they don't do any good. These people die anyway. I think they don't help at all. They think they do, but they don't.

D: *Well, you have been lucky in your travels. Have you ever gotten sick?*

L: A few times. Not anything very bad. Most of these people in the city die by the time they are forty. This is old in the city. I am fifty, and this is amazing to people that I am in such good health. My hair is getting white now, but I am in good health.

D: *That is considered old then.*

L: Very old, very old.

D: *But you're still able to walk and travel.*

L: Yes, yes, I am in good physical condition. I do not have a horse. I do not want the responsibility of taking care of anyone but myself. Even though that has been done for me.

D: *I was thinking if you had a horse you could travel faster.*

L: This way I do not have to worry about feed for my horse, or lodging. I can just go at my own speed and stay as long as I want and then leave. Sometimes I hitch a ride, but not very often.

D: *But you travel on boats though.*

L: That is a necessity because I could not swim that far. That is just a necessary thing to get to another place.

D: *Are the boats very big that you travel on?*

L: Sometimes. I have traveled on a big ship with many sails. And other times I have just gone in a small boat. It depends on who I can hitch a ride with.

D: *You don't have to worry about money that way, do you?*

L: No, isn't that amazing? I would have never thought that I could have traveled for so long with no money. It is amazing.

D: *Do you carry any clothes or anything with you?*

L: No. When my clothes get tattered, someone always comes along and gives me new ones. And someone feeds me. I do have a big stick that I carry with me. It is like a staff. It helps me go up and down hills. It has become my old friend.

D: *Do you think you will ever find this young man you are to pass the knowledge on to?*

L: I am getting a little concerned now, because of my age. I was not previously concerned. I just felt that he would be shown to me at the proper time. But as I grow older I am becoming concerned that I will not find him in time. You see, I have much to tell him. And it is not something I could tell him in a day or a week. I have very many things to tell him, and this will require some time. I will have to stay with him. I must be able to teach him while I have my health. This is a very big concern of mine at this time. Although I have been told not to worry. It has been taken care of. And thus far all things have been taken care of that have been told to me. So I guess I should stop being concerned. I do not feel myself as an old man. Only when it is drawn to my attention.

D: *Your body doesn't feel old then.*

L: Not to me inside. But to those outside I am very old.

D: *But you're going to Spain next?*

L: Yes, I have never been there. And I understand that it is very beautiful. So I thought I would look and see for myself. I have been east of there, and I have been north of there, and I have been west of there. But I have not been south of there. Maybe I will go there this time. I am usually directed when I get up in the morning to leave, in which direction to go. I am told to go east or northeast or whichever road I am to take. I am told to take this road, and so I do.

D: *You don't ask any questions. (No) All right. Let's leave that scene. I want you to move ahead until you have arrived in Spain, and tell me what you think about it. Did you take a boat?*

L: Yes, I took a large vessel this time. I met the captain at the inn, and he was very taken with me and let me ride on his vessel. I stayed in his cabin. It was very beautiful. It was a very large ship with many masts.

D: *What do you think of Spain?*

L: There aren't very many people here so far. It is very warm. Such a change. It warms my bones. It was very chilly in Liverpool, very damp. And the sunlight feels very good on my body. The air is very fresh, and the breeze is just perfect. All of the stories I have heard are true.

D: *Are you going to stay there for a while?*

L: I think I might. I would like to visit with these people for a while, to see what their philosophy of life is. They seem very friendly. They don't seem to be as frightened. These people are open. They are not as steeped in tradition. And they seem to be more independent in their thought than what I have been seeing.

D: *Maybe you will find your prodigy there.*

L: I don't think so. I think my prodigy is very far away from here. I don't know why I think that now. I don't think I will find him. I think he will find me. I think now I will stay here in Spain for a while. Maybe they will send him to me. It is so refreshing, and is such a change. I may rest a while here.

D: *But do you really think that someday you will find him?*

L: I have been told that, and I have no reason to believe otherwise.

D: *You have devoted your life to doing this. As long as you believe it, there must be some truth in it.*

L: Yes. It is a very big lesson that I learned a long time ago. A lesson of faith.

D: *So if it is intended to be, you will find him. (Yes) All right then. That sounds like a very beautiful place, and you can rest for a while.*

I then brought Linda back to full consciousness, and left Bartholomew in his world, knowing we would join him again soon and continue our story.

CHAPTER TWO
THE LESSONS BEGIN

After the first session we stopped for a few hours to have lunch, rest and visit. We went back to work around 2:00 p.m. Using Linda's keyword again, I counted her back to that life. I had finished the background about Bartholomew, and now wanted to proceed with obtaining the information. My curiosity had certainly been aroused, and I wanted to discover the knowledge Bartholomew was supposed to pass on to his prodigy. I intended to return him to the craft and pick up the story from there.

D: *I would like you to find Bartholomew once again when he was in that strange room, and he was going somewhere. I will count to three and we will be there. 1, 2, 3, we have gone again to that scene. You had just left your bedroom and found yourself in this strange place with things going by outside. What are you doing and what do you see? Tell me about it.*

L: I am the only one here. (Almost in awe.) I am sitting in a chair looking out into the universe, watching the stars and the planets go by. I was awakened and asked to go on a journey. And when I agreed I was told that I must put on these clothes. Then a beam of light enveloped me, and the next thing I knew I was sitting in this chair by myself.

D: *Didn't you say you are older now?*

L: Yes. I am very old. I am almost sixty by now. I am very, very old.

D: *Were you still looking for your prodigy?*

L: Yes, I was. I felt I had failed my mission in this life. I tried to trust, knowing that I would be given the piece to the puzzle in the proper time. But as I grew so old, I began to doubt and I began to fear.

D: *Did you ever find anyone in all your journeys on Earth that you thought you could trust with the information?*

L: No, not one. I thought maybe the eastern culture was more understanding and open and receptive. But they too are covered with their own traditions and belief system. I was very disappointed. That was when I began to lose faith. It was only this night that I was told this would be my last journey. And I would be given the final piece the end of my search.

D: *What was the last piece?*

L: The final piece is the sharing of this knowledge with someone who is akin to me, who is open to ideas they cannot fathom. Someone who is able to examine these things without fear, without prejudice, without bias. Just accepting the facts, and examining them carefully. Just to share your knowing, and that is all.

D: *Are they taking you to your prodigy?*

L: They are taking me to a new place. They call it the "colony". It is a new experimental place where they are hoping pure truth will pervade, and not be distorted in any manner. These people are of a pure heart and mind. I will be their teacher. I will give them the knowledge I have accumulated over these very many years. They will be the keepers of this knowledge. Because of their purity they will not misuse, hoard or color it in any way, shape or form. They will be the keepers of the knowledge of the universal truth.

D: *Is this where your prodigy will be?*

L: Yes. He then in turn can be sent at the proper time to enlighten the planet Earth when the time is right. Until then he will stay at this place with the others and wait. The others have their places to take this message also in the proper time.

D: *Why couldn't you pass it on to someone on Earth? That was what you thought you were going to do.*

L: Because there was no one of a pure heart that could keep it without distortion or misusing it. At this time the evolvement of the planet is not at a space in time that humanity is ready. They have so many, many lessons they must learn before they could use any of this to the proper advantage of humankind. It would be distorted, misused, and eventually destroy the entire Earth.

D: *So in this way it will eventually be brought back to Earth.*

L: That is correct. This prodigy will live here in this "colony". This place knows no time or space. They will not age or change in any way. It is a holding place. And I will leave here when my job is done, and go to my place for rest. I will not stay here, nor will I return to Earth for quite some time.

D: *If you consider yourself to be old, will that make a difference where you are going?*

L: No. But I cannot stay at this colony. My soul pattern is different from these ones on this place. It is not compatible for a long indefinite stay. I would not be comfortable here. I do desire to go to my rest when my job is done. I need to be at rest for some time. I need to be with the All.

D: *Are you saying that you will come back to Earth in this body after you have finished giving your messages and knowledge to these other people?*

L: No, I will not return to Earth for many, many generations. I will go to the "All" for rest. I will return much later in a different capacity.

From his answers it sounded like he was referring to going to the spirit side and entering the resting place for a while before being reincarnated into a different body. This place is described in my book *Between Death and Life*. The only problem I had understanding this was that he had not mentioned dying. He still apparently was in his physical body. And everyone knows you can't take your body with you when you die.

D: *I'm trying to understand. ou still have your physical body. It is inside this room sitting on the chair.*

L: Yes, it is my body. I've never asked what would happen to it. I guess I should. But it just didn't seem important.

D: *All right. Let's move ahead till this vehicle or whatever it is, this machine that you are inside, reaches its destination. You said you are traveling to where the colony is. Let's move ahead till you have reached your destination. Tell me what happens when you reach there.*

L: It is a very bright place, and I am sitting in my chair hovering over this bright place. All of a sudden a very bright light envelopes my body. It starts from the top of this room. It is cylindrical in shape, and I am in the center of it. In an instant I am with these other spirits. I am no longer in the room. I am just transported by this light into the presence of these beings. They are all very, very happy to see me. They look like beings of light. Each one different but yet alike. They are very bright beings.

D: *They have no physical characteristics?*

L: They do, but they are so bright. When I try to look into their faces I am blinded. It is like looking into the Sun. I can see that they smile. They must have a mouth. I feel they are smiling at me. But they are covered in such bright light that I cannot distinguish their body forms.

D: *Are you still in your physical body? (Pause. Maybe he wasn't sure.) What does it feel like?*

31

L: It feels very light, very light, like I am floating. Like there is no weight, no force of any kind. I am just free. I don't think I have a body. I think I am just me.

D: *Do you think these other beings are physical?*

L: (Pause) Maybe. But I think they are probably pure energy. I see them, but I don't think they are human bodies.

This was said with a sense of curiosity, of wonder, as though trying to understand something strange and different which he was unprepared for.

L: I think I have come to a different plane of existence. It started as a physical trip, but I think I have come through the physical plane and entered somewhere I don't know about. Yet I feel I could leave here if I chose, at any time, and return to that room.

D: *Do you think you could find your physical body in that room? (Yes) You said you were going to share your knowledge with these beings. Is that correct? (Yes) Once before I asked if it would be possible to share your knowledge with me also. And you said you would have to get permission. What do you think?*

I felt expectation, hoping I would be allowed to receive this knowledge. My curiosity was eager for this to happen, but it would all depend on forces outside myself forces of which I had no knowledge.

L: I asked my friend, and he said perhaps you could listen in on my teaching assignments.

I felt a thrill of joy.

D: *That would be wonderful if I would be allowed to do that.*

L: He said there would be times when you would not be able to hear certain things, but most of it will be made available to you.

D: *Why wouldn't I be able to hear certain things?*

L: Because there are only a few more things to be put in place before a plan is implemented into existence on the Earth. And those very few things must be kept until the plan is implemented. And once implemented you will be given the remaining information.

D: *Then if I sit in on the teaching assignments I will be able to share in the knowledge?*

L: That is correct. You are given this chance because you also are one of the very few who will not color or distort. You are pure in heart and will not use this for yourself.

Linda's breathing was becoming faster. She showed signs of discomfort.

D: *I see those are important requirements.*
L: Yes. Not everyone could do this. Only a very, very few.

During the last few sentences I noticed her breathing was irregular, faster and a little labored. This made it difficult for her to speak clearly.

L: The air here is going to take adjustment. It is very heavy on my chest. (She was still breathing heavily.) It will be a few days before I will be adjusted.

I gave suggestions to dispel any physical discomfort. My main concern is always for the comfort of the subject.

D: *The physical body I am speaking to will be able to adjust with no problems whatsoever, even if the entity that is speaking to me is having problems. Do you understand?*
L: (Her breathing was returning to normal.) I understand.
D: *All right. Are you going to begin your classes?*
L: Soon. There is a welcoming time now. A time of rejoicing. A time of being together.
D: *Have they been expecting you?*
L: Yes, they have been waiting for me, and they are very, very happy. They are cheering me. They are hugging me. They are very happy for me.
D: *It sounds like a nice place, a nice environment.*
L: Oh, it is very nice. It is very warm.
D: *Can we move ahead to when you start your classes, and I am able to listen? Do you have any plan or order you're going to give your classes in?*
L: I had not considered. I at one time had a plan, but it has been so long I have forgotten. I have now decided to first start off with questions from my friends. And then I will lecture on their questions. I feel this is probably the best way at this time.
D: *I agree. But because I will not be able to hear their questions, will you repeat them? (Yes) Are you at the point where you're going to begin? (Yes) All right. Go ahead at your own pace then.*

L: I am pointing to... Artness (Phonetic. maybe: Ardness) has asked me, (Slowly as though listening and then repeating.) "What happened on the Earth plane to make people so narrow in their belief system?" Many, many eons ago people who came to the Earth came with vast knowledge of the universe. There were others who were already living on the Earth, who were not as knowledgeable as those who had just recently come. And it made those who were just coming examine the issue of power. It was something they had not experienced until this time. And they liked that feeling. It gave them an exhilaration they had not known. So they decided to keep their knowledge to themselves and not share it, as it was meant to be. And they enslaved those who were not as knowledgeable. They told them things that were not so, to frighten them into serving them. They were thought of as gods. They became the gods. The general people, the ordinary people that were here first, thought they were gods, because they could do unusual things. It was not meant for this to happen. And when they got into all of this power and greed, they did not want to leave. They wanted to stay. And so they did. As they passed from this lifetime, stories were handed down about these gods and their great powers. And fear began to take hold. Fear that if they did not do as the gods had said they would be destroyed. It was a very dark time for the planet Earth.

D: *What did these beings tell them that frightened them, that allowed them to be enslaved?*

L: They told them they could rule the wind and the light, the Sun, the moon, the rain. They ruled it, and if these people didn't follow their rules, they would be destroyed. The people would have no water, no Sun. They knew they needed the Sun and the water and the wind, the rain. They had to have these things to exist. And the gods had control over all this, so they had to obey or they would be destroyed instantly. They did not know that their being, their spirit, lives forever. They could only see the here and now. The original purpose of these light beings who came to Earth was to share this information, so that the fear could be removed and the people could understand.

D: *Did these beings perform wonders to make the people believe they were gods?*

L: Yes, they did. It was all a trick. They did it with lights and magic, but the people thought they were gods. I want to say that this is a perfect example of human nature, of the constant fight within against fear and self service. To serve the self.

Power.

D: *But the beings that came were the ones that caused the problem.*

L: Yes. They did not do what they were told. They fell because they came to serve themselves and not humanity.

D: *You said this was an example of humans, but yet the problem was not caused by the humans.*

L: They were sent to bring the level of the Earth beings to a higher existence. They were sent to teach those that were here, not to make them slaves. They failed in their assignment. They were supposed to make humans understand and live on a higher order of things. They got stuck.

D: *What do you mean, they got stuck?*

L: They became involved in power and lost the light that was to be given to the human element on the Earth. The Earth was a place to experience new things. And those who came here in hopes of raising those who were already here up to their level, got stuck and were brought down to a lower order instead of vice versa.

D: *In other words, that was integrated into the human species? (Yes) Is that all you want to say about that question? (Yes) Do you want to take another question from the group?*

L: We are rather going into historical background here, so that all may understand what has evolved over many eons. I think this is probably the best way to explain it. To show what has happened in the past and then progress from there. The question was, "Why weren't more sent to help those who had gotten stuck? Why were not some sent to bring those home who were misusing their trust?" The reason being: at that time frame we were afraid if more were sent they too would fall into that pattern. So the decision was made that we would wait until this generation passed, and then send in a new influx with hopes of turning the project around. So that is what happened. The first people who came to Earth were from the planet Tyrantus (Phonetic: Ty rant tus). It is very similar in some respects to the Earth's magnetic field. So it was not difficult for these people to be accepted into the main stream of life. They would not be looked upon as oddities. They looked very much like the Earthlings. Unfortunately they failed.

D: *Those are the ones that wanted power?*

L: Yes. They came first. Some bred with the Earthlings amongst themselves. The second wave that was sent was from (She had difficulty with the name.) Iranius. (Phonetic: Iran i us) These folks were different. They did not look human, and so therefore they came in disguise. They came as animals.

D: *Animals?*

L: Yes. And their job was to very quietly work with selected beings to turn the project around. There were some chosen ones who were given instruction from these animals, as they were thought of. It was on another level, this instruction from these beings was imparted to them in their dreams. They were were instructed on concepts of love, immortality and cooperation among the species. It was done very quietly and subtly. Unfortunately this project also failed, because there were only a few that could be indoctrinated into these new thought systems. And they were scorned by the populace. They, because of the fear of the general populace, were afraid to accept what was being given to them. And of course, the ones in power wouldn't accept it, because then they would lose their power. So by this time man had sunk to the lowest level, and it was a very disappointing situation.

D: *These beings came as animals so they wouldn't be noticed?*

L: Yes, because they were not humanlike.

D: *What did they really look like?*

L: They were very small, and they had large round heads and little bodies that were withery. They had arms and legs, but they were very pliable. They weren't like human arms and legs. They thought they would be too noticeable, and people would be afraid and put them to death.

D: *So they had this ability to make themselves appear as animals?*

L: Right. They had the ability to take on the look of an animal. They disguised themselves. They stepped into that existence.

D: *And this way they could influence people through their dreams, you said, in a subtle way.*

L: Through their dreams. Right. It was hoped that if they could influence enough people that the project could be turned around very quickly. But evidently it was too subtle, too slow, so it failed also.

When I was researching Indian legends for my book *Legend of Starcrash* I found many stories of animals appearing to humans in the earliest times to impart knowledge. This is very much a part of American Indian culture. Other cultures throughout the world also have similar legends. It is interesting to note that in modern day UFO/Alien sightings the extraterrestrials often appear as animals as an overlay or screen memory so the human will not be frightened.

D: *Are you receiving any more questions about this?*

L: The question was, "Why were not more Iraniusans sent to the planet Earth? Since they are a very strong intellectual race, they could overcome all those who were on Earth at that time." And the answer to that, my friend, is: force never ever works. That is not a viable solution. Those on Earth must come to the realization through their own choice. Force has been used too often as a solution to many problems. This never ever works.

D: *That's a good answer. What is the next question?*

L: "How long did this interim time of degradation last before more were sent." It lasted for ten thousand years. The decision was made to allow the Earth to grow a little while on its own, and maybe find something for itself. Things didn't change for a very long time. People grew, but grew in darkness. There was very little light in their hearts.

D: *What were the people doing that was dark?*

L: They were very primitive. And there was not much love. There was much killing, much hate, many power struggles, which continued on for many centuries, many eons. The darkness pervaded for a very long time.

D: *Do you have another question?*

L: Yes. The question is, "What about Earth changes during this time." There were many changes on the surface. There were very many who were taken from the planet in hopes of recruiting lighter energies.

D: *What kind of Earth changes took place during that time?*

L: There were floods. Water, water everywhere. Continents that were together broke apart. There were times of intense heat. Heat so hot that those who were here expired. Some traveled to other parts to escape. Those who did escape started new colonies, praying for guidance and knowledge.

D: *What caused the continents to break apart? And why was there so much water?*

L: Beneath the surface of the Earth there are things called "grids" which hold the earth together. And when all of this was happening, these things within the Earth's surface changed their position and made the continents split apart. The water came from the heat melting the frozen water. When these continents split apart many were lost. Humans, plants, animals, they were lost. Then came the cooling off period after this intense heat. As it cooled much new vegetation began to emerge. New life began to evolve, and there was great hope of having the Earth come into the light. They thought now they had learned that love and acceptance of one's neighbor would thrive. And it did for a while, but not for very long. People tire of a peaceful existence, and look for something exciting and different. And this is what happened eventually.

D: *You mean it was the nature of humans to not be satisfied when things were going good?*

L: Yes. And that is what was hoped to change. But it didn't.

D: *What did they do when they wanted something exciting?*

L: They at first would play games, and then games became a test of strength and will. And one thing led to another, and they were back to the power thing. The "I am important. I am stronger. I am better." This has been very hard for people to understand and learn from. They keep falling into the same trap that is set for them.

D: *Do you think that's because the blood of the ones who came here is integrated into the people? Is that where it came from, or is it human nature?*

L: It is human nature that is magnified on the plane of existence through the intermixing of the cultures. The people from other lands, other places. They came and sought to make the world better, but were taken in. So therefore what they chose to destroy and make better only magnified through them into the Earthly existence.

D: *So their genes helped to make this trait stronger? Would that be a way to say it?*

L: Yes. And they were sent to do something different for the planet. That is why it was a long time before anyone else was sent, because of the fear of magnifying it yet again.

D: *All right. I think that's all the time we're going to have right now for questions. But I can return in a little while and ask more.*

L: That would be fine. I will be here.

D: *And we can continue the story from that point.*

L: We have only touched the surface of the beginning.

D: *We have to begin somewhere. I have many, many questions.*

I then brought Linda forward to full consciousness. She wanted to tell me about an image that remained in her mind. I turned the tape recorder back on for her description.

D: *You said you could see the inside of the world?*

L: It was as if it was hollow, and there were things that held it together. I don't know what they were. They were moving inside. And it was like a lot of stuff was going on top. (Hand motions.) Going like this, up and down. In the middle of the Earth it looked like a hollow ball. And these things on the sides of the ball were moving up and down. I don't know what they were. They were things that held it together. Those people who came the second time had big round heads, and they were silver. They had bodies, but they had these extensions coming out of their arms and in their middle and their legs.

D: *Extensions?*

L: Have you ever seen those statues and drawings from the eastern cultures of some of their gods? They had human faces and bodies, and arms coming out in different directions?

D: *I've seen some that have all these arms.*

L: Yeah, right. Except that these people were very little, and had huge round heads. I don't remember the faces. They had no hair. Then they had all these arms and legs coming out in different places.

D: *Then these were real appendages, real arms and legs.*

L: Right. They were little people. Their whole being was shiny. I don't know if they wore suits or whether it was the people themselves. It was silver all over, one solid color everywhere.

D: *And they knew they couldn't present themselves that way to people, because they looked so different. It would have been too frightening. (Right) Did you mean they could go into an animal or make themselves appear as an animal?*

L: I understood it that they came down and went into the animal somehow. Into their intellect or however they did it, I don't know. They did it so they could be in close proximity of the human being.

D: *I was thinking if an animal started talking to a human, no matter how far back in time, that would have startled them. But it wasn't that way.*

L: No. It was done through the mind somehow, or through their dreams. But the reason they went into these animals was so they could be with the humans in close physical contact. I guess these people must have had pets, because I saw these people sleeping and these animals lying in close proximity.

D: *Could you see what the first people looked like? The ones that were made into slaves?*

L: I saw them in the form of a human being. They were dark. I don't know whether it was the context that they were of the dark side or lower in intelligence or growth or something, but I would see them in dark. And these first beings that came down looked very human, but they were light skinned. You know, in our religious background we're taught that Adam and Eve came and propagated all the other people on the

Earth. And from what I'm getting from this, it is different. There were lots of these people on the Earth. But yet when I picture these dark people they're groveling on the ground. And there again I don't know if that was a synonym type thing for light beings and dark beings. But it was very obvious to me that these light ones were up here and erect, and there's this groveling mass of dark down here.

D: *Of course they must have been very much in awe or frightened of these people. I wonder if they were primitive to begin with, and that's why they were easily enslaved.*

L: I would assume, from what was being said, that they had very little knowledge. And these other beings were here to enlighten them and bring them to a higher level of existence. So from that I would perceive they were very primitive.

D: *There would be a lot of fear and awe, and they took advantage of that. Whether these beings were human, humanoid or whatever, they were not evolved to the point where they couldn't go on a power trip when people were falling down on their knees. So it shows that even somebody that advanced can be corrupted.*

L: They weren't perfect beings, but they were knowledgeable, and I guess that's why they came, to bring their knowledge. They looked human and very regal. Very tall and quite confident. And I remember saying they made gods out of them.

D: *You can see why they would.*

L: And those light beings on that planet that he's telling the story to. They were very bright, white light. It was like a blob. The globs of light. They reminded me of the shape of that Casper the Ghost cartoon. Except that it was very bright intense light, and they were very peaceful, very happy, loving. They just like to share love.

Linda expressed her impatience that we were not getting more information faster. She thought it would only take a few sessions. I reminded her that there was too much information to just pour it all out in an hour and a half. It was also taking longer because she was speaking slower. I was accustomed to working a long time (several months in some cases) to compile information and put it in order, but of course, Linda was not. My part in these projects was to have patience and try to organize the sequence of events.

We stopped to eat supper, rest and visit with Patsy. We began our last session well after dark. We knew it would be late when we finished but it didn't matter to me, because I was unsure of when I would be able to return to Little Rock. We wanted to try and get as much done in one day as possible. I figured she could sleep late the next day and so could I.

The keyword put Linda into the deep trance state once again, and we returned to the same scene we had left a few hours before. Bartholomew continued as though there had been no interruption.

L: I am standing on a platform in front of my students. I am taking questions at this time.

D: *Before we take questions again, I would like to clarify something you said earlier. Those first people that were here on Earth when the others came. Do you know where they came from?*

L: They were here. They were Earth beings.

D: *Were you told what these original beings looked like?*

L: I assumed they were humans like me. I never asked.

D: *All right. Then we had taken the story up to the time where you spoke about the catastrophe with the Earth's continents breaking up, and the people moving to where they would be safe. We were at that point when I was called away. Do you want to take some more questions from your students now?*

L: Yes. My students want to know why these people were dissatisfied with their situation? Why they disrupted the peace they had known for several years? The answer to that is very confusing to me. I was told that they wanted to experience an emotional state of a higher nature. They were tired of the calm. They wanted excitement in their life. And when the games became war, this provided that outlet for them. Their hearts became darkened, and there was much killing, much trauma. It was something they desired for themselves to experience.

D: *They were tired of peace. Bored, so to speak?*

L: Not bored so much as, it did not afford them much emotional outlet. They felt that extremes in behavior promoted their emotional needs. It gave them experiences they wanted to explore for themselves. Not realizing that when they allowed these emotions to rule, they were losing the light within themselves. It did not leave, however it became very, very dim. And all because of wanting to experience the exhilaration of emotional states and trauma.

D: *Didn't you say the space beings decided to leave them alone, and let them try to work things out for themselves?*

L: Yes. At this time there were not many of these people, and they were not a danger to anyone. So it was decided to leave them to their own resources. And they would either grow in this experience or they would be demolished. And then the planet could be given over to others who wanted to live a life of good.

D: *Were the space beings watching the people all this time through their history?*

L: Yes. They would just shake their heads in amazement at the black arts, wondering why.

D: *Where were they watching from? All of these things must have taken a long period of time.*

L: Their time is much different than our concept of time. They could tune into it through mental projections, or sometimes they actually visited the planet in a physical manner. This was not done very often because it was not safe to do so. People here at this time were very bad, and they killed others with no second thought. There was much murder.

D: *Why were these space beings so concerned? Couldn't they just go away and forget about Earth?*

L: No, because there was a master plan for this Earth. It is the most beautiful planet in this universe. It was designed in beauty as an experiment. Unfortunately it never evolved in the way it was designed. It was to be an experiment in emotion and physical pleasures. Things that many other places do not have. It was designed to be an experience for those who came here, and then to leave. People would come here on holiday to experience the Earth, the pleasures that it would give. Physical pleasures that these beings would normally not experience.

D: *You mean, they came here like on vacations and such before the situation got bad?*

L: It was before people inhabited this Earth. Then some of them got so involved in this physical pleasure, they got so mired in it, they did not leave. They stayed to experience it further. The longer they stayed, the less they were able to leave. They lost the ability to leave. So they were here when the first set of beings came. The ones who were supposed to help those who were mired in the physicalness of this planet, to help them regain their light spirits. They also were caught up in it.

D: *They were supposed to help them get back what they had forgotten, but it didn't work that way.*

L: No, because they too were caught. So they stayed also, and became intertwined with those that were here first.

D: *You said it was part of the master plan in the beginning. Can you tell me anything about that?*

L: In the beginning the plan was a beautiful plan. The plan would allow souls to come to Earth to visit the beauty, to

take pleasure in Earthly things, as a reward for things they
had done in other worlds. It was meant to be a short vacation,
short vacation, a pleasurable experience, and then to leave
and go on about their existence.

D: *That was the master plan?*

L: Yes. It was like a reward for a job well done.

D: *It seems like everything went wrong, didn't it?*

L: Yes. It was sad.

This was not the first time I had heard this. In other regressions
dealing with other subjects, Earth is mentioned as a vacation spot,
a holiday retreat, where beings from many different worlds and
dimensions came in the early days before the world was contaminated
by humans. This was said to be before souls became entrapped in the
physicality of Earth.

D: *Does anyone have another question?*

L: When the flood came, and the continents broke apart. He
wants to know if that was an abrupt change or if it was a
gradual thing that happened. In some instances it was very
abrupt. But the heating of the planet was a gradual thing.
What was abrupt was when the flooding began. It destroyed
a great deal and came very quickly. There was practically
nowhere on the planet that it didn't touch. Most inhabitants
were caught and lost. Only very few survived. It was hoped
this would make them see the error they had made previously,
and they could be thankful for the peace that now visited them.
But they soon tired of it.

I wondered about the flood legends that are prevalent in every
culture of the world. But this might have been a very ancient and
primitive time in Earth's history. Apparently the Earth has shifted
several times, and floods of great severity are not uncommon in our
history. The Biblical flood and others may have occurred at a later
date. It is as though there is really nothing new in the physical history
of the world, but a repetition of a series of events. Some of these things
have been recorded in ancient records, and some probably occurred
before our conception of record keeping.

D: *Is there another question? We are following the history very
well.*

L: "Why did the people who were left not leave the planet if
they were enlightened enough to be saved?" The answer is
that they were not enlightened beings. They were still Earth
beings, and they had no desire to leave. They did not know

of an existence outside of their own daily life. So they were not aware of the fact that there was a choice. Therefore they did not know they could leave. And probably it is well they didn't. Question: "Do you think if they had left it would have contaminated other places that they went?" That is a possibility, because their motives were not as pure as some. If they visited places that were receptive to their way of thinking, they might have influenced them. However, there were so few of them, I doubt whether that would have been a possibility. Question: "When was the decision made to send in more light beings?" It was not until many years later, when the Earth was again visited by a ship. There were many people on this ship, and they came, not to stay, but to instruct many who were here. They were not allowed to intermingle with the Earth people. They were only to teach them enough that would stimulate their thinking process to evolve a little more into the light. Question:....

D: *But first, what did those people look like who came this time? You said there were many.*

L: There were very many. They were human like in some ways. Enough that they would be accepted. They were very, very tall, and had funny feet.

D: *Funny feet? What do you mean?*

L: They didn't have hands and feet like ours. They were kept covered so as not to be noticed. They wore shoes and gloves at all times, so as not to frighten anyone. Their eyes were very large, and dark. And they only had holes in their face instead of a nose. They had a mouth although they did not use it in ways that we do. They did not speak a language or eat food of the Earth, nor did they drink liquids.

D: *What did they use for sustenance then?*

L: They have a system totally foreign to human concept. It is an energy system of light, promoted, vitalized, revitalized through a series of light.

D: *You mean it was light that kept them alive?*

L: Yes. Without it they would die. They brought their lights with them on the ship, and would have to rest in a chamber from time to time to become revitalized. They only had to spend a short time in these little places, but it was crucial to their health that they do this on occasion.

A similar concept was reported in *Legacy From the Stars* where beings lay down in a sarcophagus to take a light bath. This was also their only sustenance, and they said the light originated from the Source.

D: *Did these beings all come to one place on the Earth?*

L: No. There were satellite? (as though it was an unfamiliar word) satellite ships that left the main ship and went to different areas where there were people. They kept in contact with the main ship periodically comparing notes on their progress.

This was all said as though repeating information either memorized or hearing it from somewhere. As though it was strange and unfamiliar. A mere recitation of facts.

L: Some were more successful than others. Some failed completely. Most were successful however. They taught very many things to the Earthlings. Things that would enhance their physical existence. Philosophies that would enhance their spiritual and philosophical outlook, hoping to plant that spark of light that might grow.

D: *What kind of things did they teach them to help their physical life?*

L: They gave them knowledge of agriculture: times to plant, times to harvest, how to plant, which they did not know. They were hunters previous to this, and did a lot of killing. The mission was to divert their attention from killing to a more positive mode, such as growth and harvest, another source of food and energy. This also would keep them stationary or in one place, rather than living a nomadic life. They would have more time to think and develop their reasoning powers if they were stationary. They also taught them how to use animals other than killing them. They taught them to be kinder to one another, and to live a more harmonious existence. Unfortunately the people looked upon the teachers again as their gods. But this time the teachers remained true; they were not caught up in the Earthly existence. Their purpose was to come to teach. And when their assignment was finished, they all left together. This experiment was considered a great success. The Earth people were given a better existence, and a reason to expand on what they had. They were taught and they were given a more stable existence than any they had known in a long time. And a chance to use their minds in a way they had not thought of before.

D: *These were very good things.*

L: Yes. It was a very good project, and many were happy and rejoiced for some time over its completion.

D: *But you said some of the teachers went to places where it was a total failure.*

L: Yes, because those people were so steeped in their Earthly pleasures. They could not nor would they accept any help, so they were left to their own devices, to evolve as they would or to be lost. To die off, which many did. Because they didn't listen, they were lost.

D: *Were there any specific races that may have died off because of this? Races that no longer exist on Earth?*

L: In this time the Earth beings were all alike. It would be some time before there would be a difference in color and look. At this time they were all similar, and there were not very many at all.

D: *Do you want to go on with the questions?*

L: Question: "When did the changes come that made the different colors and the different languages, dialects that are spoken on the Earth?" This happened sometime later in the Earth's evolvement. It had to do with other seedings that took place in different areas. People came from all over the universe. Some stayed and intermarried with the Earth beings. This was a long process before it developed into what we know exists today. In my life it was a very long time before I realized there was another color of skin besides the one had known. In my travels I only saw two other colors, but I was told there were more than what I had seen. I had seen the eastern, the yellow race, and I had seen the brown race. I am told there is a red skinned race, which I cannot imagine how that would look on a person. I have been told there is a black skinned, which I could imagine that being. And I am told there is another color which I have not seen. It is like my skin but different. It is more white. I have not seen this either.

D: *Have you been told of any colors that used to be on Earth that no longer exist? (No) But these skin colors occurred because of other beings coming from other worlds?*

L: Yes. It was a slow evolvement.

D: *I had always thought some of it was caused by hot and cold climate. That's not the only factor?*

L: No. That may have happened afterward, but previous to that it was caused by the intermingling of the people. At one time we were all alike. There was no difference. And then we started to marry beings from other worlds, and that is when the changes started to evolve.

D: *What were we like when we were all the same?*

L: When we were all the same, we were brown colored skin. That was the color. It was a very warm brown.

D: *Did we have hair?*

L: No. No hair.

D: *Did that come through the intermingling?*

L: Yes. We intermingled with people from other planets, and also with some animals. We wanted to have the strength of these animals, and thought we could get it by mingling with them. It was a very bad idea, because there were many strange looking beings that evolved from these matings. And it affected our speech and our capacity to think rationally. So it was stopped, because it was very, very bad.

D: *It caused the humans to regress rather than progress.*

L: Yes. They became more animalistic than human. And we had already gone backward enough. So it was forbidden to do any further mingling with animals.

D: *Were there any certain animals that were bred with more than others?*

L: Yes. Ones that were very strong and large were the ones usually chosen, because of the physical strength and the greatness of their stature.

D: *But you said it created some very strange looking beings.*

L: Yes, it did.

D: *Were those traits passed down? They didn't all die off, did they?*

L: No. Some did, but some strengths stayed.

D: *But they were not positive traits.*

L: No. Except for, it did give the Earthlings larger stature than they had previously. They were small in stature, and this did bring about a change in size. And also added physical strength they had not had previously.

D: *But it had enough of a negative side effect that it was forbidden after that.*

L: Yes, it was not good, because these first offspring cared nothing for their families or life. They only sought solitude and physical existences, sheer survival.

D: *It was not what the space beings wanted.*

L: No. The purpose they had in mind was to teach the Earthlings to get along with one another in a more open and loving existence. And these creatures were loners. They did not interact with other beings unless it was necessary for their physical survival. The second generation from these these beings was a little better. They had at least participated in a community.

D: *These space beings that came from many places and interbred, and eventually created the different races. Did they come with good motives?*

L: Some did. They brought with them technology and a philosophy of good intentions. Others came to explore, only to explore. They did not come to teach or to help, but just to see. These people unfortunately could become entangled in the Earthly ways by accident, and it would be difficult for them to want to leave.

D: *So there were different reasons for coming. Was there a reason they were all coming at about the same time?*

L: Because the first experiments in agriculture were successful, and those beings left en masse. And it was thought that the Earth would progress more rapidly if it were given more experiences. The breeding program had been stopped, and it was felt that now was the time to come in and assist in a higher form of existence. Some genuinely came to do this to work. Others came because of the curiosity of it. Others came for selfish motives. They came to conquer. They were warriors in their own existence. Theirs was a very small planet, and most other people did not associate with these beings because they were too self serving. And so they were isolated from the others. They saw this as an opportunity to advance themselves in the universe. You see, no one was allowed to come to Earth for a long time. Then the permission was given to come to the Earth at this time. The first people who came were from the planet Syrus (phonetic: Sy rus). They were the ones that were successful and left. And because they were successful it was felt that maybe others could help also. But that was not the case. Some did, some did not.

D: *These ones that were like warriors, why weren't they forbidden to come?*

L: I think they came without asking. It was unexpected.

D: *I was thinking there might have been some group or someone who would be in charge of this, and keep the undesirable people from coming here. Do you know anything about a group like that?*

L: Yes. It has been in existence for a very long time. However, it was felt that the Earth had so many problems that it wouldn't matter. They were here, they did not ask for permission. They just came. And once they were here it was like they would just integrate. And it couldn't be any worse than what it was.

D: *I see. I thought maybe someone would have ordered them to leave.*

L: They did have some good qualities along with their negative ones. They were highly intellectually evolved. They were

motivated in the wrong direction by their intelligence. They
were dynamic leaders in developmental skills.

D: *Do you have another question from the group?*

L: "I would like to know why these people on Earth could not
be taught a better existence through the aspect of love and
refinement of spirit?" The answer is that they could be
taught these things, if they desired them. But at this time they
did not desire to be any more than what they were. It is a
universal law. One may not infringe on another without
permission. And these people were satisfied with the way
things were, not wanting any changes at that time. It is very
hard for me to understand why a person would not want a
better life if it were offered to him. But that is the way it was.

D: *Didn't they consider it an infringement when they brought
them agriculture and technology?*

L: They accepted these things as gifts. They wanted these things
for themselves. They did not want a new philosophy. They
were only interested at that time in the physical aspects of
their existences.

D: *The material things to help their lives?*

L: Right. They were not interested in anything beyond what
they could feel, see or be. It was only hoped that the planting
of that small spark would allow it to grow, even so slowly,
but at least it was a start. It would take very many eons for it
to be awakened.

I had received this same information from others. It is mostly
presented in *Keepers of the Garden*. In the beginning of my work I
thought the concept of the seeding of the planet Earth rather radical.
But it has been presented through many subjects, and I always think
the repetition of evidence adds validity, because the people involved
have no way of knowing what I have already received.

It was now time for me to again bring the session to a close. "May
I come again and ask more questions, and listen in on your lessons?
You have much to teach me, as well as the others."

L: Yes, you may. It sometimes is confusing to me, these things
that I know. I only hope that I can explain them to you so
you will know the truth. Many distortions have occurred
over the years, and so we have much misinformation about
these things. It will be my pleasure to clarify the things and
to show you the progression, in the hopes that the light will
shine brightly and everyone will see it for themselves. In
this way our planet can evolve and be a part of what it was
destined from the beginning. We will become beings of light

also, if we will only allow ourself to reject all that is not of this light. All that is not of the perfect essence from which we all, at one time, evolved. To get back to that place in one's destiny would be most wondrous.

I then brought Linda back to full consciousness, and Bartholomew once again receded. It was very late when this session was over, almost ten o'clock, and Linda was obviously tired. Toward the end of the session there were longer than normal gaps while she was speaking, almost as though she was falling asleep. A few times I had to prod her by repeating what she had said, to get her to proceed. But when it was typed it all fit together and made sense. We were both tired after this, even though we sat and talked with my friends until after eleven. I knew I would have the same schedule on the next day with Janice. But at least we were able to get a lot of work done in one day.

I intended to try to return to Little Rock at least once a month so I could continue working on these stories. But that did not work out. During the next months I was busy with the final editing and the galley work on the Nostradamus sequel (Volume II). I also had several radio shows. I did not have time to go anywhere or do anything else. Our next opportunity to work was several months later.

CHAPTER THREE
THE ENERGY DEVICES

I did not see Linda again until she and her husband came to my area for the Ozark UFO Conference in Eureka Springs, Arkansas, in April, 1990. We wanted to have at least one session while she was there. I had many things going on and the only time we could get together was between the end of the conference and the banquet. The session was held in her motel room, and we knew there was not time to have a full session. I put an hour tape in the recorder and thought we would try to get as much done as possible. Anything was better than nothing. All during this session I kept watching the clock, knowing we had to quit in time to get dressed for the banquet. I would have liked to continue the story, but I think I got most of what she wanted to say without feeling I was rushing her.

Her husband, John, sat in on this session and seemed to be supportive and quite interested. He said later that he knew this information was not coming from her, because she was not that smart. It was a joking, chauvinistic remark, but it proved a point. He was positive she could not have been making any of this up. She didn't have the imagination, in his opinion.

I used the keyword and counted her back to the same scene when Bartholomew was teaching the glowing globs of light.

L: I am on a platform and I am lecturing to all of these light beings who have waited for me to come to impart my knowledge to them.

She was continuing as though it were the next instant, rather than several months later. It was as though time had stood still waiting for our return.

L: I am telling them the history of the Earth. How it has evolved over the eons, and how many people came from various planets and universes to help the Earthlings progress.
D: *Are you telling them about any specific time in the history?*
L: I have just finished telling them of a time when many teachers came to endow their knowledge to those of the

Earth. They did not stay but a short time to teach them agriculture and building techniques.

D: *Are those the main things they taught?*

L: Yes. They taught how to plant grain, how to irrigate, how to harvest, when to plant, when to harvest, how to store the food so it could be used at a later time. They taught some building techniques that had been unknown to them, so they could build places to live, places to meet.

D: *What type of buildings did they have before that?*

L: They were made of wood and animal skins. And they were taught how to use the resources of the Earth to make brick, to use stone. How to put it together, so as to have a more permanent place that would not be subject to the elements, and so easily destroyed.

D: *Did they teach them anything else?*

L: Only a very few were taught how to use the elements to their benefit. How to use the Sun and the moon and the stars for benefit to the people on this planet. How to use the Sun's energy.

D: *In what way did they teach them to use the Sun's energy?*

L: They taught them by certain devices. How to capture the energy during the day with these devices, so it could be used later as a source of energy. This energy could do many things. It could move things. It could light things. It could preserve things, such as food stuffs. It had many, many uses that the Earthlings were not aware of, because they did not have the proper equipment to capture this energy and put it to proper uses. There were only certain people who were allowed to have this knowledge, and they were sworn to secrecy. These people were looked upon as priests or gods, and they were the only ones allowed to know of these things. They were, however, allowed to choose students to carry on the work that was being done.

D: *Can you describe this device that could do all these many wondrous things?*

L: It was made of a substance from another place, not of this Earth. It looked like a piece of bronze, however this was not what it was. It was long, and it had a triangular shape to it. It laid on the Earth's surface, and had to be manipulated at a certain degree between the Earth and the Sun, at a specific time and place that the Sun was in the sky. It had to be at a particular time of day, and it was crucial that this device be placed at a specific radius and degree between the Sun and the Earth's horizon.

D: *That's all it was, just a piece of metal?*

L: It looked like metal and it was in the shape of a triangle. It was probably five feet long by three feet tall, and it was V shaped in the middle.

D: *You said they also taught them how to use power from the moon and the stars. How was that possible?*

L: The moon has much energy also. Human beings have never understood this. It is a very passive form of energy, totally unlike the Sun which is very active and strong. However, the passive energy of the moon is equally as strong as that of the Sun.

D: *We think of it as being cold.*

L: Yes. It is a different type altogether. And that is why humans think of it as cold, but it is not.

D: *What type of device did they use to capture the moon's energy?*

L: It was shiny and bright like a piece of glass.

D: *Could you see through it like glass?*

L: No. It was silver and shiny, and sat on an arc shaped pedestal. It was concave in the center, and rotated in many directions. It was much larger than the instrument used for the Sun, because of the nature of the energy. It was fifty feet in diameter, and twenty feet in height. It was very, very large.

D: *That's probably why it had to have a pedestal to turn it.*

L: Yes. It took many men to move it.

D: *What was the energy from the moon used for?*

L: The energy of the moon could be used to alter the effects of time on the human form. It could be used for healing the human body. It could be used for many things.

D: *How would it alter the effect of time on the human body?*

L: As a person ages, there is a breakdown in the cellular communication throughout the system. And because of this breakdown, it causes the organs of the body to age and to not function efficiently, therefore starving vital functions of the body. This device rejuvenated the cellular structure, allowing it to function normally, as in a younger age. Only those who were chosen were allowed this knowledge, and this was given to them so they could remain on Earth for longer periods of time to direct the Earthlings.

D: *The energy would have to be stored, wouldn't it, not only directed?*

L: Yes. It was stored in secret places. People were told that these were temples of the gods, and they were made fearful so they would leave them alone and not explore what was inside. They were not allowed to enter these places.

D: *Then the energy of the Sun and the moon were both stored in this type of place?*

L: Yes. In separate chambers, because the energy of the Sun would be destructive to that of the moon.

D: *You also said they used the energy from the stars. How was that done?*

L: They captured bits of light from certain stellar configurations.

D: *The stars are so far away. How were they able to do that? The stars wouldn't have much power.*

L: No, it was not so much the energy, as the placement of the stars in the sky. They were charted and kept track of, so as to learn more about prophecy. More about the spiritual nature of things.

D: *Then it wasn't so much the energy from the stars, it was a study of the stars?*

L: A study of the stars for projections (had difficulty finding words) of other times and... I do not understand. Other... projections of prophecy. Prophecy. I'm confused.

D: *It's something you're not familiar with? Is that what you mean? You don't understand it?*

L: Yes. The placement of the stars in the sky gave them information on prophecy, things that would happen.

It was obvious she was trying to describe astrology, but apparently the entity, Bartholomew, didn't have a word for it or didn't understand the concept. Another example that we were using his mind and not Linda's.

D: *It would seem like a very wonderful place and time, if they were given all these wonderful things to make their lives better. What happened?*

L: It was wonderful for some time. These priests used their knowledge wisely. They helped their people to progress. They were kind. They healed their broken bodies. They protected them. They taught them many things. And then, as has happened many times, negativity takes place and grows like bad weeds in a field. It eventually smothers the wheat or the grain. And these things were lost.

D: *Just a gradual thing, or something sudden that caused the negativity?*

L: It was a gradual deterioration.

D: *And this caused the loss of the knowledge?*

L: Yes. These wonderful things that were given to the Earthlings as gifts were destroyed because there was an uprising amongst the common people, who wanted to have the energy of the Sun. They found out it was stored in this certain temple of, what they thought was the gods. And they wanted it for the masses. They thought this would make them powerful. And they raised an army to overtake the temple, and the priests were slaughtered. And when they entered the temple they were, of course, not able to use the energy properly, because they did not have the knowledge. And it was destroyed. There was huge devastation, explosions, fire, and mass destruction. And it was lost.

D: *This would have destroyed the other energy from the moon also, wouldn't it?*

L: Yes. There was no danger of explosion from the moon's energy. However, because it was kept in close proximity, it was also destroyed.

D: *Were the original devices also destroyed?*

L: Yes, because they were kept in this place.

D: *Couldn't the people who originally gave them this knowledge come and give it to them again?*

L: No, because they had been gone from the Earth for a long time, several hundred years. They had gone back home. They were not aware of what had taken place.

D: *That group of beings seemed to be a positive group. They were trying to give humans some knowledge they could use.*

L: Yes. They were very saddened when they found out, but it was a long time after it had happened. And the decision was made not to replace it at that time.

D: *But there must have been survivors of that group of people on Earth.*

L: Yes, there were those who were in outlying areas, and were not involved in the actual siege of the temple. They were away from the center of the upheaval. They were the very old or the very young, and they thought it was the anger of the gods of the temple that caused this destruction. So they were not aware of what really happened.

D: *I imagine their life was quite different after that.*

L: Yes, it was, because they had to rely on what little knowledge they had. They could only plant when they remembered. They had no direction from the priests. However, they managed. They did very well with what little resources they had.

D: *They were probably never able to get back to the other state where they had all the power and energy to help them.*

L: No, they didn't. It was a major, major setback. Many things were lost. Much technology and many secrets.

D: *Did the survivors return to primitive ways?*

L: Yes. However, they continued to build homes and to plant fields, and they continued to trade with other people, as they had previously.

D: *Then they still remembered how to build with the rock and stone.*

L: Yes. However, they did not have the devices that they had previously to move the stone. It had to be all done by hand. There was no energy to move it.

D: *Was this the Sun's energy that was used to move the stones into place? (Yes) Was some of this done by levitation? Or do you know what I mean?*

L: Yes, I guess you could call it that. This energy entered the stone or whatever was to be moved, and it drew it like a magnet to whatever position was calculated. And when it reached that station it was released, and it just stayed there.

D: *So after the destruction of these energy sources it had to be done by hand.*

L: Right. Because they didn't know how it was done.

D: *They retained partial knowledge but it wasn't enough. There are many lessons to be learned from these things.*

L: Yes, there are very many things to know. Some of them are very, very sad.

I brought Linda forward. This session couldn't be as long as normal, because we had to get ready to go to the banquet, and we were really pushing the time.

When Linda awakened she drew how she perceived the devices. In the case of the one for the Sun she took a piece of paper and folded it in half to show the angle of the triangle.

Because of the final editing and galley proofing of the Nostradamus sequel, I was unable to work with Linda again until I went to Little Rock in June, 1990, for a writer's convention.

* * *

I drove to Little Rock in June, 1990, to attend the Writer's Convention. In addition I intended to work with both Linda and Janice, even though I had a full schedule. I was able to have only one session with Linda.

Using the keyword I counted her back to the time of the glowing beings and Bartholomew's continuing story to them.

L: I am surrounded by these light beings. They are bombarding me with questions. There is so much to know, and we are very excited about being able to absorb all this knowledge for safe keeping, to be given to others at its proper time. We feel very blessed to be chosen for this work. There is much chatter. I must calm everyone so the work can progress. (Pause) I have now accomplished this, and we are ready to continue on this mission.

D: *Can you repeat for me the questions that they ask?*

L: There were many, and everyone was speaking at one time. We are going to continue on from where this excitement began to cause such disruption. It had to do with the energy sources that were received from the Sun and the moon. (Two months had passed, yet they continued from the last instance.) This is what caused all the excitement. Because there are many Suns and many moons in the universe, and they all contain this power and energy. It is the same on many same on many planets, and this energy can be harnessed as it was on the Earth, for use for mankind and all interplanetary journeys.

D: *It can be utilized as a source of power, you mean?*

L: Yes. It can be used for many things. Not only as a propellant and a source of power and energy, but it also has many other uses. Plus growth of spirituality of the beings who inhabit a particular planet or area. It has the potential for healing and with this healing comes spiritual growth and knowledge. This is what caused the disruption, because it was so exciting.

D: *Had they never heard of that before?*

L: Some had, but most had not. They had thought about these things, but did not know for sure. For some this was a verification.

D: *Of course, the problem is always how to harness the energy to make it work in these ways.*

L: That is correct, but it is not a very difficult process. It is a very simple task. However, not very many know of this, because it is so simple. It is a process of magnification, of absorption of the energy through magnification from the Source. The energy is collected and magnified tenfold, and then absorbed into a collective device to be distributed at the proper moment. The magnification process is the most important part of the process. And unless this is understood and done properly the process will not work. The collection and the distribution cannot be accomplished unless the magnification has taken place properly. This is where many have failed. They have tried very hard, but have missed the simplest aspect of the process.

D: *What is that simple aspect?*

L: The simple aspect is not size, but the quality of the material used in the magnification of the energy. This material cannot be found in very many places in the universe. It is only available on certain planets. The Earth is one of these places where this substance is readily available. And that is why the universal pact with the Earth people was so important to everyone concerned, even though the Earthlings are very primitive. And it has been tried very many times to help them evolve to a higher understanding, which has failed many times also.

D: *What kind of pact was made?*

L: A pact was made with the Earthlings on several occasions to allow intergalactic flights to come and trade for this material. From time to time there were disruptions in this trading, because of the warring nature of the Earthling. Things were destroyed, people left, and new pacts had to be renegotiated. Most times these were made with the leaders in particular areas on the Earth. Sometimes they could be negotiated with private citizens who had charge of a particular area.

D: *I'm thinking of a pact as usually negotiating for something in return. (Yes) What did the Earthlings receive in return?*

L: The Earthlings received technology they had not known before, or a help in technology they were developing in a very primitive stage. In these pacts they were given more information to help them develop what they happened to be working on at that particular time. It just speeded the process up a great deal. And more knowledge was able to be put into practice.

D: *What is this material that they wanted so badly?*

L: This material is a mineral found just beneath the Earth's surface. It is a fine, powdery substance which can be taken, and once put under pressure it is formed into thin sheets. These sheets are used in the magnifying process, and must be constantly changed as they filter the energy, shortly after use. So they must constantly be replaced. There is a great deal of this substance in many places around the Earth. And it is very easy to access it with the right tools.

D: *So it is very common. What color is the powdery substance?*

L: It is gray, varying shades of gray. Sometimes it could be mistaken for dirt, but it is very fine in consistency, almost powdery.

D: *In the construction of these sheets, you said it's put under pressure. Does it have to be heated, or are there any other steps in the process to convert the powder to the sheets?*

L: No, it is just tremendous pressure. While in this pressure chamber, because of the degree of pressure, it becomes very hot. No heat needs to be added. It just becomes hot from the pressure exerted on it.

D: *And then it is formed into sheets?*

L: Yes. Very thin sheets, very pliable sheets.

D: *And then this is used in the magnification process. (Yes) And then you said it was absorbed into a collective chamber? (Yes) You said propellant was one use. If this was going to be used on some kind of a craft, would it have to be onboard the craft?*

L: Yes. There is a collective portion on the craft, within the belly of the craft. Much energy is stored here for long trips. It is not a very large space that is needed for this container, because the energy is very powerful and can take it for long periods of time.

D: *Then it can go for long distances and long periods of time without being replenished?*

L: Yes. Many, many years.

D: *Then the craft must eventually return to the source of the energy to be recharged?*

L: Yes. However, they are now working on a portable device that can collect this energy from different moons and Suns, by having these sheets onboard. However, this has not been very successful, because the sheets are very.... (Long pause) I think the word is "fragile". And they have to be kept in a certain manner and temperature control. If it varies very much one way or the other, it destroys the ability of the sheet to magnify the energy without filtering it. These sheets are not made very far in advance, because they lose their ability. The substance of which the sheets are made can be stored for long periods without losing its ability. But the sheet, once made, must be used within a short period of time.

D: *When these are in natural conditions, such as on the Earth, are the sheets more stable?*

L: No. It is the same problem. The actual powder can be stored for long periods. Once pressurized into the sheet, it must be used soon.

D: *Is it dangerous for humans or any beings to handle this substance? (No) So it is a perfectly safe component or element?*

L: Yes. It is what you will call "inert." It has no particular properties until the pressurization process activates it.

D: *So this is what the beings wanted when they made these pacts with Earth.*

L: Yes. Otherwise the Earth would be left to its own devices, because those who people it are very unpredictable and have tried the patience of many from other lands.

D: *Is it one group that has learned to use this element as a power source?*

L: No, there are many who know of it, and they visit from time to time. However, they are controlled by a council. There are representatives from each place who sit on this council. And they make the decisions: who may visit and what they may give and take from the Earth. It is all decided beforehand before any contact is made. No one may come without permission from this council.

D: *I have heard of this council before, and I have always been curious about where it is located. Do you have that information?*

L: This council is located in a place that is inaccessible to anyone but a council member. And they must be a being in high respect of their peers. No one knows exactly where it is.

D: *But it is a physical place?*

L: No, it is not a physical place. It is on another plane, and is only accessible by those who are evolved enough to go there.

D: *Then they give permission to come and get this material. And to trade knowledge with the Earthlings.*

L: That is correct.

D: *Am I correct in assuming that other groups have also come for other reasons, besides obtaining the material?*

L: Yes. Some groups come to learn why we do the things we do. They come to observe our ways. Some come to try to teach us how to be a more peaceful people. There are many reasons There are many reasons why they come, not just for trading purposes. Some come just strictly out of curiosity, but not very often, because this permission to enter the atmosphere is not given solely for curiosity.

D: *They must have a purpose then.*

L: That is correct.

D: *Do any of these groups ever come for negative purposes?*

L: Not very often, because the council is very wise and they do not permit it. The Earthlings have enough negativity for many lifetimes. However, sometimes people who visit get involved in the negativity that is here, and react in such a manner as to make them seem negative. When removed from this atmosphere they are not.

D: *Then this is one way of collecting energy and creating propulsion for crafts. Aren't there other ways?*

L: There are many ways of making propellants for crafts for energy. This is only one way. However, this way, even though more critical in its collection, is less harmful to the environment of most planets. It is such a powerful method and can be stored very easily in small spaces, that it makes it very desirable.

D: *Then there are other methods that are dangerous or harmful to the environment?*

L: Very much so, as you know from what is going on now in the Earth's time that you live. This is being worked on in your time, and when people become more aware of what can be done, many things that you now use for energy will no longer be available for use on the Earth. But it will take an awakening. There are many people who do not want this change.

D: *Did these beings use these more dangerous types of power at one time?*

L: No, not the power that you are speaking of. Nuclear power was investigated, but never used. It was discarded as being too pollutant to the galaxies. It was not a good source as it was very volatile.

D: *So they found the safer methods. I was thinking if that element was so rare and hard to find on other planets, they might have developed other methods that were more convenient for them.*

L: This is true. They have found other planets where this material is readily available. However, the Earth is a closer source than some of the others. And that is why it has been pursued. Otherwise it would have been left alone. It was just more convenient.

D: *And the Earthlings could develop this themselves if they understood the process?*

L: Yes. This process has been given to some, but it has not found very much acceptance, because there are many who benefit economically from the other ways. And the other ways seem to be, to the Earthlings, a better source. It is something that has been here longer, they think. But in reality this is not so. These other energy sources have been used here before many times. However, they were lost many times also.

D: *I thought maybe it was because it was so simple that they didn't believe it would work.*

L: That is part of it, but it goes much deeper than that. It has to do with power and greed. There is a question from my students. They want to know how the material was discovered by the visitors. I am telling them that starships once again came to the Earth to visit. It was by accident that they discovered this material they have been using for energy. It was quite a revelation, and they were very ecstatic to find it, because they had been journeying far into other galaxies to collect this mineral. The expedition this time was to give medical knowledge to physicians who were practicing medicine very archaically, and killing many people. They came to teach them some basic knowledge of the physical biological makeup of the human being. It was a much needed operation in order that life could progress on this planet. While here there was a great plague and many were dying daily. They were trying to decide what to do with the corpses. It was during this time frame that the mineral was discovered while they were digging mass graves.

D: *The space people or the Earth people?*

L: Earth people. The space people were observing what was going on at that time. They never interfere with the day to day life of human beings. They only observe and provide avenues for humans to learn their technique.

D: *But if they didn't interfere, how were they giving the humans, the doctors, the information?*

L: Through mental telepathy. Doctors thought it was something they had discovered on their own. They needed to know how diseases were transmitted from one to another, and how it lived in the blood. Blood is very crucial to the life force of a human body.

D: *And the humans, the doctors, didn't know how the disease was transmitted?*

L: No, they weren't aware of the necessity, the value, of the blood flowing through the human body. It was very necessary to the life force of the human for this blood to be in the body. And they did not practice good hygiene.

D: *At that time period they didn't know about germs either, did they?*

L: No. This was what they were trying to convey to them, about bacteria and allowing the blood to leak out of the body.

D: *To leak out?*

L: They did not stop the blood from leaving the body. They did not know it was necessary. And so if one had a wound and bled profusely, they did nothing to stop it. They did not know that it was necessary for living, to maintain a certain amount of blood within the body. This was one of the mistakes they were making. And the lack of cleanliness caused bacterial infections. It allowed bacteria to enter the body and the blood stream. It was unknown at that time about disinfecting and washing and being clean. They had no knowledge of chemicals. The first step was to teach them to use water to wash themselves thoroughly. And to keep the environment clean.

D: *Were they able to transmit this knowledge through one doctor or....?*

L: Through many. The seeds of this knowledge were planted through minds, from one mind to another. Most of the doctors thought it was their own idea. It was not given in such a manner that they felt they were given this knowledge by another. It was just something that occurred to them.

D: *I was thinking if they just gave it to one man, he might be feared or considered unusual.*

L: No. The many gave it to many. And when they compared notes, they agreed that this was a good idea.

D: *But didn't the beings think this was interfering?*

L: No. They gave it as a gift, and it was up to the individual whether he wanted to take it or not. It's not considered interference because they had the opportunity to decline. Something had to be done. Many were dying.

D: *Did this plague happen at the same time they decided to give them the information?*

L: It was occurring when they came. That is why they came. Many were dying. And it was feared that the balance of life would be affected, and eventually the human race would die out on this planet. And this was not what was desired. This group was sent here for this mission. And because they did their mission well, it was a gift to find a better source of energy than they had known previously.

D: *Then this material was not something they were using at that time?*

L: They had experimented with it. However, it was unavailable to them where they were, and it was a long voyage to obtain it. So the idea was discarded because of unavailability.

D: *What type of energy were they using up to that time?*

L: They were using light. And this was all right. However, there are times when it is not available and runs out.

D: *Where did the light come from?*

L: It is collected on sheets. (Slowly as though she did not understand what she was seeing.) On panels. Sheets. However, some places that were traveled had no light to revitalize their panels. And therefore they ran out of power, and had to be rescued by another vehicle.

D: *Where did the light source come from originally?*

L: From the Suns in various galaxies.

D: *But these would have been very far away if they were traveling in space.*

L: Yes. This was the disadvantage. (Slowly, as though studying something.) Some of these panels had magnifying lenses that were able to transmit the light from these Suns at very far distances. But it took very large pieces of machinery to do this, and it was not feasible to have these on crafts. So they only had their panels for energy, and could not travel very far distances lest they run out of fuel.

D: *What about crystal power? Did they experiment with that?*

L: No. At this time it had not occurred to them to explore that possibility. They were looking for another system, because when they were traveling at great distances it was not good if they went out of range of a light source.

D: *So this new material had great magnifying properties. Is that correct?*

L: No, the material itself did not have these properties. However, they had the ability to transform it with the magnifying abilities they already possessed. It was a very simple process to transform these granules through their system, and have the ability for storage in small containers, so that travel at great distances could be achieved with the least amount of package.

D: *Was the source of the power still light?*

L: Yes, light is necessary and utilized. However, these granules were used to store. This was the missing property in their whole energy system. It enabled them to store their energy in very small containers, where previously they had to have very large panels in order to propel their vehicles. This revolutionized their entire energy system, and they found various ways to use it. Not only for vehicles, but for many varied operations. At first they just took it. But then they had to negotiate for it, as time went on. What they were doing was discovered, and they had to barter for it. But for a very long time that wasn't necessary. At first when they were discovered they just moved to another area that was not inhabited at that time. But as the populace grew on the Earth there was very little area in which they could obtain this mineral that was not populated. So negotiations have been made with several governments all over the Earth, not just in this one place. It was feared they would be stopped, so they made agreements in several different places.

D: *Could we return to the history you were speaking of? You said they made pacts with the people to help them obtain this material. And they would reward them with technology of some type, knowledge that they could use in their lives at that time.*

L: That is correct.

D: *Then what would happen to break the pact?*

L: The pact would be broken on several occasions when the physical nature of the human being would allow power and greed to take over. To want to use this technology for purposes of war, of destruction, rather than to help mankind. When these things would occur, the humans would try to conquer the beings who came. And when this occurred, those who came here from other places would leave for a time, until a new generation could evolve and a new pact could be made.

D: *So the Earthlings would take the technology that was given them, for whatever purpose or benefit, and turn it into warlike things. Is that what you mean?*

L: Yes. Many times this happened, many times.

D: *It seems strange that they would turn it on their benefactors.*

L: They thought if they had this power, they could control the benefactors and make them do as they wished them to do. They felt they had the only source available to these other planetary beings, but they were mistaken, because there were many other places on the Earth.

D: *So then the beings would withdraw?*

L: Yes. They would leave. And many times, depending on the transgressions made, they would remove all their technology, or they would destroy it so it could not be used in a negative way. Then the people would regress. This has happened very many times over the life of this Earth. It seems like mankind evolves to a higher state and then they allow power and greed to completely absorb them and what they have learned. Then they are destroyed, and they take many, many steps backward.

When Bartholomew entered the world of the little glowing light beings he apparently transcended our concept of time, or rather, time did not exist there. In the beginning he was supplying information from the mind of Bartholomew, information that had been given by his strange friend. The longer he reported he began to have access to information from future times that would not have been available to Bartholomew. He had truly transcended time and was in a place where past, present and future were all one. This is the only way I can explain his access to information pertinent to our present timeframe. His mind (in conjunction with Linda's mind) had been expanded in its ability to access and assimilate complicated and relevant facts.

But what was the purpose of teaching these little beings? What part would they play in our time?

L: Humans have not been able to learn enough from past transgressions to allow them to evolve past a certain point. This has been a very serious problem throughout many these lifetimes. The beings are hoping sometime to help these Earthlings in their evolution past this one space. Once they evolve past this space, they will allow themselves to evolve further along the way. That one obstacle continues to cause major regressions into past mistakes. This is why we are meeting now, to find a way to close the gap, so that mankind can make that leap forward in their evolution. And we are helping to do this. All of these beings here today are wanting to help close this chasm once and for all. So that mankind may evolve into what has always been there for them. And through their ignorance they were unable to close it for themselves.

D: *How are they able to help us?*

L: Many, many will be sent soon to work in everyday things. To enlighten in a subtle manner, to send a message of love, so that this can be closed once and for all. Many will choose not to stay on Earth. But those who do will work very hard and will be granted many wonderful things for their work.

D: *You mean these little energy beings would come to Earth to help? (Yes) How will they do that? Will they remain in their energy forms of light?*

L: Some will remain as they are. Others will have the ability to enter many human bodies. One light being will have the ability to enter ten human bodies at one time. And lighten the human body itself, to allow a progression of thought and spiritual growth that to this point was an impossibility.

D: *Will they enter bodies that are living on Earth and occupied by another spirit?*

L: Yes. They will not disrupt any natural law or take over the body. They will only be a speck of light that will lighten the physical body itself, and enable it to grow.

D: *I thought you meant they will enter as a soul and live a life from the baby onward.*

L: No, no. This is not possible. These light beings are so light and so evolved they have no need to take on a physical existence. This is not what they were designed to do. They are beyond your concept. They are not a soul, as you would consider them to be. They are light beings evolved from a God of all creation. The Source.

D: *But our souls also evolved from that.*

L: Yes, that is true. However, there are many, many different sources from the One, and they were all designed differently for different purposes. Yet they are all part of the same.

D: *But if they enter the human body for a little while you said it would not possess or take over, but to help is it allowed to do that by the rules of the universe? I'm thinking of the soul as being the guardian of the body. Is something else allowed to enter?*

L: Yes. It may enter if it is agreed upon beforehand. These light beings are so pure that they would not impose their will upon another. There will be many souls who are waiting anxiously for their assistance.

D: *Is this permission between the two given consciously?*

L: No. It is given on another level.

D: *So the conscious individual does not know what is happening?*

L: That is correct. They know something is changing, on a conscious level. However, they do not know exactly what. As they accept this in their conscious state and allow the evolution, they will find the answer and they will then know what I am telling you. At first they will only have a feeling of change of thought patterns. And they will wonder about this. But it will be a strong feeling that they must change, even though it is not understood why or how.

D: *But this will not occur with every individual.*

L: No. Only some, and these will bring others along to their way of thinking. Some will choose otherwise. Some are unwilling to change. They will fight this vehemently, and will cause much pain and trouble. But these negative ones will be eventually overshadowed by the majority who want to make the transition. And they will be forced to leave, because they will be very unhappy in the environment being made.

D: *These are probably people who wouldn't make an agreement for the being to make this entry anyway.*

L: No. I want to make it clear that these light beings in no way will interfere with the human body or soul or purpose in which they are to live this lifetime. They are only there to enable a certain growth to take place. They are not there to change anything that has been agreed upon or established thus far.

D: *That would be an invasion of the free will of the individual.*

L: That is correct. They are only a spark to allow the human to cross the chasm and close it once and for all, so that this back sliding into primitive ways can be stopped.

D: *Is this the reason they are coming as a spirit form, so to speak? Because the physical beings have not been able to accomplish this on their own?*

L: That is correct.

D: *Other beings tried many different ways, and like you said, they were caught up in the physicalness of the planet sometimes. And they also failed in many other ways.*

L: Yes. And this is why these light beings were created.

D: *To perform this task in a different way.*

L: Yes. For no other reason are these beings here.

D: *Is this the reason why Bartholomew has to teach them the history of our Earth?*

L: Yes, they must know how many times this has occurred. They must understand thoroughly human nature, so they will not transgress in any way. The human element must accomplish this for themselves.

D: *When they make an entry, so to speak, does the human have to be more open at that time? (Yes) Is this accomplished in a certain way? I'm thinking of a human having natural defense systems subconsciously.*

L: Yes. This will be a transition made very simply. All that is needed is a desire to grow. Not a walking in, not a taking over, but a blending, a merging, an adding to, a combining. An element being added that enhances but does not diminish.

D: *That makes sense if it won't work any other way. Are there any other spirits or beings that are planning to come to Earth to help in all of this?*

L: At this time it is a wait and see. It is hoped by the council that once Earth beings have evolved, that a coming and going of many from other places might be accomplished. And a trade network set up on an open policy rather than a hidden policy. Earth can be a more open place to visit.

When I received this information in the beginning of my work I thought it was complicated, but over the years it has been corroborated by many other sessions from all over the world.

SECTION TWO

Continuation From "The Custodians"

CHAPTER FOUR
JANICE'S OMITTED TRANSCRIPTS

When I was writing my book *The Custodians* I was focusing on my research with UFO and suspected abduction cases. It explained how I began (as most other investigators do) with the simple cases of sightings, landings, and abductions. It traced my work as it progressed from the simple to the complex. The last section of the book involved my work during the late 1980s and early 1990s with one young woman who lived in Little Rock, Arkansas. She supplied a great deal of valuable information which allowed me to discover that the extraterrestrials were not only coming from other planets and galaxies, but from other dimensions. Some of the concepts they gave me were mind expanding, because they had not been reported by others.

A strange phenomenon occurred when I worked with Janice. After we were into the session and she was in the deepest possible level of trance (the somnambulistic level) her personality would disappear, and other entities would speak through her. These were often beings onboard the spacecraft she was taken to. This curious phenomenon also occurred with other subjects I worked with, as though I had established some kind of direct pipeline to these beings. The information that came from Janice was so voluminous that it took up most of *The Custodians*. These beings would answer any of my questions and supplied information on a large variety of subjects.

My concern was that *The Custodians* was growing into a huge book, and I knew some information would have to be deleted. I found that in portions of the sessions Janice was moving away from UFOs and spacecraft, and exposing new ground into more complicated metaphysical concepts. We were no longer communicating with only beings that operated spaceships and conducted the many experiments in the Earth project. We seemed to have contacted more advanced beings, familiar to the space people, but unknown to us. I then decided to delete those portions from that book, so it would remain true to its original concept and the focus would remain on my work with extraterrestrials.

I had been accumulating information for many years during my normal regressions that overstepped the line into an area of the paranormal that I was unfamiliar with. To remain true to the focus of the books I was writing at the time, I did not include these concepts. I also knew I could not destroy that information just because I did not understand it. I put it to the side, knowing at some time in the future it would have value as my understanding increased. I did not know if and when the general public would be capable of understanding some of this, so I decided to write a book that would strictly deal with this information, and hoped there would be people who liked having their minds expanded. It certainly did expand my mind, and rearranged my pattern of thinking. Every time I would smugly think I had all the information, and had formulated a way of understanding the way the universe works, "they" would slyly supply information that expanded the concepts and started my mind exploring in another direction. "They" have always done it gently, spoon feeding me a little at a time so I would not be frightened off, and be able to digest the next tantalizing morsel. I could have refused, saying that I did not want my beliefs challenged, that I was comfortable with my own theories and did not want my line of thinking upset, but I am too curious for that. I want to know what's around the next curve in the exciting journey. Even if I didn't understand it, maybe there would be those out there who would. So my exploration has been aimed at those who like their minds bent like pretzels. My books are designed to make people think.

* * *

The sessions with Janice occurred during the late 1980s and early 1990s while I was heavily involved writing the Nostradamus material. In 1986 I was asked to become a UFO investigator in Arkansas, and that was my first exposure to this fascinating subject. All this was told in *The Custodians*. I would travel from my home in the mountains of Northwest Arkansas to Little Rock to work with two women who had proved to be excellent subjects, and were supplying wonderful information. Since it was a four hour drive I tried to have as many sessions as possible while I was there.

I would stay at my friend Patsy's house where I had the privacy of an upstairs bedroom for the sessions. Janice came there and I tried to have several sessions with Janice in one day. On one of these trips it appeared that three sessions in one day was too much for both of us since the sessions lasted late into the night. After that we tried to see how many we could do without overburdening either one of us.

On this trip in 1990 we intended to explore another event of missing time Janice had the month before. She was invited to a Saturday afternoon dinner with many friends at a house outside of Little Rock. She called her friend before leaving the house to be sure she didn't need any last minute items, and then got on the freeway. When she arrived, her friend was quite aggravated with her. The party was over and guests were leaving. Her friend said, "At least you could have called and told me you would be late!" Janice did not know what she was talking about, until she discovered four hours had elapsed since she had left home.

This was very similar to the office lunch incident reported in *The Custodians*, where several hours disappeared without her knowledge. It was definitely creating problems with her social life. Janice had reached the point where she avoided making social commitments in order to keep from being put in the embarrassing situation of having to explain these oddities to friends. It was made more difficult because she didn't have any explanations herself, until we started working in 1989, and discovered she was being taken (car and all) from the freeway. After the incident she would be deposited back on the freeway, confused, but unaware that a large block of time was missing from her life.

In our work we discovered that Janice had been working with extraterrestrials all of her life, unknown to her conscious mind. Her experiences had progressed from early reproduction experiments to participating in complicated classes onboard the wonderful and enormous "mother" craft, where she could study any subject in the universe. Of course, all of this teaching was never available to her conscious mind. It was being held in her subconscious mind until the time was right for it to be released. One part of her knew there were important things happening to her on another level, but that didn't help the confusion it brought to her normal waking life.

I began the session by using her keyword that put her immediately into the deep level of trance. I then had her regress to the day the missing time event occurred.

She relived the details of getting ready to leave the house, but she had some apprehension, because she felt something was going to happen. "I can feel the presence of my friends. They've been here for days. I had a premonition of... I knew I was going to do some work, and I just didn't want to be at the dinner, because other people were going to be there. And I don't want to be exposed. It's a private thing, not to be sensationalized by a bunch of people who don't understand. So I don't want to go, because I know I'm going to have an experience. It's coming, but yet I don't know when. So I thought I should stay home and let it happen where I was by myself."

These feelings must have been on a subconscious level, because consciously Janice normally only felt uneasy sensations before an event, without knowing where they were coming from or what they meant. The connection was always unclear, mostly because it was happening on another level inaccessible to her waking conscious mind. Only later would they be associated with the missing time episodes.

She left the house, but the apprehensions continued. "I was beginning to feel the strange sensations. And I've learned that it's okay to drive when it happens. I don't have to worry about having a wreck or anything. In the beginning, I was sometimes afraid I wouldn't be able to drive. It seems scary to not be able to know." She had not driven very far on the freeway when she whispered, "Ohhh! There they are!" Her facial expressions indicated something was happening.

J: (In awe.) Huge! Huge ship! It's in front of me, but it's above me. I'm looking, and I think, "What exit?" I was only on the freeway for a minute or two, and there it is.

D: *Do you see other cars around you?*

J: I know there are other cars, but it's like I'm the only one. It's like I'm in a corridor, for lack of a better term. It's like I'm in my own "space," but it's separate from the other cars' space.

This phenomenon of being separated from the outside world when these events occur was explored in *The Custodians*, where no one else seems to see anything. I have learned it is an individual experience and is invisible to anyone that is not involved.

J: I've seen large ships, but this one is just astronomical. Whew! (She was definitely in awe.) It's a gray color like the sky looks on a cloudy day. There are different sets or lines of little windows, because it's several stories up. It's just huge!

D: *Then what happens?*

J: I'm just blipped. (I didn't understand.) Swhooosh! Just snap your fingers, and it's just blip. Poof! It's an instant thing. It's almost as fast as a thought can be. One minute I was on the freeway, and then I wasn't any more. I'm up there.

D: *Is your car up there too?*

J: Oh, yeah.

D: *Tell me what you see.*

J: It's like you have your own city there. It's just so big. And we leave the car right there, and I go with them. You know they're waiting for you, and they take you where you have to go. This place is so big you would get lost. You couldn't even find your way around. It's so big.

Her escorts directed her to get on a strange contraption. "You're tilted. It looks like a seat by itself. There are no wires. I was looking for the wires."

There was then a sharp intake of breath, and she seemed uncomfortable. I could see she was experiencing something that was an unfamiliar physical sensation. It seemed to take her breath away. "How does that thing go like that? It moves very fast."

She reported becoming dizzy, so I supplied instructions to alleviate any physical sensations. For several seconds she described the sensation of moving very fast, and literally had to keep trying to catch her breath. This was punctuated by vocal exclamations. She could not describe the appearance of the area she was rocketing through because it became a blur of color, and the sensations took precedence.

> J: Oh, goodness! Ooohh! It was really fast. Really, really, really fast. My body feels weird. (An almost hysterical laugh.) Oh, it tingles all over.

I continued to give suggestions of well being as she took deep breaths. I was trying to move her ahead so she would arrive somewhere, and the sensations could subside. After a few seconds her breathing was returning to normal. Then her next remark surprised me.

> J: (Whispering) You're so loud. You're so loud!

This was confusing. I had not increased the volume of my voice. This is not done because that could break the trance state if you alter the pitch.

> J: It's like a megaphone.

She was sighing and moaning, obviously still recovering from the frantic ride. I gave instructions that she would perceive my voice in a normal manner.

> J: Thank you. It was like a megaphone for a minute.
> D: *What do you see as it slows down?*
> J: It's not slowed down in my mind yet. Physically I am, but it's still fast. It's still fast.
> D: *Things are returning to normal, because we don't want you to have any kind of discomfort.*
> J: It's not discomfort. Don't misunderstand. It may be necessary to feel it. I'm participating because I want to. It's not discomfort. It's an experience. You can't do that here. Oh, my gosh, it was fast! See, you have to go fast to get past the speed of light.
> D: *But it won't bother this physical body.*
> J: Well, the physical body's been adjusted. Its tolerance level has been.... There's another word, besides adjustment, but I don't know what it is.

She was breathing heavily again. Then she became hot, and moved around to get out from underneath the cover. I helped her. This sometimes happened and indicated a fluctuation of energy. Sometimes the subject can shift from hot to cold and back again. She went through several seconds of alternating discomfort as though she was still feeling the acceleration. I was still trying to get her to the end of her journey so we could continue with the story. After a few seconds of suggestions she took a deep breath, relaxed, and began making very graceful hand motions.

D: *Why are you making those motions?*
J: (Softly) It's a greeting.
D: *Who are you greeting?*
J: A being.

She continued with the hand motions, almost reverently, and indicated the being in front of her was also making the same motions. Almost oblivious of me, she was concentrating on her motions. I had to get her talking again. I asked for a description of the being.

J: The being is an area that is light, but it's a body. Like it's not physical yet. The light is very bright. It is the absence of color. You would say it is the brightest light you have ever seen.
D: *Is he conversing with you?*
J: Yes. It's like instructions of some kind. Explanations and instructions.
D: *Can you repeat what he's saying?*
J: Well, I don't hear them. (Sigh of frustration.) It's not in words. It's like if you saw dust coming, or you felt it going into yourself. I mean, it's more than your brain. It's more.

I have received letters from many readers who have strange experiences of receiving information through symbols that seem to go directly into their brain. This sometimes occurs after or while having a UFO sighting. At other times it has occurred while the person is lying on a bed or sofa, and geometric symbols appear to enter their brain through a beam of light coming through a window. I have received too many of these reports to dismiss them as fantasy. This was also reported in *The Custodians* as the aliens said information was being imparted very quickly on a cellular level. They said the information would come forth into the conscious mind at a future time when it would be needed, and the recipient would not even know where the information came from.

D: *Do you know what the instructions are pertaining to?*

J: (Sigh) It's too fast to know.

D: *Maybe that's the only way a great deal of information can be transmitted. Just going directly into your body and your mind.*

J: It's everywhere. I feel like a sponge.

D: *Do you feel comfortable in that presence?*

J: I feel very humble. I asked to see it, and it turned into a person. The light can be a person if it wants to. It can be anything. Wow! Oh! It's standing in front of me as a person. (In awe.) It looks like a human, but it's different. He can be like a soft light. You sense the skin is soft. Like a light being... like a light bulb that's frosted.

D: *You mean his face and body look like it is made out of light? (Yeah) Glowing from within?*

J: Yeah. I asked, "Are you just a light? Is that all you are? Just a light?" And right before my eyes it just formed. I was really overwhelmed to see that happen. To realize that a light could turn into a person.

D: *Can you ask it who or what it is?*

J: I'm so awed that I don't ask. It's as if you know to be quiet. (She appeared to be listening.) Things are happening to you. Things are happening to you, and if you said anything it would be chatter. Like you just don't talk. You're talking, but not in any way that I know. I just allow whatever is necessary to happen, for it has to do with something else.

D: *Well, let's move ahead. You can speed up that sequence. Is that all that happened? Did you just stay in his presence, and absorb information?*

J: No. We went around to a different place.

D: *Did you get out of the chair?*

J: I wasn't in the chair then. I don't know where it was. We went out onto the planet, or whatever this is. We're not on a craft anymore.

Apparently the chair took her out of the craft to another location. (Another dimension?)

J: (Big sigh) It's very bright everywhere. It almost hurts your eyes it's so bright. It's very quiet. We went on what we think of as a tour of your city. The way we moved was interesting, because we weren't walking. Just moving. No wires. I was looking for wires. (Chuckle) Just very smooth. No bumps. Just moving through the air.

D: *Tell me what you see as he gives you the tour.*

J: I don't know. (She was frustrated at times trying to explain what she was seeing. She had no concepts for it.) It's light. And you move through the light. And then it changes, because there are areas of the light. And then you move into it, and it becomes not solid but it changes from an area into something. And then you move to another area, and it's different.

D: *What does it change into?*

J: (She had difficulty) You know, like you're driving in a subdivision, and then you change and you're in another one, except it's different.

D: *You mean like buildings or objects?*

J: They're not buildings, but that's what they live in.

D: *He's showing you places where they live, among this light?*

J: The light is the sum total of the.... Gosh! I can't explain this.

D: *Can you describe one of them to me?*

J: There's no way, because I don't know anything that they look like. It's like nothing I've ever seen before.

D: *Well, I think of a house or a building as like a container with walls or something. (Her facial movements indicated disagreement.) It's not like that?*

J: No. You know that's the home like the light turns into the person. And then you know the light.... I can't describe it.

D: *Can you ask him to help give you the answers? I'm sure he has the answers, and maybe you have the vocabulary that he can help you to explain it. (Long pause)*

This is the way it happened in all the other circumstances. When I needed an explanation that the subject could not supply, another entity would come forth if I requested its help.

J: It's not time to understand it.

D: *Will he tell you why he is showing you these things?*

J: This is the first step.

D: *First step of what?*

J: I don't know.

D: *Can he tell you?*

J: It's not time.

D: *This place is not on Earth, is it? (No) Another planet?*

J: They don't call them planets.

D: *What do they call them?*

J: I can't say right now.

D: *Is it physical?*

J: What do you mean?

D: *I'm thinking of our Earth as physical, solid. You can touch it. (Big sigh) Or is it different?*

The voice changed. It became more spontaneous, where Janice's was confused and faltering. This one sounded authoritative. Maybe now I could get answers. This was the type that had supplied answers before. Her subconscious? Or maybe the mind of the other being?

J: It's a different reality and it's a different dimension. And it's not considered... (Confused) solid.

D: *So it's different, but nonetheless it is real. (Yes) But do the people, the beings that live there, need bodies? (No) Was that a body that was shown to Janice?*

J: Yes. It was a body that was shown to her, as our bodies can be shown. It is not a shape that we maintain all the time.

D: *It is not a solid body like hers, a physical body? (No) Is this because you don't need a body?*

J: That is correct.

D: *I'm trying to understand. This place where you are, is that like a higher state of evolution?*

J: It is a much higher state of evolution.

D: *I've been told about some of the dimensions. The spirit states where people go when they leave the physical body on Earth. Is this like that, or is it different?*

J: It is like that.

D: *But more evolved than what I've been told about?*

J: I do not necessarily understand your question.

D: *In my work people have reported when they leave our physical dimension, when they die, so to speak, their spirit or their essence moves to different levels. And sometimes those levels are much like Earth, only in a different spectrum. Then as they move higher sometimes these objects, whatever you want to call them, change. (She was shaking her head.) It's not like that?*

J: Some of the functions could be termed to be the same, in that the properties involved are those that would lend themselves to those levels which you have been made aware of. However, at this infinite point of the beingness, one does not need house. One does not need body. For the existence is at a much different... (Softly) the terminology is just ....

D: *I know it's difficult to find words. Let's see. Vibration? Frequency?*

J: (With certainty.) Vibration!... That's not correct, but as an element that you can relate to, we will use vibration. For

what you understand is incomprehensible in comparison
to what I'm trying to tell you at this point. And it is simply
evolutionary to the point that one must be able to
comprehend what I'm saying. And I must be able to
communicate it in your language. And this cannot be done
through words.

D: *The language is insufficient. I've been told that before.*

J: I could do this in another manner, but it will not take place at
this point, for you.

They had indicated earlier that they could communicate directly
through me (as channeling), but I preferred this method so I could
remain an objective reporter. Or he may have been referring to the
same method of inserting symbols directly into my mind. In which
case I would be limited in my ability to extract them and convey the
meaning to others. I might understand but be unable to transfer the
knowledge.

J: Languages are very limiting. But the type of communication
used by our people is much different than language.

D: *She said she was getting a lot of information, just flowing
into her like a sponge. Is that the way you communicate?*

J: That is one method. That is a very intense, and a very
thorough method of assimilation of information.

D: *What other methods do you use?*

J: I believe she has spoken to you of the... symbols. But that is
not the word.

He was referring to the symbols she had been receiving while in
a relaxed meditative mood.

D: *But it's a word that we understand, in our limited way.
Would we be able to try to interpret those symbols?*

J: That will be decided by someone other than myself.

D: *Can you say why you are giving her this information?*

J: That is not allowed at this point. I must know you better.

D: *That's perfectly all right with me.*

J: And she must be ready to hear it.

D: *Yes, because oftentimes if you hear things and you're not
ready, it can be quite startling.*

J: Correct.

The voice continued to sound deeper and more masculine than
Janice's normal voice.

D: *Are you giving her this information more or less on a subconscious level?*

J: Nothing to do with the subconscious, and everything to do with the subconscious. In that when I speak to you of selves, then we are speaking in terms of the subconscious, the conscious, and the physical, the non physical, the entire state of the being.

D: *So it's much more complicated, much vaster, much more than we can understand.*

J: Perhaps.

D: *Well, is this information that she will need to know later?*

J: Very definitely.

D: *Will it help her in her Earthly life?*

J: Very definitely.

D: *Will it help others?*

J: Very definitely.

D: *Would we be allowed to share the information later?*

J: It will evolve, and it will be brought forth. But it will happen in a timely fashion. Some of it will come forth in a natural state. Some of it you will be allowed to access. So the answer to your question would perhaps be "yes", but not at this point in time.

D: *All right. I have a lot of patience. I intend to put the information in the form of writing so other people could share it, and be helped by it.*

J: That will be determined by many other factors. I cannot answer your question "yes", for that will be determined by the outcomes of various planetary and interdimensional interactions.

D: *I was thinking if it would help the people of Earth, maybe we would be allowed to explore it.*

The voice not only sounded masculine, but now sounded old and very wise. The enunciation of the words was very careful and exact. There was an occasional pause and mumbling as it searched for the proper word. That was the only time there was any faltering. I felt as though I was in the presence of an entity possessing great wisdom.

J: There are, and will always be, peoples of Earth whom it would not help. Whom it would hurt. By hurt, is to say, because they will never be ready to know or assimilate any of the information. And that is why it cannot be brought forth except through certain rare individuals who are able to assimilate and integrate it into the being. And these... we do not find many on your planet. Therefore it is imperative that you understand the protection of any information you would gain if you come to this point of infinity in the future.

D: *Do you think I will come to that point at another time?*

J: It will be determined as we go. I am not at liberty to discuss with you many things at this point in our interaction. However, it is I'm having difficulty communicating. It is my problem. It could be done in another manner, but you need to remain as you are. Therefore, to communicate with you I'm... I hope you understand that I seem to be faltering and stumbling, when it is very difficult to slow to the level of vibration that forms word language. And therefore, it is difficult for me interacting with you. So we will come to develop a comfortableness of sort, perhaps if you and I should meet again.

D: *Then you think it is wiser that this is the only way that I communicate with you, through another person.*

J: Presently. I could communicate with you now in a different fashion. I could do that. But I won't do that, for it would be of no value to you if you did not hear the words.

D: *That's the way I have to communicate then?*

J: It's not the way you have to, but it is the only method that would suit your purposes and be productive for you.

D: *I think that is correct. It would be better that I get the words through another person, another vehicle, with the work that I do. I feel more comfortable with that method. I understand what you mean that some people will never understand it, and it would harm them. I was told many years ago that some information is as medicine, and other is as poison. That it could be misunderstood and taken the wrong way.*

J: Very definitely.

D: *I was told that some of this information the world's not ready for. They also said not all of my questions would be answered, for that reason. I think you can see that I do understand, and I don't intend to push.*

J: Yes. I'm sorry that more cannot be given presently.

D: *The important thing is that Janice is absorbing whatever she needs to know. She will use it at another time, and she doesn't need to know it consciously.*

J: And she knows that. It is the rare individual on your planet who is able to be secure enough to come to this point of infinity. It takes a very secure person to come to this point and return. And secure is the word. It would be important for the being's intelligence level to be understood by us, because this type of individual can communicate on many levels. That is only one reason that this interaction is taking place at this time. Plus there is another factor involved, in that the person is very trustworthy with being careful to protect the work. It wouldn't benefit the world to be told of this point of infinity, for they would never believe it in the first place. In the second place, they could never understand it. And in the third place, they would commit Janice to an institution.

D: *I would never want that.*

J: It would never happen either.

D: *But in my limited understanding are you at what we consider the God level? The Creator level?*

J: It's the point of infinity, yes.

D: *I've taken many people to different levels, and they speak of some that are higher. Although maybe there isn't any such thing as direction.*

J: It is direction only in the sense of movement of the being. For really "higher" is merely a reference point from which they have come.

D: *Yes, in our linear way of understanding.*

J: Correct.

D: *So this would be the level we all hope to attain some day?*

J: There are levels past here.

D: *There are? Then this is not the ultimate.*

J: This cannot be discussed at this moment. Except to tell you that interaction from this level requires purity of body, mind and spirit. Purity. These interactions are not that prevalent on your planet. Although they do happen, it is not known. For most individuals are not able to carry knowing.

D: *She said she doesn't listen to these tape recordings that I make of these sessions. Maybe is it better that she doesn't know what's going on?*

J: She knows what is going on. And that was my statement to you, in that she can carry what she knows. For being able to carry it is the key to attainment of the different other states of beingness. And it's very important that she be developmentally taken to stages. You must understand one thing. This individual has worked very, very hard with many beings. Her work with UFO energy is only one facet of what she does. She is not of your normal peopled world, although she is very much a part of your peopled world. Functionally, her properties are totally out of the realm of comprehension by measured science. What you must understand is that this person operates at the physical level, and is a very physical human being. But at the same time operates at many other dimensions and levels interdependently.

D: *You said there were other levels above this, but yet you call this an infinity level.*

J: It is an infinity level.

D: *To me infinity means forever, like there's nothing beyond that.*

J: There's the point of infinity, and then there's past the point of infinity.

D: *Does she have to come to this place very often?*

J: It's not a matter of having to come. This is an interaction which is necessary for.... (Hesitancy, searching for words.)

D: *Her work or what?*

J: Hmmm. Many reasons. One is comfort to the individual.

D: *So she experiences comfort when she comes there? (Yes) Even though she is bombarded by information, and the feeling of speed? (Yes) It is still comfort.*

J: You see, to reach the point of infinity you must go past the speed of light. Past light. So past light is faster than light. Then you enter into another type of beingness.

D: *Well, I think we have been doing this long enough. I am very protective of how long we do this. So I want to thank you very much for allowing me to speak with you.*

J: You wouldn't be speaking to me unless it had been preapproved by other than myself. I thank you for allowing any faltering communication, for it is difficult. And I merely wish to thank you for your patience in my stumbling.

D: *That's all right. I appreciate it that you have spoken to me. And maybe at another time in the future we may speak again, if you're willing.*

J: Perhaps things will have been evolved to the point that we could have a more indepth discussion. But it is not warranted at this time.

D: *That's all right. I have patience. I will wait until the time comes. I will take anything I can get in the meantime.*

I oriented Janice and brought her forward to full consciousness. As usual she took a long time to be able to sit up. She was always able to talk to me, but seemed so relaxed that it would be impossible for her to get up and walk for several minutes. Even then she was wobbly until she was fully awake. This seemed to be her normal pattern, and nothing to be concerned about. While she was composing herself, we discussed some of the session. She always had total amnesia of the session.

***

After eating and relaxing with Patsy we went back to the bedroom for another session. It was agreed that two would be enough for this visit. We have had three sessions in the past, but these often prove tedious and tiring, moreso for me than the subject.

Before we began we discussed what we wanted to find out. Janice was still wondering about the symbols she had seen flooding into her mind the week before. I explained that the being said it was not time for her to know, and we couldn't have the information yet. Although she was disappointed, I knew from past experiences that you could not force this. They would allow the information to come through when the time is right. It would do no good to try to override them anyway. I always had to maintain their trust or all information would be shut off and my research would stop.

We finally decided to explore a strange incident that had occurred the night before. She had gone into a darkened parking lot to get in her car. As she started the motor she suddenly saw what appeared to be smoke or fog rising around the car. Thinking something was wrong with the car, she got out and walked around it trying to see where the smoke was coming from. The smoke then settled into an area in front of the car. In the center of it she could make out a cat. The last thing she remembered was walking toward the animal into the fog. When she became conscious of being back in her car preparing to drive home, it was several hours later. So we decided to focus on this event in this session.

After using her keyword she immediately went into a deep trance, and I took her back to the previous night when she was leaving a meeting and going to her car in the parking lot. She began reliving the scene.

J: I am trying to see if it's smoke that's coming out of the hood. It isn't exactly smoke colored, but I could see it just kind of move up. And it was in front of the windshield, and on the hood of the car, and all over the front of the car. It isn't thick like smoke, it's vapory. More like mist. At first I thought it was the car overheating, but I had a sense it was something else. I stood there and waited. And I thought, well, I'll just see what happens. And then I saw there was a cat there. And I said, "I knew it. I knew it. I knew it." And then I was moving toward the cat, but the cat wasn't a cat. The smoke and the cat were just there to get me out of the car. And then I moved toward the cat. I knew the cat was going to move, and when the cat moved I'd go away. That's how it works. You have these sort of things that happen, and you know it is not what it looks like.

D: *What happened when you walked toward the cat?*

J: I was locked in. It's like you lock into a frequency. You look in the cat's eyes and you're locked in. It's like you move from being in the now to a frequency. It's like changing channels on a TV, except you do it differently. And then it's like you're on a beam, or you're in a corridor. But you know you're moving. I don't know if I'm physically moving, or just mentally moving.

D: *When you became locked in on that, did you see anything besides the cat?*

J: Yeah. It turned into a group of beings right before my eyes. I knew I was moving toward it, but sometimes I move toward it and then I find myself in the ship. They were standing there, and yet they couldn't have been standing there. Anyway, I kept moving toward them, like I was drawn, like I was on automatic. Then I heard a sound, and I knew what was happening. And I began to feel myself go, in another way. You feel very fluid, and you go like that. And they were waiting for me to come.

D: *Who was waiting?*

J: There was a whole group of beings there. I wasn't sure that I really recognized them. The guy in that green robe, I know him though. I was trying to look at everybody, but I was moving too fast, so I couldn't look at all of them.

D: *You said it was somebody you recognized?*

J: I recognized the clothes from another time. When I was at a big meeting, and I was in an auditorium. This same guy was standing down on a stage giving a lecture. And I was sitting there, except I was in a vapor state. If you looked over at something, you saw the physical of it, but then it's right back to vapor. It's a different way of seeing. We were all there in this big place, and he was down there, in front of a whole bunch of us. And he did his part and he left, and then somebody else came.

D: *And you thought it was safe to go with them, because you knew him?*

J: Because I saw him and I knew it was okay.

D: *Where have you gone?*

J: I don't know where I've gone. I'm laying in the air. I'm just laying. It's not on a table. I don't understand it, but I know I'm not on the Earth.

D: *Can you see anything around you?*

J: No, right now I can't. You know what the night sky looks like. You know it's there, but I can see the stars. And I don't think there were stars last night.

D: *Can you sense anything around you, if you can't see it?*

J: I know they're there. I know that they are the preliminary to where I went. So I moved through them to get to where I am. They stood between me and where I am. I'm safe and I'm okay. And they tell me I know I'm safe. It's like I had to lie down after I got there.

D: *Is anybody with you?*

J: I sense there is, but I don't see them. There's a big purple light over my face. It's pulsating. It's moving. It's like a heartbeat, except it's not a heartbeat. It's huge. And sometimes all outside of it is green. It's like a glowing thing, almost an indigo iridescent center. I've seen it a lot, and I don't know what that is. Then in the light came some different shapes again, but I've never seen them come in that light before. I've seen that light a hundred million times, but I've never seen that. This has never happened. Shapes. Patterns. Shapes. Patterns. (She repeated these words over and over at an increasing speed, indicating they were occurring rapidly.) Like I'm watching what's happening inside... it's integrating in me. Shapes, patterns, shapes, patterns. Patterns, shapes. Snowflake pattern shapes, six sided pattern shapes.

D: *But does it have a good feeling?*

J: Oh, it feels as if you were cramming for a test or something. You know what it feels like when you study really hard. Except I don't really have to study it. I'm just absorbing it. But it's happening to me. (In awe.) Oh, my goodness, look at that one!

D: *While you're doing that, is there anyone there that can answer our questions? And we could find out the purpose for this?*

J: It's like the group's between us.

D: *Do you want to ask someone if they can come forth and answer our questions? While you're doing the viewing of the shapes they can talk to us.*

J: The light went away. The shapes went away. I'm hearing some talking. I don't know what they're saying though, cause I don't understand that talk.

D: *Can you ask for someone to help us with information?*

J: (Pause) They're not listening.

D: *Maybe you can do it mentally.*

J: I'm trying to. (Softly) I just don't know what's happening. (She was mumbling and seemed to be communicating silently with someone.) They sound like they're all busy and they're talking. (Pause, mumbling again.) Now they're just around me.

D: *What are they doing?*

J: Exchanging information.

D: *With you, or with each other?*

J: Both.

D: *All right. Can you mentally ask one of them if they can answer our questions while this is all going on with you?*

J: It's hard to ask while this is happening. There's so much going on right now. It's just a major.... It's a lot of... (Confused and a bit overwhelmed.) So much coming in, it's hard for me to even ask. (She made hand motions pointing to different ones around her.) This guy does an exchange, then this guy does an exchange, and this guy does an exchange, and this guy does an exchange. (Repeated over and over).

D: *And they're all mentally doing this with you?*

J: I don't think it's mental. I don't know how it's done, or what it is. It doesn't feel mental.

D: *Well, can we move past that, then you won't have so much going on in your mind? Let's move to when that is finished.*

J: My head hurts!

I suspected the discomfort may have been because of too much input into her brain. I gave suggestions that when I touched her head any discomfort would disappear. (She gave some relaxed and relieved moans. I could tell it felt better.) Let's move to where you don't have so much input going on, and you can discuss things with me. (A long relieved sigh.) Can you mentally ask someone now to come and answer questions?

J: Okay. Now they're discussing who's gonna talk to you. I'm trying to see, but I can't see. (A sudden gasp.) Oh, a pyramid came down to me. With the point down. And it has lines on it. It just came down.

D: *What is it, a light or what?*

J: I don't know what it is made out of. It's now moving. It's more like one of the video games that you see. It's coming down to my head. I see it's coming into my body. It has different levels. It's divided, and it has rings around it like a tree would have rings, except it's a pyramid. And the point comes down, and it goes in to a certain point. And it stops. Then it goes again and stops.It moves again and stops, moves again and stops. It's like my whole body's in it. It's spreading out in the whole body. My arms feel funny. It feels like my body's going away. (I was momentarily concerned.) It's fine. It's okay. It's not hurting. My body's just going away. It's just dissolving. Ohh, it's just dissolving.

D: *You can always hear my voice no matter where you are. Is there anyone in that group that can answer our questions, and explain this for you?*

J: Please. (Deep breaths) At this moment it's not possible to answer your questions. They will answer your questions, but not right now. It can't happen right now.

D: *Okay. But it's a good feeling?*

J: It's a good feeling, yes. It's just that my body's dissolved. It's completely....

They wanted me to wait so I used the time to give more suggestions for well being.

J: (Long pause) We can understand that you wish to have some communication input. However, we are doing some work, and taking an opportunity and perhaps liberty with your session. A continuation is in effect of last night's work. And you are wishing to gain the information of the evening before, when what is happening now is an entirely new development of information for this person. To know more of the product of involvement which she is being led to do.

The voice had definitely changed. It was always easy to tell when one of the beings spoke, because the change was immediate.

J: I will now explain it to you. What do you wish to know?

D: *She's curious about the purpose of the shapes and images she has been seeing.*

J: This is an entire language of I cannot discuss with you from where. However, I can tell you that there is a method of communication that is important for humans to have at their disposal. And yet it is at this particular time impossible to communicate it to you in a language you would understand. There will be a way to do that when Janice gathers more experience in functioning in this manner. Presently she is, you could say, receiving guidance and other methods of communication, because of some work that will be done in the future. Perhaps the best way to explain it to you would be to say, you go to school and you study French, so that you can go to France and speak French. She's learning it for future developments. And she's learning it for her own protection.

D: *These symbols will be a way of protecting herself?*

J: The symbols are a way of protecting herself from being able to communicate things which should not be communicated at the human level at this point in time. However, it is important that they be imprinted, so that in the future when they are called to the forefront of her consciousness, then the imprint will have been there to be activated. At that time when she will need to know and need to explain and need to teach.

D: *At a future time would she be able to draw these symbols for me and explain them?*

J: Perhaps. That is a liberty which I cannot give permission for. That must come from a level of development that is not present at this time. You could have asked it in your earlier session, and gotten your answer.

D: *I did, and they said I couldn't have it at that time.*

J: Then I would give you the same answer.

D: *She also wanted to know the purpose of the group of various beings that are gathered here.*

The voice changed again. This one sounded more authoritarian and professional. "*I* will answer you. The purpose of the group of beings is that each member of the group has a particular level of expertise. So! What you have is a group of you would perhaps term the 'cream of the crop' in various aspects of development. Much as you have your master's program of college professors that teach in the master's program. They are not the same professors that would teach the freshmen in your college classes."

D: *She said she couldn't see them all, but they did appear to be different.*

J: Very.

D: *Some of them she recognized. Well, among this group of people, would you be one that could answer some questions?*

J: If I am not the one to answer the questions you have, the one to answer your questions will come forward. For it is agreeable with the group to interact with you. If there are any in the group who do not feel that it is proper to interact at this time, it will not be done. If that should take place, we ask that you understand that although anyone in the group can answer, it will not be done. If the authority feels that the answer should not be given, no one else will answer for the authority.

This had also occurred when working with Phil in *The Keepers of the Garden*. At that time a group of twelve entities were communicating with me and giving me the story of the seeding of the planet Earth. They also said they were only allowed to give information that they all agreed upon.

D: *I always take whatever I can get. If you don't want to answer, just let me know. There is a mystery occurring on Earth at this time that many people are asking questions about. This concerns the crop circles in the fields in England. They call them Corn Circles, although it's really wheat and other grains. They have been occurring over the last few years. Can you give me any information about that? Where they're coming from, and how, and why?*

J: I can tell you that there are several reasons for the circles. And there are different reasons for them. And at different times different reasons apply. Now, you understand spirals? (Yes) And you understand windows? (Yes) At a particular time these are used by certain energies to interact with the currents of your Earth, the vibrations of your Earth. I am trying to answer you without being technical. I cannot give you all the information on this. But I can tell you that some of them are made by ships that land. And they are made due to the method of propulsion or travel that fuels the ship. And it has to do with the gravitational force of your planet. There are other reasons besides anti gravity.

D: *They are not all made by ships, are they? (No) Some of them seem to be in patterns. They have circles around circles, and different designs.*

J: That is correct. You are speaking of their interrelationship to each other. (Long pause) I'm sorry. I have your answers, but in your next meeting I will give them to you. I cannot do it now, because it is a timing problem. Meaning that it is important that it not be understood at this time. I can tell you only that there is a project that certain people are working on. And these are a part of that project. Just believe that there is no harm to come from these circles. It is in conjunction with other aspects of energy flow. It is very important for them to be there. And just as Janice is learning the symbols of language, every effort is being used in relation to the fragile planet Earth's mantle stabilization. If it needs to have a reverse circle circles are very powerful, you know. And they are also used as a transmission focal point. So that is what I can tell you.

D: *Do the patterns have significance?*

J: They do have significance.

D: *Is it significant that many of these have been found around the old monuments such as Stonehenge?*

J: Of course. When you think of Stonehenge, when you think of your old monuments or your so called "sacred places" on your planet, then you must know that to become sacred does not happen instantly. Time is a carrier of the energy. And we have worked with these particular locations for centuries.

D: *But it seems to be a new phenomenon with the circles.*

J: It is only visible. You couldn't see them before, but they have always been there. You can see them now, because of a dimensional shift that has now taken place.

D: *Then they were on the ground?*

J: They were below the surface of the ground. They've only surfaced. The Earth is changing so much that... (Big sigh) The shifting on your planet has been another manner that has caused them to come to the surface.

D: *Then in the past the energy they were creating, or the function they were serving was being done beneath the surface. (Yes) And now is being applied to the surface?*

J: Yes, because things have changed.

D: *Many people are thinking maybe it's a form of communication.*

J: It is. I explained earlier to you that they were used as a focal point for vibrational... perhaps I didn't say it. You see, that's what happens when you communicate in a different manner. You tend to believe that everyone knows what you're thinking. What I'm trying to tell you is that, they are a focal point for energy entrance. Now, energy entrance in a pattern, in a spiral, comes in and is slung up.... (Confusion about how to word it.)

D: *Out of the same place? (Yes) Rather like a bouncing effect? (Yes) All right. She had been told she was part of a project where they were using energy.*

In *The Custodians* it was explained that Janice was part of a project where her energy is being used to help balance the energies of the Earth. There are many people involved in this project, although it is totally unknown to their conscious mind. I was informed that I was also a part of this, and my travels would take me to many parts of the world, because my energy would be needed there. This project does not create any depletion of energy to the participant involved.

J: It is a different phase of the same project.

D: *But this sounds as though energy is ricocheting or bouncing. Would that be correct?*

J: There are different.... May I answer that? (Her question was soft and was obviously not directed at me.) Yes. I answered that? (This was soft, and I didn't understand that she was not talking to me.)

There was a long pause, then another voice, a softer, almost sweet one. Obviously feminine.

J: Perhaps I can answer you. It is not time for you to understand everything about this project now. It is important for you to know some details, which you will be given by members of the group. One of the things that you need to know is that there are circles in Peru. There are circles in other places on your planet that people do not realize. We are making an effort to allow mankind to begin to know other ways of communication. However, there are those that can be communicated with through those circles. The circles of energy also go through the Earth, so it's a part of the same project. It's just a different phase. Now, another thing to know is that your Earth is spinning in space, is it not? (Yes) And how does it spin? What direction?

D: *I'd have to think. Is it going counter clockwise? (She made hand motions.) Clock wise, all right. I don't remember that part of it.*

J: Well, actually it wouldn't matter if it were spinning end over end. The point of the circles is simply to create an opposite effect. And this is another area of balance. That's one purpose, and only one. But they are used and energy is circulated through them. If you could see into another dimension, you could see the spiral. You would see the effect of that swirl, for it is in movement and motion. You cannot see it, but it is moving. Constantly moving. Just as a top moves. Clockwise.

What direction do crop circles go? The ones I have seen and been in go in both directions.

D: *I'm thinking of a top. The top is rotating and moving. And these would be places where it touches down on the Earth?*

J: Perhaps you could think of a vortex.

D: *All right. I'm thinking of it being in space, and then coming toward the Earth and touching down.*

J: That is correct. Actually the beam is transmitted to the center of the circle and it rotates out. Remember the focal point I spoke to you about? The beam is transmitted to the center of the circle, and swirls.

This was something I noticed when I was in the Crop Circles several times in England. In my mind it appeared as though there was a central focal point, and the circle swirled out from that. Almost like the visual image of someone focusing the nozzle of a high pressure hose, and then opening it up to rotate from that central point. I know it was not done with a hose, but probably with the focus of energy, but that was an analogy I could identify with.

D: *And this is part of the project that is helpful in stabilizing the Earth's movements. In the plates?*
J: Yes, it is.
D: *And it seems to be directed at only certain places, or they're more noticeable there.*
J: They have surfaced there. It is an attempt to cause mankind to ask. It is an attempt to also allow those beings who are able to comprehend it, to begin to know and understand it.
D: *In some cases there will be a circle where all the grain is going one direction. Then a circle around the outside where the grain is going in the opposite direction.*
J: This is my point.
D: *Why is it in the opposite direction in the outside circle?*
J: Because it is necessary to balance the inner intensity.
D: *This must happen very fast. Is that right?*
J: Very fast. You can't see it.
D: *They say it appears overnight. Where is the beam coming from?*
J: I cannot... (Fast breathing, and the voice was disrupted and distorted. It sounded strange on the tape, almost garbled at this point. An energy flux?) ... tell you.
D: *You can't tell me?*
J: (The entity seemed upset.) "No."
D: *All right. I was wondering if it was coming from space, coming from a craft, or....?*

Janice was reacting as though she was uncomfortable. I thought she might be getting hot again, as in the earlier session. I was trying to make her comfortable by adjusting the covers, and giving cooling suggestions. But something else seemed to be occurring. She was breathing uncomfortably fast. After several seconds of suggestions her breathing slowed down. She was relaxing again, so I continued with the questioning. The being interrupted me.

J: (Softly) Please ....
D: *What is it?*
J: Allow the being a period of adjustment.
D: *Okay. Because she got very hot just then. (Yes) Was that because of energy?*

J: Yes, it is. The body came in touch with the full force of the phase of that project. You must understand that when we are communicating with you, the body is a vehicle to do so. However, because of the level of involvement of this body in this project, it is sometimes impossible to prevent the experience from full force. The being will experience the work being done mentally. Mentally. Perhaps you could understand "mentally," but it's not really a mental process, as the physical can become affected. And it happens very quickly. The words that you used to cause that to take place was, you said, "This must happen very quickly." So the word "quickly" was a trigger. Communication at this level becomes very delicate.

Actually, after listening to the tape recorder, I had said "very fast," instead of *quickly*, but apparently it was interpreted in the same way through their use of Janice's vocabulary.

D: *I'm sorry. I had no way of knowing.*
J: It is an impossibility for you to know. And we wish to interact with you. We wish to give you guidance in your work. We wish to have you continue to work with the being. And it is important for you to realize that there are times when a leveling out must be affected by us and by you, for the being to be able to continue to be involved in your session. You must understand that the level of operational energy is very... (Confused, searching for the word)... delicate.
D: *I know she reacted. It seemed like a burst of heat.*
J: That is because when this individual is located in the center of one of the circles, the particular rotational force can cause in the physical a vast amount of heat to be generated in an instant. We are trying to share with you, and coming here to speak with you, because it is important that these things be discussed. However, we will need to teach you some methods for helping the individual sometimes continue.
D: *Yes, because I had no way of knowing that any of my words would trigger anything. And I certainly didn't want that to happen.*
J: The individual's physical body will not suffer. You will perhaps believe because of your physical eye observation that the body's physicalness will suffer. This individual has been.... (Unsure of word again.)
D: *What's the word? Conditioned?*
J: That's close. But it's more than conditioning. (Hesitated.) Prepared. Yes. There's a way to explain to you. Through

the years, because of her long term involvement in this project that has gone on for her entire lifetime here, she has developed to a point of being able to withstand physical energy levels that are incomprehensible to the common individual. And also impossible for their physical body to experience without some disintegrational effect.

D: *As long as she can handle it, because I certainly wouldn't want to do anything to harm her. Do you think it wise that we discontinue talking about the circles?*

J: There's more to it than just talking about the circles. The circles are an integral part, because what you have yet to experience is the pyramids. You have your physical pyramids in Egypt. However, there are pyramids much as your circles, that you have yet to see on the surface, that are also operational. This is just another method of energy work. Energy work is vital to the maintenance of your planet. And what you must also know is that there are crafts who come, and upon landing on the surface, can cause a physical imprint to be made in much the same manner. So there are circles, and there are circles.

D: *But those landing sites don't have the same energy effect. They are just caused by the propulsion of the craft.*

J: Yet once they are made they are used.

D: *What I was asking was, were the beams coming from space or from a craft? Where are they being directed from?*

J: I'm not allowed to tell you that. We will discuss that at another meeting. There are beings who have not given you knowledge, who are present if you wish to ask your questions.

D: *All right. But I never know if I am touching on subjects I am not allowed to know about.*

J: You will.

I was about to proceed with the questions, when I was suddenly interrupted. Something had occurred that the group considered an emergency. It took precedence over what I was doing.

J: (A stern voice.) Supply the suggestion!

D: *What?*

J: (It sounded impatient.) Supply the suggestion!

D: *What do you mean?*

J: The being is in pain. Supply the suggestion!

Janice was holding her head, so I started to give my normal suggestions to alleviate something like this, by touching the center of her forehead. But the entity interrupted the process and commanded that I apply pressure with one finger. I tried to do as it suggested, but it interrupted again. "You are in the wrong location!"

D: *Show me where.*
J: (She pointed to the location.) Lightly! I will guide you. (She took my finger and guided it to the correct spot in the middle of her forehead.) I will guide you. Continue to talk and supply the suggestion.

As I continued to give suggestions it still did not satisfy the entity.

J: Let me have your hand! Do not operate your hand! This is important! (Sternly.) Do not operate your hand! Allow me to have your hand. This is important to the being. Relax your hand! Give me your finger. (Softly) Give me your finger.
D: *You have it.*

There was a long pause as she directed my finger to the proper spot on her forehead. I relaxed my hand, and gave suggestions to relieve any discomfort as she manipulated my hand.

J: I will allow you to know when I am finished. I am sorry to be so forceful with you, but there was an emergency.
D: *Can you tell me what caused it?*
J: (Pause) Do not talk! (Long pause.)
D: *Are you using the energy from my body? (No)*

There was a long pause, then Janice appeared to be more relaxed and breathing slower again.

J: (Mechanically.) Thank you. I am sorry to have been so forceful, but because of the emergency it was necessary for us to be able to have that physical touch with the being. And from where we are operating that is impossible.
D: *I'm glad I could be of use, because I care very much about her safety also. Can you tell me what caused the emergency?*
J: In a moment. We must stabilize.
D: *Then it's not my energy, it's just the physical touch.*
J: Yes. It has nothing to do with you or your energy. And if you are feeling anything, we will remove it.
D: *No, I'm not.*
J: I didn't think so.
D: *I'm just trying to relax so you can use my hand.*
J: That is very difficult, and I appreciate you. It is very important.

There was another long pause as she moved my finger to other points on her head. She gave several big sighs.

D: *Can you tell me why you're applying pressure to those different areas?*

J: These are meridian points. These are much as your acqupressure. What is happening is that the individual is able to connect to me through your touching, although your body is not involved.

D: *I want to put this on the recording. You were touching the forehead and several places: the eyes, the area just in front of the ears....*

J: (Interrupted) Give me your hand! Hold your arm stable.

D: *It's the way I'm sitting. Okay. And you were touching in front of the ears, and under the chin, and the top of the crown of the head. Then just above the bridge of the nose in the middle of the forehead.*

These actions were repeated over and over again. Then she relaxed and lowered my hand. Apparently the emergency was over.

J: Thank you.

D: *Is it better now?*

J: (Her normal voice.) Yeah, it's better.

D: *I'm glad I could help. I didn't know what I was doing. I was sitting in a strained position, so it was hard for me to relax.*

J: (The stern voice was back.) Thank you for the use of your hand.

D: *What was the emergency? Can you tell me?*

J: It is a residual effect of the circles. What you must realize is that you are interdimensional at this time. The being is interdimensional. When you very quickly move dimensionally then if the proper alignment is not affected, in that a point is not reached prior to that dimensional shift, there can be pain or short circuiting in the physicalness of the being. And we (had difficulty finding the word)... preceded ourselves, so to speak.

D: *Went a little too fast?*

J: It is a matter of timing. Cosmic time, Earth time, biological time. When you are incongruent in those times these things can happen to the physicalness of the being. Now, what you must understand is that when you discuss the circles, the being is living it.

D: *I didn't know that.*

J: We know. We thought perhaps it would be something you need not know.

D: *But in order to insure her safety and freedom from pain, I'd like to know these things.*

J: It was handled in a manner in which you will be instructed in the future. It will not be, unless necessary, to advise you in the future pre given. This particular kind of transference of information to you is very unusual for this group of beings. What you must know is that.... (Big breaths, and she seemed uncomfortable again.)

D: *Is she experiencing heat again?*

J: We are trying to see if this is possible, so that we can speed up the process of communicating with you. There will be some adjustments necessary, as we are discovering at this moment.

D: *Okay. But if it causes her any discomfort, I don't believe it is worth it for my sake.*

J: It is not a matter of your choice of it being worth it. Actually, either you choose to do the work or you don't. I do not mean to be forceful. I simply mean to tell you that this is very important information. And it is a matter of finding the proper medium to deliver it. And as the group works with you a kind of equilibrium will be established that is not present at this time. So we have some minor adjustments of equilibrium between the being and the group, and the group and you, and you and the being, and the being and the group. When we move very quickly into a very serious subject like the circles, then things can happen very quickly. And there is that word. But we have taken care of it with the individual. You see, we were not aware that "quickly" would cause the same reaction. So we are learning at the same time how this individual reacts.

D: *That's what I mean. When I am speaking, I have no way of knowing how it will affect her.*

J: We can fully understand your predicament, and are sympathetic. And we appreciate you being able to understand that if we are forceful, it is not due to being upset with you. It is due to urgency. (Long Pause)

D: *Are you listening to someone?*

J: (Her voice sounded more normal.) Yes. It's somebody that wants to speak to you, but they can't talk English, and I can't talk that. And we're trying to figure out how to do it.

D: *Can they have someone else communicate it?*

J: They're looking. They're talking. They're having a little discussion. They're in the corner. It's like they're trying to decide.

D: *Tell them we're running out of time here. I really want to get the message, because they were giving me instructions. (Confusion) Maybe they can relay it to someone else who can give me the message.*

J: That's what they're doing. (Softly, as though talking to someone else.) Okay. (Big sigh.)

D: *Are they ready now?*

J: (Another louder voice.) Perhaps.

D: *Because I have no way of knowing if I'm breaking any regulations, if they don't instruct me.*

J: (She started to talk, then cleared her throat, as though the being had to adjust to her vocal cords. The next voice was definitely feminine and softer.) There have been no regulation violations. But we would caution you to be extremely careful in your casual discussions of the phenomenon. You must be careful with whom you share casual information. There are sensitive areas. It is important, I repeat, just casual information and sharing is not allowed. You have done well, and we are thankful. One of the problems could be the nature of the information, and the timing. It is not a matter for everyone to know everything. You are very good at being able to determine who should know what. That is a level of your expertise that allows us to work with you well. It is not a matter of trusting or not trusting you, as much as it is a matter of timing. Time to know, time not to know. So, whenever you are given information in the future there will sometimes be instructions not to divulge it, until you are given further instructions. Perhaps you can find a way if it is necessarily crucial to something on which others are working, to advise them. But do not divulge your source. We will be orchestrating their knowledge, so that anything that is shared with others will be of a nature that it is preapproved.

D: *Then I'll abide by your instructions.*

I had learned in the past that I had to listen to them, or they would find ways to keep the information from being published. In *The Custodians* I reported how four tapes disappeared for eight years because it was not time for them to appear in writing. It has been over ten years since this session, so I believe it is now time to bring the information forth. They were correct about another point also. Several times during the years of my work I have been given sensitive information and told not to publish it, either for my own protection or because the time was not yet right. So I have learned to abide by their instructions.

> D: *I think we're running out of time. And the vehicle has been*
> *through an ordeal with this today. But I want to thank all the*
> *members of the group who have spoken to me today.*
> J: There are others who will speak to you at the next time.
> D: *And I'll try very hard to do what you want. If I make*
> *mistakes it's because I don't understand.*
> J: Oh, we are well aware of your capabilities, and appreciate
> and thank you. It is just that sometimes it is necessary to be
> in a bit of an urgency. And being in that, we can sound very
> harsh, and it is not our meaning.
> D: *But please understand that I am trying very hard. And I*
> *won't betray your trust, because I don't want the connection*
> *to end because of any fault on my part.*

I began reorientation suggestions to bring her back to this world, but she was making hand motions instead of following my instructions.

> D: *What does that mean?*
> J: (Very softly.) We are saying "good bye" to you.
> D: *I don't think I could duplicate those hand movements, but I*
> *appreciate it.*

I then brought Janice back to full consciousness. She had no memory of anything that transpired, and seemed to be no worse physically or mentally from the ordeal she had put both of us through. I had learned a lot from the entities in this session. When working in such an unusual field I often have had apprehensions that there might be some danger to the subject, mostly because we were treading new waters and did not know what to expect. I also carefully monitor the person's physical body signs so I would be warned of any problems that might develop unexpectedly. The entities told me earlier not to be so concerned about it, that they would always tell me if any problem was developing. During this session they proved true to their word. They alerted me to a situation that I had no way of knowing could possibly occur. I had learned a valuable lesson, but I also learned that I would never have to rely on my own expertise alone. I was definitely being guided in my work by forces from elsewhere, a higher dimension.

***

If I thought what occurred in the last session was confusing, I was certainly not prepared for the information that came out in *this* session.

I only hope the reader can follow more complicated concepts.

There had been a lapse of over a year since our last session. On one occasion when I was in Little Rock Janice was unable to work with me. She knew she had been somewhere the night before, and it had affected her to the point that she could not leave her house and definitely could not drive her car. In the past she said that sometimes she would get into her car and not even know where to put the key or how to start it. The simplest things would suddenly become very complicated, as though her mind would be totally blank and confused.

On this trip in September 1991 I was in Little Rock to interview some UFO cases for Lou Farish, so I would be trying to do everything in the same weekend. Before working, I went to dinner with Patsy, Janice and some other friends. We mostly discussed our personal lives, and mentioned nothing about UFOs or how my work was progressing. The main topic of Janice's dinner discussion centered around an old boy friend who had recently come back into her life, and things were getting serious. She seemed extremely happy, in spite of the continued UFO activity that remained in the background of her life. After dinner we went to Patsy's house and had this session. There had been many paranormal experiences in Janice's life since we last met, but it was decided not to single out one to explore. We thought it would be better to just see where the session led. Each of my sessions with Janice were always full of unexpected surprises and twists and turns anyway.

After she laid down on the bed I used her keyword and started the induction, but she interrupted and said we had to wait until a certain time to begin.

J: At 11:16 we can continue. Exactly.
D: *Okay. According to my watch it's about another minute anyway. I just hope my watch is correct.*
J: 11:16 please. We will know. For the information will not be able to culminate if it isn't.

This was the first time an entity was present even before the session began. Normally we had to search for them. I continued with my induction suggestions as I watched my watch.

J: You need to give her the word again.

I turned the recorder off as I said her keyword, so it would not be on the tape. I turned it back on when she appeared to be under.

D: *Do you know where you want to go, or would you like me to direct you?*

J: We will go to a juncture in time. Time has junctures, you know.

D: *Yes, you told me that. Why do you want to go to a juncture in time?*

J: Because that will be the beginning of an experience. It will deal with many things, because it's a multi faceted juncture.

D: *Well, we are at the time that you spoke of earlier. 11:16.*

J: I'm at a moment, you are at a minute.

D: *What do you mean?*

J: We are talking of the coordination of several different kinds of time. You see, when you speak of mankind's time you are talking in minutes and hours. But when you speak of time in other realms it is not measured by minutes and hours. But in order to bring information through dimensional time, you must be at a particular point in mankind time. Otherwise the information that comes will not be total, and it will not be coordinated elementally.

D: *But that's often hard to know. When we have sessions, we just do them when we can.*

J: Yes, but if you find a subject who is working within interdimensional time, then they will know that is important. And that everything must be done not a minute or a second before or behind. For it can be missed.

D: *Like a doorway or a gateway? (Yes) Do you want to direct it where it has to go?*

J: We will find it as we travel.

D: *How are you traveling?*

J: I'm traveling as a beam. As a particle. I am a particle. Just a particle of light. Very small, tiny.

D: *Where are you traveling?*

J: (A big breath.) Among the stars.

D: *What do you see out there?*

J: Oh, it's wonderful! It's just total, total suspended peace, quiet. Touch the velvet.

D: *Can you see where you're headed?*

J: No, but I know where I'm headed. I don't need to see it. I know I will feel when I am there.

D: *I was wondering if it looked like anything.*

J: No, because I'm not looking in the physical. I'm looking in a "see" field. You see a pattern, and you know it's a place. And if you go to the pattern, you are at the place. And the place becomes you, and you become the place. So much so, that you don't need to see it, because you're being it. So therefore if you wish to see in the physical, you ask and you can look in the physical. Otherwise you experience it in a totally different manner. There's a color, a rose quartz color. And then you know you are becoming closer to it. And closer, and closer, and closer to it. And it's moving very fast. You're going very, very fast. Very fast. But yet you feel mentally at a different speed than the physicalness that the particle is traveling, because the particle is traveling so fast you can't see it.

D: *You mean it became invisible?*

J: Yeah. It's right there, just swoosh! (She seemed to be distracted by something she was seeing.) (Softly) Okay.

D: *What?*

J: It was a cross. (Distracted) It was a... okay. A junction.

D: *Like a crossroads?*

J: Yes. Just like on a map when you come to that point.

D: *What happens when you come to that point?*

J: You stop. You stop.

D: *Why do you stop?*

J: For different reasons. It depends on where you want to live.

D: *What do you mean?*

J: At that point you can gather information, or you can go into a different dimension and be in a totally different lifetime.

D: *Do you want to gather information?*

J: We've only begun, but I want to gather information at this point, because it's a gateway to where we're going to find our information. You see, what's happening is that we have stopped so that mankind's time can be in accordance with this time. I realize this is perhaps not making much sense, but it cannot happen any other way. You see, if your time is out of joint with this time, then the connection cannot be made. So therefore you must allow that stop, that stop, and you will shoot forward the instant it has coincided. If you take two circles and you place them next to each other, and they come together until they lock, you can't pass through them.

D: *But if you pass through them, will you be going to a place where information is?*

J: I can go to the ancients. I can go to wherever you wish to go. Or I can go to where we need to go. And I can go to Creation. Or I can go to the God source.

She took some deep breaths and showed physical reaction. Something was occurring.

J: It's an infusion of information. And it's also a teacher who wishes to speak to you and to Janice. And to tell you that

you have passed time and space. (The voice changed.) First
you must understand some basic principles and foundations
with regard to source energy.

D: *I'm always willing to learn.*

J: The particle that you discovered was actually a source
particle. Everything begins with a particle of light.
Everything that is begins as the most minute pore of your
skin. If you could imagine a molecule, you could see a
pinpoint of light. You would know that in the ultimate
source, that is all you are. So what I am telling you is that,
that, within that source of "All That Is" the interconnections
between particles form a source energy. If you see a type
of pattern within a particle, and you place that particle over
another particle, they will totally match in every minute.
Now, as energy becomes matter, from that source upon
energy, it travels down the beam or out the beam depending
upon your concept, or how you wish to relate to it. And as
it implodes, explodes out, it divides as a cell divides, to
form different individuals. It can divide many times. It can
divide once. It can divide millions of times. As it divides it
becomes either male, female, or male male, female female,
male female. As it continues to divide out and travel through
dimensional shifts, it becomes in each dimension what it is
ultimately at its source. And it begins to grow. And as it goes
through universes and galaxies, every place it goes it still is.
When you bring the particle down to practical reality in Earth
terms, you have human beings who are: as in mates. You have
human beings who are: as in sub divided particles. ie: You
have similarities in human beings. You have strangers who
instantaneously become total friends, because they sub
at the source level. Rarely do the people become fused. Only
when there is a higher purpose would that union take place.
Because mankind has a way of altering reality in such a
fashion that rarely does the highest ultimate possible reality,
in this Earth plane level, become realized. So what you have
depends on planetary purposes. A common purpose for the
ultimate benefit of mankind must be realized and depends
upon the choices. The highest possible ending. You are locked
into an energy pattern, and will ultimately return to the source
in that same energy pattern from whence you came. I am
speaking of beyond time and beyond space and beyond
creation. I am telling you that I am talking to you from
beyond creation. Creation is the circle of which I spoke,
through which mankind can come. And mankind can return,
knowing how, to their source. However, before that happens

you do have some work to do on that planet, because it is time. As I spoke to you in relation to time, as I spoke to you in relation to mankind's time, and in relation to interdimensional time. I'm trying to explain time to you. You have to understand time. And that is your job. Because that is what you are dealing with in your books. You are dealing with interdimensional time.

D: *And also with very complicated concepts.*

J: Complicated concepts that it is your job to simplify, so that the man on the street can read it and go, "Oh!" So that people will begin to learn to live lifetimes at the same time. Understanding that everything they do here in the physical on this planet affects every other lifetime. Their line goes all the way. That trail of energy from where we are now, what we are saying now, what you are saying from where you are to where I am, will always stay. The difference is, as you move from dimension to dimension.

D: *I keep thinking that I'm being led to lost knowledge, to lost information.*

J: It is lost.

D: *I feel I have to get it back.*

J: That is my point. That is what I am telling you. When you were led to the Nostradamus prophecies that was only the beginning. The tip of the iceberg. You have touched only the surface. When you talked to him, for him it was reality, because his reality is where he is. And his reality exists, just as your reality exists. It will never cease to exist. It's only a shift. It's a mere shift. Do you remember initially we began to talk at 11:16. We talked at 11:16 because 11:16 is connected to.... (Pause) I think perhaps I must tell you on paper.

This has happened before during sessions, but this time I was not prepared for it. I talked to her while I opened my case and hunted for a tablet and marker that I have learned to carry for just such occasions. I brought the materials back to the bed. She sat up, and I handed the marker to her and placed the tablet in her other hand. She opened her eyes with difficulty and stared at the paper.

I witnessed this phenomenon several times in the early days of my work. It is always fascinating to observe, because the subject has the glassy eyed appearance of someone who is not awake. They always are oblivious to their surroundings and have all their concentration on the paper, and what they are drawing or writing.

J: (She began to draw.) This is you where we are, where you are, where I am with you. This is fluid. This is constantly moving. It never stops.

D: *What is that?*

J: Levels. (Pause as she drew.) I'm going to explain dimensional time. (Long pause as she drew lines.) There are more, more.

D: *What do those lines represent?*

J: Time. Periods.

D: *Time periods? (Yes) Different years, you mean?*

J: Yes, except it's more complicated than years, because it can be universes and galaxies within. Depending on how far out you go. You can go out in either one of these time periods to a point of infinity. (She drew as she talked.) Infinity, infinity, infinity. You, me, everybody on the planet in the physical....

D: *On that dot. Okay.*

J: Then... the God source.

D: *Over there in the fluid. Okay.*

J: It's all fluid. (She was marking down dates.) Oh, well, it really doesn't matter what years I put down. You begin to move. At all times energy is going this way.

D: *Forward?*

J: And this way.

D: *Forward and backward also.*

J: And so is time. And so is time.

D: *Backward and forward at the same time?*

J: The same time. Once you master dematerialization, then you can become that particle from which you started, while you are in the physical. You may go to here, because you were here. When you came from here to here, you moved through everything that exists. And you always move through everything that exists. It is complicated. However, what you need to know is that, as you move, in particle form, you go to here....

D: *That year or time frame.*

J: And you can move out to whatever lifetime within that period, because there's more than one lifetime in each period. So, what I'm saying to you is that, it is entirely possible, as a particle, to go to where Nostradamus is. Because he exists past time. Because here this is Creation time stops! Man made time periods stop.

D: *At creation?*

J: At creation. Your mankind's history says God created the heavens and the Earth.

D: *It would seem that was where time started, instead of stopping.*

J: It starts for mankind, but it stops for these dimensions here. Because you have equal dimensions in both frames. You have equal dimensions. You have mankind's time starting here. All time. All time time. But our kind of spirit time is totally different, but yet congruent with. The mechanics are totally different. You say, "One o'clock." And we say, nothing! Because we don't need time. Because we are everything. We always were. Nostradamus is here being everything he's ever been, and continuing his infinity. Even though death caused him to cease to be here, it never caused him to cease to be here. So actually, in reality what you're doing is, you are coming to the point of his death. You are transcending his death. You are connecting with him living his infinity. And that's the information and the concept in reality that you are bringing back from him, back through creation, back down to here.

D: *When I take people back into past lives, is it this particle that is going to those lives and reliving them? (Yes) Because it is as though that personality in the other life never dies.*

J: It never dies.

D: *I can contact those other personalities at any time.*

J: Correct. What you're doing is, you are vibrationally connecting this particle that exists here with this particle that exists here. Much as you say, "Oh, I remember what happened Christmas of 1964. Oh! We sat around the Christmas tree. Oh! I got a doll." That's in this lifetime. But you're talking about this vibrational rate. Right here. (Drawing.) This vibrational rate. Only you tuned into Earth 1945 this lifetime. This lifetime started in 1945. This is a time period in this dimension. But at death the particle travels all the way to here.

D: *Back to the source, from which it started.*

J: But, more complicated is that, depending upon what happened here, it can perhaps return to here. (Pointing at dates.)

D: *If it wants to pop back into the 1800s, it can do that.*

J: And come back from there. So we're getting off into some physics here. There's a little more. But what you need to know, with regard to the Einsteins and the Nostradamuses.... There is an area. (She was drawing.)

D: *What's that?*

J: It's all knowledge. Ancient, all knowledge. What has happened to people like Nostradamus and Einstein is that they began here.

D: *In that area of all knowledge?*

J: Yes. But they took an area of specialization with them to the planet. Now they haven't necessarily returned to here (the area of all knowledge), but it's irrelevant, once you pass the point of Creation, where you are.

D: *But they retained more of this knowledge in their subconscious? Would that be correct?*

J: Exactly. But that was their purpose for coming, to bring it.

D: *To our time. Okay. Would it be correct to call that little spark "your soul"?*

J: You might call it a soul, but actually in true reality, you should call it your "source energy." A soul is mankind's name for that source energy, because everything is energy. Every, every, every thing is energy. Now, this.... (She was drawing again.)

D: *The fluid part.*

J: God source or the fluid part. The spark is everything this fluid part is.

D: *Would it be like our concept of God?*

J: It could be. Yes, if you wish to, it could be God. It could be the ultimate. It could be called by any name. It doesn't really have a name. We don't do names. Actually, we are all fluid once you pass this point. Actually you exist in that way. And you also can merge here and here and here. And you can also know everything, and come out. (Drawing) You see, I'm saying that these overlap.... (Drawing)

D: *All these little dots. They all overlap.*

J: And then when each molecule has overlapped, they redivide into their three. (Drawing) And they are everything that the other energy was. Everything.

D: *But the main thing is that we are focused on this part of our life right now. Is that the idea?*

J: When we go into each other's lives here, we take with us part of what they were and part of what they are. We do everything here in the physical that we do here.

D: *In the spirit.*

J: It is no different.

D: *But we don't know about the others because we are focused on this life and what we are doing now.*

J: Because of our vibrational rate we are here. All that happens when you move is, energy speeds up. It speeds up when it goes this way (Forward). It slows down when it goes this way (Backward).

She seemed to be finished with the drawing, so I helped her lie back down, and had her close her eyes again. I looked at the paper as she moved around to get comfortable again. I thought it would be useless to keep it to put in a book later. By the time she had finished with it, it was a meaningless jumble of lines and dots, making no more sense than a child's scribbling. I knew the important description would be captured by the tape recorder.

J: We have exposed Janice to different sorts of communication patterns. It is the beginning of a totally different concept of communication, of which Einstein was well aware.

D: *She talked about the time when she was lying on the couch in her house, and all this information seemed to be coming through the window on a beam of light and bombarding her. Images? Symbols? What was that all about?*

J: Energy patterns.

D: *What was the purpose?*

J: Energy patterns are coded with information. Each pattern contains a different set of knowledge. A different concept. And maybe perhaps a whole history of a planet.

D: *In these designs and images?*

J: Yes. Because her mental capacity is such that she can carry the knowledge, and it is much as a timed release vitamin capsule. Whenever the juncture of mankind's time with interdimensional time coincide, an interplanetary... (searching for the word) overlapping, if you will, will cause a set of circumstances to evolve. Such that it will be recorded, and perhaps by you. Your connections that you are making are because you are trusted to record properly. And you have pure intentions.

D: *Yes, I was told not to censor anything. Just to report it the way it came.*

J: And you have not censored. (Softly) Except in a couple of instances.

D: *Sometimes it was necessary in a few parts, but the bulk of it has remained pure. That was the purpose of all this bombardment.*

J: No, that was not the total purpose. However, that was one of the purposes. There is another purpose. And the other purpose is so she may carry a particular vibrational rate with regard to the project of which I spoke to you earlier. It is also an activation for other information she already possesses. And it is also an integration of times within her, because she does understand the importance of junctures. She is to become active in obtaining... (searching for the word) activation of some concepts that already exist within her, because of   we do not use the word "implanted", but they have been placed within her memory bank. So that when it is presented to her in the physical, it causes the knowledge to come forth into the conscious mind, and an integration of the time frames take place. And at a source level, at an energy pattern level, the vibrational rate of the planet is interconnected interdimensionally all the way to the source. That is why it is important for mankind to not destroy his planet, you see. Because interdimensionally it will have an affect all the way to the source. Now, what I have not explained is that, when I said she had a choice, that meant we placed information in her path. And she pushed it away. That was her choice. We led her to books designed to activate certain memories. And she did not read them, so the memories did not become active. We give her physical stimulus for concepts that have been placed in that memory bank. But if she chooses to ignore her opportunity, then we must wait for another juncture in time for that to be restored.

D: *So you think that is why she was supposed to work with me, to help her release this?*

J: Yes. What I want to explain to you is that, Janice is a multi faceted individual who is capable of tuning into different dimensions. She does have a full understanding of time in relation to interdimensional junctures. With even fine tuning that knowledge to understand things, such as the solar eclipse, can change the history of your planet. If every person who is involved in the Triangle Project is located at the point on the planet at which they need to be at a particular point in time, the history will change. If one person does not locate himself, then that moment, that juncture, that mankind minute hour time in relation to multi dimensional time, will never come again. And it must be projected into future mankind time, interdimensional time, in order to have an opportunity for the change to take place. Otherwise it will not happen.

D: *But we're normal people. We don't really know that we're supposed to be in a certain place and do certain things.*

J: Yes, you do. You do. You do. She does. You are being prepared. Janice has a connection with you, and you with her. Any others you work with have a connection. And you will always know when it is time. You will think, "I need to do this. I need to do that." And you will try. Remember my explanation to you with regard to junctures. You cannot set it. Your subject cannot set it. It is already pre set. And what you need to know is that it will be, not in relation to your time or the subject's time. It will be in relation to planetary universal importance, much as your Nostradamus information came.

D: *But it came as a total surprise the first time.*

J: But it was pre set. You began at a juncture. You couldn't have done it at any other moment. It would not have happened. But what you must understand is that your UFO work is right now more important than your Nostradamus work. I am telling you this because I want you to be prepared. And I want you to get organized. You're not finished with your work on UFOs. And much of the work that you have done with Janice in relation to relation to UFOs is for your own understanding. Because as you move through your UFO contacts, there will come a point in your lifetime when you will see your connection in the whole picture. So some of the information is not for publication. You will be allowed to use some of the information. But there is a great part of it that would not be beneficial at this time, in that it would cause future developments to be altered, because of the knowledge and what would happen vibrationally as it is disseminated. What you don't understand is, as your information is disseminated, as your books are sold here, there, here, there, here, there. What is happening? Have you thought energywise what is happening?

D: *Well, I know I am connecting with many people.*

J: What is happening at the energy level? We're speaking of energy. What is happening? Nostradamus' energy goes through every person who reads that book.

D: *Many people write me and tell me they feel something.*

J: That's because I am talking to you about what they are saying. They are saying to you what I am explaining.

I was coming to the end of the session again. I never have a subject in trance beyond an hour and a half. Longer than that produces some undesirable affects, including lethargy and confusion.

D: *I think it's about time for us to leave this session now. So I will continue to work, and when the time is right the other information will come through. I want to thank you, whoever you are, who has been giving me the information.*

J: I am speaking to you from beyond time. Beyond Creation.

D: *Beyond Creation. Past the beginning of Creation?*

J: Yes. You are a wonderful being. And we are around you many times. And we guide you in directions to gather the information.

> For in actuality you are our translator, the same as you are
> Nostradamus' translator, because his knowledge comes from
> this level of knowing.

D: *I am trying to put it together the best way I can.*

J: And you are doing a wonderful job.

I then asked the entity to recede and the consciousness and personality of Janice to integrate fully back into her body. It was obvious when the other entity left because Janice began coughing and moving around, when before she had no such symptoms. Then I oriented her and brought her forward to full consciousness.

***

This was the last session I had with Janice. She continued her life as I continued mine. Her main concern was having her identity protected, and this I have done by changing her name and profession in both books. I will always be grateful for the wonderful information she gave me, and the concepts she exposed me to, that will forever change my thought processes and the way I view the world. It will also forever affect the way I conduct my work and gather information. Janice's information has given me a different way to view the world we live in, and shown me that we do reside in a truly convoluted universe where anything is possible.

CHAPTER FIVE
THE REPOSITORY PLANET OF KNOWLEDGE

Part of this session was included in *The Custodians*. In the beginning of my work dealing with abduction cases when a subject had missing time they found themselves onboard a craft interacting with extraterrestrials. As my work progressed and evolved things began to change. I found cases where, instead of going onboard a physical craft, they found themselves in otherworldly situations. An example was reported in Chapter 4. I have come to the conclusion that we cannot make assumptions about anything in this type of work. Once I think a pattern is established, I find cases that deviate from that pattern and lead in a different direction. These end up broadening my understanding of the unknown world I have been investigating. I included the first part of this case in *The Custodians* to illustrate a dramatic situation of missing time, but since the rest of it did not follow the norm, I decided to save it for this book and tell the story in its entirety.

During 1997 Clara had written and called several times asking for a session. This has been happening so often that I can no longer work with new subjects unless I am going to be giving a lecture in the city where they live, and only provided I have the time. I cannot work with everyone and still conserve my own energy. In the beginning of my work I often drove great distances to have sessions with people, and tried to help anyone who asked, but times and circumstances have changed. There are so many people now wanting sessions that I stopped doing them at my home, and on the day I am going to give a lecture. I find my energy is divided if I do too many different things on the lecture tours. I only conduct sessions on days when little else is planned. Usually I tell people they will be put on my waiting list, and the next time I am going to be in their city we can schedule an appointment.

Clara found out I was going to be in Hollywood in May 1997 for a conference, so she called and asked for an appointment. She lives near San Francisco, but she was willing to drive down to Hollywood. Under those circumstances I felt I could not refuse her, especially if she was willing to go to all that trouble.

The conference turned out to be a disaster. Lack of publicity and planning were the main reason. Although the speakers were all there, there were no participants. Several talks were canceled because there was no audience. It was the worst one I have ever attended, but as a result I had more time on my hands than I had anticipated. Phil (my friend and subject in *Keepers of the Garden*) was now living there. He turned the trip into a sight seeing tour and showed me the Hollywood I had wanted to see ever since I was a teenager dreaming dreams in a darkened movie theater. I had never had the time to really see it before, since I was always confined to my hotel or the convention center. After a conference I always had to go directly to the airport. We decided to make the best of a bad situation, and I really enjoyed seeing the glamorous side of the town.

Thus when Clara arrived I was relaxed and had plenty of time to spend with her. She came to the hotel room. Phil would arrive later and wait in the lobby until we were finished so we could go to eat supper.

Clara is an attractive blond woman in her forties, active, intelligent and in good health. During the talk beforehand, where I try to determine the problem or the reason for the session, she said the main thing troubling her was an episode of missing time that had occurred a few years earlier. She occasionally goes to Hawaii for conferences relating to her work. On this occasion she was driving on the island of Maui. It was almost dusk, but still light, and she was looking for a hotel she had been to before. It was located on the beach, and she wanted to eat supper there to enjoy the ocean view. As she drove looking for it, she discovered she had gone past the entrance, and decided to drive a little further down the road to find a place to turn around and go back. This part of the island had lush tropical growth and palm trees shading the two lane road. There were few houses, and they sat back away from the road hidden from view. She finally found a driveway to turn around in, although she mentally noted that she had never noticed it before when she drove the same route. When she pulled in she found herself in a small housing development composed of modular homes. They were sitting among palm trees in very pleasant surroundings. The only odd thing was that Clara could not remember ever seeing this community on that road before. She pulled her car into the driveway and was turning it around and that was the last thing she remembered.

The next instant she found herself on the other side of the island driving down a busy four lane highway. It was now pitch dark, and she had no idea how she got there.

A year later when she returned to Maui for another conference, out of curiosity she drove down the same road looking for the driveway she had turned around in, because the strange incident had never left her memory. She drove all over the area, and although she found the hotel again, she never found the housing development of modular homes. This had confused her ever since, and this was what prompted her to have a session. She wanted to discover what happened that night, and how she so mysteriously got to the other side of the island with no memory of having driven there.

She proved to be an excellent subject. I had no trouble getting her immediately into a deep trance. She remembered the date of the event, so I counted her back to March 1994 when she was on the island of Maui in Hawaii. She found herself standing in front of her hotel, the Maui Sun, about to walk through the glass doors. She had just arrived for an annual workshop where she liked to combine relaxation with work. She admired the vibrant colors of the flowers surrounding the hotel. After she checked in, I moved her ahead in time to when she was driving to the other hotel to have dinner.

C: I've never been there to eat before. I've just passed by it. It's right on the water, where my hotel is up the hill a little bit. And I really wanted to experience sitting in the hotel with the windows all open, and hear the water crashing on the beach. I've wanted to go there for a long time, but it just never happened.

D: *What time of the day is it?*

C: It's just about dusk. I don't know what time it is by the clock, but it's getting darker. It's hard to see because there're no streetlights. And I'm going past the Astland. That's a real big place, and I miss that driveway. There's a lot of trees. And the driveway seems like... well, not camouflaged, but I just miss it. (Aggravated) I just can't see it. So I go on down further, to find a place to turn around and go back, because I really want to eat dinner at that hotel.

During this part she seemed at times to be talking to herself as she drove, and then also answering my questions.

C: I'm driving. And I find this place... Okay. So I see this place. It's a cul de sac. Yeah, this looks like a good place to turn around. Hmmm. I've never seen this place before. (Confused) Hmmm. It has beautiful palm trees and flowers, and a fence, but it's one I can see through. And there are all kinds of... (had difficulty describing) modular homes, or very fancy mobile homes. Yeah, okay, this is a beautiful place.

D: *And do you find a place to turn around?*

C: Yeah. It's a cul de sac, and I'm turning my car. (Softly) And I see these bright lights. (Pause, then confusion.) It's like... blinding lights.

D: *Where are they?*

C: (Her breathing became faster.) They're coming down from the sky. And it's like a funnel of light. A funnel, with the wide end down toward me. It's almost like... from the sun, how you see through the trees this bright, bright light. And I feel a lot of very powerful energy from this light. (Deep breaths)

D: *Is it a solid light?*

C: It's like beaming light. Streams of light.

It was evident from her voice and her breathing that she was experiencing something unusual and mildly disturbing.

D: *Are you still driving your car?*

C: No! I just am. I just am.

D: *What do you mean?*

C: (With disbelief) It feels like I'm part of this light.

D: *Are you still in your car?*

C: No. I feel like I'm floating. And just like I'm part of the light. (Deep breaths.) I'm just light. It seems like a transcendence of time and light. Like I'm moving. I'm going somewhere, but I don't know where I'm going. And it's okay. (She was definitely caught up in the experience.) The feeling of floating. Of moving. Through colors, through time, through space, through.... (Deep breaths.) It's very pleasant.

D: *Is that all you can see, is colors?*

C: (Sluggishly) Colors, and golden light. And it's just very peaceful. (She let her breath out in a very relaxed manner.) The feeling is that I'm everything, and everything is me. All that is is there. All that is is here. All that is is.

D: *Do you have the feeling of moving or going somewhere?*

C: Yes. Going up. Ascending. Of moving to another place and another time.

D: *Let's see where you're going.*

C: (Hesitation) It's like I just kind of landed. It looks like a place where... (Deep sigh.) It's very hard to describe.

She had difficulty finding the words to describe her surroundings, but she seemed to have landed on very flat terrain where there were several spires. "They are like buildings. Gray like granite. It's sparkelly in color, but more gray. Sparkle like granite."

D: *Do you want to go over there?*

C: I do, but I feel a reluctance. This is so awesome. (She became emotional and started to cry.) To be here! It's like it's.... (She was openly crying.)

It was hard to understand why seeing this scene should make her emotional.

C: I never thought I'd see this again. (She was sobbing and crying.)

D: *Explain what you mean.*

C: It's like I'm coming home. (She was crying loudly.)

D: *And this is a place that you know?*

C: (Sobbing) Yes. I know it. But it's from a far distance in time. And I wasn't sure I would ever be here again. (Sobbing) It's a very good feeling.

As I tried to calm her down a chill ran through me. It was like *deja vu*. This sounded like the same scene and the same emotional experience that Phil had when he unexpectedly went to the Planet of the Three Spires. This was the place he called "home", and he knew he had been away for a long time, and thought he would never see it again. This was reported in *Keepers of the Garden*. Could Clara have gone to the same place?

D: *Do you see any people?*

C: (Sniffling) No, I don't see anyone right now. I just came... (She was trying to pull herself together.)

D: *It was a surprise, you mean. Unexpected.*

C: I'm very surprised. I... I didn't think I'd ever be here again. And it seems so sudden to be here. Like I came a long way. And through a long time. (She was still emotional.) To be at this place. (Crying)

D: *It sounds like a special place. (I knew I had to get her past the emotion before we could continue the story.) Tell me what happens.*

C: I'm looking, and it's as though I came on this light to this place. And... (Pause) I see people.

D: *Where are the people?*

C: (Calming down.) It's a group of people, and they're coming from around the buildings.

D: *Do they see you?*

C: Yes. And I look very strange to them. (Sobbing again.)

D: *Why do you look strange to them?*

C: Because I'm not gray like they are. I'm light. I'm this being of light. And they're curious. But I'm curious too. To see what this is like.

D: *What do they look like?*

C: They have brown heads, and... (Hand motions) Their heads look like this.

D: *(I tried to decipher her motions) You mean, kind of oblong?*

C: Kind of oblong. And their chin comes down almost to a point. And it's almost like it's all head, and there's not much body. You just see the head.

D: *Can you see any facial features?*

C: I mostly just see the intelligence. And it's very....

She was having difficulty explaining, but at least she was not sobbing and crying anymore.

D: *Are they wearing anything, or can you see that?*

C: It's like a body suit. All one color, gray, shiny.

D: *And you said this group of people see you as glowing?*

C: I'm just light. And they seem to be curious about my being of light. They're very close. They try to touch me. And I'm a little bit apprehensive. I don't know what is going to happen. They try to touch me.

D: *Can you see their hands?*

C: Yeah. They're a little spindly, just... oh, the fingers. I see three, and then there's a tiny little finger. It's almost nothing, like a stub. And they just want to touch me.

D: *Are they able to touch the light?*

C: Yes. It just feels loving.

D: *You were apprehensive.*

C: Yeah. And as they come closer it's.... (Her facial expressions and sounds were of having a pleasant experience.) They're very curious.

D: *But now it doesn't bother you.*

C: No. It's okay.

D: *Do they understand what you are?*

C: They seem to know what I am, and who I am. And so we walk together back toward the buildings. They're telling me that I am one of them. But I have gone out from this place as an investigator to gather information. And that I go as a being of light over time. And now I've gathered the information, and I've come back to bring this information to this land.

D: *Had you been gone for a long time?*

C: For a very long time. A very, very, very, very, very long time.

D: *But they still recognize you?*

C: It took a while. They said they were curious. They were not sure that it was I, the one that was sent to gather information. Now they recognize. They know that I'm the one that was sent.

D: *Are many people sent to do these things?*

C: One about every millennium or two.

D: *Why did they want you to gather the information?*

C: To retrieve the knowledge that is beyond this place, so that the knowledge is kept. That it's not lost.

D: *You mean it is knowledge that is not part of their history?*

C: Yes. The history and knowledge of another time and space.

D: *Why are they interested in retrieving it, if it's not their history?*

C: Because they had heard of this other place, and that they can learn from that knowledge. It was not to be lost.

D: *Then they wanted you to find new information they didn't have?*

C: New information from the other place that they didn't know. That they could gather.

D: *Didn't they have any other way to find the information?*

C: From time to time these beings select their chosen. And they choose to go to other galaxies, to other times and places in space, for information about time and space and place. And bring it back to this space of being. To learn. To grow. To expand. Because as this time and space learns to grow and expand, it separates. It becomes another time and space.

D: *You mean it can only expand through knowledge?*

C: Through knowledge.

D: *Do they have ways of traveling to other places to gain knowledge?*

C: They go on beams of light. The beams of light sometimes are oblong, round spheres. From one dimension they look silvery and long, oval. And from another direction they look round. And they're like a silver disk. And you just slide through the air.

D: *Are they solid, physical?*

C: Yes, yes.

D: *Because you also said they were like beams of light.*

C: They are. They can be solid, or they can be pure energy. Whatever is appropriate for the place. We can be pure energy, or we can be a solid disk, to get to where we need to be.

D: *Weren't they able to use this kind of "equipment" to gather the knowledge themselves?*

C: They could. But a being chose to go, and a being was chosen to go, for the experience.

D: *You mean, if they went with their machinery they couldn't experience?*

C: No. The being goes and it can be the disk, or the vehicle, or can just be the being. The being can be the vehicle, or the vehicle can be the being.

D: *Then it doesn't have to have a physical form? (No) But yet you're seeing them in physical form.*

C: They are becoming physical form so that I will recognize them as they were in the time that I left.

D: *Then since you left they no longer need this physical form? Is that correct?*

C: They do not need the physical form, but they became the physical form, so that I would recognize they have escalated since I have been gone, to a place where they can be pure energy. So that I will recognize them as I did at the time I left. Then I was a being like them.

D: *And since you've been gone they have changed to where they don't need the body anymore.*

C: If they choose to. If they choose to be pure energy, they can be pure energy. Or they can be the body, or the disk, the vehicle.

D: *But they still need something to travel in.*

C: Not necessarily. I came back on light as pure energy from the other time and the other space. The object they show me is so I will remember coming back into this stratosphere, this... there's not atmosphere. It's just....

D: *This dimension, or world that they live in?*

C: Yes. This world that they live in, so I will recognize that we have used the disk. We can still use the disk if we need to go to another world. We can use the disk, or we can just use pure energy. It's for my remembrance of the time past when I left.

D: *But still the best way to gain the knowledge is to have someone like you go and absorb it? Is that a good word?*

C: That's a good word. Absorb it, yes.

D: *And now you have come back to share it with them. But you're not back there to stay?*

C: That will be determined at another time, whether I stay or whether I go on to another world to gain more information or knowledge.

D: *All right. But you said they're taking you somewhere.*

C: We go into this room which is round. We sit at a round table. It's like a council of beings. And there I share the information that's gathered from these other worlds that I've been to.

D: *How are you sharing the information with them?*

C: We're sitting down in... like a physical form. (She had difficulty explaining, yet she was smiling.) We can share the information on a telepathic level, or we can talk verbally. The thought patterns... our thought communication is sometimes interrupted by someone speaking up in the group, and saying something that is... (smiling) humorous. A little interplanetary humor there.

D: *Something you said that they find humorous?*

C: Yes. And they are saying something that I find humorous. So that is done in an auditory way. And it's as though my being is feeding information into a computer bank. It's telepathically transmitting the information gathered and learned into their computer banks, into their systems.

This also occurred with Bonnie when beings took her car from the highway into a huge craft. With the help of a device that they placed on her head they duplicated and transferred her memories into a type of computer. This was reported in *The Custodians*.

D: *Can you see these systems? Are they in the room?*

C: No. It's in their brain, in their mind and their being.

D: *So the information is being transmitted from your mind to their mind. (Yes) The information of all of the worlds you have visited since you left. (Yes) All the lifetimes you have lived, or just from worlds?*

C: Just from worlds.

D: *Then you didn't actually live on all of these worlds you're discussing with them?*

C: There are other times when I've been to other worlds. But this time I went to just one world to gather information and knowledge about that culture, about that world, and about that system. And to bring it back. This seems to be a place where information is gathered from all of the other worlds. Then brought to this place. It's like a giant place where all knowledge is stored from all the universes, from all the galaxies, from all the places that exist. Like a gathering place. Like a huge library of information from all times and all spaces.

D: *Who has access to this information, if it is stored there?*

C: Everyone does. Everyone in all galaxies do, if they know how to tap into it. It's a resource center. Everyone can tap into it. It's just having the key to do it.

D: *And you're part of it right now by transmitting the information you have found. But if you went to one world, you said, to gather the information, what world was that?*

C: That world was Earth.

D: *Did you have to live lives on Earth to gather the information? (Yes) Then you've been gone a very long time. (Yes) You must have a lot of information to share.*

C: (Deep sigh) More than I thought could be possible.

D: *But it sounds as though it's being transmitted very quickly.*

C: Yes. It's faster than the speed of light. Because though it took much, much time and lifetimes to gather the information, at this resource center or this place that I am now, it's as though it can be disseminated very quickly. It can be transmitted. It can flow through my system into that place that it needs to be, in a very quick time and space, because here everything is now. Everything here happens now.

D: *And the information is safe there because it's stored with these beings?*

C: With these beings, and within everything that exists here. In the rocks, in the buildings, everything absorbs the information. It's as though everything is a computer bank. Everything absorbs this knowledge. Everything becomes this knowledge. Everything becomes everything that I'm bringing back.

When Phil went to the Planet of the Three Spires he also said that all knowledge was obtainable there, and it was stored within the planet itself. This information was in *Keepers of the Garden*.

D: *If someone like myself wanted to find the information, how could it be retrieved?*

C: It's a special key. A key to just going inside yourself, because going inside yourself is the key to that knowledge, and this is the place where all the knowledge is. And anyone, any being from any time and any place, can access that by their own desire.

D: *You mean they have to desire the knowledge first?*

C: Yes, and the knowledge comes through love. You don't have to go to this place where I am, where these beings are. Just ask for the information, and it will be given.

D: *It sounds as though you are performing a very important duty.*

C: That's what my purpose is. That's what I came into being to be and do.

D: *Then do you stay there with these beings of energy very long?*

C: Always.

This was a shock. If she stayed there, what about this body of Clara I was speaking to that was lying on the bed in Hollywood? Could a part of her stay there, and also be here at the same time. I always worry about causing any harm to the subject, and this was a strange answer.

D: *I mean, do you just stay there until they have retrieved the knowledge?*

C: No. I will be here until I am on another assignment to another place or another time. It may be gathering information from another world like Earth, another place.

D: *But I am thinking of the body that I am speaking to on Earth at this time. The body of Clara. Will this energy that I'm speaking to, return to that body? Or is it separate? I'm trying to understand what happens.*

C: It's one and the same.

D: *But yet you said the energy would stay there until another assignment?*

C: That is correct.

D: *But yet it is also part of this body on Earth?*

C: That is correct.

D: *How can it be in two places at once? Can I understand that?*

C: (Deep sigh) She doesn't understand it.

D: *Is there any way you can help us understand?*

C: (Purposefully) She was sent to be in a body and to gather information. I am a part of her who has gathered information and is now bringing it back to this place of knowledge. This resource center. This library. She has great difficulty understanding and learning that she can be there gathering information, and that I can be here disseminating information, or bringing information back. And so there is a time where there is for her a splitting of energy. Not knowing if she's in one place or another.

D: *Does this happen to other people also?*

C: Yes. There are others who experience similar lifetimes.

D: *The feeling of being in two places at the same time.*

C: Yes, yes. Because there are numerous beings that are sent. It would be a tremendous responsibility and job for one person to gather all that information.

D: *It would be almost impossible, I think.*

C: Yes, yes. So there are many beings. And there are other beings who are going to other worlds at the same time that I'm here, and that Clara is there in that form. I hope she's gathering more information in that physical form to transmit to the part of her that's me, that's bringing the information here.

This was getting beyond my understanding, and would take further study. I thought I should get back to the experience we were investigating in the first place.

D: *Are you in a position to explain what happened when she was driving down the road in Hawaii, when this transference took place? Is her physical body still in that car at that time? (No answer) We're reviewing that time, when she was driving down the road, and came upon that park.*

C: She was sent there at that time and that place. Because that was the place that materialized for her benefit, so she could go into that space, so the part that I am could leave and bring the information here to the resource center. And then it was not appropriate at the time when the information was disseminated here, that she return to that particular place. So she was taken to a place that she, in that physical body, knew on this highway, Pelanoni (phonetic). A place that she knew, so the car would be there, and she would know how to get to where she was going, when the part that I am left her physical body.

D: *Then the transference had to be at a certain place in Hawaii at that time?*

C: Not necessarily. That was just a place that she felt comfortable with in the physical body. And the place that was created for her to be, was a place of great beauty for her. And so it was a place where she could be totally and completely relaxed, so the transference of the part that I am of her could leave her body and come up to transfer the information.

D: *Then the car and her physical body in the car was physically taken to the other highway on the other side of the island?*

C: That is correct. It was just simply demateralized and then materialized back at another place.

D: *Is this common to move cars and people from one place to another?*

C: Oh, yes. Oh, yes.

D: *It happens often?*

C: Very often, very often.

D: *When it happens, is the physical body dematerialized and rematerialized also? (Yes) And no harm occurs to the body.*

C: No harm. It becomes pure energy.

D: *And she and the vehicle were just moved from one place to another.*

C: That is correct.

D: *So when she was once again conscious, she was in a different place on the island. And was driving at that time. (Yes) And she had no memory until now of what happened.*

C: That's right.

D: *Is this the only time this has occurred in her life as Clara?*

C: It has occurred many times. But this time she was at a place and time in her life when she was open to investigate, to see what occurred, and how it may have occurred. The other times were not a time when she was ready to have an understanding, or at a growth time in her Earthly physical life that she could have an understanding of what was happening.

D: *Also it was probably not as noticeable that it made her remember it.*

C: That is correct.

D: *So this was a time when something unusual occurred, and made her remember it.*

C: That is correct.

D: *Is it all right for her to know the information now?*

C: Yes. She should know the information. She has been longing to know the information. She will understand it now. It is to be a joyous benefit for her.

D: *That's very important. Would it be all right if I came at another time and communicated with this part of her?*

C: Oh, yes. We like communicating. That's what our work is, communicating.

D: *Because I've been told by others that if I wanted information I could have access to anything I needed to know.*

C: That's right. You have a special talent and a special gift that has been given to you. To gather information that has been silent, that has been suppressed, that has been hidden, that has been covered up, for eons. And it is the time now, and we are making this communication through this vehicle to you, so that you know and that you be aware, that you are doing a great work. And it is at the appropriate time on the planet Earth, that you disseminate the information in the way in which you have been chosen to do. And to allow this knowledge to come through these resources, that others will know that everyone is capable of diving deeper into that which is, to learn more about themselves. And the past and the future, and all that is happening in all universes. So, yes, you have access to all the information in the resource center. And we acknowledge you.

I then asked the other entity or portion or whatever it was to recede, and I had Clara's personality incorporate fully back into her body. The release or change is always noticeable, because the subject breathes deeply at this point. I oriented her to the present time, and brought her back to full consciousness.

After Clara was fully awake I called down to the desk and had Phil come upstairs. I thought it would be important for the two of them to meet, because their experiences were so similar. Phil was puzzled when I introduced him to Clara, because he knew that I was very cautious about revealing the identity of my subjects, in order to protect their privacy. But when I explained what had just happened they both became very emotional. It was as if two souls had met and instantly recognized their connection. They talked and described similar memories of this strange planet of spires. It was a very emotional and logically unnatural scene, because we all knew they had returned "home" for a brief period, and the feelings were overwhelming. There will be other sessions in this book where subjects found their "home" to be an unnatural place far from Earth (Chapter 10).

In the last few years, 2000 and 2001, I have found other cases where the person appeared to be in two places at once, or reporting from another perspective. In one of these a woman, instead of going into a past life, went to the spirit realm where she was attending a meeting of teachers, guides and masters. She said this part of her remained there always, and part of its job was to monitor her progress on Earth and try to give advice on a subconscious level.

As this book was going to the printers I found another similar case i n 2001. Whoever is running this show from the other side apparently has decided it is time to release this information. A woman regressed to a past life as a man in a remote part of Greece. He did not belong there, but was observing and listening. I took her backwards to see where she came from, and she found herself on a dark planet. It was all gray with a few buildings and no trees. It seemed to be mostly underground. She found herself in a strange body. She described it as a fish body, but it seemed more lizard-like with a large mouth, huge eyes, an unusually shaped head with a bump on the back and a tail. She said she was an observer and was sent to Earth at various time periods in history. At those times she took the shape of the existing being, and was an observer and accumulator of information. When I attempted to take her to the last day of her life, she said there was no last day. Her present personality was still the observer. That was her job.

There has been much talk about shape-shifters. If they are real I think they are these beings who are able to exist in several suitable forms. (Also energy beings can create any shape or body they choose.) My conclusions are that these shifters would not be in positions of power or decision-making (as has been suggested), because they are observers, accumulators and reporters. This is similar to Bartholomew, so it appears to have been going on since the beginning of time.

So it seems as though this part of us that is living a life on Earth is only a small piece or splinter of a much larger us. That we are many rather than one, or rather pieces of a more complex whole. We are only able to focus on the splinter we perceive as our totality. That is a good thing, because if we were aware of the complexity of it we would not be able to function in this world or reality. We are only allowed to see the facade that masks a much larger picture. Only now are we being allowed to peek behind the veil.

***

Clara wanted to have another session when she heard I was going to return to California. I had to come back the next week to speak at the Whole Life Expo in Pasadena. This time Clara flew down from San Francisco instead of driving, and we were able to have one session. I wanted to especially focus on questions dealing with Earth mysteries, since we had been told we could have access to any information we wanted. I didn't tell Clara what I was interested in exploring. Of course, in the past I have found that the guardians of the knowledge do not often give you everything you ask for. I have learned to not press it, and take what I can get. I always have plenty of questions, and I can always move on to another topic.

During this session I asked about many different unexplained topics, and the answers will be included in the section about Earth Mysteries. I was refused information about the Pyramids because the time was not yet right, but I got other information that is pertinent to this topic.

D: *The reason I asked about the Pyramids was because you said the planet of the spires, the entire planet, all of it, the rocks, every part of the planet, had been turned into a storehouse. (Yes) And on Earth this is not the case?*

C: Everything on Earth has the knowledge. It's all in the mind of man, if man will open to the expansiveness that the mind has for man. Man or humans on Earth, as the development of his mind is now, must have a tangible place they can touch and feel, like a library, for example. That is a place where knowledge is. It's stored. You can go there. So it is a feasible thing that all the knowledge for man, and all the creation, all the knowledge of the Earth and the universe, would have a storehouse on Earth. And that's in the Pyramid. Should man be able to open up his mind to full capacity, then he would know that all knowledge is within himself.

D: *Yes, that's true. I've found in my work, that it can be tapped by this method. (Yes) But consciously people never realize that. It's only when they're in trance and doing subconscious work.*

C: That is true. And that is why you have been chosen to show humanity, to show people on the Earth, that this is a way of expansion of the mind, to know that all knowledge that is within. It's being able to find that way of tapping into that knowledge. And by your methods, you show that this can be done. There are people who will not believe this, but as you begin to allow the information to flow through you in the manner in which you have been able to do, then the acceptance will be on a grander scale. And eventually in time more and more will accept this as a way of being able to access that which is within all. And perhaps at some future time hopefully near future time people will be able to tap into this type of knowledge on a more conscious level.

D: *I've always believed that. That the knowledge has not been destroyed because the people have died over the centuries. It is still stored in the subconscious mind.*

C: It is stored into the cellular level of the DNA. So even though a person might make a transition from a physical body into a pure energy body that which I am you never forget.

D: *So it is always available once you find the method to contact it.*

C: Yes. It is within all. The information is there.

D: *I've often suspected that the pyramids and the monuments in Peru that I just visited were much older.*

C: Macchu Picchu?

D: *Yes, I've been there. I could see a combination of structures there that I thought were from different time periods.*

C: There are different time periods at Macchu Picchu. Some are much newer than others. It's as though two civilizations were there. And in fact they were.

D: *This is what the shaman told us. That the Incas did not build the main ones with the huge blocks.*

C: That is correct. The Incas came many generations, many, many, many, many years later after the original -- ruins, as you know them now -- the civilization, the cities, were built. They were built much, much earlier than the Incas. The Incas inhabited them after the other civilization had already left the planet.

D: *That's what I thought. That's what the shaman believed too. That the Incas came and just utilized what they found.*

C: Yes. They found a very nice habitat. And so they said, "Why should we create something when it's been created for us already."

D: *And some of the buildings they built were of much lesser quality.*

C: That is correct. Because they had lost the knowledge that the earlier civilization had achieved.

D: *What happened to the original inhabitants? They just seemed to disappear and left their cities. No one knew what happened to them.*

C: They had evolved to a vibrational level in which they no longer needed a physical form. They had reached a level of such purity that they became pure energy. And just, as you would say, "disappeared" from the mass, or the density of the human body. Or the physical form, as you know it. These cities were built by people who survived Atlantis and migrated to Peru. So they were already at a higher evolved level. When they came to this planet they were already at a higher vibrational level. And those who then went out and created other communities, and other civilizations, lost some of that higher vibrational level, because they separated themselves from the whole. The whole being the civilization as it was. As it had been created when it came back from the stars. And then as they went out and created other communities and other little civilizations, as you would call it, they began to lose their higher vibrations. Their vibrations became lower, and therefore became denser, and denser and denser. Until we have the dense physical form as you know it today.

D: *The highly evolved ones more or less raised their vibrational rate to where they just changed?*

C: They totally changed form. There was no density any longer. They became light.

D: *Did they still exist on Earth when they changed to light?*

C: They still exist today.

D: *Why can't we see them?*

C: Because they're vibrating at such a high frequency of energy, that they no longer need a physical form, as you know it. And it is not a visible form.

D: *But what are they doing? Are they still living a life?*

C: They still are living a life. They can be oftentimes a spirit guide, as you know what a spirit guide is. If a being or an energy would appear to you, it is very possible it could be one of those who has reached such a level of vibration that they become what you would call "an ascended master." This whole civilization, as a group, was one unit. And as one unit they evolved to a place where they no longer needed a physical form.

D: *What happened to the bodies when they evolved?*

C: The bodies just dissipated.

D: *And this place they went to, was it like a land, a city?*

C: Yes. They can be in any city. Any city, any place can be their home. Also there are what you would call "etheric cities." Cities just like your cities, only they are on a vibrational level which is at a higher note that humans, as you know it, cannot see. But they exist.

D: *And they exist in this light form.*

C: In light form, yes. Should you be able to raise your consciousness to a level such that you would no longer need a dense physical body, then you would be able to see the cities. You would be able to move in and out, and go about your daily whatever you do, as though you were in a dense form. But your vibrational level is of such a pure thought, shall I say. Your thoughts are so pure. Your life is so pure, that it is all positive. And you reach a level where your sensitivity and your vibration, your energy level is at such a high note, that you no longer need this. So you go to that place, which is still in existence.

D: *But in that place, it sounds like they wouldn't die, if they were pure light.*

C: No, you do not die. You never die. Even in the dense form you don't die.

D: *I know you just change forms.*

C: Yes. You simply change to a different vibration. And it is a possibility that you could go to that vibration at some point. You might transcend. Because even though you leave a dense physical form, as you know it, you still have stages in which you can grow and develop to other vibrational levels. There are many different levels of vibration.

D: *Then even at that level, if they transcended and went there en masse, do they still have karma to repay?*

C: When you reach that level of vibration, that would be far beyond the fifth dimension, as you would think of dimensions. You have worked out all karma that would need to be worked through. So when you get to that level of vibration there is no karma.

D: *Then they could stay there for eternity?*

C: For as long as they wish.

D: *Even if they don't die, could they decide to go on and do something else?*

C: They could decide to come back in physical form. They decide, "Well, gee, that was so much fun, why don't we try this again."

D: *But then they can get caught up into karma again.*

C: That is a possibility, yes.

D: *I'm trying to put this together with some of the other things I've heard. It's different than the spirit level, where people go when they die on Earth and leave the physical body. Is this a different place that these beings are at?*

C: It can be the same. It depends on the growth of the spirit. If it's someone who has just made a transition, they could be at a vibrational level where this community is. Or it may take more growth to get to that place. It depends on the state of enlightenment at which that person is at the time of that transition.

D: *Then the majority of people on Earth today, when they die and leave the body, are working out problems in karma, so they have to keep going back and forth. So apparently these in Peru were coming from a different place when they crossed over.*

C: Yes. That group was a civilization that did it in group form instead of as an individual form.

D: *So that is probably what we are trying to attain, to reach that level where we don't have to keep coming back.*

C: That is the ultimate goal.

D: *I've heard the ultimate goal is to return to the Creator, return to God.*

C: That's what it's all about, going to the light which is the source, that is what you would call God.

D: *Yes, there are different names for Him.*

C: Many different names. It is what you choose it to be for you.

D: *Then these people, I suppose you would say, are as close as you can get to the Creator.*

C: Very close. Very close. Because a civilization went in group form, and they went as one, with no separation between, what you would say, the bosom of God. Which is being one with God, or being one with all, being one with everything that is. Being everything that is. Because the ultimate goal is to be one with God. And you are not one with God when you realize there is a separation, because man has tried so hard to to be separate from God. The ultimate goal of the soul is to to be back with God, from whence we came from the beginning.

D: *Yes, that makes sense to me. Are there other civilizations that have made this transition en masse?*

C: Many have done that.

D: *Are there any that we would be familiar with in history?*

C: Not in your known history, no.

D: *It was back before that?*

C: Before that, yes.

D: *It sounds as though the people of Atlantis died violently. So that would be different circumstances when we have mass disasters.*

C: (Interrupted) I will say one thing about the mass disasters. If it's a civilization, or if it's a group of people, those souls, those beings chose that at that time, as a way of going to another level. Or to another place where they could grow in a different way. It is choice.

D: *As you can see, I have many questions.*

C: Yes, you do. You have very good questions. And that's why you have been chosen. And that is why we wish to share the knowledge with you, so that mankind, as you know it today, will have the information and the secrets that have been locked up from ourselves. We wish to talk with you some more. Clara is doing much like what you're doing, but in a different sense. In that you will be reporting it to humanity. She comes in contact with humans, is taking information, and reporting it back to us. And that is why you have been sent many varied and different peoples to gather your information through.

D: *But the information is becoming more complicated as I work.*

C: That's because you're opening more doors. And as you allow yourself to open more doors, as you step through the doors, then other doors open up, so that other realities and much more complicated material will be given to you. It will be an honor to explore them with you.

D: *I will try never to violate your trust.*

C: We know that or we wouldn't come to you.

I oriented Clara back to the present time and brought her forward to full consciousness. Upon awakening she described her feelings while she was talking.

C: I had the feeling I was in now. I felt like I was in future time, past time and now. It was like all time was right now.

D: *It was all combined. Kind of like you were split?*

C: No, it didn't feel split. It felt very much unity, being in future time and yet in ancient, way past time. Many, many civilizations ago. It felt like this entity knew no boundaries of time. It was like all time was now.

D: *Well, you can see how we can get information that way, because it doesn't have any boundaries.*

A unusual occurrence happened after this session. Clara went back to her hotel room. After a few minutes she called me and asked me to come to her room. When I got there she showed me the back of her neck. When she was brushing her hair she saw a red mark on the back of her neck. (In the bathroom at this hotel there were mirrors on both sides of the wall. Thus Clara could see the back of her head as she brushed her hair up. She wore it up in a tight ponytail.) The red mark extended up into the hairline at least two inches, and then down beyond the hairline that's where she noticed it about a half inch. It was very red, and looked like a stripe. In the area below the hairline it was about a half an inch to three quarters of an inch wide, tapering upward to about an inch and a half at the broadest part of the red mark inside the hairline. I got my camera and took some pictures of it. But it was already beginning to fade by the time I was trying to take pictures. There is no way anything could have caused any irritation in that part of the body, because she had been lying perfectly still on a pillow. She said it didn't hurt or itch or anything, it was just red, and she was curious about it. This could go along with the other people I have worked with, who had marks and blotches appear on their body when working with types of energy as this. These cases were reported in *The Custodians.*

***

This contact with a planet that holds all knowledge, and is always accumulating more is very similar to the accounts of my other subjects who have been told they are reporters. Many humans have implants in their body that act as transmitters. Everything they see, hear and feel is being sent to computer banks that are recording the history of our planet Earth. Are these two separate projects, or are they connected some way to the whole? I have found that one of the main functions of the subconscious, or perhaps our very soul, is to accumulate information from all the lives we ever live. Our ultimate goal is to return to the Source, our concept of God, the Creator. When we have completed all the journeys and adventures through all our many variety of lives we are supposed to return to the Creator with our accumulation of knowledge. It is then absorbed. In this way we are considered cells in the body of God.

Knowledge and information seem to be the main purpose of the human species, and thus nothing can be right or wrong. It is only positive and negative. We learn lessons from it and it enables us to work out any karma so we can complete our assignments and return to whence we came. In that respect in the final analysis all we have and are is the sum total of our experiences and our knowledge.

***

A disturbing thought went through my mind when I heard about the entire civilization in Peru that transcended en masse to a higher vibration so they were invisible. It was said this has also happened to other civilizations in the past. There is much talk now about our present day Earth changing its vibration and moving to a higher vibration and changing dimensions. That some would go and some would be left behind, and those that are left will never know what happened. Is it the same thing that happened to these civilizations in the past?

SECTION THREE

Earth Mysteries

CHAPTER SIX
ATLANTIS

One important mystery that has tantalized the minds of men for ages is the existence of the civilization of Atlantis. Many have called it merely a myth, a legend, yet it has persisted. I have always thought that even a myth or legend has some basis in truth, and I have verified this time and again in my work with hypnosis.

When my subjects are in the deepest level of trance we can access the subconscious directly in a variety of ways. I have discovered that all knowledge is available once you tap into the wisdom of the subconscious mind. Often the person is given the information directly through past lives, and other times they are taken to places where they can access the information and interpret it for themselves. This is often done by visiting the Library on the spirit side. In this wonderful edifice all the knowledge that has ever existed, and all that will exist, is contained on every conceivable subject. This is my favorite place in the spirit world because I am always searching for "lost" knowledge. This place is usually managed by a guardian whose job is to screen those wishing to have access, and to determine their purpose. I have been told that I can have access to anything I wish, because I have proven myself by reporting the information as factually as I can, without distortion or censoring. Of course, there is always information that cannot be given, because the mind of man cannot handle it at the present time. Although, I have noticed in over twenty years of regression work, that information is now being leaked that was forbidden in the early days of my work. This gives me hope that the mind of man has finally advanced to the point that it can comprehend complicated concepts.

Over the years when I had a subject in this deep level of trance my curiosity required me to ask as many questions as I could about many, many topics. When I have access to knowledge, I will never turn away from that opportunity. The information in this section came forth over fifteen years. I put it aside and kept accumulating more until it is now time to put it into this book.

Some of the information on the subject of Atlantis may seem contradictory at first glance. But I do not agree, because I think the various subjects were seeing it at different times in its existence. I have found that Atlantis was not a single continent, city, or place. It was a name given to the world as a whole at that time. The name has become associated with the most developed part of the civilization. But all of the world was not at the same level, similar to ours at the present time. This remarkable civilization existed for thousands of years, so it underwent many changes as it rose to the highest advances mankind was capable of achieving, and then descended in its gradual deterioration and downfall. One only has to look at the history of our own world over the past thousand to two thousand years to see a parallel. Our world has also undergone a myriad of changes and advancements, some good and some not so good.

I have been told that many, many people living today were also alive at the time of Atlantis. We have returned at the present time because mankind is once again approaching that precipice that could plunge our world into the same abyss that claimed Atlantis. Operating as a spiral, time has brought similar circumstances into our present time, and we are proceeding down the same path. We have returned to make sure that mankind does not make the same mistakes again. By living in this tumultuous time we can repay karma that would normally require ten lifetimes. So we all volunteered to be here during these times.

Brenda gave us information about Atlantis during its glory days before it began to deteriorate.

B: The history of Atlantis stretched over many thousands of years. We could start by giving you general terms of how things developed. And then later as you desire more details, we could organize them and give it to you in the various aspects of the history.

D: *Was this the first advanced civilization on this planet, or were there others before that?*

B: It's hard to say, they stretch so far back. It looks like before Atlantis arose, the main civilization on this Earth was from the galactic community helping mankind. They helped Atlantis to develop, so that mankind would develop their own civilization. Which is what mankind needed to do in order to eventually join the galactic community. They were upset because when Atlantis was destroyed, mankind was on the verge of joining the galactic community. And when it was destroyed, it shook mankind so severely and knocked them so far back, that they could not join the galactic community then.

D: *Where do you want to begin? I always like things in order. It makes it easier for me.*

B: Yes. As I have just mentioned, it was various settlements of the overall galactic community that helped Atlantis get started. They had been watching mankind and trying to help them advance, but they remained basically hidden. Mankind was doing basic things like agriculture and they had fire, and were building simple cities. And they felt that mankind was far enough advanced to handle the knowledge that there were others that were not of mankind. They saw there was a group on Atlantis that was the most advanced. They had the highest developed civilization in the production of goods and art and literature and such as that. A very urbane type of people. They started helping these people to advance the civilization further. They had a way of stimulating these people so they could come up with inventions at a faster rate. They knew the type of energy that was conducive towards creative thought. And they stimulated the people's mind with this energy. When they saw it was working, they started doing this in other civilized centers of the world, which gave rise to the other civilizations. You asked specifically about Atlantis, so I shall try to stay with that story.

D: *Was Atlantis just one place?*

B: It started out being one place, but then as the civilization grew, its influence spread. And so what was considered to be Atlantis started to include more than just the land originally called Atlantis. Its civilization spread so that whoever was in the influence of this sphere was considered to be part of Atlantis.

D: *Are we correct in calling it that?*

B: It's a good name. It's a correction of the original name. As you know when a civilization is spread over a large area different dialects of the major language will appear. And in the dialect that developed in the south, the name was pronounced closer to Atlanta, which has been further altered in pronunciation in your language. But it is accurate enough so.... It was a direct progression and it poses no problem in relating that name to the civilization I'm speaking of.

D: *There were other civilizations, but you want to zero in on this one at this time.*

B: You seem to desire the information about this one. So I will make references to the other civilizations. The development was steady in all these civilizations. Atlantis was slightly ahead because they started developing first. But the other civilizations developed as well, so they could all work together. For the good of mankind, it was necessary. So the civilization continued to advance. The people were a pretty people. They were generally happy, good featured. They were emotionally healthy as well as physically healthy, which helped to make them a fair people. Not meaning necessarily light, but fair as in pretty. Your language is very imprecise with its descriptive words.

D: *I know. I've heard that before. Did they have any general coloring or features that were predominant?*

B: Not really. At first, yes, and then as they spread they came in contact with other peoples. It became a general mixture much as it is in your country. They could tell someone's general ancestry, where their ancestors came from, by their coloring, sometimes. But it didn't matter to them and so they didn't worry about it. They started out being basically reddish blond headed with a few brown haired. Of a light olive complexion, between light olive and creamy. And with usually green or hazel eyes. And then later on, they came to be people who were blond or black headed, brown eyed, light skin, dark skin, a general mixture. And they tended to be tall and well formed.

D: *I wanted to get a mental picture.*

B: They did not base their culture on metal, the way yours does. They believed in using materials as close to the original condition as when they obtained them. So they used a lot of stone and clay for their buildings. And their sciences developed directly into the manipulation of energies, so they could manipulate all types of energy, including such things as gravity. Hence they were able to erect buildings using huge blocks of stone that seem impossible to you with the basis and mind set of your civilization.

D: *Then they didn't use machinery or equipment?*

B: Correct. Because it was not necessary. They knew how to manipulate these energies using what seems like plain and simple instruments that would be impossible to do such things. But they knew how to tune in to different types of energy flow and cause them to interact in such a way to cause things to happen the way they wanted them to happen. Which sounds vague in your language, but that seems to be the best that I can state it.

D: *Did they need many people to do this?*

B: It depended on what was being done. Usually one person could do it with the tools on hand, but it had to have the consent of all, so that the energy would be flowing in a positive direction.

D: *Everyone didn't have to be concentrating or sending the energy?*

B: No. But they had to give their general consent, so they would not be blocking the energy by disagreeing with what was going on. It's like your concept of positive thinking. You don't have to concentrate too terribly hard for positive thinking. It's just a general mind set that you try to achieve. In the process of learning about these energies and manipulating them they developed their psychic abilities to the peak. So many things our civilization depends upon were simply not necessary in their civilization. Things like telephones, governmental red tape. The administrative type things were very direct because people could communicate through telepathy. And whenever something needed to be done and needed the consent of all, they would just ask them through telepathy and they would give their consent. And it would be almost instantaneous and that would eliminate many of the problems present in the modern world.

D: *Was this the only way they communicated, just through the mind?*

B: No. They also communicated verbally, but it was a mixture of both. And they just took it for granted. They never really differentiated whether they were communicating verbally or mentally, because they would be doing both simultaneously.

D: *Was this something they had to learn, or did it come naturally?*

B: All human beings have the natural predilection for this. It was bred into the race, but it was a matter of developing it. For example, all human beings generally have hands with five fingers. These hands are extremely skillful tools and they can do very delicate manipulative type work, but only if you develop the muscles and use the hands. It is the same way with psychic abilities. All human beings have psychic abilities, but the only way they can be developed is by using them.

D: *But this was something that came naturally to these people?*

B: No, they had to develop it. It was just considered part of the normal maturing process, but they were more conscious of it than people in general are today. They considered it to be a normal part of a child's development, developing muscular skills as well as psychic skills. They didn't ignore the signs the way they are ignored today. It was there waiting to be developed, but they did have to work at it, like they would have to work at learning how to walk. The ability had always been there, but it took them a while to realize it was consistently there. Early humans relied on it for survival, but didn't realize what they were doing. Then later when humans became civilized, many times they would forget about it, but it was still there. And then when their civilization developed with the help of the galactic community, they realized it was something that could be developed. Their science pointed out that they needed to be a harmonious whole themselves to be in harmony with the universe in general. And this was part of yourself. And if it's not developed, you would not be balanced and you would not be a harmonious whole. Upon the rare occasion that one would fall ill, their psychic abilities would help them locate where they were out of balance from the basic energy levels of the universe. And so they used their psychic abilities in countless ways in the smallest details of everyday life. It would be impossible to list all the ways. We would be here for a long time just listing different ways their psychic abilities could be used. The psyche is much more dexterous than just the mind, although it is functioning through the mind. It is a different aspect of the brain than mind is. Mind and psyche are two different aspects that work through the organ called the brain. One is basic and takes care of the necessities of life, and the other adds the details and finishing touches. It can be very precise and do things that the mind would be incapable of doing, because it is not fine honed enough.

D: *Were the majority of the people in the world at that time developed in this way?*

B: The ones in the civilization, yes. The ones in the backwoods did not have their psyche as well developed. They just relied on it almost as instinct.

D: *Did they have a government of any kind?*

B: At first yes, but then it changed as the civilization developed, because the original purposes of the government became obsolete, due to the psychic powers. And so the government gradually altered and changed to where it had another purpose. They put organizational structure to better use elsewhere, like organizing research.

D: *The scientific community? Or was it considered that in those days?*

B: It really wasn't considered that because the research being done was mostly based on mystical and psychic things. And so it was considered individual quests. Whenever people had insights about things they would report it to this organizational body, so they could keep track of that fact and see how it fit into the whole picture, because they considered every fact to be pertinent. And they would collect all these facts together and organize them and fit them into the whole picture, to try to better understand the nature of the universe. This involved every single person. It was very complex and the organization was needed. So that's what happened to the original governmental structure.

D: *Did they keep records of some type?*

B: Yes, they had to keep very extensive records. Due to the nature of this civilization they did not have computers per se, but they had a way of storing information using the basic energy of the universe, that could be tapped into with psychic abilities. (Perhaps similar to the way we were collecting information.) That was their major storage area, and that is why your archaeologists have not found anything. Their information is still stored there and ready to be tapped into. You need only to develop the correct psychic abilities to be able to tap into it. They had paper like products for teaching the children to read, and illustrating how to develop their psychic abilities and such. And that rotted long ago.

D: *I think the scientists are expecting to find something written down or carved or some kind of record like that.*

B: Yes. The record is there, but it's on the psychic planes. It's very organized and it's stored and it's ready to use. And it will be of great benefit to your world. It's almost lke Akashic records, but not quite, because Akashic records are part of the universe. They took that concept and found it could be used to set up a different sort of records. It exists on a sort of energy level.

D: *I was thinking of the pyramids or something similar. If they might have access to the knowledge in a physical place.*

B: No. However, the pyramids and other types of megalithic structures that are aligned to the heavenly bodies by that I'm referring to things like the mysterious stone circles in Europe are devices to help focus this energy, so that one could tap into it. Because the energy had to be organized and focused in order to be used for this purpose.

D: *If someone went to one of these ancient sites, would that help them have more access to it?*

B: Yes, it would. Some of the stone circles would not be as finely tuned as they had been, simply because of the procession of the equinoxes.

D: *You mean the sky and the Earth changing?*

B: Right, and so they're slightly out of alignment now. But others that had a strong solar alignment would still be functional. For example, since Atlantis was destroyed the major focusing center now is the pyramids of Egypt. And they are still in perfect alignment, the way they were when they were built, hence their power has not diminished. That is why people have had hallucinatory experiences upon spending long periods of time in certain interior parts of the pyramids. It is because that is the center of the focusing of the power. And you would have to be deaf, dumb, blind and retarded, not to be able to pick up on these emanations. They had similar megalithic structures on Atlantis. If your archaeologists find anything, it will be these megalithic structures, and they are no longer aligned. They were badly damaged at the time Atlantis was destroyed, and naturally their alignment was messed up. Your archaeologists will figure out they were aligned with the Sun at one time, using the precedence of the existence of these other megalithic structures that are undamaged. These were like a gigantic stone computer, using the natural energy flows of the Earth and surrounding space. And focusing them in certain ways to be able to use the different energy levels of the universe.

D: *You said the people of Atlantis used no metal?*

B: Very little metal because they found that the more something is manufactured and altered from its original form, the more out of harmony it is with the universe, and the more vibrations it loses. And if you take something from the Earth and use it without drastically altering its molecular structure, it will still be in tune with the energy levels, and can be used for this purpose. Hence they tended to use a lot of stone in their structures, since this was just solid chunks of Earth cut up and transported to another place without being subjected to melting, like you do for the refinement of certain metals.

D: *Then all their buildings, even the private dwellings, were made from stone.*

B: Either stone or clay or wood, and such. Some of the furniture in their homes was carved from stone. I used "carved", for that's the word in the language, but it's not really a good description of the process. When they took stone out of the Earth, there was a way of temporarily altering its energy fields to where it would become flexible like clay. And as a result, they could shape it like you would clay, into anything they needed. And then they would let the energy field return to its normal state and it would become rigid like stone again. They had all the ordinary comforts of life that you would expect in a civilized community.

D: *What about food?*

B: Just a regular balance of food. In the process of learning about the energy, they learned how to stay balanced with their eating. Which eliminated many medical problems that your civilization has problems with, and various diseases caused by unbalanced eating. So as a consequence, most of the people would eat mainly vegetable, high fiber type diets and very little meat. They didn't go to the extremes that some of your vegetarians have, because the body needed protein and they didn't want to eat eggs all the time. And so they would kill meat as they needed it. Some of the more advanced mystics did not feel the need for eating, because they could tap into the energy and absorb what their bodies needed directly from the universe, rather than indirectly through food. (This is the way certain extraterrestrials exist.) It's a very advanced technique. And even as advanced as Atlantis was psychically in general, only their most advanced would do it on a regular basis.

D: *Were their animals similar to the ones we have on Earth today?*

B: They were basically similar. What your archaeologists consider early civilizations, that is, the civilizations that first had agriculture and domesticated animals, were actually remnant survivors of this former civilization that had fallen. They were trying to rebuild civilization from their shattered remains. That's where the domesticated animals came from, cattle, goats, sheep, camels and certain types of horses. The breeds were different and they looked different, but that's because mankind is always doing selective breeding to change the appearance of their domesticated animals. But basically they were the same animal. For example, it's like the difference between a dairy cow and a brahma bull.

D: *Did they have any type of transportation?*

B: Oh, yes. The type of transportation they had has come down to you in legends of magic carpets. (I gave a surprised laugh.) Basically, they could levitate with no problem, because they knew how to manipulate the energy and gravity. And so they did most of their traveling by levitation. Now, sometimes if they wanted to take something with them but didn't want to carry it, instead of using the additional energy to levitate it separately, they would get a rug or something that they would sit on and just levitate themselves and the other objects on the rug.

D: *Ah ha, just like the Arabian Nights.*

B: Right. They learned to manipulate this energy to accomplish many things, and this included traveling over the surface of the Earth. If they just wanted to go a short distance and didn't want to tap into the energy, they would use an animal. But as a result of being able to tap into this energy, there was no need to develop automobiles or airplanes. And the galactic community was very excited about this. For this ability seems, as best I can see, to be very unique to our race. And it would be one of the contributions we would make to the galactic community. Becuase the other planets developed through the use of machines and vehicles.

D: *Like we have done this time.*

B: Yes. And the galactic community is somewhat concerned that we have not developed our psychic abilities this time, but they know these abilities are there waiting to be developed. And they remember how it was with the other civilization. If we are not successful in tapping into this psychic information ourselves, they will undoubtedly prod us and help us to "discover" it, the way they have with other past discoveries. This type of energy was used mainly for personal transportation over long distances, and for transportation of the blocks of stone and such as that. There are certain mystics in your present day civilization that can still do this, but they're in isolated areas of the world. Certain ones deep in the jungles of India. But the ability is most prominent among the Lamas in the high mountains of Tibet. They were able to preserve it because they were so isolated. They were the least affected by the devastation of Atlantis being destroyed.

D: *Did they do anything for entertainment?*

B: Oh, yes, that's a basic need of human nature. It depended upon what civilization it was, and according to their individual cultures. For example, in Atlantis, one thing that was very popular would be: a group of people would attach colored streamers to their arms or to articles of clothing. And then they would all levitate around each other to perform pretty colorful patterns with the streamers streaming behind them. And the children would love to watch this. They would do whatever their imagination could come up with. They had drama and plays and music. They tended to prefer live performances, but if they wanted to see something that was not being performed locally at the time, they could tune in psychically to where it was being performed and watch it with their psychic abilities. So it was like TV in a way.

D: *It appears they were very highly psychically developed.*

B: Yes, but the destruction of Atlantis frightened them very much. It gave them the equivalent of a mental trauma. Like when an individual suffers a severe mental trauma in their younger life and it affects them the rest of their life, unless they become aware of it and work it through and resolve it. The entire human race received the equivalent. And also, the way in which Atlantis was destroyed, and the way the psychic focusing centers were destroyed, it gave everybody a temporary psychic burnout. It would be like accidentally seeing an explosion too closely and your eyes would be temporarily blinded.

D: *And this affected them for several generations.*

B: Yes. The ability was still there, it was just numbed for a while. Then it gradually started getting its feeling back. And it didn't take as long as you might think. But humankind in general subconsciously remembered this and so they avoided developing psychic abilities for several thousand years, afraid they would get burned again, so to speak.

D: *That would make sense. Well, did they stay in that type of development for a long time?*

B: Yes, that was the major impetus of their civilization. They used crystals for focusing certain types of energies, for contacting the galactic community. They could do it mentally, but to help amplify the mental energies they would use certain types of crystals. Their science of crystallography was extremely advanced.

D: *You said they used this for contacting the galactic community?*

B: Yes, for long range communication. Instead of sapping everybody's energy by tapping in on everyone's telepathic abilities, they would use these crystals. Because not everyone in the galactic community was attuned to this, it would be like trying to speak with a deaf person. One had to use a different means of communication.

D: *And they understood the crystal communication?*

B: Right. And so they would use the energies generated by the crystallography for interacting with the galactic community. It was complimentary and compatible to both their civilization and the various civilizations of the galactic community.

D: *Could one person focus these crystals or did it take many people?*

B: One person could do it because these crystals could draw upon the various energies and energy fields of the Earth. Such as the electro magnetic fields, gravitation, sunlight, what have you. What needed to be done would depend on what kind of energy the crystals would draw upon. And there would be different types of crystals for different purposes. And some of these different types would be specialized for drawing upon certain kinds of energy.

D: *Did they have to be carved a certain way or shaped a certain way?*

B: Their molecular structures, the matrices, the latticework of the molecular structure would have to be designed in a certain way. And yes, many times the shape of the surface also had an affect. But they would start at the molecular level and do something similar to the crystals as they did to the rocks. They would alter the energy field so they could redesign the lattice work of the molecules so they would focus a particular energy in a particular way. And then reset the energy fields so it would stay that way.

D: *Then this was how they formed certain shapes for different purposes?*

B: Not shapes! The internal structure. The molecular structure of the crystal. And then, yes, they would alter the surface of this crystal to shape it the way it needed to be. But it was first important to get the internal structure, the molecular structure correct or you could do all the shaping in the world and do no good.

D: *I thought it had something to do with the facets or the different shape how it would be focused.*

B: You first have to get the molecular structure correct. It's like the structure of a snowflake, but carry it down into infinitely small levels of energy. And you must have all these shaped correctly, or it would do you no good.

D: *Did it matter how large the crystal was?*

B: It depended on what it was used for as to how large it would be or the shape of it ultimately. But their major concern was the molecular structure. And since they could control the molecular shape of these crystals, that's one reason their science of crystallography was so far advanced. And that's why they were able to use crystals for so many different purposes. Because they had specific controlled molecular structures, as well as controlled shapes or sizes.

D: *I've always thought that the larger they were the more powerful they were.*

B: Not necessarily. There was one crystal they had for focusing a particular type of energy that was about three inches long and very slender. It was lens shaped, pointed on both ends. And if you looked at it endwise, it had the shape of a five pointed star or something similar. And it was only about an eighth of an inch across at its widest point. It was very slender, but it was a powerful crystal due to the type of energy it focused. I can't find the information of what it was used for, but I can see that shape of crystal.

D: *I see. Then they had to be aware of the energy they wanted and what the different energies would do.*

B: Exactly. I think you're beginning to see now. They had different crystals for focusing different kinds of energy for the different purposes. For example, they had certain types of crystals that could focus cosmic rays, and ultraviolet type radiation and starlight to make visible light at nighttime. And these crystals could also use infrared heat like from body heat to help make light at nighttime. Your archaeologists have found some of these crystals in the jungles of Central America. They have not been maintained in many centuries, yet they still glow at night and produce light, but not as clearly as they used to. And they appear to the archaeologists to be simple stone balls. They can't understand what they were for or how they worked, because these are a specialized type of crystal. They have found balls of different sizes. And there have been rumors about how they glow at night. That's why they are so prevalent and are found everywhere. In the places where they found them they were used for providing light at night. Like most civilizations there are things going on at night too, and you needed a fairly widespread source of artificial light.

D: *They were like huge streetlights that illuminated the cities?*

B: Yes. Street lights, interior lights, spot lights, depending on what kind of lighting was needed. And there were other types of crystals that radiated heat to help warm houses. So they did not have to cut down their forests to build fires. They could use these crystals instead and save the forests for articles of furniture, or simply for growing and oxygenating the air.

D: *What types did they use in the houses for light?*

B: Stone balls. They came in all sizes. And they have found them in all sizes in Central America. You personally have only heard of the large ones, but they have also found smaller ones about the size of a bowling ball or slightly smaller, that could be carried in two hands.

D: *Those are stone, but you're calling them crystals.*

B: As I have already said, your archaeologists call them stone because they appear to be stone, but they are a specialized type of crystal.

D: *I think of crystal as the kind you can see through.*

B: Some you can and some you can't. They are referred to as crystals not because of their outward appearance, but simply because of their molecular structure.

D: *I see. Then these smaller stone balls were used for illumination in the houses?*

B: Right. There would be a pedestal protruding from the wall that they could sit on. Or a type of holder in the ceiling much like a setting for a stone on your jewelry. There would be a setting, so to speak, like this, protruding from the ceiling where they could implant one of these balls, or more, depending upon what kind of arrangement they wanted.

D: *Were the ones used for heating similar?*

B: They had a different structure and so they appeared differently. They would come closer to looking like your perception of crystals. And they could be obtained in different colors according to how they wanted to fit in with their interior decor. And they could do one thing with the light balls which you have not thought of. Since the balls came in different sizes, they could get some that were very mall, say, one to two inches across. And make them into a pretty arrangement, as a decoration as well as a source of light.

D: *This is getting away from Atlantis but it's bringing up something in the book I wrote about Jesus when He lived at Qumran (Jesus and the Essenes). They had a mysterious source of light. It sounds very similar. Would you know about that?*

B: It appears that the source of light were from old crystals that were left over from the earlier days that were passed down from generation to generation. Since they no longer had the knowledge to make more of these, they treasured these.

D: *They said they came from the Old Ones, the people who had lived many years before. They had many things that had come from them.*

B: Yes. They were passed down and taken care of and used from generation to generation. And they passed down the knowledge of how to maintain these, because as long as they maintained these crystals they could produce light practically forever. It was simple maintenance.

***

I worked with Phil for many years and the information he provided has been spliced into many of my books. Instead of going to the Library on the spirit side, he gained his information from the Planet of the Three Spires, which seemed to be a storehouse or depository of all knowledge. Often a group of twelve entities would also supply missing pieces or he would be shown scenes and try to interpret them with the help of these entities.

We had access to this information by using an elevator method, rather than the cloud method that is very effective with most of my subjects. Phil would visualize himself in an elevator in an office building, and would stop at the appropriate floor that contained access to whatever information we were looking for. In this case we had discussed the possibility of finding something about Atlantis. The method doesn't really matter, gaining access is the important part of the work.

The elevator had stopped and I asked him what he saw as the door opened.

> P: There are bright shimmering lights. They are the energy of the level from which we work. And I'm passing through the lights. I can see what appears to be a flying craft, or a flying ship, flying above a field of green grass. It has a somewhat pointed shape in the front, and a somewhat oval shape toward the rear. And there is room for two people to sit. There are other craft in the sky which could hold many. There is in the distance, from my point of view, a city that sparkles in the Sun. This is one of many cities at this time.
>
> D: *Do you know where we are?*
>
> P: This had been discussed earlier. The questions were related to that time on Earth. This is merely one city on what was then called the continent of Atlantis.

It may seem a contradiction that he saw flying craft while Brenda did not see these. As has been stated the civilization at that time existed for thousands of years, and underwent many changes and advancements. By this time apparently they had developed mechanical devices, and had moved into technology. We were also to discover other changes.

> D: *Can you tell what that craft is made of?*
>
> P: It is an aluminum alloy, very similar to that in use in the present.
>
> D: *Can you tell how it is powered?*
>
> P: By what is called crystal power. There are in place across the land rays of crystal energy, which are directed to various other parts of the continent. And these craft merely align themselves on this ray and are projected along it. Similar to the concept of highways in use throughout your country today.
>
> D: *Do they also have craft that leave the planet, or travel in space?*
>
> P: Yes, however, they were not of this same type of construction. There were those people who were allowed this possibility. However, they were the high priests or highest functional order, who were in communion with those of the star nature. These were not common experiences among the general

populace. Those who were of the highest moral character and understanding were allowed this experience, as a part of their learning and spiritual evolution. It was not a pleasure type of experience. It was given in the context of learning.

D: *Are there any parts of the original continent above water today?*

P: Parts of the Atlantis continent are indeed rising again, and will once again rise to and above the surface. However there is not at this time what one would call parts of the original dry land. That is, nothing significant.

D: *I've heard that part of the United States was part of it.*

P: That is not accurate as we perceive it. You asked for land which was considered a permanent part of Atlantis, and the entire continent of the United States was, in fact, part of the ocean floor at one time.

D: *Do you know where Atlantis was originally located according to our geographical map as it is today?*

P: It was in the Atlantic Ocean. There are those areas which were, at that period, above and below, as well. There are areas today which were above ground at that time, which subsequently sank for a period of time, and have since reemerged. There are those areas which were, at that time, submerged, which are now above ground. There have been many Earth changes since that period. Many times being one or the other, that is, land or sea.

D: *Then the majority of the continent is below water now.*

P: That is accurate.

D: *What about the rest of the world? It couldn't have been the only populated continent.*

P: There were in that one particular area many different civilizations of peoples. A social structure, not that far removed from what you on your planet have in place today. That is, there were many different types and classes of people. There were the low or poor working class. And then economically speaking, the middle and upper classes.

D: *But there were other continents besides Atlantis?*

P: That is accurate. There were areas, not as continents, in the sense that they were given or ascribed one particular name or designation. For at that time the imminent and premier area of population was called "Atlantis". However, not accurate to say that was the only populated area at that time. It was the showcase or center of civilization at that time.

D: *The other areas didn't have names.*

P: That is accurate. There was not the necessity to incorporate these into what would have then been called the "world government."

D: *Did they have the same cultural advancement as this continent of Atlantis?*

P: There were those areas which were technologically somewhat superior. However, morally none was surpassed in that area of Atlantis. It was the crowning achievement of civilization at that point. At that time on your planet, it was the epitome of the search for truth.

D: *Had mankind been in existence a long time when Atlantis developed to this state?*

P: There were many, many generations previous to this. The evolution of the spiritual manifestations were to a high degree, more highly evolved than even to this day.

D: *I was wondering if this was the highest evolvement that man had reached at that time.*

P: That is accurate, and since. For the moral character of your planet to this day has a great distance to go to reach this pinnacle of success.

D: *I was thinking there might have been other earlier civilizations that we didn't know about.*

P: There were indeed other civilizations and continents previous to the Atlantean culture. However, none have surpassed that which was found in Atlantis at that time, speaking strictly from a moral and character standpoint.

D: *Then were there times whenever man would evolve so far and the civilizations would be destroyed, before the Atlantean continent was formed?*

P: There was, as the sands of the desert shifting the shifting fortunes of man. For there were always those advances which would preeminent that particular culture to a level of distinction among its peers. Through various types of what could be called "misfortune" these cultures never seemed to establish a firm foothold on the civilizations in place at that time. And so there was a continual loss and rebuilding, and then loss again. Until suddenly there came the great advancements of that continent of Atlantis. There were previous to that many cultures which were in excess of the spiritual character of Atlantis. However, none taken in the context of the overall population as a whole. There were individuals in other cultures who through diligence and self denial, and training, reached those levels of awareness, which were above the general population of Atlantis. However, we speak here of a general overall population awareness. That is, the culture or population in general had reached the high area of awareness. And there were cultures previous to the Atlanteans who were of a higher moral character, but yet had not the same type of culture or inner connectedness about it. It was more of the individual basis.

D: *But each time mankind had to start over again from a very low level?*

P: There were always those who were keepers of the knowledge, for that was a jealously guarded secret. The knowledge was protected with much reverence and dignity. However, it was not available to the population in general. And so there were always those of the higher moral standards, who were the keepers of the knowledge.

D: *Then the Earth had changed, continents had risen and disappeared, before this time of Atlantis.*

P: That is accurate. This was caused by various cataclysms natural to the planet. For in that time period the Earth was still making adjustments, and settling into a long and prosperous life. The Earth at that point was somewhat younger than now, it was much more unsettled.

D: *Our scientists tend to think there were no people in those early days.*

P: Not so, for there were people in days when scientists believe there was no life at all. However, they simply do not have the perspective of hindsight that would be necessary to confirm the existence of these people. For with each change there was the obliteration of those who existed previous to the change, such that their cultures were lost with no trace. Not that the peoples themselves were decimated such that there were no humans left, but that there was no trace left of their accomplishments. Simply because of the cataclysmic destruction which followed each natural Earth change.

D: *Then there has always been some who have survived.*

P: That is accurate. For it has always been known that the change was imminent. And those who were attuned and aware would make preparations, and so would survive intact and continue on. There was always that level of awareness which states that the greatest possible achievement in man's history is that which is at the present. This has been prevalent throughout man's history. There were many previous civilizations which unfortunately held this same viewpoint. That is only human nature.

I have had regressions where entire civilizations were destroyed by dramatic Earth changes. Sometimes by walls of water, sometimes by volcanic eruptions that produced walls of mud and debris. I was told these were before Atlantis, and mankind has no knowledge of their highly advanced accomplishments. The scientists have no records of them because any remains are buried either underwater or under mountains of Earth. Our world is like a restless old woman who constantly frets and twists and turns.

I returned to what Phil was observing.

D: *You said you could see a city in the distance?*

P: That is accurate. The keepers of the knowledge are based or emanate from this city. The Elohim of the ancients, the keepers of the moral physical laws of truth. That is the highest form of awareness of the natural and physical laws of mankind, in conjunction with the spiritual awareness.

D: *Then the ones that had these so called mental powers were only a few in comparison to the whole population?*

P: Not so, for the city as a whole was very aware. It is as if this city itself held some type of energy, which seemed to elevate these people to far greater potentials than were normally seen throughout the rest of the country.

D: *What makes the city shine?*

P: It is of the crystal nature, from the building materials which constitute their construction. It is as if the concrete you use today were of a crystalline nature.

D: *Are you at the city where you can look around and observe?*

P: There is a somewhat reluctant attitude to go nearer to the city. For those who are not of the highest energy were not allowed in, for it would cause considerable damage to the physical and spiritual entity, as a whole. The energy level of this city was such that it would overload those who were not familiar with how to channel this energy. And so it is a somewhat precautionary measure that we observe from a distance. For the energy is much too powerful to attempt to channel at this time.

D: *I appreciate you telling me that. We won't do anything that will harm you in any way. Can you get information by observing it from a distance?*

P: That is accurate. There are those who are aware of our presence on the perimeter, and can channel this information to us without causing any type of physical disturbance in the vehicle. There are those who would see in their mind's eye that there is something to be learned from this contact. And so they would journey towards this city drawn by some invisible force which would lead them to this area. There they would intuitively feel the connection with those who were the Watchers of the Truth. And who would then contact these individuals. And the communion would be given that would establish that which is truth to the individuals seeking it.

D: *But we really are from their future. Have they normally spoken to people in different times?*

P: There is always the possibility of bridging that which is called the time barrier, for in the truest sense there is no such barrier. It is always possible to relate to those who are of this higher order, merely by thought. There is no barrier to thought. They are most pleased that you would attempt to do this, for it is of the higher order of thinking that allows you to do this. Were it not so, then it would not be allowed.

D: *Yes, I'm always searching for knowledge. Then if we stay back so you will feel safe and protected, I would like to ask some questions about the city.*

P: There will be given that knowledge which is safe to the vehicle involved, and to the general mission, as you would call it. That is to bring this information forward to your time period.

D: *If this city's energy was so powerful, what about people who didn't live there. Would they be allowed to come in?*

P: As we said earlier, there were those who would attempt to come towards the city. However, the level of energy was such that they intuitively would not come much further, for they could know that this was an area which was off limits. The awareness of that which is on a higher level would tell them they need approach no further, lest they bring harm to themselves. It was an innate and intuitive awareness. There was no need for guards or centurions, for the awareness was such that those who were appropriate to approaching this city would not feel the need to turn away. It was an automatic safety feature, which would turn away those who were not of the higher nature.

D: *Is this the only city of this type in existence at that time?*

P: It is one of several. Each was unique in the particular aspect of its energy. The knowledge and level of people there was somewhat unique. However, the cities as a whole were very similar, in that this same type of manifestation, the energy levels prevalent throughout and about, were common.

D: *Then each of these cities were used for different purposes?*

P: That is accurate, for there was the learning of physical natures, the elements of personality, for example. And there was the awareness of spiritual nature, the elements of spirituality. There were cities which would integrate these.

D: *What type was this city used for?*

P: This was of the health and nature type, or awareness of that which combines physical and spiritual in order to maintain health and balance of physical and spiritual awareness.

D: *Can they give you information about the types of buildings? You said they were made of crystal.*

P: In the construction there is the powder of a crystalline nature, which would appear to be separate individual crystals. It was as if the building itself were made of crystalline material, such that the building as a whole would then become a crystal receptor.

D: *At first I thought it was made entirely of huge crystals.*

P: Not so, they were of a powdered nature, such that the individual grains themselves were of a crystalline nature.

D: *I didn't think you could find crystals that large anyway. But this powder was mixed with something to make the walls?*

P: That is accurate. They were mixed with a base or mortar content, which would cement them together in one solid form. They were poured in a concrete form and allowed to harden. They were somewhat self heating in that the energy given off was of the temperature of Sun shining on it in the midday Sun.

D: *Were they large buildings?*

P: There were structures which would rise several tens of stories, perhaps thirty stories, if necessary. There was the knowledge available to construct these buildings. There was commerce and industry, and then there was the office space, so to say. The areas of which knowledge and information was assimilated and distributed, much as you have in your society today.

D: *Then all the buildings in this city are built of the same material.*

P: All of the city as a whole, so that the entire city and those inhabitants within it, were irradiated by this energy.

D: *But the normal cities on the planet were not built of this material?*

P: The lesser cities were built of more common forms of materials, such as the clays and stones and woods which were prevalent.

This sounded more like the city that Brenda saw.

D: *That would explain why this one gave off a different energy level.*

P: That is accurate. It was as if the city itself reflected the higher mental character of those inhabitants.

He described the furnishings, but they were made of similar materials that we use today. There was also nothing unusual about the people and their clothing, except they wore mostly tunics or robes.

P: The lighting itself was done with crystal energy, such that the crystals for lighting would give off a light energy, but a bright somewhat blue tinted light. There were at that time crystals which would when excited through cosmic energy give off, or translate that energy into physical light. It was simply an energy transducer.

D: *Are the floors and walls also this crystalline material?*

P: That is accurate. It was as if the entire city were built of this material.

D: *Is there any other type of vehicle besides the one you saw in the sky?*

P: There are many which allow for transportation. Many of a utility nature, as opposed to a transportational nature. For in construction and rebuilding it was necessary to haul great loads of materials long distances.

D: *What do the ones used for transportation look like?*

P: It could be described as somewhat of a shuttle craft in appearance. We refer here to the two man craft which was presented earlier. Somewhat egg shaped when viewed from below, and somewhat larger in the rear as opposed to the front. There was an area to the front in which the individuals would sit. There was a viewing area, which allowed for observing the areas around and below and above. There was no need at that time for frictional mechanical conveyance, as you have at this time. It was more of a levitational nature. These were powered by crystals. It was necessary to increase the amount of energy output in order to compensate for the additional payload. The arrangement of the drive crystals could be in multiples, which would allow for a combined output, which would be sufficient to propel that payload.

D: *You mean it had several smaller crystals, according to how much of a payload it had to pull, or propel?*

P: That is accurate. There were more of one common type of crystal, arranged in such a pattern that their total energy output would be multiples of a single form. These crystals were, as a whole, naturally occurring. However, they were manufactured to a certain specification, such that their energy output could be directed.

D: *You said these were powered by rays of energy that were projected out from somewhere, like highways?*

P: That is accurate. For long distance transportation, there were beacons of crystal energy. A radiator of crystal energy which would be aligned so that the path would lead to another beacon, which would be stationed at some distant point. It would then be simply a matter of aligning one's craft or transport along this beacon of energy. And then being driven or propelled along this beacon. It was necessary to redirect the energy, so that one would be moving forward or backwards, to one point and from another. It was simply a matter of rearranging the crystals themselves, the propulsion units, such that the propulsion would be in one direction or another. The beams or beacons were broad enough that there could be multiple craft occupying this beacon simultaneously, and traveling in perhaps opposite directions. It was not, as has been interpreted, a tight and narrow beam, but a broad and general beacon.

D: *Then these beacons were placed at various places on the planet?*

P: Not so much the planet itself, because the knowledge and awareness necessary to utilize this form of transportation was not prevalent throughout. They were throughout the continent at various strategic or important places, not randomly. For there were those areas which were in need of such beacons, and those areas which were not.

D: *Then the vehicles within this city operated differently?*

P: There was energy available throughout the entire city so no beacons or beams were necessary. The energy available in the surrounding atmosphere or ambient energy was sufficient to cause these craft to be able to fly in whatever direction the occupants desired.

D: *They were able to tap into the energy caused by the crystal buildings and the city itself.*

P: That is accurate.

D: *Then if you wanted to go out of the city you had to use the other type of vehicle.*

P: That is accurate.

D: *What about communication within the city?*

P: It was telepathic in nature. There was no need for phones in the sense that one would interpret them today. The inhabitants were very telepathic in nature, and could be aware of, and communicate with anyone they wished at any time. However, there were what could be called "machines", somewhat similar to your computers. These were distributors and accumulators of knowledge and information. These were used mostly within the city itself, for the more accurate communications of information.

D: *Were the people able to communicate over long distances telepathically?*

P: Quite accurate. There were those who could communicate between different areas on the planet. There was no need for artificial forms of communication. It was not necessary to limit oneself only to the planet, for there was the ability to communicate with those who were on quite distant planets, simply by telepathic means. This form of communication is still available to this day, were it to be recognized as such.

D: *Reactivated, to a certain extent.*

P: That is accurate.

D: *Did everyone on the planet have this ability to communicate?*

P: Not so. For there were those who could not care less. Perhaps they felt no need for such forms of communication and were not interested in learning what was necessary to allow for this type of communication.

D: *Then the entire planet was not that highly evolved.*

P: That is accurate. There were those who desired the dedication and the knowledge that would facilitate this communication. The communication was not in and of itself the focal point of the search for knowledge. It was not the end to the means.

D: *Why were they communicating with other planets?*

P: There was information given that would allow for a higher understanding of one's self, with respect to one's self and others as well. It had been made available by the progress of the inhabitants' social awareness. A more complete understanding of social functions on a planetary level.

D: *People from the other planets contacted them whenever they had evolved to the proper state?*

P: Not so. It was simply a matter of the evolution of awareness, such that the awareness of those on the planet soon reached a level at which they were aware of far more than simply their own kind on their own planet. Their awareness broadened and increased so they were then aware of communication between other planets.

D: *Did they also have physical contact with people from other planets?*

P: Yes, as we have said earlier. There was given that ability to communicate with directly or to meet in person those who were of the other nature.

D: *Yes, you did say that certain ones were allowed to go off the planet.*

P: That is accurate.

D: *Did the people from other planets also come here?*

P: That is accurate. For it was seen there could be given that knowledge exchange which would be beneficial to both parties involved. So that their learning was more complete and grounded.

D: *Do you know if this communication had been going on for a long time before they were aware of it?*

P: There was in other areas of the universe communication going on far previous to the appearance of the planet as a whole. However, the awareness reached by that specific part of the population allowed for the communication between those on other planets and themselves.

D: *I was curious if the people from the other planets had been coming to Earth before they were noticed, so to speak.*

P: There was, for quite some time previous to the Atlantean incarnation, those visitations which allowed for an awareness of the planet in other areas of the universe. It was not unknown that the planet was evolving in such a manner. And it was seen that the evolution was such that eventually telepathic forms of communication would be established in which those beings left on planets, who were not traveling, were soon to be able to contact directly these inhabitants of this newly evolving planet.

D: *Were there any other types of machines within the city?*

P: There were again the communication types of machines, as well as the information retrieval and storage. There was that level of machinery which would insure the comfort of the buildings themselves. There was the preservation machine, so that the food and articles of clothing and so forth, were kept healthy and in a clean and high state of appearance.

D: *That's an interesting term "preservation machine." I think of our refrigerators. But it couldn't have been that if you mentioned clothing also.*

P: We speak here in a broad category, and not so much a single concept. It is indeed very similar in concept to the refrigerator and washing machine so common in your society today.

D: *Then they've always had need for such things, I suppose.*

P: That is accurate. For the need for cleanliness and preservation has been prevalent with man for many centuries.

D: *Are there any animals within the city?*

P: It was not deemed appropriate in this crystal city to allow for the wanderings of animals throughout the streets, as was common in some other areas of the continent at that time. Animals would not be able to adjust to the tremendous energy power of the city.

D: *Were the people's lifespan about like ours?*

P: It was somewhat shorter than is common in this time frame today. However, not due to ill health. Being in this energy shortens somewhat the life expectancy. However, the accumulation of knowledge was such that one learned in a far shorter time that which may take many, many years in subsequent lesser lifetimes. It was as if the learning process were speeded up. And in living with the energies the physical bodies were used far faster and greater than those who would live outside of the energies. The disease and ill health prevalent in other areas of the planet were, to a great extent, non existent in that particular type of city.

D: *Then other people on the planet had different lifespans than the ones living in the city.*

P: That is accurate. Those living in the energy cities had lifespans somewhat shorter than is considered average. Possibly in the forty and fifty year age bracket would be average. Those living outside who were of higher order and were aware of cleanliness and diet could expect to live into the sixties and seventies. However, there were those who were somewhat more primitive, whose lifespan was much less.

D: *I suspect much of this had to do with medical advances too.*

P: That is accurate. It was simply a level of awareness which dictated the life expectancy.

I decided to end the session since I felt we had learned enough about the crystal city. I asked if I could return at another time and get information about their knowledge and abilities.

P: We will attempt to give you that which is most appropriate to give at that time. We would wish that you understand that the appropriateness factor is the constituting guideline in each of these sessions. For that which is appropriate at one session may perhaps not be at the next.

D: *It's according to what energy answers the questions?*

P: According to the energy of the overall situation, for there are many participants in this endeavor, not simply your own, which has an affect on the overall operation. It is this overall sum total of the conditionals of the energies, which constitutes the appropriateness factor. We shall protect him in his efforts to understand his self, as well as his life, which can, as always, be very distinct and separate. For oftentimes people feel that they are their life. And yet in fact one's life is really an extension of one's self. One's self can become quite separate from one's life. Here defining life in the social societal cultural aspects, and not in a physical sense. The experience of living then is one's life. And so one filters through this life concept those experiences which are the experience of life itself.

This was a difficult session for me. There seemed to be an energy emanating from Phil even though he was not in close proximity to the city. It gave me a slight headache, and disturbed my line of thinking and questioning. It was difficult to form questions and to concentrate. It was also strange that when I left this session and went to John's apartment for a session on the Nostradamus' material, I had another strange experience. This was the day that the evil Imam zapped me with his energy. This was reported in *Conversations With Nostradamus, Volume II.* Two occasions in one day of being exposed to a strange type of energy. Coincidence?

***

Continuing information came forth from Phil during another session when I was asking questions about Earth Mysteries.

D: *I am tying up loose ends about the history of Atlantis. They said the people of Atlantis had evolved a great mental ability. That they could do many things with their minds that is impossible for the people of our day to do. Can you tell me the abilities the people of Atlantis had on the mental level?*

P: There are those things in existence which were more apparent to those who you would call the Atlanteans. The people were more attuned to the breath of existence, and were able to perceive more. The talents of these individuals were more highly motivated by a desire to learn, as opposed to a desire to earn. Which is what you find in your society at this point in time, as you define it.

D: *What could they do that we can't do today?*

P: There is nothing that was done then that could not be done today. However, the motivation is perhaps lacking in a majority of the people we see on your planet at this time. There are many who are trying to regain that lost knowledge.

D: *But what powers did they have that we have lost?*

P: The ability to metamorphosize has become unused and forgotten. That is, to change one's existence from one particular being into another. It is simply a matter of reassembling one's atomic structure to identify more closely with another already established and identified set of atomic harmonies. The ability to do this has much more to do with the acceptance of life models than what is commonly known today. The concept is that in the formation of a physical planet there are agreements between the energies which constitute this planet, that such and such energies shall be such and such. And other energies shall be such and such else. There is an agreement that rocks will be rocks, and trees will be trees. This is in harmony with the needs and desires of the individual energies. There are however those who have the ability to change their accepted realities so they may then model themselves as another creature of reality. This is not a transgression of universal law, but merely an application of universal law. There is the ability to do this in many people on your planet today, who are afraid of this talent. They are somewhat aware of it, and conscious of the ability to do this. But are bound by many different types of fears and loyalties so they refuse to acknowledge the existence of such a talent. It was however common in those days of Atlantis.

This was the first time I had heard of such a concept outside of Hollywood's version. I wanted to clarify it.

D: *Do you mean instead of the spirit entering the body of an animal, they actually change the existing body of the human into the form of an animal, and back again?*
P: That is accurate. It would be simply a remodeling of the overall general harmony of a particular existence. Such that it then became another overall different type of existence. It is different vibrations. To change one's vibration from that of a tree to that of a stone would simmply be a matter of adjustment. There are those entities which can do this at will, for some purpose. However, it was found that during those days of Atlantis, before the breakup, that many were using this talent and ability to cause much destruction and harm. Not only to those around them, but to themselves. The higher order and harmony of this ability was discarded in favor of personal aggrandizement or gain. And therefore the talent was lost.
D: *Why would someone want to do that? It sounds more or less like a game.*
P: There are no games in life that do not teach. However, there are those "games" that can be used in a manner that is not healthy and wholesome. It would be then seen that those games which were being played and were causing death and destruction, were then not games but were becoming liabilities to the consequences of the individuals involved.

D: *But how could metamorphosing, switching from different forms, cause death and destruction?*

P: The act of deceit and treachery was not unknown in those times. And therefore you can see that the mischief rained upon a civilization by the individuals who could change into another person, and imitate that person, could be very apparent; even in your lifetime if you could represent yourself as someone else and cause mischief in the guise of that individual. When one takes that to a level of cross personalization between one species to the next, then there are many who would become confused as to which is their true identity. And they therefore would become lost as to what and who they truly are.

D: *So you mean they were using this for the wrong purposes.*

P: That is accurate. The purposes for which these talents were given were being discarded at an alarming rate. And so it was seen that this ability would necessarily have to be removed, in order to prevent the wholesale destruction of the civilization at large.

D: *Does this go along with the legends of half human and half animal?*

P: That is accurate. Minotaurs, for example. There were those who would change into that which had become one, and yet retained aspects of that which is another. And then became confused as to which of the two they were, and so retained a portion of both. This ability then degenerated into a confusion of the identities of both realities or existences, such that there was the danger that there would be a general loss of identity of all species. Therefore it was seen that this identity crossing would not be allowed.

D: *I've also heard they might have been doing this to other people without their permission.*

P: In order for this to be accomplished, it was necessary for the awareness of the individual to know, not only that from whence he came, but of that to which he was going. Therefore there would necessarily have to be the conscious awareness of this process, in order for it to be enabled. We see that there were instances in which there were given instructions on how to change this individual into that figure. And then were given further instructions on how to chnage that individual into another, such that the original identity was then lost. It was seen that this was one way to remove one from the picture, so to say, to change one into something that was less threatening or neutral.

D: *But this actually would be going against moral laws, and also the laws of the universe.*

P: The technique was in line with the laws, obviously. It would not be possible to do this, were it not already an established law. The fact that this was possible suggests that it was already established as a law. The moral implications of such actions were however in direct conflict with the charter given to this planet at the time of life bestowment, such that the advancement of the race would be enhanced, and not hindered. It was seen that this cross mutation was hindering the progress, and therefore it was taken away.

D: *Was there anything else they had the ability to do with their mind, that we have lost or not developed at this time?*

P: There were many, many different talents, as you would call them. However, they are simply recognitions of universal truths. In time there will be given again the awareness and the ability to recognize and to use for lack of a better term these realities.

D: *This was one of things I heard, that they began to abuse their abilities and the laws of the universe. That was one of the reasons why they had to stop.*

P: That is accurate.

***

This portion came from another session, and I am not sure if it is speaking of the same thing or not.

D: *One time when we were talking, they said that in the very beginning when spirits first began coming to Earth to inhabit bodies, they entered the bodies of animals. And I believe you told me it was no longer allowed to do this. Did something happen? Why was it no longer allowed?*

P: There was given the opportunity to experiment with, what you might call, a transmigrational experience. Or perhaps more simply, the implanting of consciousness and awareness in animal bodies, so that an animal then would perceive and have the consciousness of, what you call, human awareness with it.

D: *Do you mean the animals were more aware than they are at the present time?*

P: We mean only that the animal bodies had at that time the awareness and consciousness of the animal bodies you call "human". It is not that the animals themselves were changed, speaking from a strictly physical point of reference. However, the awareness, the consciousness, which is distinct between animal and human, was given at that time to the animals. It was simply an allowance of awareness to integrate into an animal body.

D: *Did this make the animal behave differently?*

P: From a strictly spiritual sense, the awareness was not so much changed, but was allowed to experience the inhabitation of an animal body or a different life form. It would be as if your consciousness was allowed to enter into that of an animal. You yourself, your awareness, would not so much be changed. You would still retain your identity. However, the expression of your physical would be different. You would then be aware in an animal body.

D: *You would be limited by what the animal could do.*

P: Through the physical limitations of the animal vehicle, that is correct.

D: *I've asked questions about the life force that inhabits the animals today, and I was told it is different.*

P: That is accurate. It is not as aware or perceiving, or on the same level as that intelligence which you yourself inhabit. It is in itself an animal or life force, however, it is not of the same energy as that consciousness which you carry.

D: *Then in those early days it was different?*

P: It was not so different from the intelligence inhabiting your animal body. It is simply that the intelligence was given to more than one physical type of body, in that time.

D: *Then this was just a form of experimentation?*

P: That is accurate. There is always, in the realm of experience, the need for that which is new, and that which has not been done previously. Therefore, it was allowed. Those who were ministering the planet at that time allowed these transmigrations, to enable those intelligences to experience life in a physical environment through many different types of physical expression. It was seen that this could enhance the ability to express oneself in physical or on a physical level. The added abilities of expression would enhance the capabilities of the intelligences to we find thisdifficult to translate, for there is no concept given on this level. However, the intent of the expression was to learn.

D: *Then this was going on when the spirits first came to Earth?*

P: That is not accurate, for it was well after the original seeding of the planet. However, it was in an advanced state of habitation of the planet, in the Atlantean experience, in which there was a high degree of awareness of the life forces.

D: *I was thinking maybe there weren't any humans at the time this was done, there were only animals.*

P: That is not accurate. For there would not be given the ability to transmigrate in this way, had there not been the human development previous to this. That is, the experience of human incarnation.

D: *Then at that time, you said the Atlanteans were more aware?*

P: That is accurate. They were extremely aware of the life force, and the implications of life forces in animal or physical bodies. It was as if this was a science which was taken to a high degree. And so they were allowed to experiment with more vehicles, to understand better this phenomenon of the intelligence or awareness inhabiting an animal body. It is simply an allowance that this happened. It was however abused and misused, to the extent that the animal expressions were muddying the waters of genetic pools. It was creating disturbances in the harmony of physical expression. Had this experiment been kept to its highest moral code, it would have allowed for many of the highest expressions of intelligence in many different forms of animal life. However the introduction of disharmony into this experiment condemned it to failure.

D: *One point I am trying to understand. Did they die first and then enter the animal body, or were they doing this while they were also in the human body?*

P: It could be done simultaneously. For it was shown that the awareness could be migrated from one vehicle to another. It would be as if one were to meditate, and remove oneself from one's body. And then place oneself into the physical body of another animal.

D: *I thought if they were doing this as an experiment, they died and then came back as an animal, which is true transmigration.*

P: There were those experiences in which those from the other side were assisting those who were yet in physical. And so it could be said there were those instances in which an incarnation was allowed to take place. However, not in the classical sense of rebirth, such as you have here on your planet now.

D: *Then the Atlanteans were so developed mentally and intellectually, they did these things as an experiment.*

P: It would be more accurate to say they were far more aware, not so much intellectually, as simply open minded. For there seems to be quite a distinction here. There are those who could perhaps be of not the highest intellect, and yet be very aware. And there could be those who could be of genius level, and yet be closed off to all but that which is of the five senses. There is no distinction here between which is better or highest in achievement.

D: *I thought maybe they were highly developed.*

P: The one need not be attendant with the other.

D: *I'm trying to understand this correctly, so I may say some things that sound naive. But it seems as though they were playing a game?*

P: That is not accurate. For there was no frivolity involved in this. It was indeed a serious effort on the part of discovery. Or to more accurately portray it, serious research into the consequences of intelligences inhabiting animal form, or physical form.

D: *But they were able to, more or less, project their awareness into the animal. Then they could come back to their own bodies when they wanted to.*

P: In those instances that is accurate. In perhaps more instances it was a migration of the intelligence from one form to the other.

D: *This was a complete migration?*

P: That is accurate in some respects. However, there are subtle differences which cannot be totally given at this time. We perceive there is a lack of complete understanding in the physical consequences of simultaneous awareness, on this level at this time. However, there were those instances in which one would choose to leave one's previous physical body, in order to inhabit that which was of a lesser or different nature.

D: *But in those cases they wouldn't return to the original body.*

P: That is accurate.

D: *Wouldn't the original body die?*

P: It could perhaps be inhabited by another or different intelligence. It would be as if they were swapping places.

D: *But it wouldn't be the animal intelligence entering the human. Trading in that way.*

P: Not so, for there was not the intelligence in the animal to begin with. There is not what you would call an animal intelligence. The intelligence was of a spirit nature, which was simply trying on new forms of physical expression.

Apparently this had to be willed or desired by the intelligence, and the animal would not be advanced enough to have the will or desire to trade places. Also, as I discovered in *Between Death and Life* the animal spirit is different from the human spirit, because it is more of a group spirit similar to colonies of ants or hives of bees.

D: *You said this created disharmony?*

P: That is accurate, for there was the integration of those different forms of life within common groupings. And so there were mutations. It was such that the true forms or... we find this concept hard to translate here, for again there is not an accurate understanding of the realities of life forms inhabiting physical bodies, at this time. Therefore, we must use that which is known at this time: the building blocks available to us, in order to portray as closely as possible that which we perceive as the ultimate reality. In other words, we would use your knowledge available to you at this time. However, we feel you can see that the picture portrayed would not be as accurate as we would wish. And so we must sacrifice somewhat in the translation, in order to convey that which is closest to what we perceive as truth. We would ask that you also understand that we could not allow this to be translated if it were to be portrayed in what we would term a false or misleading manner. Therefore there are some areas of which we cannot speak, simply because of the fact that there is nothing with which to convey on a conceptual basis. For any attempt at conveying this conceptual basis would, because of the nature of that which is available for conveying, be translated giving a quite inaccurate and misleading picture.

D: *Just do the best you can. I appreciate anything you can give me along that line.*

P: We then would ask that you simply state what you wish to know.

D: *Well, you said they were able to mutate the bodies...?*

P: The bodies mutated, not that they mutated. The distinction being between the physical and spiritual aspects here. In other words, the bodies then would express or reflect that which is or was of the spirit nature. For it is known that the physical is merely a reflection of the spiritual. And therefore, in cross mixing these spiritual energies there was the mutation or cross reflection of the physical to the spiritual.

D: *I was thinking that after they inhabited they may have interbred with other animals, and this was what you meant by mutation.*

P: That is accurate. However, it is important to understand that the cohabitation itself is and of itself not the sole determining factor in these mutations. Were one to experience and to assimilate the life form of one type of animal, and then migrate into that vehicle which is of another animal form, in so crossing the distinctive boundaries of physical aspects there would be a carrying over of the properties or assimilations of one form into the next. And it is here that these mutations arose.

D: *I have heard that animals normally cannot interbreed with another species. And I thought that was what you meant by mutations.*

P: We mean here to convey the idea that the physical expression again is merely a reflection of that which is in the spiritual sense. Therefore, were half of one reflection commingled with a half of another expression, you could see that the result would be a mutation.

D: *Then by doing this, were they able to somehow influence the genetic....?*

P: (Interrupted.) That is accurate, for the genetic is wholly influenced through the spiritual. It could be explained thusly, that the expression of human is a spiritual expression in nature. And the physical form which forms around this expression is simply a reflection of that which is spiritually human. And therefore, it follows that this human form is found in many different parts of the universe, simply because of the fact that this is a similar expression. The human form is expressed in human form, be it here on this planet or any other planet. There are other expressions. Those expressions which are not human, but which are aware, were they to express on this planet, would express in a quite unfamiliar and possibly terrifying way. It is simply that the human form is one form of physical expression that is an expression in the physical of the spiritual.

D: *This has brought up two lines of questioning. We might be able to cover both of them. Would this explain some of the legends of strange beings, half human half animal?*

P: That is accurate. There was indeed this cross expression. The muddying of the waters.

D: *That's what you meant by the disharmony?*

P: That is accurate.

D: *Then these were true physical creatures.*

P: That is accurate. They were castoffs in their own society. For there were those who considered themselves pure and looked down on these creatures that they termed of "less pure" expression. There then became somewhat of a caste society, such as you have in India today. There are those who are considered to be of a higher nature, and those considered of a lesser nature.

D: *Then when these forms appeared, like half man half horse and different ones of this nature, were they able to reproduce of their own kind?*

P: Not so, for theirs was not a genetic blueprint. They were merely expressions of that which was of the spiritual nature, and not in and of themselves a race of beings, such as you have now. There are those races of beings, be they human or animal.

D: *Then they were one of a kind.*

P: That is accurate.

D: *There seem to be so many stories about different types.*

P: That is accurate. For there were more than singular events of this cross migration. There were multiple events. However, they were not in and of themselves what you would term "a race" of creatures. To explain this further, we need to perhaps give you a short discourse on this awareness of spiritual integration. In the physical or human expression, there are those energies which in and of themselves are human in nature. We speak here strictly in a spiritual sense, disregarding any type of physical component. These are human energies. In physical expression these human energies appear in physical as you know them, in human form. The reality here is that the physical is simply an expression of that which is spiritual. The human form, physically speaking, is merely an expression of that energy which is human in nature. The life force which is peculiarly or particularly human in nature translates down to the physical level in human form. There are those energies, such as that which you would call "grass" energy. A blade of grass is simply a physical manifestation of that energy which is of the blade of grass nature. So you see there are many forms of energy. And these different forms of energy translate differently into the physical level. The universe is made of energy. The physical universe is simply an expression or a translation of these higher energies. So you see, the reality of the universe is based on spiritual energy. The physical universe is nothing more than an expression or a translation of that which is spiritual in nature. Therefore, when one takes a spiritual energy and translates it down into a physical expression, you have what is perceived as a physical form, which is simply reflecting or translating that spiritual energy of which it is a contingent. So when you look around and see these physical forms, you are in fact seeing nothing more than reflections or translations. These are reflections or translations based on, or derived from, these energies of which they are a component of reflection of. So that in transmigration, one finds a mixing of these energies. The energy that is peculiarly or particularly horse energy mingling with or mixing with that energy which in expression is human. And so in this mingling or mixing of energies, the expression then naturally becomes part horse and part human.

D: *Then in that way you're using the centaur as an example they would usually look alike. This is why we have this legend of the half man and half horse?*

P: That is accurate. However, the proportions of mix were not consistent. There was the general agreement that this was half horse or perhaps half human. However, there was no law or dictate that demanded that the human part extend from where the neck of the horse perhaps would be. The expressions were not identical in all cases, however they were similar.

D: *Then the legends just gave a generalization.*

P: That is accurate.

D: *Then the stories of mermaids and the harpies: half bird and half female, all came from these actual happenings.*

P: That is accurate.

D: *Then at that time these creatures did roam the Earth, but as you said, they were looked down upon.*

P: We would not say they roamed the Earth. For they were not spread throughout the entire population of the planet. They were in fact localized or segregated into those areas in which the experimentation was taking place. In those areas where the culture had reached that high state of awareness, so that these experiments could manifest.

D: *This is why these legends are, more or less, in certain cultures today.*

P: That is accurate. The experience was known to many throughout the evolution of the planet. However, the actual physical manifestations were somewhat localized to the Atlantean incarnation.

D: *What about the stories of magic, where an individual, a wizard of some kind, could turn people into animals?*

P: Perhaps this would be more accurately regulated to the areas of fantasy and desire. The wish to have more control over one's life. For in that time period in which magic was quite prevalent in the human awareness, there was the desire to have more control over the physical environment. And so these stories lent credence to the possibility that people did indeed have more control over their environment. It was simply a manifestation of a psychological need to express one's majesty over the elements. And so, in telling and believing these stories, it was vicariously lived by these persons. They then could imagine they had some of this magic power, and could then be more in control of their physical environment. It is not so different in this day and age to see the use of science in taming that which is of the physical environment. It is again this same type of need to be in control over those elements.

D: *Then in these cases in Atlantis, these were people who wanted to experience this other type of reality.*

P: That is accurate.

D: *Then you said it was forbidden after that?*

P: It was seen that this was causing more disharmony than realizing any benefit. Therefore it was decreed by those energies and levels of energy far above those which were on the experimental levels, that for the good of the race, and for the good of those individuals, that this not be allowed.

D: *Then this was causing disharmony to the spirit, the energy, that was inhabiting? It was somehow distorting their personality or their own spirit.*

P: That is accurate. And it was then given that we search here for the accurate translation as the mutations returned to the spiritual, there was not allowed any further manifestations such as this. This was simply not an appropriate allowance at that time period, and so this disallowal has stood to this day. That disallowal may, however, at some point be removed. However, considering the state of affairs on this planet at this time, it would seem unlikely this would be any time in the near future.

D: *But the memory survived after the destruction of Atlantis, and that is why we have these legends?*

P: That is accurate. It was in written accounts, which were passed down to the succeeding generations. And so changed over the centuries that it soon became legend.

D: *Did that disharmony create more karma for the spirit?*

P: Perhaps in the sense that karma could be interpreted as disharmony, or perhaps disharmony could be interpreted as karma. There was the need to work off this disharmony, and so straighten out one's energies. In this sense then it could be seen as karma. For we feel that in your context, karma then represents a disharmony or a misalignment of energies, which through experience must be realigned. We feel the karma concept, as it is understood, is not accurate in this portrayal, for it is not a vengeance type of factor. We feel that the understanding which is prevalent of karma at this time is one of punitive or punishment type of effect, and we feel this is indeed a totally wrong perception. It is simply that in generating what one would call "bad" karma, one is simply dealing with energies that have become out of tune or misaligned. And so we feel it would be more accurate to say that when one is straightening out one's karma, one is in fact realigning one's energies.

D: *Was the misuse of this type of ability part of what led to the downfall of Atlantis?*

P: It would be more accurate to say that this was a reflection of those conditions which led to the downfall. Not that this was in and of itself the direct cause of the downfall. However, those conditions which were in place and which caused the downfall of this culture, had as an element or a manifestation, this type of condition, or this experience.

D: *There was one more question I wanted to ask, before I forgot it. This life force apparently was able to genetically change the appearance of the animal, by the manipulation of the genes or however it was accomplished. Does that also mean that we have control over our own bodily cellular structure?*

P: That is accurate. You should understand that this control is not to a great degree on a conscious level. The physical expression is an accurate representation of the energy of which you are. And therefore you cannot in and of your free will change your reflection. You may change your energy, which then would cause a related change in your reflection. You however cannot change your reflection in the mirror. You may change your appearance, that is, your body, and your reflection then will change in like manner. However, you cannot change merely the reflection and not change that which causes the reflection. It is important to understand that the physical is merely a reflection. In order to change the reflection, you must change that which causes the reflection.

D: *You mean we can't physically change our appearance.*

P: If it were to be allowed that you could again, as was previously to commingle these energies, then it would be possible. For example, to commingle the energy of a lade of grass with a human energy were this allowed the effect could possibly be a human who had blades of grass instead of hair.

D: *(Chuckle) I can see where all of these stories come from. That they imagine these things are possible.*

P: They are entirely possible. However, to be allowed is quite something different.

D: *If we had genetic control we could change our appearance to look like a different type of human being.*

P: It is important here to understand it would be of little value to change the reflection merely for the sake of changing the reflection. The worth of such an experiment would be in joining the energies which caused the reflection. You must see that the true value would be of a higher level, than in simply making interesting reflections.

***

I found that over the long existence of Atlantis the people developed their minds to a much higher degree. This accompanied with scientific curiosity to discover what was possible took the intermingling of species even further. These scientifically advanced people seemed to be trying to decipher the secrets of creation itself, which sounds ominously similar to our present day. Maybe the twisted experiments were caused by boredom when they reached the pinnacle of discovering what the mind could do. Then instead of using it for creative and beneficial purposes they misused these powers in nonbeneficial ways.

When I placed John in deep trance he was always able to access the magnificent Library on the spirit plane, located in the Temple of Wisdom complex. Most of the information he provided in my many books came from these archives. As always when we entered the building we were greeted by the guardian of the Library who wanted to know our intentions, and informed us of restrictions.

D: *Can he locate any information from the volumes or whatever they are, on the continent of Atlantis?*

J: Yes. He says we have a lot of research on Atlantis. He said you can go into the viewer.

D: *What is that?*

J: He's taking me into this other room, and it's like a viewing room. It's as if you just call attention to Atlantis, and all kinds of images come in. They're on the walls.

D: *Like a screen on one wall?*

J: Not really like a screen. It surrounds you, and I'm in the middle of it watching it. Oh, it's this beautiful, beautiful, beautiful city. It's gold. It's looks luminescent, as if the light is coming from within the walls of the city. And it's dark, and the stars are out. There's this beautiful full moon. And it looks like they know how to use the moon's energy. It's very beautiful. I'm surrounded by this scenery. And I'm starting to see the people. I'm coming up closer. The people are just beautiful.

He said upon awakening that the city seemed to be arranged like a pyramid from a distance. One central tower or highest point, and the rest of the buildings gradually increasing in height as they surrounded or led up to this point. There were ramps that joined these various levels.

D: *What do the people look like?*
J: Oh, they are like us, but they look like movie stars. They all have perfect teeth, and beautiful hair. They have experimented with different hair styles and hair colors and designs.

He said later the hair had parts that were different colors, bright colors like birds: reds, yellows, greens and blues. And the hair was braided and twisted to form various designs. I remarked that it would be similar to punk styles today, but he objected saying it was not that wild. This was different, flamboyant, yet beautiful in its own way.

J: They seem to be wearing... gowns, if that's the right word. No, not gowns, they wear like tunics and robes. And they're luminescent. I mean, their clothes can change color. It's as if beautiful spectrums of color are woven into the cloth, so in different lights it gives different colors. You look at a garment and it might appear pink, but you look at it in a different way and it appears a pastel blue. And you look at it again and you see it as violet. It changes and shimmers. The clothes are just gorgeous. And I see they have different types of jewelry, and there are crystals in the jewelry.
D: *What about the city? Why do you think the walls radiate light?*
J: I don't know. There are some really big buildings there. Some of them look like our version of Greek temples. There are others that look like very contemporary modern 20th century. Some of the buildings have twenty and thirty stories.
D: *How do they go up to the different floors?*
J: There are movable ramps. You get on a ramp and you're right where you need to go. They're ramps, but they're hard to describe. You see, these buildings are not built like our buildings that need elevators. They're built in stages. (He had difficulty describing.) The lower levels are staggered, that's the word. These buildings are not just all one building. They are different buildings that have rampways between them. And these rampways are electric. It's like an escalator but it's flat. They move you very fast up to these different

places that you have to go to.

D: *Is there any kind of transportation within the city?*

J: Yes. There's lots of transportation. There are cigar shaped airplanes. And there are cars that are cigar shaped. But basically they use a lot of these rampways to get around the city.

D: *Are the cars like ours, with wheels?*

J: No, they don't have wheels. They're sort of like hover craft.

D: *How are they powered?*

J: They're powered by solar energy and crystals. Solar energy poured through the crystal.

D: *What about the aircraft? Do they have wings?*

J: No, it doesn't have wings. It doesn't look like our aircraft at all. In fact, it looks like a big cigar. (Laugh) And it has windows all around the middle of it. And it seems to get its power from a big huge crystal in its tip. It draws energy from something that looks like a tower. It's like a mooring that helps the ship go up and down. So it's also energized by being part of this mooring post.

D: *It couldn't go very far, could it, if it gained its power from that?*

J: Oh, it can go thousands of miles. It stores solar energy in this battery and this is what the ship draws on.

D: *Do they have any communication devices?*

J: People don't need telephones there. They can talk telepathically.

D: *What about long distances, out of the city? Can they still do it the same way?*

J: Yes. I don't see radio or TV or anything like that. There is no need. They do have entertainment, yes. They like music. And there are arenas. (He paused and then suddenly gasped.) Oh, my God! That's horrible! They are really cruel people.

This was the first indication that something was different. Up to this point his description sounded very much like the others. Apparently everything was not all paradise. As I said earlier, Atlantis was in existence for thousands of years, and perhaps John was seeing what it was like during the time it began to deteriorate. The people and the city were beautiful and magnificent, yet this exterior hid a dark and ugly secret.

J: There are some real cruel things going on. It looks like people that are attached to animal bodies. They've got them in this arena, and they are forcing them to fight each other. It's like Roman gladiator contest type things.

D: *What do the creatures look like?*

J: I can see one creature. He's a man, but it looks like a man in the middle of a horse's back. He has four legs and the torso of a man. And he's in the middle of his back. It looks like he was grafted on. And where the horse's head would be, is just empty space.

D: *I think I know what you mean. (It sounded like he was describing a centaur.) What do the other creatures look like?*

J: Oh, there's... it looks like a jaguar... the face of a jaguar but the hind legs of a human. The back part is like a human body. Oh, it's just terrible! It's like these are genetic misfits. They're very cruel to them.

D: *Are there only those two creatures?*

J: Oh, no, there's tens of them. I'd say there are at least a hundred to two hundred. They're all in this arena. They're all fighting each other, and they're having a battle of death. And the people are kind of sitting around, and they're not clapping or yelling or anything like that. It's just amusing to them.

D: *Can you see any other combination creature?*

J: Yeah. There's another creature that looks like a bull. It has the horns and the face of a bull, and the body of a bull, but where it's legs would be there are human legs. These things are really grotesque looking. There are others. There's a thing that looks like a snake with a human face. And then there's... oh! An animal that looks like a giraffe that has a human face.

He seemed upset to be observing these strange creatures.

D: *I don't want to cause you any discomfort with my curiosity.*

J: No, it's not discomforting, it's just that these were genetic mistakes. They cannot reproduce, so why not just let them die. It's like a sport that these people enjoy. These people are very cruel.

D: *I would have thought if they were telepathic, they would be more understanding and gentle. It's not that way?*

J: No. Actually I get this feeling that they are very, very proud, and they look down on other creatures. They see all the other species of Earth as just terrible animals.

D: *Do you think they gathered these creatures, and put them here so they could fight?*

J: They do this periodically, because it's as if they can always experiment on a new batch.

D: *Do these creatures have any weapons, or do they just attack each other? I'm thinking of gladiators.*

J: No, they use their natural instincts. And the people enjoy watching this, but they don't clap or show any expression. They don't yell or scream or show any emotion. They like watching it. It's entertaining to them.

D: *It seems hard to understand someone having entertainment and not showing an emotion of some kind.*

J: Yes, they don't show any emotion. It's so different. These people are really not nice people. I mean, they're cold. They're superior. They have a real distaste for other lifeforms. Now they're walking into the arena. And they have something like guns, but they are made out of crystal. And they're directing them at the heart centers of all these animals that are left.

D: *The ones that didn't kill each other?*

J: Yeah, and they're killing them. There's a beam of light that comes out and centers right around their heart. It looks like a laser, except that it's a beam of light, not a laser. (Sounds of disgust.) And now I'm being taken into another place where they make these animals. These people are gathered before a drawing. There's an animal in a chamber separate from them, and they're visualizing a man's face on this animal. They're looking at a drawing of an animal with a human face, and they're manifesting that on this animal, with their minds. They're concentrating on this. And this is to teach them how to manifest. There's a live animal in there. It looks like a dog. It's very painful for the naimal to go through this. This is why I consider them cruel. There are four people that are doing this, a woman and three men. It takes their combined concentration. They're concentrating on putting a human face on this animal in the chamber.

D: *And they are able to do this just with their mind power?*

J: Yes. They are able to concentrate so hard that it will happen. But their concentration is on the restructuring of the animal's face. They're concentrating on working on the cellular structure on the animal's face, which is very painful for the animal to go through.

D: *Are they doing this as an exercise in mind control?*

J: Well, probably that. But also they're trying to find some type of pet, like we have dogs and cats. A pet that has human like characteristics.

D: *Are there any type of machines or anything in the room that help them with this?*

J: Yes, there's... it looks like crystal glass. And there's stone, but the stone is malleable. I mean, it's like rubber. You can bend it and manipulate it. The stone is used in the interior of the room.

D: *Is this stone part of a machine?*

J: No. It's just used in the lining of the room. Instead of having painted walls, it has dressed malleable stone.

D: *Then the crystals are part of whatever they use.*

J: Yes, they have crystals all over the place. Big massive crystals, and different colors. And I see a control board with the crystals. And then the light is coming from star clusters of crystals on the ceiling.

D: *Is anyone operating this machine?*

J: They're doing it with their minds, but they attune with the crystals.

D: *I don't know if you have access to this knowledge or not, but when they change this animal to half human and half animal, does this affect the animal in any way? The way it thinks and acts?*

J: Well, the animal hates it because it's hurt. It's painful.

D: *I mean, does this make the animal gain more human characteristics?*

J: Yes, it takes on more human like attributes, although they're not really good human qualities.

D: *I was wondering how this would affect the life force, the spirit, so to speak, within the animal.*

J: The reason they feel they can experiment on these animals, is because they're a lower life form, and they're a superior life force. Their attitude toward the animal world is, "We're superior, so we can do whatever we want."

D: *But doesn't this make the animal less inferior when they do this?*

J: They're not trying to evolve the animal, no. They don't see the animal having a soul. They have the souls and they can do whatever they want because they're gods. And they are, they are gods. They can do so much. They can create and restructure that dog's face to make it look like a human.

D: *But it's for no purpose, is it? If they just put them out in the arena and let them kill each other.*

J: No, they use some of these creatures in servitude. They believe they are a low form of life, so it's okay.

D: *They just wanted them to appear more human. It sounds like they're playing games.*

J: (He frowned) I don't think they're playing games. They're not nice people. I don't like them.

D: *Well, I didn't want to cause you any discomfort to watch something like that.*

J: Oh, it was painful to see these poor animals kill each other. But they're in agony all the time, because their molecular structure has been upset.

D: *It seems like it would be going against the life force of the universe, their environment, to do something like that.*

J: This is why Atlantis was destroyed.

Atlanteans were described as perfect people. Maybe they had already mastered or perfected the art of genetically altering the human body. There were no more challenges left. So they ventured into altering and combining their genes with animals. It was a new challenge steeped in the adventure of the unknown.

D: *Can you see anything else they can do with their minds? Perhaps not that destructive, but any other powers they have?*

J: Yes. (Gasp) They can bring a person to orgasm very easily just by thinking it. (He found this rather amusing.) That's something they like to do, greeting and talking and loving other people. (Laugh) That's a game that they do play. They can influence other beings on the planet. They're very superior minded and think they are the best, and that everything functions for them. As a result, they have contempt for lower forms of life. This is why they experiment on the animals like that.

D: *Do they have any constructive way of using their minds?*

J: Oh, yes. They can create these cities with their mind power. They can lift heavy objects and teleport them.

D: *Levitation? Well, that would be a positive attribute.*

J: They're so self centered. That's what I'm trying to say, I guess. Everything has to respond to them.

D: *I'm also interested in this malleable stone.*

J: It's a certain type of stone that they use to build their cities, and these electric ramps.

D: *Does it occur like that in the natural state?*

J: I really don't know. I'm asking about that right now. I'm being shown that it's stone that has been treated by mind experimentation, so that it can become malleable. They're very, very intelligent people. Yet they really have contempt for other life. (Pause) Oooo, that's gross! (He interrupted emphatically.) I don't want to stay here! (An expression of disgust.)

D: *That's all right. I don't want you to. You can journey out of that city. Do the rest of the people on the continent live in cities like that, or is that only a small group of people?*

I was trying to remove him from something that was obviously unpleasant to watch.

J: No, some people live in the countryside. They live in beautiful houses, and they have beautiful gardens. (Suprised) There's no insects like we have. I've noticed that, there's no insects. They can stay outdoors, and there's no real bothersome insects.

D: *Do you know why?*

J: (Surprise) They created many noxious insects in their experimentations. I just don't like them. They're also cannibalistic, too. I saw this party of them eat another person.

D: *Do you think it was one of these animals?*

J: No, it wasn't one of these animals. They captured this man and ate him. This was outside the city. There was a party of them. They went in the airplane. And they captured one of these people and they cooked him and ate him.

D: *Oh, my goodness! (I wanted to change the subject.) Well, what about these noxious insects? You said they did that as experimentation?*

J: Yes. This was why Atlantis had to fall, because they were abusing the life force. They just did that to be inventive. I get the feeling they were not very nice people. I don't like being here. I'd like to get out of here.

D: *Okay. If it bothers you, you don't have to stay.*

J: I'd like to leave. You see, they have this real arrogant attitude of life. That they are supreme, and that everything else is for their benefit. They don't respect the life force. This is why they were destroyed.

D: *I appreciate you looking at it and telling me the information. I didn't want to disturb you in any way.*

J: What disturbed me was the cannibalism. It was just so senseless. And this is why we have cannibalism still in the world, I guess. But they just do very senseless things for the spur of the moment.

D: *If you're uncomfortable there, you can leave the viewing room?*

J: It's blank now. I always thought that Atlanteans were nice people, with high energy and stuff like that. And they weren't. They were highly advanced, yes, but they were very, very arrogant and very unrespectful to lower life forms. It was things that we would not understand. They were senseless. They would mutate these animals, and cause this poor animal such pain just because they wanted to do it.

D: *Maybe they were bored.*

J: That's what it seemed like when they captured this man. This group of people went in this airplane, and they captured this aborigine type man. Like if we went to New Guinea now.

D: *Then they did have natives in that time.*

J: Right. They went to a place where there were natives, and they captured him and cooked him and ate him. And I thought that was real senseless.

D: *Maybe everything was so advanced that they became bored. And these were sports to keep them interested and entertained.*

J: Probably. I get that feeling.

D: *Their minds had evolved to such a point that nothing was a challenge anymore, so they wanted to try different things.*

J: The librarian is telling me, most people on Earth think of the Atlanteans as a high energy people. But why was their continent destroyed? It was because they misused the life force, and they had to be destroyed.

D: *That makes a lot more sense than some of the other things we have heard.*

***

More information was gained on another visit to the viewing room in the Library.

J: I'm walking into the library now. I am at the place where the guardian of the library is. He says, "I am here to be of service and help to you." And I am asked, "What is my request?"

D: *Before we asked for Atlantis information and were shown it in the viewing room. And it was disturbing. We would like to look at some information dealing with their positive powers, if we can.*

J: Yes. He says please step into the viewing room. He was confused because he thought the information we wanted was to watch the sinking of Atlantis, and why it sank.

D: *We'll get to that another time.*

J: He says this is why the information was disturbing to the vehicle, because it was one of the reasons for the downfall. He says there is a sense of justice. And when one uses one's negativity so strongly, one attracts negativity. And this was how the Atlantean civilization finally collapsed.

D: *Even though it was disturbing we thank him for giving the information. This time we want to see anything about their healing powers of that time, to see what heights they attained with those kind of powers.*

J: He's showing me this beautiful crystal room. There are thousands of crystals all over this room. It's almost like frosted panes of glass, but they're all made out of crystals that they manufacture. They take a gel they have discovered, and mix it with sand, and this forms these most perfect crystals. But there's a special apparatus that it's in. It's almost biological looking. He is showing me this wonderful area that has different colored lights. There are green, blue, red, violet, yellow, orange and white. And each one of these, he says, represents a different part of the body to heal. The white is to heal the etheric body and astral body. The green is to heal the physical body. The blue is to heal the emotional body. The red is to heal the causal body. These are all different bodies of the person. By sitting in these colored rays, in the harmony and in its sequence, one would be healed of any difficulty that lies within himself. Also there are terminators of crystals arranged in different patterns around a board that the person lies on. It looks sort of like a stone board, but at the same time it's very comfortable. It has a cloth covering that looks very thin, yet it's very strong in resistance. It looks like one of those space age blankets, it has that silver metallic color. But yet it's different because it feels like foam when you lie on it. This bed travels underneath these different colors. And the colors have to be done in the right sequence. If they're done in the wrong sequence, it could cause ill health, so there's a certain sequence. But he hasn't given me that sequence yet. He says that is not important right now. He says this was the highest healing chamber in Atlantis, and was used to treat people of the aristocracy or the elite ruling government.

D: *It wasn't for the ordinary person?*

J: No. He says they had other places that were very similar. But this would be like a hospital for the elite in your own country and time.

D: *Then individual ailments didn't have to be treated?*

J: The healing of the whole bodies had to be treated. Not just the physical body but also the emotional, the mental, all these bodies had to be healed.

D: *If you had an injury or an illness, it wasn't treated as a separate thing.*

J: No. This was mostly for spiritual development and healing of past wrongs and things of this type. It was sort of like a psychiatric approach. He's showing me the areas where people had broken bones mended and things of this nature. And in a way it looks like our regular operating rooms, except that they're using crystal like instruments that have been refined and sharpened to razor point perfection.

D: *You said the machine you saw in the other room, that healed the different bodies, was almost biological. What did you mean by that?*

J: It looks alive! It looks like it is alive. It's a computer terminal that looks like something in the plant type family. Because it looks like it can grow and expand, just like a plant can grow and expand. And it has a light greenish color to it. But it also has a crystal liquid display unit that looks like something out of a science fiction magazine. But it looks like it can grow and multiply itself.

D: *Who would decide if someone had a disorder that needed to be treated in this room?*

J: The people of the time were very aware. This was the center where one would come after the transition of a close relative, to wish them good bye, send them love. This is a healing process for many things. Grief. They were highly advanced people at this time who knew basically their manipulations and motivations. People at this time are not judgmental of each other.

***

While I was putting this book together in 2001 I had a small piece of information given in a session in Memphis. A woman described a frequency machine used in Atlantis that used light to regulate frequencies to bring the body into harmony for healing. It was operated by the person's mind and was pure energy. It was real, and it was effective. But after a while it sat unused, because the scientists developed another machine they thought was more effective. They preferred to use crystal machines which were powerful, yet they distorted the energy. The crystals were in boxes with some type of fluid. Light shining through the boxes generated the power from many people's minds in the room. It degenerated into being used for the wrong purposes (especially sexual) and produced distorted effects.

As the Atlanteans learned more about the use of energies and their knowledge expanded they were fascinated by the manipulation of energy. They discovered new ways to experiment with it and direct it. They lost sight of using it for positive purposes in their life such as healing and balancing. When the energy (multiplied by many people concentrating and giving it increased power) was used for negative, it became misdirected and distorted and turned destructive. It became so powerful it turned in on itself. This was one of the reasons for the destruction of Atlantis.

We continued to gain more information when we returned to the Library.

J: The guardian asks, which subject would you like to discuss?

D: *We are still interested in Atlantis. I'd like to ask a few questions about the time of Atlantis whenever it was happy, before it went into its downfall. When it was at its height. We would like to know something about the family life of the people during the good times of Atlantis. Can you see that?*

J: Yes, he's showing me pictures of Atlantis.

D: *Did they have individual families and a family structure?*

J: Yes, they had individual families. The families were really connected. People lived for a very long time, so there were large amounts of people. A family would fill a whole town. Or not a whole town, but it would be like that in our time. But they were interconnected and each member of the family was very important. They all had different skills and techniques to be of help for each other. Basically though they didn't live communally like we do. Everybody had their own individual space, but they all met together at different times for meals and talks and things like that. Even husbands and wives had separate rooms or separate areas. Their houses were spacious, and had many rooms for every member of the family, and they were all interconnected, sort of like courtyards. I see courtyards with different people. They're all related but they're still very individualized. And I see the older people working with the children, and these older people are hundreds of years old. They're not just a hundred, they're hundreds of years old. And they seem especially to like working with young children. And I see that people go about their different things. There are people that are meditating. There are people that are working on different scientific experiments and things of this type. And they all had their own sense of space, like their own room where they do their own thing. A sense of individuality was very important to them.

D: *And you said they would come together to eat?*

J: Yes, they come together at different times for entertainment and to eat and to dance and to sing. They did get into group activities with the family. There were holidays and things like that, but basically everybody lived rather individually.

D: *What about art and music and things like that?*

J: Oh, yes, they had beautiful art. They mixed ground crystals with their paints, so everything had a luminous quality. And the styles of paintings had something like spirals in them.

Little spiral things that made them really pop out at you. And they had all these processes where they used crystals for music. It looks like some type of machine that spins the crystal into a spiral thread. It goes like that. (Hand motions of a spiral.) And they were stringed instruments that they played on. They take the crystal and they spin... it's not like the crystals that we have now, rock crystals. They were originally that, but they were mutated in laboratories that they had throughout the continent. And they spun it to a degree that it made like a spiral wire. And this spiral wire was used as an instrument on guitars, but not like our guitars or anything like that. They're very different looking types of instruments. There are string instruments. There are flutes. And then there are these things made out of huge long crystal like things. They're all made out of a crystal type of material. And they play in special areas, so that it resonates. It really opens up their heart and muscles, because the music is so beautiful. It's very relaxing and spiritual. It makes you feel at peace. And people dance and sing. And I see many ropes of flowers around people. And that's how they dance with ropes of flowers, entwining themselves with them. It doesn't look ancient Roman or Greek. In fact, everybody has these beautiful colored garments on, in reds and blues and greens and yellows. And they're dancing with these flowers and garlands. It's sort of a combination of synthesized music and classical music. The sounds are very similar, but it's very pure in tone. It's not synthesized, it doesn't have feedback. And they use it in their rituals. And it's used in churches not churches, temples that they had. As for art. Art is everywhere. Everything is painted beautifully. It looks like ground paint. It's more like a solid rather than a liquid, that they use. Some are on canvas type things and others are on walls. And other things are partly sculptured into the wall and then colored.

D: *Do you see any type of light source they would use in their houses?*

J: There is this malleable rock crystal energy that they have. It radiates everywhere, so it's always light. But by moving their hand up or down they can make the radiance even more brilliant or darker. When they sleep, to make the room at peace, they put their hand down like that if they want dark. (Hand motions, like moving his hand downward slowly.) Towards the wall. And it's their vibration that the wall picks up and darkens the room. Everything is controlled by their own energies.

D: *What about their cooking or eating habits.*

J: They have these areas that are like big vineyards and gardens. And they have these strange looking beings taking care of all that. They work the fields and gardens. They look like centaurs and mermaids and goats. And all the food that comes into the kitchen area is then processed by these creatures. They do all the planting and harvesting and picking of the fruits. And they're given food in return. Most of the Atlanteans love them very much, like a good farmer loves his horses and takes good care of them. These strange creatures are treated like benevolent animals.

So in some parts of the continent these creatures were created and appreciated.

D: *I'm curious about those animals. Where did they come from?*

J: They were created for that purpose. They were genetically engineered.

D: *You said there were mermaids?*

J: Yes, the mermaids go into the waters and bring back baskets of fish. The people come and they laugh and they sing and they stroke these animals and kiss them and hold them, and let them know that they're loved and that they're grateful for what they're doing. And the creatures prepare the food as well. Not the mermaid. The mermaid stays at this pond type thing because she's half fish. While the little centaurs bring in these wagon loads of baskets of food and fruits and things of this nature, that goes into a central kitchen. And there is one being that has an upper human body but has goat feet. And there's a kitchen type of atmosphere, but the kitchen doesn't look anything like our kitchens. It has cupboards though to keep things in. But basically the food is not cooked as much as it's processed live, like fruits are sliced up or peeled. The fish and things of that type go into a thing that cooks them very quickly. It has different areas of it. It's like a microwave type of thing but it isn't a microwave. It looks like a crystal chamber where the foods are put that need to be cooked like fish. I don't see any meat there. I just see the fish and crustaceans, like scallops and clams and things like that. And they're just heated to the point where they're not alive anymore. And then they're eaten.

D: *Were these creatures created genetically to be servants?*

J: Yes, they were created to be the servants of these people. They're loved though. When one gets hurt or anything like that, the whole family gather to energize on that injured animal's part. They're treated like servants, but loved servants. Like the way we would treat a cat or a dog, show it love and care. They're very grateful for what these animals do, because they're considered more like animals than humans. Parts of the body are more like an animal, but basically, their faces are humanlike.

D: *What about their behavior or their intellect.*

J: Oh, they can speak and take instructions. They know simple things, yes, but nothing like the rest of the people do.

D: *They're not as intelligent as the other humans, although they do look partially human.*

J: They're not gross looking or anything like that. They look very natural, and they're taken good care of. And they were very appreciated, and were told they were loved. I see this one servant that made up the fruit platter. And this woman takes it and kisses her and strokes her head, because in the head area there are little horns. And she rubs those horns like this, (hand motions) and she says, "Oh, you're so great. Look at this, this is wonderful. It looks so pretty. Everyone is going to love it. And why don't you come on out afterwards and..." And they all come up afterwards and they're loved by the rest of the family. They're treated like a loving pet would be.

D: *Can these creatures genetically reproduce, or are they one of a kind?*

J: No, they can't reproduce. People buy them. Each one of them is individual, but they are mass marketed. They have places where you can go and buy these creatures so that they'll be of service.

After awakening John described the creature in the kitchen, which was the last thing he remembered. It had a face that was part cowlike and part human. As though a human had the nose of a cow and small horns coming out of its head. It was wearing a bib type garment over the top part of its body, because it was apparently female.

***

Phil: There are far more uses for crystals than is available now to your human comprehension. That which is unknown far exceeds that which is known. However, when your level of awareness increases to accept and accommodate these realities, then the uses will be manifest. It can be seen that quartz in some form magnifies and intensifies that energy which is human energy. We find here the translation is difficult, for the true energy concept is not understood. However, a blending of energies, both human and non human is quite possible and readily accomplished with these crystals. They can be used as blenders and differentiators or separators, depending on the direction of the energy given by the person or persons using or directing this crystal. They are a filter, useful in many different ways, limited only by the imagination of those who would use them.

D: *When you speak of a stone filtering cosmic rays, what would be the purpose of needing to filter cosmic rays?*

P: There is the filtering and focusing, which can be separate or simultaneous. There are four specific reasons or purposes. Specific energies which are best suited. This would be for the filtering or focusing aspect. Focusing merely focuses or condenses the energies to one singular area. Different stones may do each or special stones may do both, depending on the purpose. The cosmic energies are a very powerful, as yet untouched, source of energy, which this planet has yet to discover an abundant source of raw energy many millions of of times more powerful than any raw materials here on this planet.

D: *The problem is being able to uncover it.*

P: The problem is raising the consciousness in order to accept the concept and simultaneously to sharpen the responsibility in order to use it. This energy was prevalent on this planet at one time, but through lack of responsibility the knowledge of its use was lost.

D: *Was this at the time of Atlantis?*

P: Yes, that is correct. Much was lost at that time. There was much misuse in the Atlantean times of many different types and forms of energies. For there was initially a high understanding of these energies which constitute physical reality. There was then the misuse of the understanding of these energies.

***

Clara received information from a place that sounded very similar to Phil's Planet of the Three Spires. Hers was also a planet with strange spire like structures, and the information was contained in the entire planet, as though its composition was a storehouse of knowledge. This was the same description given by Phil. Clara also emotionally called this place her "home", as did Phil. The complete story of how she located this place was told earlier in this book.

D: *Can you tell me anything about Atlantis? Is that part of the records?*

C: Atlantis went into the sea.

D: *I would like to know about it before it went into the sea. What kind of a civilization was it?*

C: It was very sophisticated. Very green. And very technologically advanced, beyond where Earth is today.

D: *Was this civilization in existence for a long time?*

C: A very long time.

D: *Can you tell me some of their technological advances?*

C: They had the ability to shift and move energy through time and through space in a much more sophisticated manner than technological how do you say? advances are done today. (Had difficulty) Hmmm, what is this word you use for advanced machinery? Like computers and communication devices. This equipment was very vast. It was done very, very minute. Even to the point where some information was accomplished at a telepathic level.

D: *How was the machinery or the computers powered?*

C: It was all done by solar. Everything was done by the Sun. The great central Sun.

D: *Then they didn't have electricity like we have today?*

C: At one time they did. But nearing and in the latter years of the time that it existed it was all generated by the great central Sun.

D: *Is this the Sun we know of in the sky, or is it something different?*

C: The Sun that you know.

D: *Was the equipment similar to what we have today?*

C: Much more sophisticated. You have giant and mammoth solar panels, and solar equipment, which is far greater than what was used in Atlantis. Theirs was so advanced as to be utilized in a more efficient manner, and not taking up as much space. Their technology was more in tune with the central Sun, which gave off the energy. They were as though connected to a greater power. They were connected to the stars, and to the powers from other stars.

John had mentioned that they also knew how to utilize the power of the moon. Bartholomew also mentioned that ancient people had this knowledge.

C: They communicated with beings from other planets, from other stars. And through their communications they exchanged information, which they utilized in the technology of their machinery, their computers, and their other technological advances, whatever that might be.

D: *So the other beings from the stars helped them?*

C: Yes. It was a cooperative effort.

D: *I have been told that the scientists developed the power of their minds to achieve some of these results.*

C: That is correct. In development of their mind, when they began to open up to all possibilities, that indeed there were beings on other planets, then they were in contact in a way that was unlimited. They then had the ability, by leaving the limited way of thinking, and feeling and believing, to receive that which came from other universes and from other planets. And those planets in turn would feed information to them in such a manner that it became very telepathic. They would communicate from a mind to mind level without needing long lines of communication, like your telephone lines. And therefore, they took this telepathic ability and advanced that by communicating with many planets. It became a a global community, as opposed to one sector of a human race.

D: *They were able to accomplish a great deal more. Is that what you mean? (Yes) I've heard that Atlantis was not just one country, but it was the entire world at that time.*

C: It was the known world at the time that Atlantis existed.

D: *Were all of the parts of this known world advanced?*

C: No. Not all parts. There were areas that were primitive, where people had not opened themselves up to the communication. The entire planet was not completely elevated to a higher level of vibration. There were some places and some populated areas that chose not to open thier hearts and endorse a new way of living, a new way of being. So they became, what you might call, outcasts. They were those who did not believe they could go beyond their limitations. The ones who chose to live a limited life, chose themselves to live in a different area of that planet. Whereas those who opened their hearts and their minds to an unlimited way of living, soared and advanced. And communicated with all planets.

D: *It was as though they didn't have anything in common with each other.*

C: Exactly.

D: *Can you see where the more advanced, the scientific community, lived in relation to the way the world is today? I know the world has changed a lot.*

C: It has changed very vastly. What was the known world at that time was comprised in an area which you would now call the

Atlantic Ocean.

D: *Are there any remnants of that civilization left that mankind might find at some time?*

C: Only on an etheric level.

D: *So it can't be found at a physical level?*

C: At this time there is a possibility if man opens himself up enough to believe truly, in a conscious way, that it can be found. Then it will be found.

D: *Some people think they have seen things under the water that might be remnants of the cities, roads and buildings.*

C: That is not true. What they're seeing is remnants of other newer civilizations, since Atlantis.

D: *I've also been told that the Atlantean scientists reached the point that they were doing physical experiments. Do you see anything like that?*

C: What kind of physical experiments?

D: *Genetic or anything like that?*

C: Everything that is being experienced now on this planet was done during the time of Atlantis. However, it was done many centuries prior to the demise of Atlantis. Genetically, they cloned animals. They cloned humans. But they found that this was not the appropriate thing to do. For it interfered with the DNA of the human race, and the human race would suffer greatly should they continue. So it was shown that they were to stop.

So genetic experimentation was done in addition to the use of the mind to affect the physical. I never found out which came first, or if they were both going on at the same time. It seems that their curiosity held no bounds. An echo from the past being repeated in our present time.

D: *Was it just as an experiment, or did they have a purpose?*

C: It was experimental. Their purpose was to see if it could be done. And when they discovered that it could be done, they ran into many difficulties and many troubles with the outcomes. It was not desirable, and so it was felt best by those that made the rules, that it should be discontinued.

D: *What kind of problems did they come across?*

C: Forms appeared unlike humans. And there were many experiments of how do you say? interbreeding? (She questioned that word.) Inter cloning? Mixing up. And the outcome was more like animal. It reversed the process of evolution. And disease occurred. It was not for the purpose of the planet for that to continue. So it was decided that, for the best for the planet, that it be discontinued. That it be stopped, or it would destroy humanity.

D: *That sounds very drastic.*

C: It was drastic. It is drastic.

D: *But then instead of doing just exact clones, they began mixing the DNA, the genes, just to see what would happen? Is that what you mean?*

C: Yes. The curiosity. Experiment. Let's do this and see what comes out. Let's do this and try this and see what happens. In the plant kingdom they had made hybrids of different plants and different vegetables, and trees. And so they thought, "Wow, we were successful doing that. Why not do it with humans?" So then they started. And it became, "Oh, well, let's see now what we can do with this, and this and this." And it became a massive disaster.

D: *So when they began cloning and mixing the different genes, you said it became more animalistic than human?*

C: It was as though they were reversing evolution. But it became very grotesque, and very evil.

D: *So they began to get combinations that were not desirable.*

C: And had never been before.

D: *But apparently they were viable. They did live.*

C: They lived for a while. And they went into a state of what you would call "crazy". And destruction occurred, because they became like monsters.

D: *Why did they become crazy? You mean because it was not a normal process it affected the mind of the creature?*

C: That's part of it. But part of it was the mixing of genetics of the animal kingdom with the human. And so it became such a plaything for the scientists. To see where we can go, and what we can create. We can now become gods, and create that which we choose to create. That which had never existed before. And so disaster reigned.

D: *But you also said disease was introduced.*

C: Diseases that had never been known before were introduced.

D: *How did that come about?*

C: By mixing the genes. By mixing that which was sick with that which was well. And that which was.... (Had difficulty finding the word.) What you would call "foreign bodies" to the human race. Which could be animal, or whatever of any kingdom that they wanted to try to introduce. That's what they did. And so if one particle of the DNA from one strand, or from one race, had an inkling of some type of disease, it was introduced into the whole, which created a whole new line of disease.

This could be a dormant type of disease that the host body was carrying and was probably immune to. But when the cloning process awakened it it also changed it.

C: The disease would mutate, and then it would mutate into something else. And if one disease would be introduced by one DNA strand, and another disease would be introduced into the same thing, the combination then would introduce something that could be and was very destructive.

D: *So not only were the bodies and the physical appearance and minds of these creatures changing, also any I want to say bacteria, molecules, were also mutating and forming different diseases. (Yes) Going off in ways that had never happened.*

C: That is correct. And it became so massive that they had to shut down all the experiments, because they saw it becoming quite rampant. And that it could destroy the entire human race.

It was during 1997 that the first official cloning of a sheep in England was announced. After this session in August, 1997 the authorities were openly discussing the dangers of cloning and the ethics of it. From my work I have discovered that the cloning of humans has already been perfected. There are many things that the public at large is not aware of. It is as though the first crumbs of information are now being dropped (especially with the recent announcement of the first successful cloning of a monkey [our nearest relative]) so we will grow accustomed to it when the official announcement is made of human cloning.

Scientists said they could clone animals and introduce human genes into them to produce better meat, and make a better animal. They also recently began introducing human genes into special pigs so their organs could be used in human transplant operations. If the donor pig had some human genes then the host human body would not reject the organ, because normally it would reject anything that was not human or compatible.

One scientist raised the objection that introducing and mixing human genes with animal genes could create unknown diseases, that would start with the animal and possibly spread to the human. The pig, for example, had diseases that were unique to it and could not be spread by handling it or eating its meat. But the scientists worried about what would happen if the donated organ were a permanent part of the human body and blood was constantly flowing through it. It could be carrying the germs of these diseases throughout the host's system, and they could mutate into unknown diseases that could spread throughout the population. There was enough concern to temporarily halt the donor program until further research could be done.

It sounded like history repeating itself. Mankind was making the same mistakes we had made in the bygone days of Atlantis. Maybe that was the purpose of this information coming forth at this time in our history. A warning bell from the past.

D: *Then the diseases were not only just in the genetic experiments. It was beginning to spread to the rest of the human race?*

C: It was confined to the genetics. But scientists saw that, should they continue, then it would. Because those beings would then integrate into the other community. And then that disease would be transmitted throughout all of civilization. And the powers that be said, this we cannot allow to happen. So that which was, was destroyed.

D: *Were these creatures they created, sterile, or were they able to reproduce themselves?*

C: They could not reproduce themselves. They were simply "clones", with no reproductive organs.

D: *What did they use these beings for, when it first began, before it got out of control? Did they have a purpose?*

C: The purpose to start with was simply to see if it could be done, and it got out of control.

D: *Then they didn't use these beings for anything?*

C: What the beings were capable of doing, they taught them like robots. So they acted as robots at the commands of the scientists. They could be their assistants, or playmates for others. They were designed to be a housekeeper, designed to be the shepherd, designed to be whatever. Once they saw that, "Well, we should have a purpose for this, if we're going to create these."

Were these the gentle servant beings that John saw?

C: And then they thought, "Well, this is nice. So we'll introduce all these other genes with all these other animals, to see what we can come up with." And so what happened then was chaos.

D: *Then the main reason for shutting down the experiment was they were afraid it was getting out of hand and the disease would spread?*

C: That was the only reason. Because they could see that the whole civilization would be totally destroyed. So instead they destroyed those beings which they had created.

D: *And you said the "powers that be" are the ones that told them they had to do this. Who do you mean?*

C: The governments.

D: *So they knew what the scientists were doing.*

C: Yes. They endorsed it, until they saw it was at a place where it could not go, and it could not be. Otherwise all of civilization would be destroyed.

D: *It would have spread even to the communities that were, more or less, what you called "outcasts"?*

C: Oh, yes. Oh, yes.

D: *So they then rounded up the beings they had created, and had to destroy them?*

C: Yes, they did. Not in a massive way, but in a very quiet and subtle way that seemed a natural way. So the community at large would not be alarmed or go into a panic situation. So it was kept very under control. The general public was not aware of some of the grotesque beings that came out of the experimentations. It was somewhat like the way your government hides a lot of stuff from the general public. That is the way it was in the time of Atlantis.

D: *I've often suspected that many of the legends of half human, half animal, may have come from that time period. Is that possible?*

C: Yes. It is possible. It did.

D: *Then these creatures, half human, half animal, did not exist after the time of Atlantis? (No) So the legends have to be that old?*

C: Yes. It originated in Atlantis.

D: *In the times of the Romans and the Greeks and the Egyptians, you hear of these stories. So they had a basis in fact, but it went very far back in time. Is that correct?*

C: Long before Egypt and Rome were ever, ever conceived.

D: *But it was part of the memories, and they turned them into legends.*

C: Yes, that is correct. It has been handed down, so it is a memory of the collective consciousness.

D: *I've always believed that legends have some basis in fact, if you take them back far enough.*

C: All of them do. Otherwise, how would they ever come to be a legend? Once they're a legend, then each person who gets it wants to add a little hint of their own flare and flamboyance to it, to make it an even greater, more colorful legend.

D: *But it all has to begin somewhere.*

C: There is always the beginning.

D: *Was there anything else that the scientists did that they were later told they should stop?*

C: That was the biggest thing. That was the thing of significance that you asked about, and seemed appropriate at this time to mention.

D: *Because we are beginning to stumble into the same area. (Yes) I have been told that in our time, today in the 20th century, there are scientists who are experimenting on this same type of thing. Do you know anything about that?*

C: That is true. That is true. They are at the very beginning of playing with the genetics. And as the public becomes more aware of it, there will be an uprising. Of saying, "That is unnatural. Let it be."

D: *I've often suspected they have gone further than they're letting the people know.*

C: Yes, they have. They will drop a little piece of information here, and a little piece of information there. And as in the days of Atlantis, it was hidden. In today's time, as you know it, they are allowing a little dribble of information out. Just enough so that the general public will not become alarmed. And when enough information does leak out on purpose, by some from the interior then the public will rise up in arms, and say, "We cannot allow this to happen. It must not happen. Because it will destroy the human race, as we know it."

D: *History will repeat itself.*

C: Yes. But because of communication in the time in which you live, more people are aware in a faster way by getting this communication en masse at one time. If this is known that it could destroy the world, the public will rise up in arms.

D: *Have the scientists in the 20th century already begun combining DNA of different species?*

C: Yes. Very secretively.

D: *Can you tell me anything about that? I would like to know how far we have gone. I know it's a disturbing topic.*

C: (Deep sigh) It's not appropriate at this time for us to talk about that subject any more.

This same thing occurred when I wanted to explore this subject further in *The Custodians*. The aliens told me much information, but there was some they did not reveal, mostly because of the effect it would have on the vehicle it had to pass through. When this happens I cannot override these directives, nor would I want to.

D: *Okay. But I've been told that the extraterrestrials are helping our government in such experiments. Is that true? (Yes) Do they approve of what's going on?*

C: What the extraterrestrials are doing is simply controlling it and keeping it at a level where the human race will not destroy themselves.

D: *Because they, more or less, know how this works, don't they?*

C: Yes, we do.

D: *I wonder if human scientists will listen to them, or did they go off on their own?*

C: We have ways of letting the scientists know there are limits.

D: *And I assume these experiments are being done in secret places.*

C: Yes. All over the planet. But we, more or less, are helping keep a cap on it, so that it doesn't destroy the Earth.

D: *Do you think the scientists could take it out of control?*

C: It could happen. It is a planet of free choice. (She seemed uncomfortable.)

D: *That's okay. You always tell me when you can't give me any more information, and I respect that. To go back to Atlantis Can you tell me what happened at the destruction? Was there a certain event that finally culminated and caused it to sink into the water?*

C: I can't discuss that today.

D: *Why not?*

C: It is just not an appropriate time to discuss how it happened. It may, at some future time, be a time when that information can be released.

D: *All right. But after the destruction, were there survivors?*

C: There was much loss of life at that time. Earth required a reseeding.

D: *I believe in the seeding, so that doesn't surprise me. Let me tell you a theory I have, and you can tell me if it's correct or not. I've often thought there might have been survivors who came to Egypt and Peru and different parts of the world, where we have these large monuments. And that maybe they carried the knowledge of how to do these things, like working with stone. Is that correct?*

C: During the time of Atlantis we were in contact with humans on Atlantis. And so in cooperation beings from Atlantis visited other stars. And some of the beings from Atlantis, who were on other stars, then helped to seed the area where Egypt is, and where other areas are. So therefore the information and the memories of Atlantis have continued. The legend began, and has carried through because beings from Atlantis, who lived on other stars, came back, as seedlings in physical form.

D: *But as seedlings, you mean... full grown. (Yes) Because I know in the very beginning life began on the cellular stage and evolved.*

C: Yes. Not so at this time. Those beings, you might say, took a sabbatical, took a vacation from Atlantis and went to another star. And then when Atlantis disappeared from the Earth, and other areas came up, those beings came back to the planet Earth to start life again. Many that repopulated the Earth had to come from other star systems, because there was a great loss of life. Simply because of the explosive nature in which the planet disappeared. And that's all I can say about that. Perhaps at another time, if it's appropriate, and the council will release that information, then we can allow that.

What Clara said about humans being transported to other stars and being returned after the cataclysm sounded very similar to information I received, which is reported later in this book. This is a viable plan to evacuate a portion of the human race in the future if needed. Apparently it has happened in the past, and could also be history repeating itself. The aliens have always said they would not allow the destruction of the human race. Too much time and energy have been invested in its development. If we do not heed them, they will help us in spite of ourselves.

It did not concern me that Clara could not give me information about the destruction of Atlantis, because I had already received it from other subjects. I have kept all of this in my files for years until I started compiling it for this book. Then I discovered that I actually had all I needed. It had been given in bits and pieces over several years.

We had been given clues that the great civilization had to fall because of their misuse of their mind powers and their attempts to go against the moral structure of the universe by rewriting genetics. Yet I suspected that something more powerful was involved to create the actual cataclysm that sank Atlantis.

***

This information came from the librarian at the great Library on the spirit plane.

D: *Can we have access to the files on Atlantis again? I would like to know about the actual destruction of Atlantis. The last time he was telling us some of the reasons why it was destroyed, because of the misuse of mind power. But what about the actual destruction? Can he show you anything about that?*

John: Yes, he's showing me deep fissures made in the Earth. Deep fissures, because of these crystals. They used this crystal power and transmitted sunlight into the ground and it caused stress. Also they tried to tap the molten core of the Earth, and this caused a lot of pressure that helped destroy the island as well. They bored into the molten core. And this molten core blew up, and that's why things exploded.

D: *Why were they doing that?*

J: They were looking for another energy source, instead of just the Sun.

D: *Then they were using the Sun with the crystals. How were they boring into the Earth?*

J: Through heavy concentration and mind power.

D: *They did have their minds developed to quite a degree. (Yes) And then what happened? You said they made these fissures in the Earth from both of these sources, the crystals and their mind?*

J: Comets had something to do with it as well.

D: *Does he know why?*

J: No. He's just showing that comets were in the skies that foreordained that this event would happen. The scientists bored into the solid rock down to the molten core level. This put an enormous relief on the Earth's molten core. But it also affected all the planets, and not just the continents on the Earth itself.

D: *You mean the planets in our solar system?*

J: Right. Because this threw off lots of high energy, and this was why Atlantis sank.

D: *They were messing with something they didn't understand?*

J: They didn't comprehend the power behind the molten core.

D: *Then the comets didn't have anything to actually do with this.*

J: No, but there were attendants in the skies for this event.

D: *Then what happened?*

J: It created the fissures by this mental drilling. And what escaped was the inner molten core, which lopsided the world, and this is why it sank.

D: *Like a volcanic eruption?*

J: Right. It was an Earth shift.

After awakening John told what he could remember that was not recorded on the tape. As usual the clearest memory was the last thing we discussed.

J: They knew about astrology. They mastered that art. The comets appearing gave them warning that they should not be messing around with seeking this energy source from the center of the Earth. Yet they kept on boring into the Earth using mental power. Imagine a bore going into the Earth. And when it hit this molten core, this caused a huge amount of energy to be released. That caused volcanic eruptions. And it's like something burst to the surface. You know how it can bubble and burst to the surface and then....?

D: *I was thinking it must have been like a volcano, but apparently it was more powerful than that.*

J: Oh, yes, it was much more powerful. They didn't realize they couldn't channel this energy.

D: *To stop it, you mean?*

J: Right, it was too powerful. It was like a volcano, except it was like a million times. It just tore up the whole island. He was very reluctant to tell me. I think he didn't want people to get ideas to do that again.

D: *There's been talk about boring into the Earth with machinery.*

J: Yeah. He was really reluctant for me to talk about it. I could go into it more, but it was like "subject finished, file closed". That was enough.

*** * ***

More information was found in Phil's sessions when he was given knowledge of history from the Planet of the Three Spires.

D: *Can you see what brought about the destruction of Atlantis?*

P: There are many factors here that are both apparent and non apparent. However, we feel that the physical is perhaps more akin to what you are asking. The destruction was many fold. However, the most traumatic was the destruction of the land mass itself in a cataclysm of volcanic activity caused by earthquakes. The majority of this destruction was enhanced by those who were the ruling class at that time. There was given to the people an ability to destroy themselves by use of many different forms of energies. There were many different types of energies available. And they were simply misusing these, such that there became many disharmonious forces in that particular portion of the planet.

D: *I wondered whether the cause was natural phenomenon, or if the people had a part to play in the actual destruction.*

P: The majority of the destruction was an act of ignorance and dim wittedness. However, there was at some level an awareness that such actions would have consequences. And yet those consequences were ignored in favor of the immediate so called gain of such actions.

D: *But you said they used energies, and these types of energies were part of the cause of the erupting volcanoes and the earthquakes?*

P: That is accurate. There were the energies of the crystals that were focused so that the lines of force of the Earth itself were cut. So that the glue, so to say, that held that portion of the Earth was severed. And there was the disharmony that resulted from this destruction. And then the cataclysm which followed.

D: *Does that mean they didn't expect this to happen?*

P: There were those who warned that such actions would cause such a reaction. However, the majority of the people who were making the decisions at that time were blinded by their own sense of not being answerable to the laws of nature and God. And were acting in ways that were causing much destruction.

D: *So they were playing around with things they shouldn't have, in other words.*

P: They were playing around with things in ways they should not have. Not that they were playing around with things that they should not have.

D: *So it backfired and ended up destroying them and their world at that time.*

P: That is accurate.

***

D: *I was wondering that if Atlantis was such a perfect place and was developing such tremendous capabilities, what happened that brought its downfall?*

Brenda: What happened was as best I can see an unforeseen natural disaster. And this natural disaster was so widespread that it threw everything into chaos. It appears the main thing that happened was that, they were developing along really well and there appears to be a small group who wanted more power than they should have. But they had not really developed any major problematical power yet. The way Atlantis was situated, it was on two different tectonic plates. And the strain between these two plates got to the point where they had a major earthquake. I mean, very major, to the point that when the ground split, it split all the way through the crust and the magma and lava started welling up from it, not from a volcano but from the earthquake. And it was so violent it was felt all over the world. And it was collapsing buildings on both continents. It just totally destroyed Atlantis to smithereens, as this subject would say.

D: *I've heard a story, and I didn't know how true it was. That the group that wanted power used the main crystal or something and this was part of it.*

B: That probably contributed to the violence of the earthquake, because it was unstable and ready to go at any time. And they thought they would tinker around with what they could do, and it set the earthquake off worst than it would have otherwise.

D: *Then do you see, is that why the continent sank?*

B: It didn't sink all the way. It sank, but for centuries thereafter ships could not navigate that ocean because of the mud shoals that were in the way. It was too shallow for ships to navigate all the way across. And as the plates moved apart, the mud shoals gradually sank deep enough to where ships could go across without running aground. There have been some records of this in your maritime annals, that people have just chalked up to something inexplicable.

This could explain the old maps and the reluctance of sailors to sail out a great distance. There were many tales even in the days of Columbus of monsters and lost ships. Maybe this was behind the legends of ships falling off the edge of the Earth, because when they sailed out and did not return they had indeed fallen off. The people at home could not know they had perhaps struck the shoals and sunk, or became stuck and thus died of starvation. This could also explain the legend of the Sargasso Sea or Sea of Lost Ships.

D: *When it happened, was it like a sinking to the people who were on the land?*

B: No, it was confusion and disaster, with their land shaking like crazy and rivers of lava running down the streets. And it was very horrible and people ran to the ocean and swam out into the ocean to get away from the lava and to get away from the shaking land. And the ones that escaped to the ocean were drowned because the initial earthquake caused tidal waves to come back and were bouncing off the continent on both sides. And the tidal waves swept over the remains of the island and destroyed everything that was not already destroyed by the lava and the shaking.

***

I want to comment on a case I had in New Orleans in 2000. A man regressed to what he described as Atlantis, where he was a member of a group of priests. There was a high priest over them, and they were using crystals to try to counteract the negative influences of another group of scientists that were very dominant. It seemed that the other group of scientists were using their mental powers and their mind control in negative ways. And they were also conducting experiments in negative ways. Thus this group of priests were trying to counteract the negativity by using crystals and directing energy to try to negate the effects they were creating. But the priests were having problems. They had a group of crystals, and these had to be aligned in a certain order or pattern to create the highest degree of effectiveness, but it wasn't working. They kept rearranging the crystals, and using the power of their minds, and it was still not able to work.

Things gradually got worse, and the land was experiencing a great deal of seismic activity. And they knew that the continent was going to sink. I asked him how they knew for sure, and he said because of the negative things that the other group was doing. It was creating an imbalance, and everything was greatly out of balance. This together with everything else that was happening was creating the seismic activity. And they knew that the piece of land, the island or whatever, Atlantis, was going to sink. So they decided to leave the continent to go somewhere else.

He said they left in ships and took all of their group with them. I wanted a description of the ships, and they were very strange looking. He said they were like large round bubbles. They were quite large because they could hold as many as fifty people in one. When they rode in the water, half of the bubble was above the water and half of it was below the water. The half that was above the water was clear. You could see through it. The people were inside these bubbles, and were powering them by the crystals and mind control. They had taken the crystals with them, some of them on each of the ships. The group focused their minds to create the power that was propelling these bubble ships across the ocean. They were going to what would later be known as Egypt.

When the group reached Egypt they were able to use the crystals, and erected living quarters. They never heard what happened to the continent, because they never encountered anyone who survived and made the journey. There were groups of people living there who were native to the area with no advanced psychic abilities. So they didn't even mix with them. They stayed to themselves as this group of priests, and were going to continue their work and start a whole new civilization there with the use of their crystals and mind control. They intended to continue to use advanced science.

This was an unexpected example of survivors who were able to escape the tragedy and carry advanced knowledge with them. They hoped to create a new civilization that would not be carried to the extremes of the last one. Who knows how many others escaped and went to other continents? This would be an explanation for the erection of monuments and edifices that our scientists cannot explain. The knowledge was there, and was probably lost after several generations. This possibility will be explored in the next chapter.

CHAPTER SEVEN
THE MYSTERY OF THE PYRAMIDS

Every time I have a subject in the deepest possible level of trance I have many, many questions. When I was made aware that I had access to an unlimited source of information my reporter's insatiable curiosity took over and I wanted to know everything I could about every conceivable topic.

Phil had access through the Planet of the Three Spires.

P: The knowledge is not on the planet itself, but is accessible from the planet via the communication system on the planet.

D: *A clearing house, would that be a way of saying it? A communication system contact?*

P: Yes, that would be accurate.

D: *Didn't you say that the records of Earth's past were accessible from this place?*

P: That is correct. The history is here. The history is everywhere at once. It is merely available to me at this point.

D: *There have been many different theories as to how the ancient pyramids in Egypt were built. Could we have some information on that subject, please?*

P: These structures were built with the aid of levitation, which is being rediscovered in some areas on Earth today. The act of moving these stones was accomplished with pure mental energy. This is as possible today, at this hour, as it was at that time. It requires total focus and concentration. There were a group of five to seven of the priests who were schooled in this science and many other sciences. This was merely one aspect of their training. The knowledge was transferred from Atlantis. The pyramids were a gift of the knowledge from Atlantis.

D: *Was levitation the only method by which these stones were raised?*

P: There was singing of tones that accompanied this. It was a religious experience as well.

D: *I've also heard that maybe some pyramids were constructed in a different way.*

P: There is much speculation in the world. Always when the knowledge does not exist on how something was constructed, it is theorized that it was constructed in a manner, theoretically which is common to the civilization at that time. It would not be natural to suppose a construction method which would be unknown at that time. There are many ways of building pyramids. Some are more relevant than others.

D: *Another person told me she saw them being poured, as we would pour concrete today.*

P: We see they were quarried and cut and then levitated. However, we will not discredit that information, for we are not in complete control of all information. And this may be entirely accurate. From what we see however, the stones that we are familiar with were cut and quarried in distant locations and then transported by telepathy. The priest would accompany the stones on the transport and then levitate them to that point from which they were erected. The work was more mental than physical.

D: *Then they were transported by levitation also?*

I was referring to the transportation of the stones, but Phil thought I mean the priests were levitated also.

P: The priests were transported in more conventional manners, as in chariots, but would accompany the stones and keep the stones in their sight, so as to firmly keep the stones in their concentration. The stones were transported from the quarries to the site by levitation and were then moved into place with levitation. The entire raising was done with levitation. The energies used and extended in those stones during their levitation was stored. Each stone stored a small part, and so the pyramid as a whole contained much energy. The stones act as crystals in that they can store human energy as well as many other energies.

D: *You mentioned singing, music. What part did that play?*

P: This is a physical manifestation of that energy which is being focused.

When I was working on my book, *Jesus and the Essenes,* it was difficult to obtain information about certain subjects, because of the extreme secrecy code that the Essenes lived under. I was trying to find out if they had any methods of protecting themselves from their enemies. The most I was able to learn was that it had something to do with sound and there were no weapons, per se, because they were not needed. I also asked about the building of the pyramids, but I was only told the stories and legends they had in their culture. When a subject is regressed to a past life they are greatly influenced by the moral structure of the personality they were at that time. Thus it was often impossible to get the subject to reveal secrets.

Years after I had worked on this material, another woman in another part of the United States supplied some of the missing pieces that the original subject could not, because of his mental restrictions. This woman had also been a member of the Essene community in a past life, involved with the teaching of the mysteries, and also felt the extreme requirement for secrecy. Because she did not go into the complete somnambulist trance she was able to retain memories of scenes when she regained consciousness. She said even in the waking state it was difficult to speak of these things, because her body tensed and her throat tried to close up. This was impressive of how ingrained these restrictions had been in that lifetime. She consciously understood the reasons for the community's privacy and the need to protect this information, because if certain things got out and were used incorrectly, they could cause a great deal of stress and harm.

She reported the information that remained in her conscious mind, "I saw this valley where as many as a hundred or two hundred people were sitting in rows. They were using sound to levitate a huge stone creation and move it where they wanted it to be. The sound was mystical, holy, and yet at the same time it was earthy. It was all the things of the universe combined. The sound was not only created by the voice, but was accompanied by certain types of horns. (She was not sure what to call the instruments because they did not resemble anything she had seen in this lifetime.) They were very long, some were curved and some were straight. They produced sustained clear notes, and this was done in unison. The combined sound never stopped until whatever they were doing was completed. In other words, no one breathed at the same time, so the sounds could be kept constant. The number of people participating depended on the job. The more difficult or grander the scale, the more people would be involved.

"Levitation was not the only use. Sound could be used for many different things. There were different tones or pitches that would render people powerless by causing unconsciousness, or cause them to behave in a crazy, angry or agitated manner. It was also possible to kill with sound, although the Essenes never went that far, since rendering people unconscious would serve the same purpose. They could also use sound to make themselves invisible. It had to do with harmonics, the natural method of finding the mathematical equation that makes any one object tick. This could be done by one person, but if there were an advancing army, it would take several people to deal with it."

This, of course, immediately brought to mind the Bible story of Joshua and the Battle of Jericho, where sound caused the walls of the city to collapse. It is known that sound is capable of these things, such as a certain note can shatter a crystal glass. And the vibration of a marching group of soldiers can collapse a bridge if they do not break step.

I wondered why this powerful weapon was not used in later times when the Romans attacked and destroyed Qumran, and captured and tortured the Essenes. This was the time when the Dead Sea scrolls were hidden in the caves for safe keeping. Maybe they knew it was time for the ending of an era? Maybe they had forgotten how to use this method, or had not been taught it? We shall probably never know. In all respects, it appeared that the ancients had the knowledge of levitation through sound, which has been lost to succeeding generations.

I returned my questioning to the pyramids.

D: *Were all of them built in the same manner?*

P: The construction of the pyramids increased in complexity and the meaning is hard to translate but the evolution was from crude to more refined, concurrently with the attunement of the priests in their religion. There was more accomplished, more possible with the higher attunement of these priests. This was not something the average lay citizen could do. It took many years of study and concentrated effort in order to accomplish this. This was something only a select few could accomplish through years of studying.

D: *Would it be possible for people today to learn how to levitate?*

P: The answer is yes. There are no restraints, physical, mental or emotional, as to who may receive this knowledge. The deciding factor is in the person himself, whether they wish to pursue this and exert the effort necessary to learn this.

D: *What about the strange energy in the pyramids that people say can preserve things?*

P: The energy is simply an energy which is able to focus through the human body. There are those energies which the human body cannot focus, which would be out of tune with the human experience. So these pyramids do not hold this type of energy as the humans who stored the energy in these pyramids were unable to channel this energy into them. Thus these pyramids contain energy which is peculiar to the human experience. The material can be charged by any human who focuses his energies into it, as those who work with crystals know very well. The same principle applies here.

D: *I have read there are curses that kill people who break into the pyramids or violate their burial places. Is this true or is it just people's imagination?*

P: This is not what one would call a curse, in that there are avenging entities at work here. This is not correct. The pyramids are full of human energy, more so than any other object or device currently on Earth. When one enters into these pyramids, they enter into this field of concentrated human energy. They are immersed and bathed in the energy that is part of the personalities of those who charged these stones. The curse, the bad luck you speak of, is merely manifestations of imbalance in these people who cannot deal with this energy. And so cause these tragedies to happen to themselves. One who is trained and aware and open can into these pyramids, and receive from them much knowledge which is stored in the pyramid itself. If one would be open and agreeable, these are very psychic areas. A psychic building, if you would.

D: *What about the pyramids in South America? Were they built in the same manner as those in Egypt?*

P: These pyramids are from the same stock of people who migrated from Atlantis during the time of the destruction. The method used is identical, for this was common knowledge on Atlantis. These temples were used in order to worship. Many, many years transpired from the original Atlantean experience until these pyramids in the east and west were built, and many ideas had evolved in different directions as well.

D: *But it was the same principle though. What about the pyramids in Mexico, were they also built by levitation?*

P: There was a gradual loss of this art, and many civilizations attempted to copy this building technique in more conventional manners. We are searching for this knowledge, which seems to indicate that these were built in the conventional manner of bridgework and physical labor.

D: *Was that because the knowledge was being lost by that time?*

P: It was because this generation had never received the knowledge and wished to copy those structures which they had heard about or seen. There were pyramids on the continent of Atlantis. They, however, are submerged at this time. These pyramids are destined to rise once again, after the cataclysm. The knowledge stored in these pyramids is to be released to the foundation generation, the new awareness of which Earth is now integrating. This knowledge will assist in man's evolution at that time.

D: *What do you mean by the cataclysm?*

P: This is a loose term applied to the many physical changes which are now occurring and shall occur for the next eighteen chronological years on this planet. (This was recorded in 1985.) These are loosely grouped into the term "cataclysm". This is not to be considered one gigantic event.

***

D: *Could you tell me who built the Great Pyramids in Egypt, and why? And how they built them?*

P: This has been given in many previous channelings. This is a monument to the accomplishments or pinnacle of success of the previous civilization to the succeeding generations. A mile marker to their achievement, a symbol of their success. The epitome of their understanding of the nature of reality. The fact that this monument remains a mystery indicates to the successive generations their lack of understanding. At such time as this pinnacle is understood, then the technology of that generation will have achieved a sufficient level of awareness, to be given the succeeding information, of which the pyramid speaks very little of. It is a litmus test for that generation. Such that the higher energies in charge of the dissemination of energies can perceive that the generation current on the planet at that time has reached a sufficient level of understanding, that they be given the remainder of the information available. Until the complete understanding of the pyramid has been reached, it would be premature to allow the dissemination of the information which has been held.

D: *I was interested in how these pyramids were built. Can you see that?*

P: Can you see that? (Laugh) It has been already surmised through levitational means and electro magnetic propulsion of many different sorts, including the use of tones and mental resonance. To further elaborate would be useless, as your level of understanding has not been raised to the point that you could comprehend that which we would give you. Therefore when you through your own attempts at understanding, have pulled yourself up to that level, such that you can understand these higher order realities, then you shall be given a more complete understanding. You must build your foundation before you can build your house.

D: *That makes sense. I've heard it was done by music. Would that be going along with what you said about tones?*

P: Music in the sense of tones, not in the sense of song.

D: *Are these tones becoming more feasible with our synthesizers existing today? They are capable of generating tones we could not generate before.*

P: Not so in the sense of simple sonic or vibrational realities. However conceptual realities, the tone of mental energies. Your mental energy resonating at a single particular tone the concept of a tone being that your mental energy is not random noise, as many now operate on. But that your mental energy could be focused such that it is resonating at a particular tone. Not noise or even harmony. Although many chords of mental energy are possible with the further realization of the concept of mental tones. Such that these mental tones in unison generate a tremendous powerful energy which is capable of literally splitting your Earth in two, were a sufficient number of beings to join in a common effort. It would be as the destruction of Atlantis again.

D: *Would this go along with what we have been told of how the extraterrestrials are able to propel their craft? Through mental concentration.*

P: That is accurate.

D: *It's the same energy?*

P: Not the same energy. The same concept, however, practiced in a different form.

D: *Do the pyramids act only as monuments, or do they fit a useful need in the energy in nature?*

P: They are a psycho reactive element of the energy on your planet. Somewhat of a stimulus to those on your planet, who through their own actions attempt to raise their level of awareness to that level of which the pyramid resonates. It was a stimulus, not simply in conceptual terms, but in reactive terms. The energy on your planet is somewhat amplified by tuning in to and trying to understand the conceptual realities of these pyramids.

D: *Is it true that the pyramids are also a energy transmitter to other planets, or even other galaxies?*

P: That is accurate. The energy streaming on to your planet is focused by this geometric design, far more than the concept of "perfect" can even approach. However, the square, or even cube, of the concept of perfect or perfection, such that the resonance of this perfection reaches beyond three dimensional realities. The most absolute truth that could possibly be attained on your lower realities, stretching beyond simply your three dimensional realities. This truth then is sensed in other areas of your galaxy. The energies streaming to and from your planet are directed or homogenized by this truth. Truth being somewhat like a polarizing filter. These conceptual analogies are inaccurate in the sense that, in your understanding, they have no basis for common denominators. However we are simply trying to allow you to understand in terms that you can perceive, the fact that truth is not simply an abstraction. It is a reality. Truth is far more real than abstract, and can be utilized. The concept of truth, on your terms, is simply abstract. In reality there is a true cause and effect of that which you call "truth". This truth then becomes somewhat like a filter, or perhaps even a reflector. Much as you might reflect perhaps a laser beam. That laser being the coherent light of one particular wave length or spectrum even, reflecting off perhaps a mirror or seismic device on your moon. The analogy here being the reflecting device on your moon would equate to this pyramid. And the concept or conceptual stream of truth, universal truth, reflects off this pyramid. On your planet there is this reflector of higher truths, higher knowledge. Such that those who would turn their gaze toward your planet, can see this reflection of truth. Therefore someone on your planet had at some point been on this higher level of truth, your planet then or thus has a reflector of higher levels of truth. Again, truth being far more than simple abstraction.

D: *I think I got more of an answer than I planned for. (Laugh)*

***

P: The pyramids were used as observation points. For the alignment of the stars could be calculated by the proximity of the apex of the triangle to the nearest marker star or mark star. Certain stars were assigned the status of "mark star", and so by positioning oneself specifically at one point on the pyramid and looking up to the apex and thence outward to the heavens, one could find the mark star, or where the apex was in relation to the mark star.

D: *What did they use this information for?*

P: It was to allow for charting of the heavens as well as to map time. And so be able to tell exactly where one was in the Earth's revolution around the Sun.

***

D: *I'm thinking of the pyramids, and those in Peru, and in Mexico. The monuments that are made of the large stones. Did they have abilities to erect these stones that we don't have today in the 20th century?*

Clara: No. You have it. You don't use it.

D: *(Chuckle) I've been told that. It's the powers of the mind that we no longer utilize then.*

C: That is correct.

D: *How were they able to erect these large stone monuments?*

C: Let me ask you a question. Is that stone native to that place?

D: *I think in some cases it is, but in other cases, they said it had to be transported a long distance.*

C: On many stars and on many planets we simply create something into being just by energy. And simply, the stones are created. It can be created from the area. But if we have the ability to create telepathically, or to just simply materialize by pure energy, we can transport it from any place to any place. But the great pyramids were created mostly from that which was native for that particular area. So it could confuse a lot of people, as it has over the centuries. It simply came into being by using the mind, that which we do not use today. Simply by creating, cutting that stone in the manner in which you want it, cut to fit the pattern according to the architectural structure that was chosen for for that particular pyramid.

D: *I've seen some where the stones fit together absolutely perfectly, with no type of mortar or cement. And they are even curved so they will all fit together.*

C: Yes. It is done telepathically, simply by using thought. Thought is the creation of everything. First becomes a thought. And in the thought of those that were creating the structure they unified that thought in such a way that every corner would fit perfectly. Because every thought fit perfectly with every other thought. And so when every thought meshes and molds itself one to the other, it becomes the other, so that it fits perfectly in a pattern or a design which one chooses it to be.

D: *Some people think it might have been done with machinery like laser beams.*

C: Thought is the fastest laser known. Each block is a thought. So a thought can be the foundation. One block at a time is one thought at a time. And all the thoughts together, and you might say a telepathic stone is a thought. And so, every thought being a telepathic stone, or a physical stone because thought can become physical and each one is then placed one on top of the other. One beside each other. However the pattern fits to create.

D: *How were they transported or placed on top of each other?*

C: By thought. So my thought is to create this stone. I might say, "I will bring this stone from here and place it here." It was a collective construction of many people with their thoughts. So my thought is, that I have this stone to put here, and this one here. The thought becomes a reality. A living being. A stone is a being. It's just a different mass of energy. As you see it, it's a mass that doesn't move. But it is all space. I mean, it's all space, and it's all energy. So therefore, this collective group, with one mind and one unity and one goal and one construct to create, brings these thoughts together. And creates a physical construct.

D: *Then the group mind was more powerful than the individual.*

C: Much more. It always is, when there is one thought, or one goal, that wants to be achieved.

D: *I've always thought it might have been achieved by levitation.*

C: You could call that levitation. By your thoughts levitating, or saying, "Okay, I go over here and my thought chisels out this stone. So I will create it. I will bring this over." It is a good analogy. You could say, in your linear way of thinking, that it in fact could be levitation.

D: *I was also told it could be levitated through sound.*

C: That is a possibility. Thought is much faster than sound. Thought is faster than light.

D: *Do you think people used sound at a later time because they forgot how to use the minds.*

C: Yes, yes. People became so involved in their personalities, and their day to day living and goings in and goings out, that they began to pull away from the collective. Pull away from the source. Pull away from that which is. To become separate from All That Is, and to become individualized. And so as an individual person or being, they chose separation from source. And with the separation from source, then they began to forget to use the thought. And so then they began to find other ways.

D: *So it was possible at later times they did use sound.*

C: Oh, yes.

D: *Were the original group, that used group thought to build the pyramids, human beings?*

C: Oh, yes. Highly evolved human beings.

D: *Were these the ones you said were the survivors of Atlantis?*

C: Brought back to Earth from the stars.

D: *And they just lived in these centralized areas, Egypt and Peru and Mexico?*

C: Yes, to begin with. And then humans wandered off to discover new universes, to discover new planets, to discover new lands. And so, as they wandered over the land, they created more communities. And generally it was more than one person that would go, because they wanted companionship, or they wanted protection from the wilds or from the dangers that might be out there in the unknown lands over the hills or the waters.

D: *And at first they carried this knowledge with them. (Yes) But they, more or less, needed the group mind to create these big monuments. (Yes) Can you tell me the purpose of the great pyramid?*

C: It is a storehouse for knowledge, of all that the Earth is. The mystery of the Earth, and the creation of the Earth is in the great pyramid.

D: *It is trying to turn it into a storehouse that would be similar to the one of the three spires?*

C: It is a similar storehouse. Not going to be turned into.

D: *Many people think the measurements and the orientation of the way it sits could provide solutions to the mystery.*

C: That is true, but there is more. Man has lost the capacity to use his mind to the fullest. He uses only a small portion of that which is available to him. He needs to open up and accept that there are no limitations, and without limitations you can go beyond time and space. And you can know the mystery of all there is to know. You will be given more information at a future time, because the energy of the pyramids are being reactivated, and new changes will be taking place in that area.

D: *How can people tap into the knowledge that is contained in the pyramids?*

C: Man is not ready for that at this time. He's not open enough. He's going in a direction that it is a tomb. He is not willing to accept that it really carries the mystery of the creation of the universe, and all the knowledge of what the universe is. The Earth and the universe, and of the stars.

***

Brenda: The culture of the people of the pyramids was linked to Atlantis. And the stone structures they built were part of some of their sciences. And when Atlantis was destroyed these stone structures could no longer function the way they were designed to, because the central part of them had been destroyed with Atlantis.

D: *How were they intended to function?*

B: The nearest concept I can find is computer. They interacted with each other so one could use them for calculating celestial things. But also one could use them for manipulating cosmic and Earth energies such as gravitation and such, for various reasons. They were complex devices, they could be used for many things. But most of the concepts cannot be translated into this language, because they are things that your civilization had not conceived of doing.

D: *I've been told that the secret was within the pyramids themselves. The numbers and the calculations.*

B: Yes, they are. The pyramids were precisely designed, particularly the three major ones from Egypt. The way they are positioned and the way they were designed, the dimensions and every measurement there could possibly be, applied like for example, distance from apex to apex and what have you. Anything and everything you could dream of, within it contains all of the mathematical formulae that civilization had. And that includes many mathematical formulae your civilization has not thought of yet. There will be a few that will be discovered in the pyramids, that may take a while for you to understand and be able to apply. They'll find uses for it and you'll just think it's something wonderful. The pyramids are like a condensed container of all of the scientific knowledge of this civilization.

D: *Do you know what the power source was that ran these? You said it couldn't function after the sinking of Atlantis.*

B: The power source was the Earth itself. But the reason why they couldn't function is because they were no longer balanced to where they could make use of the Earth flow.

D: *We have been told they were burial tombs for Egyptians kings.*

B: When the civilizations lost the knowledge and did not know what these were, that's what they conceived they had to be. And so that was the story passed down through the centuries.

Pictures and hieroglyphics have been found that apparently show the building of the pyramids and slaves dragging rocks up dirt ramps to place them into position. Maybe the pyramids were already there and old at the time these pictures were drawn, and these were the version of the people, of how they thought they must have been built. Maybe they were as much a mystery in their time as ours.

D: *There were never any bodies found in there.*

B: There were never any kings buried in there.

D: *Then what were the rooms inside used for?*

B: They were used for much more complex purposes than burial chambers. Some of them were used for doing some of the energy manipulation. But most of the rooms were for the purpose of containing more calculations and mathematical formulae in their measurements, and their relationship to the measurements of the pyramid.

D: *Do you see how they were built with these huge stones?*

B: Partially through manipulation of the Earth forces and partially through the process that you have been told of of changing stone to liquid.

D: *The same methods they used on Atlantis then. (Yes) Someone told me they thought they might have used music in some way.*

B: One of the ways they had of manipulating the energies was the controlled use of sound.

***

Some subjects accidentally tapped into knowledge about the Pyramids when they regressed to a lifetime there.

I had a session with Steve in August, 2000, in New Orleans. He had a strange experience while visiting the Great Pyramid in Egypt a few months before. This was one of the things he wanted to explore while in trance.

He had never intended to go to Egypt and had no desire to see the pyramids. But when he and his wife went to Switzerland to visit relatives, they had a surprise for them. They had already arranged to take Steve and his wife to Egypt to the pyramids. He really did not want to go, but felt they had no choice. Surprisingly, Steve had a *tremendous* experience while they were there.

He became separated from his wife and relatives while their guide was buying the tickets. The Egyptians were being very selective, and were especially trying to keep foreigners out. They were only allowing 300 people a day to go into the pyramids. So their guide stood in line and bought the tickets for them. Then Steve was searching for the rest of his group among the crowd of tourists on the Giza Plateau, so they could go inside. There were hundreds of people, and many buses. Lots of activity.

As he walked across the plateau toward the pyramid a strange thing happened. Suddenly it was as though he stepped into some sort of time warp. As he stood there looking around, he was the only one on the plateau. He could not hear anything, no sound. And all the people and the buses had totally disappeared. He still felt the same, no different, but as he looked around he was totally alone. And a tremendous feeling came over him as he looked at the pyramids. He had a sudden surge of emotion, and it came to him in a rush that he had come "home". That this was "home", and it was a wonderful experience. He said it engulfed him completely as he looked at the structure.

Then just as quickly everything returned to normal as he continued to walk towards the pyramids. There was a sudden roar of noise as the sound came back. The activity and all the people and the buses and everything swirled around him as he was jolted back into the present. When his wife located him among the crowd she was startled to see he was crying emotionally. They proceeded to go into the pyramid, which was a wonderful experience for him. But he couldn't comprehend what happened in that fraction of a second. Time had seemed to stand still, and everything changed, and then switched back again.

After Steve was put into a deep trance we went through a normal regression, and I was speaking to his subconscious to find the answer to questions he requested.

D: *When Steve went to Egypt and saw the Pyramids he had a strange experience. He'd like to understand what happened at that time?*

S: It was a gift. He was where his spirit was the happiest. Lots of joy.

D: *When he was on that same ground again? (Yes) What happened? He said it was a strange experience.*

S: His soul was so joyful. It wanted to express that. Therefore it was a gift to him.

D: *He said it was as though everything else disappeared.*

S: Yes, it did.

D: *Did he actually go into another time during those few minutes?*

S: Partly. Consciously, no.

D: *Because the other people were not present.*

S: No, they weren't. It was to give him the strength to continue.

D: *Why was his spirit the most joyful around the pyramids?*

S: It goes back to another lifetime. He was involved in the building of the pyramid. He was one of the main people to help construct it.

D: *How did he help with the construction?*

S: The engineering of the placement of the blocks.

D: *How was it done?*

S: Different ways. He was just in charge of one way. The way to choose each stone for each placement. It was a very complicated science.

D: *It had to fit together perfectly, didn't it? (Yes) Was it done with tools?*

S: Some tools. Some mental powers.

D: *How was it done with mental powers?*

S: The brain waves tune in with the vibrations of the stone.

D: *As to synchronize?*

S: Yes, through sound and mental thoughts.

D: *Did he do it alone, or was it done with other people?*

S: It was done with highly evolved people. They performed their techniques, and we executed the construction.

D: *Were these people that lived there at that place?*

S: Yes, they lived there. They immigrated there.

D: *You said it was done with sound also?*

S: Yes. It is a high frequency type sound that could tune into the molecular construction of the blocks, and cut it the way they wanted to cut it.

D: *Was the sound created by something?*

S: Sometimes, yes.

I was thinking of a musical instrument.

S: It's like a tuning fork. It has to be done with the mind as well. Without the mind you have nothing.

D: *Can you see what the instrument looks like that they created the tone with?*

S: It was long, shiny like metal. It had many prongs on it. (As though observing.) And they touched the stone with it.

D: *Was it big?*

S: No, it was small, but elongated.

D: *What happened when they touched the stone with it?*

S: Sometimes it would levitate. Sometimes it would fracture. It was very powerful.

D: *And it created this tone when it touched the stone?*

S: Yes. Sometimes you could hardly hear it. It was like a spark almost.

D: *But the other people had to use their minds with it whenever the individual touched the stone with the instrument?*

S: Yes, that's right.

D: *Could they amplify the power that way? (Yes) You said these highly evolved people migrated there. Where did they migrate from?*

S: We're not sure.

D: *So they knew how to show the others how to do it.*

S: Yes. But you had to be able to control your thoughts. Only certain ones could do it, or it would be very dangerous.

D: *Why would it be dangerous?*

S: It could kill you. The frequency would affect you molecularly. You had to mentally block it to protect yourself from it.

D: *You had to direct it outward? (Yes) So if you didn't have the right thoughts it could more or less ricochet or bounce back?*

S: Essentially, yes.

D: *So only pure minded or the right minded people could direct this energy.*

S: Yes, only the right minded.

D: *So everybody involved in the directing of the mind energy had to have more or less a pure mind?*

S: Yes, very few people could do it.

D: *If there were many workers, could they use the mass consciousness of their minds? (No) It had to be those that knew how to direct the energy. (Yes) And the instrument helped direct it into the stone?*

S: Yes, through mental energy.

D: *And you said they brought that instrument with them when they migrated.*

S: Yes, they did.

D: *But this was the reason Steve felt such emotion when he returned to that place.*

S: Yes. It was given to him as a gift to give him strength. To empower him to continue. He was capable of very important and powerful things in the past. And he can use that same ability, because the mind is powerful. He can do anything he wants to do with his life, but he must learn discipline.

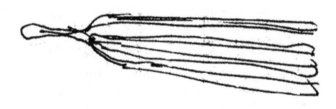

The instrument Steve saw was approximately one foot long. It was made of a metal that was shiny like a mirror. The prongs were thin and there was a crystal in the handle.

***

In 2000 a woman client regressed to a lifetime where she was some kind of male director in Egypt. She was standing in the desert on the edge of a large city watching the construction of a large edifice nearby. He was dressed in clothes that were not the type worn outside, they were too luxurious. He had golden thongs on his sandals, and a heavy golden collar with an insignia (the rays of the Sun) around his neck.

It was heavy, but he was used to wearing it in spite of its weight. He had a golden helmet type headdress with feathers (similar to peacock) coming out of the top of it. It was all heavy and uncomfortable in the hot Sun.

He was lamenting about the slow progress of the building. He said everyone was tired, so tired, of the constant building. It was all for the ego of the ruler, and it was unceasing. He said the building was in the shape of a pyramid, and the alignment was not quite right, and it was going so slowly. He said the ruler was already building two other pyramids, one was complete and the other was almost complete, yet they had started on this third one. He thought they should complete the others before beginning this one. The people were tired of the constant construction.

I asked how they were being constructed. He said the base was underground with certain chambers and passageways that had to be perfectly plotted out. This part was done by physical labor because "they" could not have contact with the Earth. Of course, I wanted to know who "they" were. He said they were the beings in the disk, who were directing the whole operation. After the base had been built then the rest of the building (above ground) was constructed with energy directed by the disk. The workers all formed an unbroken circle around the building. Then the energy was directed from the disk to him and others, then to the workers. This created an energy circle that was sufficient to raise huge blocks of stone into place. It was important that the workers have purity in their bodies (no drinking etc.) so the energy could be directed through their bodies. Afterwards they would have no knowledge of what transpired. They were just used as conduits, so to speak.

The only problem was that sometimes the disk would descend too low. It normally hovered over where the apex of the pyramid would eventually be. This was the position that the energy was directed from. But if it descended too low it would knock some of the workers to the ground, and throw them out of the circle. He didn't know if it harmed them or not, but their place had to be immediately replaced, as the circle had to remain unbroken. The description of the disk sounded very much like present day sightings: shiny gray metal with a smaller circle within the larger one. The energy came from the smaller circle. I asked what the occupants looked like. He said he could not see their faces because they wore an unusual type of headdress. It was designed to prevent the humans from reading their minds and knowing their intent. The metal headdress was thicker at the upper back of the head, because he said that was where the thoughts emanated from. His headdress was supposed to be a copy of theirs, although it did not serve the same purpose.

Although he blamed the constant construction on the ego of the ruler, he thought it was really the agenda of the beings in the disk. There was to be a series of seven pyramids altogether, and they would be built in a certain pattern. The construction had been going on for as long as he could remember, at least 50 years. He lamented that the people were tired of it, and thought it was too much.

The final purpose of the pyramids was to direct energy into space, thus the coordinates had to be perfect, and the disk directed the precise placement of the stones. The construction became easier as it reached the top or apex, because it was smaller and didn't require as many stones. After the construction was completed the ordinary workers were allowed to work on filling in some of the cracks and spaces between the stones, but even this had to be done precisely. He thought they should finish one completely before starting work on another. The ordinary buildings in the city were constructed differently and were crude by comparison. The labor did not have to be done with such intense preciseness. The directing of the energy to raise the stones was too intense on everyone involved. Yet there didn't seem to be any intention of defying those on the disk.

The ruler was an unusually shaped man, very tall and thin. He had to be old, yet he showed no signs of age. The man said he knew he would be dead before the seven pyramids were completed, but the work would be carried on by others. He emphasized that the ones in the disk could not have contact with the earth, therefore the laborers had to do that physical construction. They had to stand in an unbroken circle around the construction site in order to direct the "Earth" energy, which apparently was "collected" and redirected by the disk. This was the power that accomplished the raising of the stones. It was directed through the workers, using their bodies as "amplifiers". They would have no memory of it afterwards. That was not important, they were just used. He knew what was going on, but was also being used to direct the energy. He said mathematicians, astrologers and other wise men were used in the alignment. It had to be exact, so the eventual direction of energy (when completed) would be directed to the proper points in outer space. He was one of the few who knew the purpose of the constant construction, but he did not know how it was used in the final outcome. The beings in the disk only had contact with the ruler.

When I tried to take the story forward to a conclusion the woman jumped into another lifetime, and since I was doing the session for therapy I followed that line without returning to the story. It had all the indications that it was occurring in Egypt, but could have been Atlantis.

It is hard to say which pyramids are referred to, since there apparently were many pyramids during that time. Some of them may not have survived to our time. In another session a man was present during the construction of a large pyramid, and was involved in the calculating of the measurements. He indicated that it would be used as a communication device between Earth and Sirius.

***

Another session in 2000 took a strange twist, and although it does not deal with the construction of the pyramids, it appears to deal with the origin of another mystery associated with Egypt.

After I had gone through a past life regression with Marie I contacted her subconscious to ask questions. She had made a list of things she wanted to know about. She had had a vision or a scene of something that occurred in Egypt. At least she assumed it was Egypt. She saw herself in a room with some kind of strange device.

D: *Can you tell her anything about what that was? Was it real or was it just imagination?*

M: It was real. What she saw was only a fragment of a bigger machine. And we say "machine", but not like we know machines. It was a contained energy source.

D: *What was she doing with it?*

M: She was like a lab assistant really. Just the person who knew how to regulate how much of this energy could go back into a human lifeform to regenerate it. It actually brought life back to dead bodies. And it was experimental.

D: *Were these experiments being done on Earth?*

M: They were done on Earth, but not by Earth beings. The ones who knew how to do this were experimenting on this mass of people. I don't know how they died.

D: *Do you know what country this was, or does it have a name?*

M: The word Targa comes.

D: *Marie had the feeling it was Egypt. But you don't think so?*

M: Maybe Targa was the group. It was in the heat of the desert. It was a civilization that was like Egypt, but it was not Egypt.

D: *You said many people died some way?*

M: They are all charred bodies. And they look like mummies. They are like the kind you see mummified for a long time.

D: *Dried up, you mean? (Yes) But why would they want to revitalize, regenerate those kind of bodies?*

M: Because there were so few living bodies at this time. Something had happened. And they needed to find a way to bring back enough of a lifeforce on the planet. To have enough of the bodies alive and active.

D: *But could something like that work?*

M: It worked.

D: *They could reactivate them?*

M: Yes. But there was a gestation period, once you rebandaged them, like gave them a cocoon. You take this core material, that's what it became. It's just dried up genetic material with the bones.

D: *It would have been dead for quite a while, I guess.*

M: Right. But no body fluids. And you rewrap them, and give them a housing to reconstitute.

D: *They had to be covered.*

M: Totally wrapped. And then you plug in this hose that's connected to this energy source at the base, on the feet. And you pump it. It's got a pump sound (she made thumping noises) like a big heart sound. And pump until you see the swelling in the bandages. And then you let these packages, these packaged bodies, stay there until you need them.

D: *So it's something like suspended animation? (Right) But were they able to walk and move around when you needed them?*

M: I don't know after that. I can only see that my job there was to wrap them, to reenergize them, and house them.

D: *How were they housed?*

M: On shelves.

D: *(I found that strange.) On shelves? (Yes) But I have the impression that unless a soul, a spirit enters the body it isn't really alive. What do you think?*

M: No, there's a lifeforce that activates the body system. It doesn't have anything to do with the soul.

D: *It is more or less like a mechanical or robotic being then?*

M: You get the system going, but the activation of the intelligence and the consciousness comes later.

D: *So these people had the ability to do these things, but you were just a helper in it.*

M: Like a technician.

D: *Let me ask your subconscious a question that really is intriguing me. Could this be where the idea of mummies came from later in Egypt? Do you have access to that information?*

M: Oh, yes, that's right. But the Egyptians didn't know. It's almost like they got it a little backwards. They didn't have the equipment. The had the residual foreknowledge of the wrapping, and life returning and carrying on and continuing. They didn't know really how to reconstitute. And that's what we did.

D: *So this equipment was not available to the people that came later?*

M: Right. They had knowledge of soul travel and the afterlife, and stars in transition. But they didn't know how to really bring the physical body back.

D: *But they remembered from the times when you were there, that it could be done?*

M: They knew that somewhere, somehow, it was possible, because some of their early teachers were with us. And they knew, but they lost technology. They had other technology. They didn't have this that could bring life back.

D: *So they were attempting to bring the person back to life. And they thought this was the way it was done.*

M: I think they remembered unwrapping the bodies that we would bring back to life when needed. They knew about that. And so they assumed that wrapping the bodies would preserve the life. But then they knew something was missing.

D: *Something they didn't have. An ingredient, a piece of knowledge. But where did this technology and knowledge come from originally?*

M: People not of the Earth. I was a worker for them, but I wasn't one of them. They were very, very efficient and smart. And big.

D: *Big people? (Yes) Do you have the knowledge of what happened to kill all these people?*

M: No, I don't. I'm in this room doing the work.

D: *But they had to bring these people back because there weren't enough left. It must have killed many people.*

M: Yes, large numbers.

D: *And this was one way of getting people back quickly?*

M: Or saving the race.

D: *They couldn't just create more, or start over?*

M: Apparently not. This was very important, because it was a lot of work, and took a lot of time. But it was very spiritual work too.

D: *It wasn't just to create workers. It wasn't that kind of motive.*

M: No, no, no, no. It was so much about the love for these beings and the race.

This must have been a memory of a very ancient time, because it predated the Egyptians. Something catastrophic must have happened that killed (burned) many people. There was not as large a population on Earth as there was later. Apparently it would have taken too long to wait for the race to repopulate itself. Maybe this was a stop gap procedure. A way of preserving the people and reactivating them when necessary. She said it was the dried genetic material that was wrapped and preserved. We do know that even one cell contains all the genetic information to reproduce an identical human being. So the wrapped remains of bodies were stored until they could be reactivated. I wish we could have gotten more complete information about the procedure, but she was only a worker carrying out instructions, and could only report what she knew. It would be a logical conclusion that when this information was passed down as a racial memory the descendants knew that somehow the wrapping and preserving of bodies was the key to returning to life. They probably had memories or legends passed down to them that these wrapped bundles were brought back to life or reactivated after a long period of time. As it happens so often down through history, they had partial knowledge but not enough to repeat what these ancient beings could do. Later the reasons for wrapping and preserving the bodies were probably lost, and it just deteriorated into a ritual associated with life after death.

***

I was receiving more information on the mysteries of the Pyramid and the Sphinx when this book was going to the printers. Rather than delay the publication I decided that this new material would be put into Book Two of *The Convoluted Universe*. This confirmed to me that my journey into the unknown is still continuing. I have much more to explore.

CHAPTER EIGHT
UNEXPLAINED MYSTERIES

The following explanations of the various mysteries of Earth came from various subjects over a period of several years. Some may seem contradictory. I am including them here to cause the reader to think. I will allow the readers to make up their own minds. There may be elements of truth in all of the explanations, even though they may not be the total truth. It all depends on the interpretation of the vehicle and their understanding of the information received.

NAZCA LINES IN PERU

D: *Do you know of the Nazca lines in Peru?*

Phil: That is correct. What would you wish to know?

D *There is a mystery about where they came from and the purpose behind them.*

P: They are designs painted by an artist as he was looking down on this planet. He desired to embellish this planet at that place or point, with his artistic abilities. It was a manipulation by telepathic means from a distance. From a hover craft, not to be confused with an extraterrestrial spaceship, for this was a craft of Earth origin operated by anti gravity means. This artist simply levitated himself to a vantage point high above the plains, and from there used his telepathic efforts to draw these lines. These are simply "doodles".

D: *There are other things besides lines, aren't there? In the plains there are also drawings.*

P: Yes, this is what we were referring to, the spider, the monkey and so forth. These are simply artistic endeavors and have no special significance, other than they were one man's work.

D: *He was just more or less playing?*

P: Yes, that is correct.

D: *One author thought the lines were ancient astronaut airfields.*

P: Humph! We find this amusing, for we see this artist with black beard and white robe in his chariot of sorts. We see him clearly now, hovering above the lines, thinking, pausing, deciding his next move. It was as important as if he had spelled "7 Up".

D: *(Laugh) They thought this was where the ancient astronauts' craft landed and took off.*

P: This would not be accurate. Extraterrestrial craft have no need for lines of that dimension with which to guide them. For their eyesight is quite good and they could land on a dime were it placed on the desert floor.

D: *Do you think extraterrestrial craft have been there out of curiosity?*

P: To observe the lines? Perhaps this is true.

D: *There has been much importance attached to these symbols.*

P: Yes, for there is much misunderstanding. So naturally that which is misunderstood is either feared, or if it is also much larger than man, it is much revered.

D: *Do you have any idea how long ago the drawings were done?*

P: Would you wish a delineation in chronological years?

D: *Yes, if you can.*

P: Twelve thousand, five hundred years. (12,500)

D: *Whew! That was a long time ago.*

P: Not really.

D: *Well, it is to us. Then it was done by a person living at that time period.*

P: That is correct. A human, an Earth being. He was not extraterrestrial.

D: *It must have been a very advanced civilization if they had hover craft.*

P: That is, in relative terms to what you speak today, correct. It would be advanced in that respect. However, the medicines and technology you have today would elevate you to the status of God in their time.

D: *Oh, then we have things they were not aware of.*

P: That is correct.

D: *Well, it seems like such a long time, and the lines have not shown any sign of deterioration or....*

P: They are constructed of rock, which is most difficult to blow by the winds. These are rocks which are placed in such a way as to form this outline. There is not much rain on those plains.

D: *Haven't there been Earth catastrophes since that time?*

P: Certainly, but none which would erase it, or else these would have been erased.

D: *I thought if there had been an Earth catastrophes, the ocean would have risen over this part and deluged it with water.*

P: That has not happened.

D: *Did this man with the hover craft have any connection with Atlantis?*

P: The knowledge which enabled the craft to hover was of the same knowledge used in Atlantis. And the man himself was of the lineage of Atlantis. That is about the extent of it however. There have been other continents as well, as you are quite aware of, Lemuria or Mu.

D: *Were these continents in existence before this time period when this man lived?*

P: Concurrent with. This man was not alone, for there was a civilization there at that time.

D: *Where the Nazca lines are now located?*

P: Not in the exact place, but down the coast, so to say.

D: *There are also marks on the side of a cliff not too far from there on the coast.*

P: More doodles, for he was quite inventive. There were other lines which were drawn, but which have been lost to the elements. These however, have remained due to their position and relative shelter from the elements. There were many artists who constructed great sweeping designs of magnificent structures by this very method. However, these have been lost to time due to the elements.

***

D: Do you know where the Nazca Lines in Peru came from?

Brenda: They're very old now. And they are not as clear as they once were. A set of visitors from one of the civilizations that wanted to help us, wanted to observe mankind, but they needed a place to land their larger ships and just use smaller ships for traveling on the Earth's surface. They picked an area that was abandoned to use as their center of operation. And so they used energy beams to cut these lines into the earth to serve as direction pointers, so they would know where to land without giving themselves away by using any sort of energy devices. They would come in with all energy systems shut down and land by visual means, so they could keep their presence a secret. And hence, the long lines that go from one mountain top to another, for miles on end. They did that with an energy beam while they were flying past the first time very swiftly. They had to do it very quickly, in order to not be discovered by others. The figures of the animals and such were done by the different pilots in their spare time when they were not on duty. They would use energy devices that had low outputs so they would not be detected by the other group on Easter Island. They observed different artforms of the various peoples. Instead of drawing them with a hand held instrument on a writing surface, just for fun and to keep their flying skills in shape, they did it with energy devices attached to their personal flyers.

D: *Oh, just like playing, you mean?*

B: Yes. Their flying there was very basic, nothing to keep their skills sharpened. They were all extremely skillful pilots, and they wanted to keep their skills honed. It's like a musician needing to practice every day. So they were just doing that. And also, to relieve some of the boredom.

D: *Then these figures, the spider and the monkey etc., had no real significance. (No) There are some scientists who have spent their whole lives trying to decipher these.*

B: That was considered a very amusing point among the pilots. They were saying, "Some day these peoples' scientists are finally going to come here and discover these. And they're going to wonder what on Earth went on here."

D: *(Laugh) I was wondering why they were able to survive so long, with all the Earth changes that took place.*

B: Since they were cut with energy beams, it affected the place where it was cut in such a way so it was of a more permanent nature than it would have been otherwise.

D: *There is one design on the coast that looks like a pitchfork.*

B: That was one of the things they used as a directional beacon type thing to help them come in visually. By the time they got low enough in the Earth's atmosphere to be detected, they had to turn off their energy devices and they'd circle around the Earth a couple of times getting lower in the atmosphere. When they got low enough to see land, they were usually approaching the coast. And that figure carved on that cliff would point them in the right direction. They would fly in that direction and then over these long lines that went from mountain top to mountain top, and they knew they were heading in the right direction.

D: *Then it was a place they could land and be concealed. Is that what you mean?*

B: Yes. When they landed it was in the middle of an abandoned plateau. And there were no human beings and nobody else there. So they did not have to worry about being discovered, because of the location. So they knew they would be safe. And they could keep the ships ready to take off at any time, rather than having to disguise them.

D: *Were there any people on Earth at that time?*

B: Oh, yes! Oh, yes! There were quite a few people on Earth at that time. And there were several civilizations developing. That's why they were observing. Because the civilizations were looking very promising and they knew mankind had a curiosity and the intelligence to develop into a viable technological civilization very quickly. So they were making observational progress reports.

***

D: *Another Earth mystery we're curious about is the Nazca lines in Peru. Do you know what I'm speaking of?*

John: Yes. He's taking me there now. (In the Library) He says these drawings were only observed from planetary vehicles. This was a sacred area to the Lemurians as well. This was part of the continent of Lemuria. And these were landing sites where extraterrestrials came and helped the technology of the people of the time.

D: *I didn't think they were that old.*

J: Some were made by the descendants of the Lemurians so they would attract the extraterrestrial visitors again.

D: *Then whenever the original extraterrestrials landed there weren't any drawings at that time?*

J: There's a long history of them coming and going, and coming and going, and coming and going. And this art was passed on early. Extraterrestrials helped in making these lines. This is why they're more exact looking from the air than from the ground.

D: *What was the purpose of making these?*

J: The extraterrestrials that came to this area, came as visitors, like going on vacation. You know, "Let's see a primitive world." Rather like the way Americans would travel to New Guinea or the Australian outback to be with the aborigines. These extraterrestrials would come to Earth to observe people people and the atmosphere of that time and place. And there have been many landings even into the present time at this place. This is a part of the globe where the extraterrestrials are welcomed.

D: *Do they have any meaning?*

J: They represent different animal figures, and even one that represents humans. It was the primitive people's mentality, letting the extraterrestrials know that these were their people and animals that welcomed them. It was partly done by the local people, and partly the descendants of Lemuria. This has been a very special space age place for these space vehicles to land over thousands and thousands and thousands and thousands of years. They landed when it was part of Lemuria and now as it is part of the South American continent. They've been landing and they're still landing in this area.

D: *Can he show you how the animal designs were made? What method was used?*

J: There was an extraterrestrial that used a beam of energy coming from a space ship. And this was directed over the land. And that's how it was done.

D: *The straight lines, or the designs also?*

J: Also the designs. But it's done from up above in the air. There is an energy beam that came down. And then there was a group of people and extraterrestrials that would follow the course of it. The line would burn into the Earth and they would scrape it away. After it had passed over a certain segment it pulverized the earth and they were able to move it some way.

D: *It has been a mystery for years with people trying to figure out what they're supposed to symbolize, because they know they can only be seen from the air. Right near there on the coast, there is one on the side of the hill that they call the pitchfork. Does that come from the same time period?*

J: Yes. It's to welcome these extraterrestrial visitors. It's just like the Hawaii Islands offer people leis when they come to visit. These people offered these designs to welcome the visitors from other planets, because they were known as healers and helpful to the local man. They also brought with also brought with them grains like corn and things of this type. These originally were hybridized by these extraterrestrials to help feed these people. They were like a peace corps mission.

D: *Does this mean that corn and things like that did not originate on Earth?*

J: It's been hybridized to fit Earth, yes.

D: *Do you know of any plants or food that did not originate on Earth but were brought here originally?*

J: He's switching the file, so to speak. Certain of our crops were hybridized by these extraterrestrials. He says sugar cane, cotton, the potato, were all hybrid. They were Earth plants, but they were chemically or in some way helped by the extraterrestrials. Especially the extraterrestrials helped the natives in developing the potato plant and the corn. That was very important. Other extraterrestrials worked with cotton in India and that part of the world. They took an existing plant and helped transform it.

When I visited Peru to see Maccu Picchu I was told by a shaman that corn and potatoes are very important crops in Peru. They have hundreds of different varieties.

D: *I've always been curious about bananas, whether that might have been one. It doesn't grow from a seed, but from a root of the plant.*

J: No. Bananas existed in the time of Lemuria. They were one of the popular fruits. Many plants and animals were hybrid by these extraterrestrials from original Earth material.

***

D: *I was curious about the Nazca Lines. Can you tell me anything about those designs?*

Clara: (Long pause, yet her facial expressions indicated something was occurring.) I just needed to go up and look at them again. The original purpose for these were like the ley lines. There was this vast community. And these were particular lines that beings from other planets used to come to be guided down. To land. At different places on the designs were different communities, were different places, like ports, where they would come and put down.

D: *Then there were people living on that plain?*

C: Yes. In different places. In spots, a little ways from the plain. But it would be a port where they could go, and they would set down. And these were like guidelines to know where these different villages, and different places were where the people lived. The different communities. And some of these communities have not been uncovered, as Macchu Picchu has been. Some will never be found, and some will. But there are some civilizations, from millenniums ago, that have not been found.

D: *If the designs survived, why wouldn't the ruins of the communities survive?*

C: That's because they were not upon that plain. It was kind of a disguise, where these villages were. It was an aerial port, you might call it, where they could come in and space down. And then the big ships could come down, and smaller ships would come out. They could go to the villages in the smaller ships, from the big one.

D: *I'm thinking of the spider and the monkey the villages were not located right there.*

C: Not on the spider or at the monkey, but some places off from that. It was a disguise for the ships to be able to find a certain place on the monkey. And from that particular place they could go and find the village. And from another place on the monkey would be another village. Another civilization.

D: *I see. Rather like a navigation device.*

C: Exactly. Thank you. Yes.

D: *They think ancient tribes made these, and they don't know why. Because they can't be seen from the Earth.*

C: That is correct. They cannot be seen unless you're up in the air. So who... (pause) I'm being shut down on saying any more about that. Only that there are other villages that have never been uncovered, never investigated.

D: *Then it wasn't the original natives that lived there, who would have been very uneducated. They didn't build these things.*

C: No, they did not. It was from a higher, more intelligent source than the natives that lived around there. But they interacted with this intelligence.

D: *Then I'm assuming this would have been very long ago.*

C: Yes. Much older than the Incas. Much further, before the Incas came. This was for interaction with the villagers, because they had a communication, but the villagers did not have the intelligence as the beings from the spacecraft. But they had interaction between some of the villages. It was a common thing to see the comings and goings of the spacecraft. It was a pivotal place on the planet for interplanetary connection. As they viewed the planet Earth it was like a big landing space. A place where they could come and have protection from being detected. Their interaction of going and coming. And they still do, even today.

D: *They still come to that place?*

C: Yes, they do.

D: *Why would they come now? The villages are no longer there.*

C: That is because it has been a pattern of theirs. And they still cannot be as detected coming in and out of there, as they would in some other parts of the planet. Because of the particular geographical location in the Peruvian mountains.

D: *Then I'm assuming that these designs were probably made by the aliens. (Yes) Because the natives probably wouldn't have possessed the abilities to do that.*

C: No, they did not.

These various versions of the origin of the Nazca Lines may seem somewhat contradictory. But I think they may be simply versions of different time periods spanning thousands of years when there was activity in the area by both extraterrestrials and later civilizations.

Maybe each had something to do with the creation of the various designs.

***

FLOOD LEGENDS

D: *They say every country in the world has a flood legend.*

Phil: Much of the information has come through unchanged and is quite accurate. However, not all. The flood legend is indeed more than mere legend, but was based on realities. This was caused by the upheaval of the lands. The sinking of Atlantis would appear to be a flood if viewed from the perspective of being on the land itself.

D: *I wondered if it were related to Atlantis. Did it happen at the same time?*

P: This is an explanation of how this came to be. For in some ways this flooding was merely the lowering or sinking of the lands in some of these legends. There was however, a true global problem caused by melting of the polar icecaps due to polar changes or shifts. With the polar shifts, each pole naturally would be shifted, and so there would be the change from one pole to the other. The occurrence has happened more than once.

D: *Did this happen at the same time as the sinking of Atlantis?*

P: Yes, that is accurate. It did happen, it was concurrent with. As this was simply one of many physical manifestations of this cause.

D: *It has also been said that something drastic must have happened, as dinosaurs have been found with food still in their mouths.*

P: That is accurate. The change was so rapid as to cause a tilting of the Earth in, not quite an instant, but in a very rapid rate. Such that the atmosphere was shifted, and those winds and air masses remained somewhat stationary while the Earth tilted beneath them. And so those cooler Arctic winds and air masses which were previously over the poles, would very quickly be located over those lands in which a more temperate climate was found. As you can imagine, this was accompanied with terrific winds as the air masses rushed over the land.

D: *What about earthquakes and other phenomenon (volcanic)?*

P: That is accurate. Many lands previously above water were sunk and much land at that time below water was elevated.

D: *Then for a time was the entire Earth covered with water? Or is that just part of the legend?*

P: There was, in relating these stories, widespread flooding. However, it would not be accurate to say the entire Earth was flooded. There were those areas which were safe from flood. However, they were not of the known world at that time.

***

EASTER ISLAND

D: *There is a little island called Easter Island off the coast of South America that has many, many giant statues. People have always wondered about their origin.*

Phil: Do you wish an explanation? The monoliths were created by a race of people who were of the Atlantean culture and who migrated at the time of the Atlantean downfall. The symbolism is of looking to the east for the arrival of that race which would return.

D: *Is that why they built them so large?*

P: The physical size is a pronouncement of their respect for these people or beings. Many times it is common in human nature to relate size to respect. An interesting note to this is, how a movie star projected onto the big screen is instantly adored and revered. This phenomenon works in reverse. Those who are held in high esteem are given gigantic proportions. Those who are given gigantic proportions are held in high esteem.

D: *I see. They're made bigger than life.*

P: Exactly. And it works both ways. This is how phenomenon such as fan madness or mania occurs. It is a peculiarity of the human race.

D: *Why are the features of the statues exaggerated?*

P: This is an artistic expression, much as paintings are exaggerated to highlight an aspect or an expression.

D: *They are so large, people have wondered how they were made.*

P: There was the same technology involved which was used in building pyramids. The material was shaped somewhat differently from a block. There was the use of tools, of chiseling, such as is done today. But the method of transportation was the same. It was telepathic in nature and was done with thought energy.

There were hat like blocks on top of the statues at one time. They have since fallen off. These were made of a different type of stone material than the statues. I wondered what the purpose of these so called "top knots" were.

P: This is something which was done to accommodate the people who would sit on the top of these statues, and so would be gazing in the same plane or direction as the statue itself. This was thought to give a power or an insight to these priests, in that they would be gazing with the idols.

D: *They were gazing out to sea, watching for the others of their race to come. Is that what you mean?*

P: They felt that by doing this, the return could be hastened. That it was necessary for the energy to be put out before it would return. The statues were pointed in the direction in which to gaze. The priests would then climb to the top and sit on these stones or top knots and so direct their energy to pull in these beings. The effort was successful many times. They were visited by beings who were extraterrestrial in nature. The craft would come in from the sea. The gazing, longing, was as a beacon, which would signal to the beings a desire to communicate and so the arrival would occur.

D: *What type of craft came in by sea?*

P: There were extraterrestrials who were in hover craft. The term is hover craft, for there are many different types of craft.

D: *I thought it might have been some type of boat.*

P: Not as human would acquaint, for these hovered over the water and not on it.

D: *What happened to these original Atlanteans? Did they remain on that island?*

P: They were dispersed in time, by hardships and the change of Earth's axis, which changed the climate. The people or natives were dispersed to other parts of the globe. The present natives were of the Indies tribes, who after the climate had returned to its present state, migrated to the islands, and so found these monoliths many generations later.

D: *Of course, they did not understand their purpose, did they?*

P: No, they thought the stones were gods themselves.

D: *I've also heard there was a form of writing that was found. It has never been translated. Which tribe did that originate with, the first ones or the ones that came later?*

P: This was writing which was created or expressed by the people who erected the stones. Some of the writing in possession today is an instruction manual on how to levitate. The ideas are so abstract as to be useless to any who would read it, if they could. It requires a complete set of abstractions and ideas which are not present on Earth today.

D: *Did any of the ancestors of the Atlanteans stay there and interbreed to come down to modern times?*

P: The Egyptians, the race who have olive skin are the closest in direct descendants in a physical lineage. The olive skinned people are of the original Atlantean stock. All left the island as the climate was not conducive to support life there at that time. For the Earth is a restless old woman who turns and frets, and so people move into different areas.

D: *Did the extraterrestrials help them to depart?*

P: There was no assistance needed, for boating on the waves was a firmly established art or science.

Phil said upon awakening that he could see the priests sitting cross legged on the top of the statues watching the hover craft come in across the water.

***

John was once again in the Library on the astral plane, and the guardian asked what he could help us find. I asked him if there were any restrictions as to who could come to the Library. He said there were none per se, but that souls of a low energy level would not come there. Besides not being particularly interested in seeking knowledge, they would be repelled by the difference in energy emitted by this realm.

D: *There are many things on Earth that are considered mysteries that people don't understand.*

J: This is true. There are many things in the heavens that are also mysteries as well. He says, the conscious mind cannot always understand things. So in a sense you would say that would be a restriction. But people in their super conscious state can understand things that the conscious mind cannot understand. So in a sense, talking about restrictions, that is how it operates.

D: *You mean things would be too complicated?*

J: Yes. He says you're not at the proper energy level. You do not hand an algebra book to a three year old that's just entering preschool. He says, you do not do that. That's part of how our library works as well. A three year old would not understand the algebra.

D: *But sometimes they have given me things that I didn't think I could understand.*

J: This is true. But the knowledge is to make you grow. To make you understand more.

D: *And to open up your mind.*

J: And to open you up, yes.

D: *Well, we are trying to find some explanations for Earth mysteries that people don't understand. Do we have to go into the viewing room?*

J: It depends upon what information you'd like to talk about.

D: *There are all the giant statues on Easter Island. Can we have information about them?*

J: He says, yes, please step into the viewing room. He says this at one time was part of the Lemurian continent. And when the Lemurian continent sank, this was a sacred mountain top area. He says the Lemurians were tribal, but they were able to manifest physical laws. They were able to make these statues. And solidify them and move them with mental power and thought. And this was done by their shamans, their priests and their leaders of the different tribal units. And when the Earth shift took place, he says this was one of the places that was left. Modern scientists cannot date these things because the stone comes from a primitive period. There's something about this type of rock or stone that is unique. I can't get the word. Geologists think they know the age of these things but they really do not. This is why it is a mystery. But they are remnants of the ancient Lemurian civilization. He says they go back about twenty thousand years.

D: *Modern scientists think the statues were carved from rock taken from the nearby mountains.*

J: The rock was taken from the nearby mountains. This is true. But they were shaped by the concentration of energy forms. The stone was made malleable by energy direction. So that it was easy for stone and flint instruments to work up these different shapes. It was like a knife cutting through butter. It was very easy.

D: *They think the stone came from quite a distance from where the statues are now. (Yes) How were they transported?*

J: Again, telepathic levitation methods were used with these stones. That's why there are no tracks.

D: *Some of them have toppled over. (Yes) The ones we see now all face one direction. They all seem to face out toward the water, unless they have been moved.*

J: No, they have not been moved. He is saying they faced in the direction that the Sun rose at that time. The Sun rose in a different position than it does at this present time. And they were in alignment with that.

D: *Was there a reason why they faced the rising Sun?*

J: It had spiritual and significant religious experiences for the people at the time.

D: *What did the statues represent? They all seem to be alike.*

J: They represent the souls of man. The guardians of the watch tower, so to speak. This has been traced throughout history. They are the manifestation of the guardian spirits of the different tribal clans of the ancient Lemurians. There were 136 different tribal clans in ancient Lemuria. And these represent different factions of these tribal clans, ancestors, so to speak. They are rather a primitive people in your recommendation, but they had great spiritual gifts as well.

D: *It sounds like they also had great psychic powers.*

J: Yes, their leaders had great psychic powers.

D: *The statues seem to have exaggerated features. Was there a reason for that?*

J: Yes, there was a definite reason. This was how people looked at that time. Man, in his process of evolution, has become more refined. And in fact, he will still have a further step of refinement when we move into the golden age of the flowering Age of Aquarius. He will be more refined then.

D: *There was also what we call a "top knot" that sat on top of the head of the statues, which has since fallen off. This was made from a different type of rock.*

J: Yes. This represents sort of a spiritual cord. They would dress their hair in this manner. Sometimes they would say that they were being pulled out of the material universe by their top knot. (Laugh) So this was why they had these elaborate hair ornaments.

D: *It was a different type of a rock than the body of the statue was made from.*

J: Yes, just like the hair is different colors in your life now. There were different designs that these people believed would help them to be pulled out of their body. They believed that the spirit entity not their spirit the main spirit of the universe would allow them to go into the astral. And the way it was done was that they were pulled out. But this is ancient history in your time period.

D: *That's why it's so difficult for the scientists to understand it. They think that the statues were made by a group of more recent people.*

J: These were left over from the Lemurians.

D: *Then did other people come to this island?*

J: Oh, yes, many people came to this island. And they desecrated some of the stones. They cannibalized themselves. They were like animals of the lowest sort.

D: *These were not the original people.*

J: No, these were not the original people of this land. In fact, some of the remnants of the Lemurian civilization were still around when this invader tribe came. And they were eaten by these fierce warlike people.

D: *Did any of the original descendants survive?*

J: None of them survived. They were completely wiped out by the invader tribe. For you see, the seas around Easter Island teem with animal life, but it's very hard to support life on this island area. And in fact, these warlike tribes captured these people and ate them.

D: *Then these warlike tribes are the ancestors of the people who are living there now.*

J: Yes. The people that are descendants of this warlike tribe. The Lemurians were very advanced people spiritually and psychically compared to modern man, but they lived primitively. I mean, they did not have the type of inventions that we have. They had city like places, but they were built of materials that could be replaced very easily. Like palm fibers and natural vegetation type things.

D: *The scientists have also found remnants of what they claim is their writing, and they didn't know how old it is.*

J: These date back to the ancient Lemurians and they were carried by their descendants. And then the descendants were finally disposed of by the fierce tribes. You see, the fierce tribes thought they were good eating. They just looked at them as animals, yet these people carried on old traditions. And some of their seers even wrote about the times before. And about the Earth shift that took place that broke up Lemuria.

D: *Then they kept the writings but they didn't know what they meant. Is that correct?*

J: The descendants of the Lemurians knew what it meant.

D: *But the other people ....*

J: Oh, no, they were just animals. They were warlike. The shamans of the conquering people picked up on the spirits of the place, and maybe interpreted some of the writings. But they... I don't want to talk about this. They're too warlike and they're too mean and they're really... I want to leave. What he's showing me... they're just terrible people. They cut out the hearts of the people. Oh, it's just terrible.

John said upon awakening that he saw these people chasing the Lemurians. He saw one of them cut open the man's chest and pull out his heart. He then proceeded to eat it while it was still beating. No wonder the sight revolted him.

D: *Okay. I don't want you to have to look at anything that disturbs you.*
J: The guardian says, go on.
D: *Yes, change the subject. Let's switch the screen, so to speak. Let's show something else. We don't have to look at that.*

***

ARK OF THE COVENANT

D: *There is much written in the Bible about the Ark of the Covenant, and there is a lot of mystery surrounding it.*
Phil: Yes, we are familiar with this area. We would ask you to see this as a receiver, a radio receiver which was able to translate or receive those messages from a higher plane and convert them to a physical plane level. So that information could be channeled to these people in such a way that there could be the greatest amount of accuracy in this channeling. Because then there would be no human awareness or consciousness which this information would pass through.
D: *You mean they spoke to people this way?*
P: That is correct. It was a spoken message.
D: *Where did the plans come from to build this?*
P: This was a gift. The plans were given to build the housing for this. There were those craftsmen and artisans of the tribe who used their talents to create this housing, this receptacle. However, the receiver itself was of a design constructed by beings who were assisting in the planetary evolution at that time. There was given instructions of where to place the finished product or the housing, so that it would be activated without being seen by these people. For this was done under cover of darkness. The people were instructed where to leave this Covenant or the Ark, and it was then activated with this receiver. It attracted energy from cosmic power, which is even in this day surrounding the planet and is still available for this use. You would like to know where this Ark or receiver is at this time. And it would not be appropriate to disclose its location at this time. It, however, is in good hands.
D: *Is it still located on Earth?*
P: We would not give a location at this time.
D: *According to our Bible, it became dangerous.*

P: That would not be correct. It had become misused. It, itself, was inert and no more dangerous than a blade of grass. However, its use for political reasons or whatever expression would be appropriate, was corrupting its intended purpose.

D: *In the Bible it says that people died when they touched it. Was there some kind of power inside?*

P: There was the energy which was being processed for this good, which would cause one to simply check out, or to kill, to die from an overexposure of this energy. This insistence that death would result was to prevent the people from opening the ark and discovering its contents. And also to build an aura of protection around this device, that it would be treated with fear and respect.

This portion of the tape was badly garbled, and transcription became impossible. It sounded like heavy, loud static that completely obliterated Phil's voice. You could barely hear my questions, but not his answers. The rest of the questioning about the Ark and the beginning of my questioning about the Bermuda Triangle were blocked out. If there is some way, I would still like to use this missing portion if it can be deciphered. There may now be some way with computers to separate the static from the voice. At the end of this side of the tape the sound suddenly returned. When the tape was turned over the other side was normal. This was a strange experience because Phil had his tape recorder going on the other side of the bed, and his tape was also untranscribable. If something had been wrong with the tape I would think both sides would be affected. Also, if something had been wrong with the microphone, why didn't the trouble continue when I turned the tape over?

An electronics expert said it might have happened if the tape recorder was placed on top of a TV or some source of electronic emanations. But it was sitting on a small table next to the bed, and there was not even a radio in close proximity. That would not explain why the sound suddenly returned. If the cause was some type of electronic signal then I would think both sides of the tape would have been affected.

This has happened since with other subjects. I have had strange things happen with my tape recorder, as though being influenced by outside energy (static, fading in and out, speeding up and slowing down, two voices at the same time, etc.).

Because of the garbled condition of the tape I was going to try to recap what was said, which is usually an impossibility. The next week when I began the session with Phil I wanted to know if they could tell me what happened.

D: *The last time we visited this place we asked many questions about the Ark of the Covenant and the Bermuda Triangle, and received very interesting information. But for some reason it was not recorded on the tape recorder. Do you know why?*

P: The information given carried with it an energy vortex similar to that which the wording described. And caused a vortex in this immediate area, similar to that described in the narration. This is illustrative of the power of suggestion. For these energies which are on the planet now are of such nature that merely thinking about them creates that thought in physical. This is the nature of the energies on this planet at this time, as we move into this new age of awareness.

D: *Do you mean the planet Earth or the planet you're speaking from? (The Planet of the Three Spires.)*

P: This physical planet here, the planet Earth. The energies on this planet now are of the nature that a thought is a deed. And so this is illustrative of the caution that must be exercised in the use of these energies. For they are very creative.

D: *I knew the tape recorder was working correctly.*

P: That is accurate. The recorder was faithfully reproducing that which it received. And as you can see your recorder has an awareness above and beyond that which can be perceived by your human senses. The machinery and equipment produced on this plane is raising its awareness as well. Its level of energy is naturally being raised, since it is of this Earth and a part of this Earth and all in this Earth henceforth shall be steeped in these energies.

I said I wanted to try again and ask the same questions. Because I wanted to use the information but I would have to rely on my memory since I did not have a clear tape recording.

P: You may ask if you so choose. There is no harm in asking.

D: *I wonder if there is some way we could keep it from interfering with the tape recorder again?*

P: We shall attempt to focus more clearly those energies which are being requested for channeling, and so assist in limiting those energies which are channeled through this vehicle. There may however be some relapse of this condition, as this vehicle is in largest part responsible for those energies which are channeled through. And so, he must become aware of this broad spectrum of energies and so learn to limit that which is passing through. This is not harmful energy. This is simply energy which is coming through, and is manifesting itself on

your tape recorder. There is no physical harm in this.
D: *It's just that the machine can pick it up.*

I then proceeded to ask the questions again about the Bermuda Triangle hoping that this time there would be no interference. When I transcribed that tape everything was fine. While working with Phil over many years we occasionally had unusual things happen with the recorder, but none as drastic as this one.

* * *

During the 1980s and into the 1990s I continued to ask the same questions of other subjects every time a suitable situation presented itself.

D: *There have been stories that the Ark of the Covenant was dangerous. Was that true?*

Brenda: Of course it was! It was an energy device.

D: *Stories about people being hurt if they touched it or....*

B: If they did not know how to operate it and were not insulated correctly, yes, they could be harmed from it.

D: *Do you know what eventually happened to the Ark of the Covenant?*

B: It lasted for several centuries. It's hard to say what happened to it because at the end before it disappeared there was more than one Ark of the Covenant. One was dumped into a ravine by accident. They were carrying it on the framework that it was transported on, and they were crossing a narrow bridge across a ravine. One of the men accidentally stumbled and it landed at the bottom of the ravine.

D: *Was this during the wanderings through the wilderness?*

B: Afterwards. One was stored in a temple for several centuries. And some invaders were coming into that country and they had to hide it. A third one is still existing, but it's hidden in secret and only a very small group know about it.

D: *I didn't know there was more than one. (Oh, yes.) Did these all exist at the same time, or did they make another one after the one fell into the ravine?*

B: They made the original and they made others in later centuries. There is one still existing. The one at the bottom of the ravine is part of a glacier now. Sometimes people see it when the ice clears up. And the one that was hidden is sealed off in a cave and I can't see whether it will be discovered or not. The third one that still exists is in a private bank vault.

D: *Do you know in what country?*

B: It's hard to tell. A western country with advanced technology.

D: *If anyone ever came across that one in the bank vault, would they know what it was?*

B: It's impossible for anyone to come across it inside the bank vault, because it's a private bank vault. It's on private property of someone who's extremely wealthy.

***

BERMUDA TRIANGLE

D: *Do you have any explanation for the disappearance of ships and planes in the Bermuda Triangle area?*

Phil: Much speculation has been put forth, which is erroneous at best. This area is a vortex of energy, a vast and very powerful creative vortex of those energies now on this planet. This erratic behavior is in part due to those machinations lying deep beneath the ocean, inert and yet not totally dormant. There are in the vast rivers of energy passing through this planet, enough of the power left from this machinery to cause a focusing effect which causes these disappearances, so to say. This is simply passing through a doorway into another reality. They are not lost in a physical sense, for they are still here, they are simply elsewhere. There is the belief that they have died a natural death, but they are simply in another reality, in another plane of existence, in another time frame. This is a bend or a doorway, if you would like that connotation. These people are not harmed when they pass through, other than psychologically, mentally and emotionally by this occurrence. Their physical energy levels would have been raised by passing through this doorway. Many would find that they had become most telepathic and clairvoyant. For many have found themselves in a reality in which these super human devices are quite normal. Their manifest realities are such that they fit with those whom they are with. As the realities here could be quite different if the mind were so disposed to believe that these things would be possible. Then as surely as one thought the thought that they could be possible, then they would become reality. It is simply a matter of belief in what is real and what is not. And that is what determines what is real and what is not.

D: *There have been reports of the planes' instruments going haywire right before this happened.*

P: That is accurate. There is a disturbance in this magnetic flux. This is a symptom of this phenomenon. This flux is the result of bending of the Earth's magnetic fields and other energies unknown to man at this time. The instruments work in the presence of these fields being in their normal state. However, in the absence of a normal state of these fields, the instruments do not work as they were designed. For the fields which they work on are not functioning properly, so to say.

D: *They also said that the horizon looked strange, and sometimes, what they were flying over looked different.*

P: Many things would obviously look strange, because of the rising awareness. Not only from physical, but inner plane awareness. And so those things which in this reality are quite closed off and not seen, for the most part, would become very readily apparent as the awareness rises and the inner planes begin to assimilate that information which they are receiving, and then feed this awareness to the conscious self.

D: *Is this bend there all the time? Many people fly in and out of that area, and sail in and out of there with no trouble.*

P: It is not there all the time, that is accurate. It varies, it is erratic

D: *When these people went through this doorway, would they land somewhere?*

P: That is accurate. For there is physical mass as is in this reality. They are still here on Earth. However, they are simply in another reality, another time, if you choose to use that analogy. They would pass through to the eye of the storm, so to say, and find themselves in a place they had never been before. They would find themselves in another time on Earth.

D: *Would you have any way of knowing if these people went into the past or into the future?*

P: It really does not make much difference, for there is, to be quite frank, no past or future. This is simply a concept which is created by man to allow him to perceive those events which he can comprehend. It would not be accurate to say that they have passed into the past or future. They simply are "in another time".

D: *I thought if an airplane came down in the past, it would be quite startling to the people of that time. Then, these people probably landed somewhere or the ships came ashore somewhere, but they were in a different time.*

P: A different plane, perhaps, would be more accurate.

D: *But it must have been frightening to these people if they were not expecting it.*

P: They were, no doubt, quite taken by this dramatic turn of events. However, as we can perceive, most have adapted quite readily and find no real desire to move back into the past, so to say. For many of them have stepped headlong into your future, where the Christ consciousness is. It is a well known and observed phenomenon, such as it is on this side. People here simply disappear, people there simply appear. There is as much mystery to both, as to who these people are and why they keep coming here. And how their stories are quite fantastic to these people.

D: *It must have been a surprise to people in the future to have these people suddenly appear.*

P: From the future point of view it would not be so much a surprise. As the future already knows what has been happening in the past. It would simply be a matter of realizing that another has passed through the door. And then to welcome and to assist in allowing these people to adjust and to accommodate to their new reality.

D: *Then some of those people may still be living, or they may have grown old in that time.*

P: That is accurate.

D: *Is there any way for them to get back?*

P: At this time it would not seem possible, for the door is somewhat askew and not controlled, but is simply swinging by the winds that blow it, so to say. One would simply have to be at the appropriate place at the appropriate time and hope that the door swung in the appropriate way. This would require knowledge that is not at present on this planet. They most likely would not want to, were they able to. As the awareness they are in now causes this reality to seem as children playing with toys. For they are elevated far beyond this plane we are in here.

D: *Were these people chosen to do this, or did they just happen to come across the door, so to say?*

P: In the grand cosmic scheme, in the universal clockwork, there is a reason given for everything that happens. And so it could be said that these events were based on a very valid reason. However, it would not be accurate to say this was planned. For many things happen in life which are not planned, but which become very appropriate at the time. It is simply a matter of those things happening which are most appropriate at that time. And so it would have been very appropriate for this to happen to these people. To give an example, it might have been most appropriate for some of these people to advance. Perhaps they were ready to advance this quickly into the next plane awareness. Whereas, we must finish out this physical incarnation and then be born again, and be raised to that environment in which they find themselves. These people, possibly, had no need for such an occurrence. They were simply ready in their inner plane awareness and training for this thing to happen. And so they found themselves at that point in which they were needed.

D: *Would there be any way people going into that area could have a warning that something like this could happen?*

P: There would be the awareness on the inner planes to guide one. When one finds oneself in this situation, it cannot be said that warning was not given on the inner planes.

D: *You mean, inside their own mind or what?*

P: That is accurate. They would have to be listening to themselves, as would be appropriate for all of life, to be attuned with oneself and know oneself.

D: *Then there really isn't any physical way to tell. They just happen to be in the wrong place at the wrong time.*

P: Not entirely so, for as has been said, warning was given. However, warning was not heeded.

D: *But there was one case where pilots were sent out to search for some lost planes. They had no choice, they had to go and look for the planes.*

P: We create our own destinies. And so it would be accurate to say that these individuals created the circumstances of their disappearances, in the same manner as many choose their own deaths. For all choose their own deaths.

This concept is expanded upon in my book, *Between Death and Life.*

D: *Are there many of these bends or fields on the Earth's surface?*

P: Not in numerical terms, no. This is an isolated incident.

D: *You spoke a while ago about machinery under the ocean that was still functioning in part and that was one of the things that caused this.*

P: That is accurate. You could visualize a mirror, a once grand mirror, now broken. And a piece of this great mirror now dangling on a thread. And as the wind or water currents play with this mirror, the Sun shining overhead occasionally catches the mirror and shines for a brief instance bright and sure, through the air or water, whichever analogy you choose. You can see this is a random occurrence and is not controlled by man. In this same way these currents of energy are moving or playing with the remnants of this once great society, and causing this occurrence.

D: *Is this a real mirror or is this an analogy?*

P: This is an analogy. For the mirror itself is of crystal nature.

D: *How did it originally get under the ocean?*

P: This was not under the ocean originally. This was in the time of Atlantis. Some of the machinery of that great continent. It was inundated during the destruction, and now rests quite comfortably and securely in the depths.

D: *Is it in a building of any kind?*

P: It is on a plateau, where it had been erected originally. The entire land mass sunk and took with it all that this civilization had created.

D: *Can you explain more about what it looked like?*

P: There would be no need or use in explaining, as it would be useless to try. It would simply not be possible to give any satisfactory explanations as to what one would see visually. It simply is above human comprehension at this point.

D: *I am visualizing a crystal in the shape of a pyramid. I don't know if that would be accurate or not.*

P: Then we would say you could try to use this analogy and visualize with your mind's eye what you see, and your perceptions could be quite accurate. We will not pass judgment on this, for that is your reality, and so be it. For this, again, is of the nature of energies that are what one wishes, and so be it.

D: *But you talked as if it was broken. Would this be true, that the original crystal or whatever it is down there, is broken?*

P: It is fragmented, yes. That is accurate.

D: *How did that happen?*

P: It would be best to say at this point that it was intentional, in order to prevent those who coveted the use of this crystal from using it in a disharmonious manner. For there were those who wished nothing more than to claim this great power source for their own. And so it was seen that it was necessary to segment this crystal in order to prevent its use in a destructive manner.

D: *So they purposely destroyed it?*

P: That is accurate.

D: *Did this happen around the time of the sinking, or before?*

P: Concurrent with.

D: *Did the destroying of the crystal cause the sinking?*

P: There were simultaneous events precipitated by the disharmonious use of this crystal, by causing these energies to be used in a harmful manner. Which in turn caused to some extent the sinking of the continent. And so there is some correlation. However it is not a simple cause and effect. They were somewhat separate incidents and yet somewhat connected as well.

D: *Wouldn't the people who destroyed it know it would cause a catastrophe like that?*

P: These people were blinded by their greed and ambition, and were oblivious to the effects of their folly. And so they continued the use of these energies in this manner and then paid the price.

D: *I thought maybe they were in ignorance and didn't know this would happen.*

P: It was not in total ignorance, for there had been those who warned incessantly of the use of these energies in such a manner. There were those who devoted their entire lives to the attempted enlightenment of the people of these energies, as the awareness declined of their use and power. However the ignorance soon overshadowed the enlightenment and the disharmony overtook the harmony.

D: *Are the pieces in the deep ocean?*

P: That would be accurate.

D: *Do you think anyone might find them someday?*

P: There will be the resurfacing of this land during the time of upheaval. And that information which is stored in the temple for the future generations will once again be discovered and implemented. For it was seen that this land would be inundated and out of reach. And so this knowledge was stored for those future generations which will find access to this knowledge. And so it will be given to those who are of high character and are thus prepared and able to use this knowledge.

D: *Whenever the scientists or whoever find this knowledge, will they know what it is?*

P: One would hope so. That, however, is something which will be decided at that time.

D: *Is the knowledge in the form of a book? Or how is it preserved?*

P: In writing, in stone. It will need to be deciphered for it is simply in the language of the people who stored it. And so it would be necessary to transcribe from one language to another. However, this is not an insurmountable task, as much of the awareness will be intuitive as to how to accomplish this. There will be much more work and processing done on the mental level, than is done now through simply rational level.

D: *Is the temple still there or would it be in ruins?*

P: Naturally after being several miles under the ocean for many thousands of years, it would not be in very good shape. However, it would be in such a shape as to preserve the information. That would be an accurate assessment for now.

D: *But this will not be discovered until the upheaval of the land?*

P: That is accurate. And it will be at an appropriate time, when those who find this knowledge will be of highest order, and will use it accordingly. It will not be given until it is appropriate.

D: *Does this knowledge contain the history of what happened to Atlantis?*

P: It does. It contains the history and day to day accounts of this civilization over many thousands of years. And a summary of the final days leading up to the social collapse and physical inundation. With a recounting of such, those who find the information will understand what happened to that civilization.

D: *When this was functioning during the time of Atlantis, what did they use it for?*

P: This was a master source of energy. Many energies could be channeled at that time. Some energies could be used for several different purposes, depending on its application. There was healing energy, levitational energy, lighting, heating, motivation. Many types of energies were available, as are now and returning to the planet.

D: *Then when it was broken, for some reason it creates this time bend.*

P: It is simple random reflection or transmission of the energies. We would like to say that many who lived at that time are again incarnate.

D: *There are many mysteries, and we are looking for answers.*

P: Oftentimes people ask but refuse to hear the answers. Many ask the questions but do not believe the answers, and so continue asking the questions until they find one who will give the answer they wish to hear.

***

LOCH NESS MONSTER

D: *One mystery on Earth that people are interested in is the Loch Ness Monster in Scotland. Can you tell me any information about that?*

Brenda: The answer is complex. I'm trying to get it organized. There are several creatures of this sort on the Earth's surface. They generally live in deep, freshwater lakes. There is one similar to it in a lake in Siberia, that is considered the deepest. These creatures stay in the depths and they really have no reason to come to the surface.

D: *Is it a type of mammal or what?*

B: It's a freshwater, aquatic reptile. And it's a very ancient animal. It has been on the Earth a long time. It's much like some of the insects on the Earth. It evolved so far and it had no need to evolve any further. So it stayed as it is through the eons. It is a gentle, harmless creature, hence the protective coloration that it has, to keep others from harming it. It eats the aquatic plants that grow in the water.

D: *Are there many of them? I mean, do they multiply very fast?*

B: They multiply some. They're not as prolific as other animals. They lay eggs in the lake's bottom and mud, and the eggs hatch out. Actually they're kind of inbetween a reptile and an amphibian. They're closer to a reptile than they are an amphibian. They are mostly in cool water lakes, because they like the cool temperatures. And there are more than people give credit for. They think they're finding one here and one there, but there are more than that. Not many, but a few small communities of these creatures.

D: *Then if they're not a mammal, they don't really need to come up for air?*

B: Not really. They can. This is how they are somewhat related to amphibians, because they have gills and rudimentary lungs So they're able to surface for a few minutes without suffocating but they can breathe underwater as well. These are aquatic creatures. They have been seen on the land, but the creatures rarely leave the lake.

D: *In one case they had sonar reflections in the water. Sonar is like radar, it bounces off large objects. What were they picking up?*

B: That is true, but often sonar also bounces off where the water chnges temperature. And if there's a layer of water of different temperature, it bounces off there too. And so they would be wise not to rely too heavily on part of the readings.

D: *In other words, all those pictures and other so called proofs are not reliable.*

B: According to your scientists' standards they cannot be considered reliable.

D: *They've claimed it's like a prehistoric creature.*

B: It is. Like I said, it got stuck in evolution eons ago. There are other creatures like the one you call the Loch Ness Monster or the one on the other continent... Lake Superior? The colony in that body of water. Plus there's a colony in Lake Baykal in Siberia. There are others scattered, and there are similar related creatures that like warm water in the Amazon Basin. The natives there have reports about it but the people in power dismiss it as superstition.

***

D: *What can you tell me about the Loch Ness Monster in the big lake in Scotland.*

Phil: These creatures are land locked, in the sense that they have nowhere now to go. Where once they were able to travel the entire globe, they now find themselves locked no pun intended. However, there are no other creatures that would compare to this particular type of creature left in the free oceans.

D: *Where did they come from originally? Are they remnants of the dinosaurs, or something like that?*

P: That is accurate. During ages past there were many of these creatures among the oceans and seas of the world. However, during the time of upheavals and shifts only those who were stranded were able to survive, due to the changes in the salt content of the oceans. And therefore they could not change as did the other creatures around them. Their ability to remain in their previous state owes itself to the fact that the waters in which they were trapped did not cause them to change. They were allowed to continue as they were and are.

D: *Are they more amphibian or mammal?*

P: They are more akin to dolphins and porpoises, in that they do have vertebrae and are air breathing. However, they are more serpentine or reptilian in appearance, and do not have appendages.

D: *But we should see them more often if they're multiplying, shouldn't we?*

P: There is no correlation between the number of appearances and number of animals. The fact that they survive to this day owes itself to the fact that they are secretive, and do not cherish the upper world. There are many who believe that these are remnants of the pre Cambrian times. However, there are indeed many who are of more current heritage, but have not been recognized as such.

D: *You said they were survivors of the upheavals. Was that Atlantis, or before Atlantis?*

P: There were in those days many upheavals across the entire planet. During that time there were many creatures that were lost due to changes in climate, as opposed to changes in geology. However, when we speak here of these creatures you call the Loch Ness Monster, we would say that changes of both caused this to happen. In that the warmer seas from which they originally came turned cooler, and caused many of those in the open oceans to die from a change in climate.

However, those that were in that particular area at that time found they could survive by staying near the bottom where the water was much warmer. They did, however, over a period of time adapt to the colder climate, so they could survive in the colder water for short periods of time, such as that in the Loch Ness Lake.

D: *Then the Atlantis catastrophe occurred much later in time sequence.*

P: That is not indeed the case. However, the calamities we speak of happened over a much broader period of time than just that which befell the Atlantis culture. The entire scenario was more along the lines of a million years as opposed to a thousand years.

D: *I see. Are there some of these creatures left in other parts of the world?*

P: There are many creatures left in many different parts of the world, that are not yet known to your culture. However, they are known to other cultures which are more aware. There are many creatures on your planet of whom you are not aware.

D: *Are these all sea creatures? Or land creatures?*

P: The distribution would be such that more of the mammals exist than the fishes. So that the overall picture of that which you call "nature" today is somewhat askewed by this dark cousin of nature, that the race as a whole is unaware of.

D: *Are these animals usually in places like Africa, South America, continents that are not as populated?*

P: They exist throughout the entire known planet. However, not to say that they exist on the planet, but perhaps in the planet.

D: *They might be underneath the surface?*

P: That is accurate.

D: *Because most of the world, as we know it, has been explored. And we think there is nothing left we can find on the surface.*

P: Most of the known world has been explored. However, that which is unknown has not been explored. Therefore it is not of the world, because it is not known to exist.

D: *So under the planet there are creatures that we have no knowledge of.*

P: That is accurate. There are races and cultures that exist without the knowledge of those which you call the "surface dwellers".

D: *Are the people underground remnants of Atlantis? Or are they races that were there before that?*

P: There are each of the above. There are some who were there before, and some after. However, they are not in complete harmony with each other. And so tend to keep away from each other, and are somewhat unknown to each other, due to their own unique desires to be kept separate. The true scope of the interaction between those of the surface and those of the underground dwellers is not widespread or common knowledge. However, there are those who are common to each group who speak to neither group.

***

D: *Can the guardian of the Library give us any information on creatures like the Loch Ness Monster? Are these creatures real?*

John: Yes, they are real. They are remnants of primitive life forms that used to live on the Earth during the age of the reptilian.

D: *You mean like the dinosaur?*

J: Yes. There are creatures both in the sea, on the land, and even in the air, that man hasn't discovered yet. They took refuge in certain areas, and their lives were prolonged. And they reproduce.

D: *I'm thinking of one in particular, the one that is called the Loch Ness Monster.*

J: There are about seven in the Loch Ness tank. (Laugh) That's what he says, "tank". (Laugh) And they have reproduced over time. They live for quite a long time, hundreds of years. They don't reproduce that often. The cold water has something to do with that.

D: *How do they reproduce?*

J: As most animals do.

D: *I mean, is it mammal or does it lay eggs or what?*

J: They lay eggs under water. It takes a long time for them to be harvested, to grow into an adult. It takes almost two years, it seems. There are predators, fish and things like that, that have to be watched. But they have a lair underneath one of the cliffs of the Loch Ness.

D: *Are they also air breathing, or are they strictly aquatic?*

J: They're basically aquatic, but they can emerge for brief periods of time. Similar to the way flying fish are able to fly up and then go back into the water. They have that ability. They do not need to breathe air. They get their oxygen supply through water, for they have gills.

D: *There have been tales of them coming on the land. Does this ever happen?*

J: Occasionally. It has happened in the past and it could happen again.

D: *There have been tales of seeing them around the lake.*

J: Oh, they've been seen. They do emerge out of the lake. But they elude capture because they are very intuitive and depend on their instincts.

D: *There have been tales of seeing their images on sonar. Did it actually happen?*

J: Yes. They are in existence. There are seven of them right now that live in Loch Ness, in a cave that's underwater on a cliffy side. They hunt fish, and they're big.

D: *Yes. Some people have taken pictures of them when they emerged from the water. Is there any other specific place where there are many of them?*

J: There are two or three in a lake in Africa. There used to be twelve. There are two in the tropical Amazonian rain forest, in a lake off the Amazon River. And in southeast Asia there are four in the rivers.

D: *Are these creatures dangerous?*

J: To a degree, no, they're not dangerous. But they do eat fish and could mistake a person for a fish in water. Especially the larger types.

D: *You also said there were other creatures from this time period that have survived?*

J: Yes. Not all of them look like the Loch Ness Monster either. They're reptilian in form. Some look like a big lizard.

D: *Did you say there were land types?*

J: No, most of them are aquatic. That's how they function, they live at the bottoms of rivers and lakes and in caves.

D: *You said these were remnants, survivors of the dinosaur age.*

J: Reptilian era.

D: *Are there any creatures that survived that were mostly on the land and not aquatic?*

J: These have mutated into modern biological evolutionary animals. It's mostly aquatic animals that have survived from his period. There is one in the air that you haven't discovered. That information will be found in the near future. It's like, "Don't ask any more questions. That's a file that's still unopened." (Laugh)

D: *If it's in the air, why haven't we seen it.*

J: It's been able to make itself almost invisible. That is the reason.

D: *How can it do that?*

J: (He smiled.) I don't know. This file on this subject is unopened. And he says more information will be revealed in the future. And there's one creature on the land in the jungles of Africa. Another one on the land will be found in the Andes mountains.

He says that will whet your curiosity, but I can't talk more about this because this is an open file, and it's still being filed on.

***

YETI OR ABOMINABLE SNOWMAN

Brenda: There are other creatures that are locked in evolution. These creatures are called by several names. There are so many names in your language for this creature, it's hard to hard to choose which would be the best label for it: Yeti, Sasquatch, Bigfoot, Snowman. That is to be expected, because this creature is very widespread. Any mountainous area where there are snow capped ranges has this creature. And this creature is extremely shy and afraid of men. It's psychic in the way that it can sense other creatures from a great distance. Usually they hide whenever they sens other creatures. These are related to man in a way. They're kind of like man's little brothers. They are developing intelligence and this planet is capable of supporting more than one intelligent species, if the currently dominant intelligent species will allow it. And it would be for the enrichment of the planet and eventually for the enrichment of the galactic community.

D: *Where did that creature come from? Is it indigenous to the planet?*

B: Yes. When the ancient ones, the archaic ones were helping the species to develop on this planet, they came up with an intelligent species which is now man. While this species was developing, they were distressed at the violent tendencies it portrayed. And they noticed that a parallel line of development also had the promise of developing into an intelligent species but without the violent trait. And so they continued developing that species as well. When this species reaches its full potential, it will be equally intelligent as man, but in different ways. And both species will have to do a great deal of adjustment to be able to deal with each other. Because this species is lacking the violent streak that is in man, and so they are extremely sensitive and shy.

D: *But they are taking longer to develop than man did?*

B: No, it's just that they got started later.

D: *We hear many stories about them being violent.*

B: Usually it's the manner of the creature trying to frighten people so they can get away and hide, because they just want to be left alone. Up to their present point of development, they've not taken any longer than man has. It's a possibility that their development may be slowed down to make sure that the violent traits do not accidentally enter in. But some of the others say they may need a few violent traits to give them the energy they need to survive adversity. Because there is the violent streak in man that has helped them to survive various sorts of adversities since he has achieved his intelligence.

D: *It's not really good to be completely passive anyway.*

B: That is correct.

D: *The way man is moving out and developing more of the land, is he encroaching upon their territory?*

B: Yes, and has been for quite some time. That's why I made the statement, "If man will allow them to develop, they will." But they do a good job of hiding. They live all over the planet. They are in the very high remote mountains, as well as the deep rain forests of the tropical areas of the planet. They have adapted to differing climates and altitudes, but they prefer the isolated areas.

D: *Well, people are afraid of things they don't understand, that's one of our traits.*

***

D: *We have heard about some creatures we call the Sasquatch and the Yeti? Does he know what I'm referring to? The Abominable Snowman, those type of creatures? They're known by many different names.*

John: He says, yes, they do exist.

D: *Are they all the same type of animal, but just found in different parts of the world?*

J: No, they're not animals. He says they're evolved beings as well as you.

D: *Can he give us some information about them?*

J: He says they are a very gentle, spiritually intuned people, because they're very intuned to the nature spirits. This is why they can almost be invisible. They do have the power to make themselves blend into their scenery and surroundings. They don't actively seek out man because they're afraid of him. Thier nature spirits have told them that man has misguided this planet and misguided her resources. So they shy away from man. But they like the food that man has.

D: *Then the ones that have been found in the different parts of the world are all the same type?*

J: Yes. They were primitive survivors of the Lemurian cataclysm.

D: *From the descriptions they seem to be very animalistic.*

J: At one time we all were. (Laugh)

D: *Then they haven't evolved. They've kept the same type of body?*

J: To a degree they have evolved. But they've evolved more on a spiritual consciousness and a mental consciousness than a physical. He said they are a protected race, a protected minority, so to speak. For they're much more in tune with the lower life forms.

D: *Protected by whom?*

J: Nature spirits.

D: *From the descriptions we've had, they don't seem to speak as we do.*

J: They have telepathic communications. Something that you humans have to have speech for. So they're not as unadvanced as you think. They make clicking sounds and noises like animals do. But they have telepathic capacity that is much stronger than man has presently developed. Quite frankly, speech is a most limiting thing. Each individual word that we say to another being is understood only by that being's frame of reference of what that word means. So, in fact, we could be talking about one thing, and the person receiving the information could be getting an entirely different picture, based on their experience definition of a word. When you have telepathic communication, then you are communicating what you're thinking. It is much, much broader than verbal speech. We humans are limited to vocal speech. So we have a big, big obstacle to overcome.

D: *Many people think they are violent.*

J: No, he says they're not basically violent, but they have animalistic characteristics. They are afraid of humans. They pick up on the emotional environment. They can read intuitively or telephatically people's auras, or people's surroundings. If they felt they were to be abused, this would cause negative reactions. Also if they were being cornered. And most, whether it be a man or a beast, do not like to be cornered.

D: *What about their type of food?*

J: They eat lots of nuts and berries. Fish. They eat it whole. (He made an expression of distaste and I laughed.) They eat very simplistically off the land. They like things like butterflies and insects as well.

D: *We've heard tales of them breaking into people's chicken houses and things like that.*

J: Yes. They eat smaller life forms. They've eaten chickens. They eat rats too. (Again an expression of distaste and I laughed.) Rodents. Prairie dogs. But they don't eat carnivorous animals. They only eat animals that eat plant food.

D: *I would think if someone was evolved enough to have mental powers, that they wouldn't... that sounds primitive to me.*

J: Do not judge. (He wagged his finger at me.) The guardian's saying, "Do not judge! They are more advanced in so many things that you could not understand." Because they're intuned with the Earth and the Earth energies and the nature spirits, and they have telepathy. This is why they're able to avoid man too. He said, "Do not be judgmental."

D: *Then when they sound primitive by our standards, they may not be.*

J: No. By other standards they're not.

***

D: *Let's shift to another part of the globe. Why are the animals of Australia different than other parts of the world? There are animals there that are not found anywhere else.*

Phil: There is no real answer to the question you ask, simply because we do not see that distinction. There are indeed animals on each continent that are not found on any other continent. However, that is not to say they are unique in any way from the rest of the animals on the planet. Simply that they reside in one place, and not another. We would ask that perhaps you clarify.

D: *In Australia there is a theory that maybe the animals came from outer space. That aliens brought them, and that's why they are different there than other parts of the planet.*

I heard this during my first trip to Australia in 1994. There was a book published at that time that expounded this theory.

P: There are indeed animals that were brought from other planets to this planet. However, if we were to exclude the presence of only those animals which were brought from other planets, there then would be nothing on this planet at all.

D: I'm thinking of the original concept of the seeding of the planet, but we're not going with that idea, are we? Or not? I'm thinking of the physical transportation of an animal, maybe after the time of the seeding.

The theory of the seeding of planet Earth is in *Keepers of the Garden* and *The Custodians*.

P: There are many items, for we include here not only the animal kingdom, but the entire existence of life on your planet. It has been enhanced through the transportation of living and viable creatures and entities from other planets, and dimensions. So that the entire existence of any particular type of lifeform on your planet owes itself to the existence of said lifeform on another planet.

D: *Then Australia is not unique from the rest of the world.*

P: There have been many enhancements to the lifeforms on this planet, as opposed to the lifeforms on other planets. Not to say that one is perhaps better than the other, but perhaps were changed for the particular climate or environment they were to be inhabiting. Perhaps on your planet there are many who find the animals are perhaps a bit odd, from your perception of their abilities, in some ways, and their appearances, in others. However, we would ask that you look at the overall picture, and see that the variety is, in and of itself, not an indicator of whether these creatures were inhabiting this planet originally or from some other planet. The overall picture of similarity in your planet is much different than on other planets.

***

STONEHENGE

D: *I wanted to ask about Stonehenge in England.*

Phil: This was simply a school of astronomy. A place where those who wished to learn astronomy could do so.

D: *What race built that?*

P: It was of Gaelic origin. This knowledge was spread throughout the world at the time and sinking of Atlantis, and so many cultures benefited from the divestiture of this knowledge by those who traveled throughout the world.

D: *Was this the only place where stones were placed like this?*

P: In that exact structure, yes. There are many throughout the world whose function is identical, yet whose form is different. The pyramids in South America were used for observation as well as those in Egypt. There are several places on Earth similar to this.

D: *With Stonehenge, how were these stones raised?*

P: By telepathic means, by thought energy. In the same general function as were the pyramids. They were conducted by telepathic thought energies from their quarries to the site. This was constructed over a period of years. The original purpose was lost. However, not to say that there was not some function found in these monuments, but the original purpose was not of time, but of distance. To track the positions of the planets, such that it could be determined the location of this planet with respect to many others of known origin in other places in this universe.

***

D: *Do you know what happened to the Mayan people? They were very unique. Supposedly they just suddenly disappeared.*
Phil: The answer to this question is somewhat tied up in court, to use your analogy. The story or perhaps the ending is not complete on this subject. However, suffice to say that they did not die out, but were transported. We would not care to elaborate at this time as to the means, however, they were transported.
D: *Do you know why?*
P: They themselves chose to escape that destruction which they could foresee happening to their brothers during the Spanish conquest.
D: *Does this happen to civilizations often in history?*
P: Not that it has no precedent, however, it is not a regular occurrence. Should the situation arise that a civilization has reached a level, as a whole, that they, for the survival of the civilization, desire such a transportation, then, yes, it would happen. Not that there is any law that says it must happen. However, through the desire of the individuals themselves to protect their levels of awareness and their achievements, to better enable them to further their understanding and growth, and to protect their society, then they would be given that opportunity, were it in their best interests as well as the best interest of those around them.

***

CROP CIRCLES

D: *What can you tell me about the crop circles that have been appearing in England? I know they are appearing elsewhere, but they seem to be more defined over there with symbols and are much more elaborate. Can you tell me anything about who is making them and how they are being made?*

Phil had been in deep trance for almost an hour and had answered many questions, yet suddenly he opened his eyes, and seemed uncomfortable.

D: *You don't want to answer that question?*
P: (He seemed very uncomfortable.) No, it's just... I don't know... I don't feel very well. For some reason I feel almost ill. Something's not right. I don't think it had to do with the crop circles. Although I'm getting an impression that there was something when you asked that question.
D: *We never considered them to be harmful, because they're just in the grain.*
P: But there's something tied in with it that's hidden. I'm not sure... it's other than human. There's a definite... I don't know. This is on a much deeper and broader level.
D: *Do you think that's what bothered you?*
P: I almost felt ill, sick to my stomach. (He sat up.) I can go back. I just... let me take a break here.

Phil got up and went to the bathroom. He was unique among my subjects in that he could wake himself up from a deep trance if he felt uncomfortable. After a few moments he came back. The disturbing feeling had passed as quickly as it had come. When he laid down again on the bed, he relaxed and immediately reentered the deep trance. I did not have to do anything. I gave reassuring suggestions that he would feel perfectly comfortable, and reinforced the fact that he was protected at all times.

P: We would say that there are those devices in place which would protect both you and the receiver of this information. There would not be given that which would be harmful in any sense.
D: *But he did have a physical reaction. That's what concerned me.*
P: The need for such a device was not apparent at that time. However, the connections were getting too close for comfort, so to say, in that the establishment of such a connection would cause physical discomfort. The energies of those that were being connected to the vehicle were not compatible with the energy of the vehicle.
D: *Do you think you'll be able to answer the question now? I just wanted to know about the crop circles. Who was making them and for what purpose? And maybe how they were being created.*

P: The higher forms of communication on your planet now are understood to be in terms of binary or computer languages. In your common belief system the highest forms of communication are accomplished through your scientists, and are therefore not understood by the masses in general. These crop circles are intended to convey to the masses the information which is being given to your planet, so that the populace as a whole understands that the nature of your existence is radically different from that which is commonly believed to be the accepted point of view. That all is not as it seems. Those who would undertake such an endeavor are attempting to communicate in a way that resonates with each individual on a highly personal level, on levels that each individual is open to, and not simply given.

D: *Who or what is creating the crop circles?*

P: The entire answer to such a question would not be possible in this context, in that it would be necessary to give an entire discourse on the origins of the human race as a whole. But we should say that these symbols are relevant to the history of life on your planet. It is a geography lesson in the origins of your planetary lifeforms. And there are those who are now coming to slowly recognize the significance of these symbols, in that they convey meanings. They are not simply random acts of art. They are indeed forms of communication. Those who are knowledgeable in this form of communication will slowly come to the realization that they are being communicated to, and they then will understand the message that is being transmitted, as to the origins of life on this planet.

D: *So it is symbolism. Rather like "take us back to our roots", so to speak?*

P: That is accurate.

D: *Is it being done by people of Earth?*

P: There have been attempts to duplicate this. However, it is not possible to say that the humans are originators of this. As the knowledge that is being imparted has not been known commonly on this planet for centuries.

D: *Who were the originators? Those who are making the real ones.*

P: They are of the order of... (looking for the word)... the keepers of the truth.

D: *Where are these keepers of the truth located?*

P: Their physical location is not relevant. However, their purpose is indeed relevant. They are now presenting to you, as a race, the truth of your heritage.

D: *I guess I'm trying to say, are they aliens on space crafts?*

P: And that is what we are trying not to say. For indeed it would not be so. However, we would say that they are not of the Earth.

D: *But they are also not of the Watchers?*

P: That is accurate. Not in the sense of coming from somewhere else to here. They are of here. They are home already. However, they are not of the world as you know it.

D: *Would it be sufficient to say, other dimensions?*

P: They are of your world, but not of the world as you know it. However, there is no need to divulge their true or relative location, so that there would be an attempt to communicate to these beings. However, in time there will be given the location as to where they are coming from. Such that there will be those who may go to them, to seek higher understandings.

D: *But they are not of the spirit realm that we go to after we die?*

P: They are of the spirit realm in the same sense that each of us is of the spirit realm. However, they have manifested themselves in not quite a similar fashion as you find yourselves in. Not to say that they do not manifest certain physical forms to enable them to accomplish their purposes. However, they are not resident in physical form.

D: *So they are more or less associated with the Earth, but they're not in a form we're familiar with. Would that be correct?*

P: That is accurate.

D: *They are not a deceased spirit.*

P: In the sense that they were of physical nature and then departed, no. They are of a higher form that was not in the physical as you know it. However, not to say that they were not of physical form. For indeed they were at one time in their evolution physical in nature, but not as you know it.

D: *So they evolved beyond those that are in the space crafts and us on Earth. They more or less evolved to another level, so to speak?*

P: They are not above those of the space craft, but rather are evolved in their own right, to a level above that from which they were. However, there is still more to go, and yet there are more things to do before they go there. This communication (crop circles) is in fact part of their attempt to convey to those of your world the realities of their world.

D: *Can you tell me how the crop circles are made?*

P: The process itself is not so mysterious, but simply is being used on a scale that is not common in your world. There are those who are able to direct the energies into concentrated forms, such that the molecular structures of these plants are thus altered. It would be as bending a twig, such that the force of bending is not external but internal. It is simply a realignment of the structures themselves, and not of the environment.

D: *We're thinking it's the use of some type of energy.*

P: That is accurate.

D: *So it's not done with a machine or a craft or anything.*

P: Not in the sense as you perceive it. There is a reality in that machines are spiritual, and not physical. So in that sense, by the definition of your question, we would say machines not in the sense of physical, as you know it. However, this does not include the concept of machines on the spiritual plane, as you know it. We are not excluding spiritual machines.

D: *I guess I'm thinking of space craft.*

P: These are not machines which are used to transport from one dimension to another, or travel. But rather that the concept of machines in the spirit world is somewhat lacking. And we would say that there is indeed the reality of those which you call "machines" on the spirit plane, other than the three dimensional world. They are indeed manufactured and serve a specific purpose. However, they are not, as you say, three dimensional, but are of the higher energy manufactures.

D: *There have been reports that some people become ill or have physical symptoms when they are in these circles.*

P: That is accurate. That is the same reaction this vehicle had when approaching those energies. There are those who simply are not compatible with those energies. It is simply that the energies themselves are not in harmony with the energies of the witness.

D: *When I was in the circle I had a wonderful experience. It was very peaceful and very wonderful, uplifting.*

P: There are those who are in harmony and those who are out of harmony. However, this is not a judgment call, but rather there are some notes that are in harmony with other notes. And then there are some notes which are not in harmony with other notes.

D: *The physical reaction he had, it was as though there was something that was not good about the energy.*

P: That is accurate. That is in the sense of perception of what he understands through his experience. In the conscious filter there was an entity or energy that was unknown, and was perceived as threatening. We find it is a product of this fear of the unknown. The physical symptoms are reminiscent of that which one finds when one is in disharmony with many forms of reality.

D: *Then they are not negative.*

P: That is accurate. The misunderstanding or lack of understanding is understandable. In that there has never been requested by this vehicle to communicate on that level. It was a new experience.

D: *Then if he were to actually go to the crop circles, like I did, he might experience an uncomfortable feeling because his energies would be different, and not compatible with the circle.*

P: That is accurate.

D: *Do you know why these are appearing around the areas like Stonehenge, Avebury, Glastonbury? They say these are very, very old power points. But why are they appearing in those areas in England more predominantly than in other parts of the world?*

P: There are at this time on your planet many polar opposites of energy vortexes. There are some points where energy goes in and other points where energy goes out. It is the gates of the rivers that flow into and out of your planet. There are at this time many vortices in that particular part of the planet, that are taking in energy, an inlet. In these vortices there will be given the energies which are filters such that the energies which are allowed to enter are harmonious and aligned with the needs and purposes of the planet upon which these energies are directed. It is in these vortices where one finds the keepers of the gate, or rather to say, guardians of the gate, that these manifestations present themselves. They are bringing new knowledge to your planet at this time.

When Phil awakened he retained some memories of the information he had been receiving. There is always more presented than can be relayed to me verbally. This is why asking the right questions is so important.

D: *What was the feeling you were getting about the crop circles? You said you didn't think it was a human and you didn't think it was an alien in a space craft.*

P: But to say that they're in the Earth is not exactly right either. It's almost like they're in another dimension. And they seem to have technology, maybe fourth dimensional technology. They're actually machines. They're manufactured and they work just like machines here. But they work with energies in different ways than our machines do on this level. Their machines are much more refined, and are not so coarse in their actions. And they work with energy. I mean, they literally change the energies.

D: *Mold them in some way?*

P: Mold them. Change them. Alter them. But the machines themselves are energies that are working with energies. They're not gross physical form like ours, but every bit as much machines as our machines are.

D: *You were most emphatic about them not being the aliens on the space craft.*

P: They're from here. What I was seeing was on a higher level than where the spirits are. It's almost like a higher form of us.

D: *Living in another dimension?*

P: Maybe. I'm not sure. It's as if our energy was raised, not so high that we left the physical. We were still physical, but in an ultra physical. Yeah, that's a good term: ultra physical. Better energy. That's what it is. They're not really physical by our standards, but they're not spiritual. They're hyper physical. Their energy forms are a much higher frequency than ours. It's ultra physical. That word just fits perfectly.

D: *So they are able to observe us, but we can't see them. (Yes) We have talked before about energy worlds and other dimensions. Some of them can exist side by side with ours. If we are able to raise our consciousness, like they claim we're going to....*

P: It's more than just our consciousness. It's like our physical beings are shifting much higher somehow. I'm not sure how that is, but it's as if our atoms were vibrating twice the speed. So if you raised everything, set up the table where the elements were in place in their vibration, in terms of how many electrons there are. I don't know how to define that. But if you took the energy level of every atom and doubled it, so that they all kept the same relative energy level to each other, but everything was twice as high as ours. That's why we wouldn't be able to see them because they're vibrating too fast. I'm seeing that the whole crop circle is made at once, not in segments or whatever. The size of the machine that's doing this is not the same size as the crop circle itself. But it's not physical as we understand it. It's ultra physical.

This whole side of the discussion tape began to speed up gradually to where it was impossible to transcribe. It gradually became impossible to understand. Maybe it could be slowed down to where it could be understood. At least some of that discussion portion was not important enough to worry about. Suddenly about half way through the discussion tape it began to slow down again to where I could transcribe. I have no idea what we were discussing up to this point.

P: ...a rock is a rock and a tree is a tree. But if you actually are the master of your molecules, and you understand that there are certain agreed upon models, you can convert your molecules to another model.

Here the speed of the tape returned to normal for the first time. Several minutes had been a racing blur of noise.

D: *Well, it goes back to the idea that we can control the cells of our own body, and this way we can control illness. We can alter the cells.*
P: Exactly. And you can go even further. You can control the molecules, and yet on a molecular level or atomic level, there are patterns that are already established that cannot be changed.

During the tape of the session the opposite effect occurred. It gradually slowed down to where it was dragging. It was tedious, but at least it could be understood to be transcribed. I changed tape recorders and the effect was the same on both of them. So it was not the mechanical speeding up or slowing down of the recorder. It was definitely something that affected the tape. Was the machine being affected by the same energy flux that affected Phil and caused him to break trance because he felt ill? This was similar to the way the mere mention of the Crop Circles drastically affected Janice in Chapter 4. There appeared to definitely be a energy effect of some type connected with the Crop Circles that was not only affecting my subjects but also the machinery I use.

***

D: *There is the phenomenon called the "Crop Circles", or the English call them the "Corn Circles". They seem to be appearing around old sacred sites. Is there a connection?*
Clara: There is very definite energy patterns created, some from the other sacred sites to the Corn Circles, the Crop Circles. There is a very definite pattern to it. It's something like your how do you say? anagram?
D: *It's a puzzle?*
C: Yes, it's the puzzle, and it's written in the wheat. So the puzzle is for you to look at, and it's all done with energies. So when you look at this "anagram", this puzzle, it is for you to figure out.

D: *Can you tell me who or what is creating the Crop Circles?*

C: All I can say is that it is for positive. It is for love, it is for good.

D: *But is it alien beings? (No) Can you give me any other indication?*

C: It is the energies within the Earth. I can only say that. The Earth itself.

D: *And could it be directed by beings like yourself? (The entity that was speaking through Clara.) Because I consider you to be a different type than the ones that are in the spacecraft.*

C: (A sly smile.) What do you think? That is for you to decide.

D: *(Chuckle) I have the feeling you have much more power and knowledge. But yet some of the beings I've spoken to on the crafts are also very intelligent and very knowledgeable.*

C: Yes, they are. They are very intelligent, very masterful beings. Many of them have been through an Earth experience on their way to a higher vibration. And moved from Earth planet to another planet, whichever planet they're from.

D: *But yet I get the feeling that it is being directed from higher forces than the beings on the spacecraft.*

C: We will say that is the truth.

D: *Because I can't perceive that the Earth itself would make the designs. Maybe using the energy of the Earth, but that it couldn't....*

C: (Interrupted) That is correct. The energy of the Earth is used in this, in these circles.

D: *And it is trying to give us messages. Is that what you mean?*

C: Yes. She's been trying to give us messages.

D: *The Earth. (Yes, yes.) But some people think it's being done by spacecrafts.*

C: We will say this. It is done from a much higher source, and a more powerful source, than spacecrafts.

D: *I've been in the circles. And to me it looks as though there is definitely an energy ray or something, that swirls the wheat. (Yes) Because it seems to start at a central point and move out from that.*

C: It's a very powerful force, much greater than a spacecraft, that creates this, with the energy of mother Earth. And there is a message, if one will decipher and decode the message within the circles.

D: *Can you tell me what the message might be?*

C: That's your puzzle. (We both laughed.)

D: *When I was in the circles I felt very peaceful and a very positive energy. But I've been told when some people enter the circles, sometimes they become ill.*

C: That depends on the space of where the being is, within their own journey, within their own path. Where their journey is is what they'll feel. If their journey is in a place of peace and harmony, they'll feel wonderful and peaceful. If they're within their contract and within their path and on their journey of what they came here to do. If they're not, then they will feel a wanting to move, wanting to get out of that place. As they are in their physical being, wanting to move into another place on their journey. So if they are, shall we say, moving negatively from their contract, then they will not feel peaceful within the circles.

D: *Then that would explain why some of the people had feelings of nausea, and felt ill. And they're very uncomfortable about being in them.*

***

This session was performed in a Bed and Breakfast establishment in the north section of London. The summer of 1992 was my first trip to England, and I was greatly looking forward to seeing the Crop Circles after I finished my lecture engagements. Alick Bartholomew, my publisher in England was also on the Board of Crop Circle Investigators. He was going to take me into the latest Crop Circles that had been found near Milk Hill at Alton Barnes, and the Oliver's Castle area.

Laura was an attractive blond who was an accomplished astrologer. She had no problems and was not looking for anything specific. When the session began she regressed to a very normal and mundane lifetime. After taking her through the death sequence she was describing the spirit world. At this point another entity began to speak through her. That was when the surprise occurred. In these sessions you have to learn to never take anything for granted, and to always be alert for the unexpected. I will never pass up the opportunity to ask questions if the being appears to have knowledge.

D: *Can I ask a question? We are very interested in the crop circles that are being made here in England. Do you have any information about how they are being constructed?*

L: Yes, we have this information. They are being constructed as part of a pattern that is now being placed within the energy frequency of the Earth. The pattern will be shifted into the awareness of many people on the Earth plane. This will continue within the energy frequency around the Earth. As each and every person connects with this frequency pattern, so they will be charged up. Their own frequencies will interact with the patterns in the circle and other configurations.

D: *How are they being constructed? Are there instruments involved, or what is the method?*

L: There is an energy frequency system. And each person will become aware of their own frequencies in their bodies. You have a particular frequency. That is your own pattern. Now as you interact with other people, so you become aware of their frequency. Are you aware that when you speak with another person on your Earthly plane, you will either enjoy their company or wish to separate from them.

D: *Yes, that's true.*

L: Ah! That is the direct interaction of the energy frequencies. And as you perceive a frequency of compatibility, so that frequency can interact together with your own. And so you can get in touch with each other's patterns of thought. It is no accident when you speak of patterns of thought. Those frequencies, those patterns of thought, interconnect you with every other intelligent lifeform within the galaxy, within the universe itself. That is how you communicate, and also through the energy lines. That is what will form the crop circles and configurations.

D: *Then these are being produced by the people in a space craft?*

L: That is correct, but also through your own thought patterns. Do you understand that? Dolores, your own thought patterns will contribute to this complete communication system.

D: *Is that why I have to be here in England at this time? Or am I just assuming?*

L: No, you are not assuming. You are correct. Why else would we have brought you together with other circle investigators? Remember that every person you meet, your own frequencies will interconnect with theirs. And so the connections keep going. Certain spacecraft and capsules connect directly with the thought frequencies of all lifeforms on your Earth, and many other frequencies besides.

D: *So the designs were really being done by thought?*

L: That is one way of thinking of it. It is not always easy to convey how this communication occurs. The easiest way to think of it is in thought wave patterns.

D: *In other words, it is not being done by some kind of a machine or a ray or something. That has been one theory that has been presented. Something mechanical.*

L: It is not mechanical. There are various people who have tried with machines. They are well known. But the machine that we speak of bears no resemblance whatsoever to the rather physical machinery that is used on your Earthly plane. We have used that word as it is in your vocabulary. And it is the closest word we could find. The machinery we use is far more sophisticated and complex than you could possibly comprehend.

D: *So I am probably looking at it in a simplified manner, but I wanted to ask those questions because they have been presented to me. Then it is a combination of working with certain people's energies, that creates these designs.*

L: That is correct.

D: *People think the designs are like a language, and they are trying to communicate some message to us. Is there a message in the circles?*

L: The message that is being conveyed, is that all people have a part to play. And whatever symbol you choose to see, whatever tool we can use to attract your attention, to alter your wave patterns, we will endeavor to pursue. For some it is a beam, a ray, as you used the term. For others they are the ancient symbols. For others they are but a flattening of the corn. Whatever is needed to attract your attention will be used. For as your attention is gained, so your thoughtforms can interact with our dimension. And so assistance can be given at any time, to assist all of you on your Earthly plane.

SECTION FOUR

Vibrations, Frequencies, and Levels

CHAPTER NINE
THE AWAKENING

I had many sessions during the 1980s and portions of these were used in my many books. There were other parts that have remained in my files awaiting a logical book to be inserted in. We covered many topics with Pam while she was in deep trance. Different entities would come through during the sessions to give us information and answer questions.

During this session in 1988 she saw a robed being that reminded her of Father Time. Although she instinctively knew there was no gender to this being, she immediately thought of it as male. He was dressed in white robes, but was actually glowing from an intense internal energy. We asked where he came from, and the response was, "Beyond the beyond. Or if you wish, the Hall of Always."

D: *Do you know who he is?*
P: No. He said he is one of the essences made manifest in order that we might facilitate communication. And to make it easier for me, he has allowed himself into dense and gross physical matter, because it's easier for me to talk to a physical being than just a blank space in the air. This is not the first time. He has appeared to many others in many other time periods on this planet and others, he says, in order to, not only facilitate communication, but to inspire and to comfort. So this is not a job that is taken lightly, and this is not a solo event. But in fact for the purpose of communicating, this is rarely done. Mainly he appears in people's reveries and dreams for the purpose of inspiration and comfort.
D: *Would it be correct to say he is like a guide?*
P: He feels the term "guide" is far too limiting, but then realized that our concept of guide is limited. If we were to expand what we thought of guides, then he would accept that label.
D: *I'm trying to put him into some kind of a category, I suppose.*
P: Yes. He says that is human. (She laughed.) He said one of the problems we have as limited Earth beings is that we try to label, categorize and put into boxes and slots those things which are limitless and eternal. And that is a very limiting

thought. If we could practice thinking on space going on forever, timelessness, eternity and infinite possibilities, then perhaps we could approach thinking about how to define "guide". Just as putting a gender on a being limits in some way the way we think about the being. By putting any kind of label on anything, we limit it. He's saying perhaps "friend" would be a better way of looking at him than "guide". For he does not wish to direct us or guide us, but to assist us in any way that we ask.

D: *Has he ever lived on Earth in a physical body?*

P: No, but he is intimately associated with Earth beings who have asked for help. There has not been a need for him to have the forgetting that must accompany life in physical form as a human on this planet.

D: *Then he never felt the need to have a physical life, to have this experience?*

P: Never felt the need. He says he has but one responsibility, and that is to make manifest the principle of love. So needing to actually be a human being would delay or take his attention from his much larger task.

D: *I'm thinking of the different levels and dimensions, and trying to physically place him somewhere.*

P: If you were to view the planet as a ping pong ball. And extending outward another concentric orb, say, the size of an orange. And then extending outward from that, say, another orb the size of a basketball. And then continuing larger and larger orbs. You could call those planes or levels. And in fact some of the planes and levels are as slow and almost as dense and forgetful as the ping pong ball of Earth. But he has transcended these levels. The difficulty lies in going through these levels, because some are sticky, almost like syrupy static. Like clothes sticking to each other in the dryer. It is with loving intent that he makes the attempt to penetrate these levels to the most dense, in order that we may have this communication. But in his normal realm he is not held down to what we would consider a "level". He is light. And light can permeate I wanted to say almost all levels. His response was that light can permeate all levels. Not to qualify the statement.

D: *When we leave our physical bodies, do we also transverse these different levels, from the ping pong ball outwards?*

P: Yes, we do. As I said, there are sticky levels. We have going out from us at all times vibrations, many, many vibrations. These don't go out to X spot and then stop. They continue flowing out in all directions, intertwining with everybody else's vibrations and the vibrations of everything else. Each vibration not only has power and force that we could equate to electricity, it also has magnetism. So our vibrations are attracted to like vibrations. If, for example, a large percentage of our thoughts have been at a certain vibratory level, then we may be more easily attracted to a specific concentric ring. If however we have practiced projecting our thoughts, feelings and desires to All That Is, to the greatest power and love of the universe of the universes, he corrects then we can, like a fish slipping through the water, transcend many, many levels, because our thoughts are extremely powerful vibrations. Those extremely powerful vibrations are attracted to equally powerful vibrations. And we can definitely transcend many of these more sticky levels.

D: *Are there any barriers that keep us from going to a certain level?*

P: Our thoughts, our fears, our beliefs and our intent.

D: *Would we be able to go to the level he is from?*

P: At this time we can do that with our consciousness, which always resides in this level, unbeknown to us, who are 99% asleep. There is an enormous part of us that always dwells in the realm of light and foreverness. It is our responsibility to bring this to the "awake" state of our consciousness.

D: *I'm thinking that we are so concentrated on our physical bodies, that when we die, so to speak, and we leave the physical body, we would only go out so far and then return back to the physical level.*

P: That is absolutely a possibility. It depends on your focus. Your conscious thoughts are the power source that you and every other human possess. The thoughts that you consciously generate will be a major determining factor on where you go, and if and how soon you do return consciously in the physical form on this planet.

D: *You said we were 99% asleep? Do you mean all humans?*

P: Of course there are humans who have been able to have the realization through their thought, their loving intent, their actual belief and faith in the everlasting love light. There have been human beings on this planet who have definitely been able to transcend gross physical matter, and not "die", as you are familiar with. They have been called "ascended masters", which is a term of some humor, for it just meant they were able to transcend many of the sticky layers. It seems not possible to be actually still in physical form on the planet and operating in the light simultaneously. So in order to actually reach this state we must slough off what is material and dense, and this has been accomplished by some human beings. It would be allowing each molecule of the human body to, say, turn up the power. Each molecule would become fully light. And by turning on the light, the vibration is sped up to such a degree that the body, as well as the infinite consciousness, transcends this plane.

D: *Then the body disappears?*

P: That is correct.

D: *Because there wouldn't be any need for a physical body in the other dimension.*

P: It would be very distracting. (She laughed.) You realize that Earth has gravity that holds objects with weight to it. To travel in space you have to do something about gravity and weight. So they actually have the capability to teletransport, like swirling glitter. Disassemble and reassemble according to their conscious intent.

D: *So it's like the entire body decomposes. I don't know if that would be the right word. Disappears.*

P: Yes, disappears is adequate. It would have to be a very controlled condition, and only in the sense that these vibrations could be raised to a level which would be beyond your physical sense of sight. It has been done, however, not by people you would generally accept as normal. Some humans have realized that they, in fact, are part of the God force. Once they, in their consciousness, become the light that they are, they have the capability to disassemble their molecules. There are those of an advanced nature who could rearrange their molecules. However, this would not be normal or common. There is very little reason to reassemble the molecules into gross, dense physical form. Once disassembled, to reassemble means that you have to go back in some way.

D: *Some people think this would be a method of escaping death.*

P: There is no need to escape death. For as you can see there is no true death in the sense of anything which you would escape from. There is no spiritual death in that sense. And so the physical body would naturally not need to be raised to another level. It would be as if you were trying to take your coat with you when you died. You have no need of it, therefore why would you take it with you? It would not be necessary to attempt to transfigure a body to take it with you to the spirit plane. It would have no function or use on that level. However, to attempt this in incarnate form in the attempt to gain more knowledge while still healthy or still functioning, then, yes, it could be a tool. In the sense that it could involve many experiences far beyond that which would be considered normal or everyday experiences. However, again, in and of itself it has no real value.

D: *What about the reported transfiguration of Jesus. Was that His actual physical body?*

P: That physical body was raised far beyond a level which would decay. To accelerate the natural decay process it was as if the molecules were simply separated through an advanced process of energy stimulation, such that the molecules themselves broke down. Which is the natural decay process in a speeded up form. When Jesus appeared to people after His "death" it was possible for Him to adjust His frequency, or more accurately, the frequency of His spirit or soul to those who would witness Him. He could adjust it so that only one person out of a crowd could see Him. It could also be adjusted so that the entire crowd could see Him if necessary. And this is being done many times in many different places. It was not unique to the Jesus experience.

I have had many cases where extraterrestrials have been able to do this. They do not die until they decide to, usually because they are ready to leave and go on to another adventure in a different body elsewhere. In these cases their body disappears, or as they say "disformulates". It has been seen to break apart into a glittery substance or into separate minute molecules. I had never heard of it being done by a human, because normally the only way our souls can exit the body is by the spirit form leaving the physical body behind to decompose.

D: *When most people die they leave the body on Earth, and the spirit, the essence of them goes on.*

P: That is correct. That is the normal case. The example we are describing is someone not of the 99% asleep. This would be a person who has the belief, the desire and the intent to do that. To transcend, taking their bodies with them. Other people also desire this transcendence, but do not believe that they can do this. Therefore they cannot, and their body must physically die. Your belief system is a shaft of steel. Without truly believing this is possible, it's not possible.

D: *They seem to have an attachment to the body if they want to take it with them.*

P: You seem to have answered your question as well, that it is an important attachment to the individual. The human body has a specific purpose, and that is to experience life in that form. He says something to the effect that you asked for physical form, and each human manifested in that way. That's the importance of it. Humans are not the only "species", and that is in quotation marks and said with humor. (She laughed. But is not the only species attached to physical form. You must realize that those people who have consciously been able to let me use the term "disassemble" consciously the physical body, are not in the 99% asleep state. If, in fact, you awaken to the knowledge and belief that you can transcend these levels, or layers, of being, and have been able to achieve this accomplishment, then you have also awakened to the fact that you need not drudge on in the heavy and dense material plane.

D: *It seems to me that being able to control the mind to such an extent would be a final lesson. Would that be correct?*

P: Lesson. Learning. Seems to be a problem of semantics. And the word "final" learning, of course, is limiting, because then you think that's the end of it. But in fact it is the greatest physical learning we can possess. If, if it is accompanied by the belief of the heart. So it must go beyond the mind. The mind is a tool of the spirit.

D: *But if you learned to control the mind and the body to such an extent, it would be the final physical learning.*

P: It is difficult, because we are like children approaching the Pacific Ocean. We're like little bitty beings looking at a vast, vast sea with no boundaries. And it seems so big. His point, I think, is that we use the mind as our tool to get to the spirit. But in fact, when we release our sleepiness, the spirit is the one who has been using the mind. Each time you have a conscious thought of raising your vibration, that thought has power and force and clarity. You have zeroed in on what it is that you wish to accomplish. That thought goes out like a clear, straight arrow. It doesn't stop. All other consciousnesses who become aware of that clear, straight thought can add power to it. But the fact that you had it initially means you are shooting out those lines, those highways of harmony and "raised" vibration. Increased or speeded up vibration. So every time you make that conscious effort you are in fact accomplishing what your intent is, because you have the belief that it is possible. You can most definitely do it while you have physical form. If you can actually allow your mind to accept the fact that truly every molecule of everything is light and light is synonymous with love, you can bring this into your belief system and can then work with every atom of your physical being. You can turn up the power. You can let the light shine. By turning up the power, by turning on the light, by speeding up that vibration, you can actually disassemble your physical form.

D: *If like you said, humans are 99% asleep, what steps could we take to awaken?*

P: He said, Great question! The information has of course been given, but it certainly bears repeating. If our mind is our greatest tool, and if we do wish to use it to its fullest capacity, then we wish to consciously connect with those in the realm of light. So we send out those vibrations. We consciously practice thinking on light, on expansiveness, beyond the stars. Don't think it ends somewhere and then there's something else. Just send it out like a satellite probe. Just knowing that it will become what it is that we intend. Our intent is that incredibly strong lifeline that we can send out. It has to be done in some disciplined and focused manner, however. There has to be continuity of some kind.

D: *So what should we do every day?*

P: Consciously focus your thoughts on light. Not light just without, but light that radiates from every cell of your living body. From the planet herself, from each plant and animal, and from the very air and water themselves. Think that every single thing you come in contact with or even think of, is in essence made of light. And the core of light, the very bottom line, is love. And love is a force much misunderstood by humans, who put it into a very tiny, narrow little box.

D: *How do you think on light or focus on light?*

P: How does the human focus? He is laughing because he realizes how very important that question is, and how very obvious it seems to him. (She laughed.) He said not to try to visualize, as in seeing a movie, but to try to imagine all things glowing. Just think of glow. Perhaps that will make it easier.

D: *Like looking for the aura?*

P: What I see as you ask that question, is very much like smoke coming out from all things. Waving and swirling and patterning and dispersing, and continuing to flow. So it is as glowing smoke. Luminous fibers that are spoken of in many American Indian tales, do exist. So if you were to think of glowing threads, perhaps; if in fact you saw the aura going on forever! Most people think of it as only surrounding things, but it's within and through and keeps on going. It permeates all things.

D: *In this way we would all be connected, because if it goes on forever each individual light, so to speak, would overlap the other.*

P: That's right. The analogy of the tapestry has not been missed.

D: *How do you explain the analogy of the tapestry?*

P: Not quite as simply as I'm afraid we may view a tapestry. The tapestry does seem to be relatively flat, although composed or many fibers weaving in and out, touching at intersections, patterning and forming designs. The tapestry is in fact holographic, so it has depth as well as all the other dimensions

D: *I asked that question because I have been taken to the room where the tapestry is. (Described in Between Death and Life.)*

P: Please be aware that information is given to you through other human beings in the form they can best interpret, and then deliver the information. There is such a loving attempt to communicate to humans the incredible vastness of All That Is, that beings will use many different analogies that will become visible to the person you are speaking to. And will be very real in their minds. They are in fact analogies come to life, if you will. So to actually believe that a room of Akashic records exists in solid form is wonderful, it feels good, and it's a good analogy.

D: *Many of these same analogies have come through different people.*

P: That's correct. But he said that other loving essences "read the same books". If they have found a technique that will work to open up a human to these other possibilities and realms in such a way that they can understand and interpret the data, then they are prone to use similar techniques with differing individuals. One problem we have encountered working with humans is verifying, validating, and coming to terms somehow with logic. And this is quite limiting and quite unnecessary. The awakening is the purpose. The awakening of the fact that in essence we are light, we are love. Each cell of our bodies, each cell and molecule of everything. The power source that runs all life is light. So to awaken to that knowledge, and to desire to operate in that realm, and to believe that it is possible, are all factors that will put you there.

D: *Then we're caught on the wheel of karma that keeps us tied here, and keeps us from transcending.*

P: Absolutely. Because that is the asleep state on the wheel of karma. And that term needs much clarification also. But for continuity sake, on the wheel of karma the human is asleep, therefore unaware.

D: *They don't realize they can get off.*

P: That is correct. However, it will not be accomplished without true belief. You see, beliefs are real things, just like thoughts are. Until exposed to light, beliefs are, shall we say, like ropes binding us. And our larger Selves I must say it's very confusing to speak in terms of larger and then again larger than that, and then again larger than that self. Because the larger self that I'm speaking of is certainly not light celled and in the angelic realm. The larger Self is just one more more cognizant self, but not yet expanded into All That Is. So you see, here is where terminology is very critical to understanding. I wish there was another term we could use. Perhaps I should call it the "karmic" self. For the karmic self is the one who determines what distractions we hold on to.

D: *For the lessons we have to learn.*

P: That we have decided we have to learn, through our belief. If there were any learning that we could bring forth from this session to other people, it would be the power of our beliefs. Belief is a very difficult term even for the human to really comprehend. What is belief? It's beyond what you think about something. It's what you think and feel and have that inner knowing about. But it's even bigger than that. It defies definition. It seems that beliefs are highways. We hold tight to these highways of belief. Our job as beings who are trying to become enlightened, is to send out belief highways toward the light. Beliefs are it's so hard to articulate this very strong thoughts. I see that our friend thinks one of the problems comes from semantics. That by putting a word on something vast and limitless and without sharp edges, we tend to narrow those highways.

D: *Why is all this information becoming available now?*

P: First, there has been a call. Largely due to the fact that at this point in human history we have instantaneous mass communication. Many more people are becoming intellectually aware of the possibility that larger realms exist. Once becoming intellectually aware that this possibility exists, the curious human wants to try. So they send out desire, intent, and the clincher: asking. So at this time on the planet there are actually more numbers of people asking for communication with the invisible realms. However, it does seem an internal urgency that we get this information. There has been a desire among the angelic realms for some long period of time, to consciously have communication and contact with human beings. So this urgency is not necessarily a new urgency. The desire of the angelic realms has been around for a very long period of time. I cannot differentiate at this moment the reason for the urgency, if it is long standing or if something is imminent. To look upon a potential planetary disaster, as has been speculated by many as the reason for this communication, is not the intent at this time.

***

Pam: Seems like God, the force, the generating power plant of All That Is, known by many names but we'll just call that force God for now is also curiosity. Curiosity is an incredible force. So when you take the most powerful force that is, and use just part of it, that curiosity is capable of manifesting in physical form anything that the force puts its attention on. So therefore you have a myriad of lifeforms because the God force is a very curious force. And the fact of thought at all, thinking of anything, takes it to manifestation. The thought creates, and we are one of many, many, many, many thoughts.

***

Phil: There is life in all that there is. There is, of course, that which one would call inanimate. However, the distinction made here is of a level which is far beyond human comprehension. Nevertheless, from the higher planes of awareness, it is apparent that all is, in one form or another, aware. Here we make the distinction between aware and alive. From your vantage point, it would be difficult to perceive awareness on that level. However, it is indeed true that all, even rocks, have awareness, perhaps not on a level at which you can perceive it. And so were it to be understood, then it could be said that, yes, indeed, even rocks themselves are alive if this awareness constitutes life. There is what you would call a life force which is separate and distinct from that which we call awareness. However, from your perspective, awareness and life are somewhat interrelated in that they seem to be one and the same.

***

Pam: Music is definitely a great art form. It is a form of interstellar communication as well as planetary communication.

D: *Can you explain about it being interstellar?*

P: Sound is a vibration, as you already know. Vibrations don't extend outward and then stop at some X point. A vibration continues to go out. It's hard to comprehend going out forever, because our limited human brains don't think in terms of eternity and foreverness. However, the song of the whale is patterned, harmonious and totally planned. And this vibration continues in a harmonious, patterned and planned way. Therefore it reaches outward and those who are perceptive to receiving this pattern and this harmony do.

D: *Does this mean that interspace beings can pick it up and understand it?*

P: Absolutely.

***

Phil: It's really not necessary to eat anything. The globe that we
live upon is living in a living plasma. In this plasma are all
elements necessary for life. This is beyond what we think of
as air, water, light. But suffice it to say, that all necessary
nutrients exist in an invisible form all over the Earth. The
problem is that this plasma is affected by thought and by actual
physical pollution, and in many parts of the globe is no longer
pure. What you call extraterrestrials need not physically eat.
They can receive from the cosmos plasma, unpolluted,
undistorted life force. (This was explored in The Custodians.)

D: *Many of the space beings have told me they don't need food
as we do. That seems to be a human trait. They can live off
air and atmosphere and light.*

The aliens keep saying that our bodies are becoming more light
in order to escape the density of our dimension, and that our diet is
changing to accommodate this. Are we progressing to the state when
we will also exist on light? Is that the plan?

***

A portion of a session with LeeAnn in 1989 that we thought would
be an UFO experience, because that was what we were investigating,
demonstrates that often we do not get what they are expecting. It also
shows that often the person is not taken onboard a craft, but somewhere
else that definitely is not Earth. (Such as Clara in Chapter 5.)

LeeAnn consciously remembered seeing a beautiful golden light
just as she was going to sleep. It had a very warm, peaceful, calming
effect as she drifted off. The room was dark so it could not have come
from a normal source. She remembered snatches of a dream that night
about being in a very white, very sterile room. In part of the dream she
saw a visual image of a volcano or lava, and when she awakened the
word "hologram" was in her mind.

We had already explored other experiences that happened just
after she thought she had gone to sleep. One of these was reported in
The Custodians when she was taken onboard a spacecraft. I expected
this to be connected to that type of experience, so when she was in
trance I returned her to that night as she was going to sleep. Suddenly
it was not dark anymore, it was light, but she could not determine the
source of the light. She then saw herself seated in a place resembling
an auditorium, yet not knowing how she got there. It was a sterile

clean space, and she was sitting on steps that resembled bleachers except they were solid, molded. The rooms were divided by clear see through walls that were not glass, but they went off in a non ending fashion similar to a Hall of Mirrors. The atmosphere was very calm and quiet. She was surprised when I asked her how she was dressed.

L: Just in light. I guess like a robe. Not really dressed at all, but not undressed either. I know there are people there. I don't see them, but I feel them. So there must be someone there. I look around and I should be able to see them.

D: *If you could ask them how you got there, what would their answer be?*

L: (Long pause) This is a good one. I must be making this one up. (Slowly, as though hearing and repeating.) It's a manifestation of transcending the physical limits of your body to venture into the realms of space time. Where the oneness called -- this doesn't make sense -- the oneness of the universe The end of being ... whole. It makes no sense.

D: *It's all right if it doesn't make sense. Maybe we can understand it later. That's the answer you got?*

L: Yeah. Whatever it said.

D: *Are you there in the physical body?*

L: No, I guess not.

D: *Then you journeyed there in a spirit form of some kind?*

L: They say. Well, the physical body's not here. (Long pause) guess it's a matter of.... I don't understand it, but I want to say what's accurate. The energy of your spirit is such that you're just a force and you're able to travel through dimensions and through space, without, I guess, actually knowing how. And when you're ready, then you're ready. And it's not by will or by choice. You can't will yourself. It just happens. The more you try to make a conscious effort, the more you're beating yourself back against the wall.

D: *Then it won't happen until it's ready to happen.*

L: Right. So you need that separation. That mindset, objective and subjective.

D: *Do these beings have something to do with this?*

L: I guess they do. We're here for learning, for serving, because they shed light and they guide. And to know, so we can be of service.

D: *Those are good things. Why did they want you to come here?*

L: Because changes will occur. Changes are occurring. Within the evolution of the planet, all for the betterment of the planet Within the age we're in people have to be shown, by your example, their oneness with the universe and the father. And at that point the planet will be well. We've taken very much and have abused, and now she needs to be cleansed. And we're here to help, by example, not by preaching. And kindnesses beget kindnesses.

D: *But they told you there were changes taking place?*

L: Yeah. I really don't want to know about them, but I guess I'm supposed to.

She paused as she appeared to be observing something. Then she began to describe volcanic eruptions and earthquakes. Also explosions and fires being caused by gases coming from underground. There were many deaths, but in the middle of it all she saw shuttle craft evacuating people to a larger ship higher in the sky. They were then to be transported to other planets in other galaxies.

L: They are coming to give assistance. We raise our vibrational levels, or they raise our vibrational levels, someone does, something does. And then you're just "whoosh" on there. And since you're just an energy force you're fluctuating at a higher rate. And the physicalness of the denseness of your body is not as dense as it is right now, but still you're the same being. I guess you have to be like that, because if you would change planets I guess they have a different atmosphere. It's not so dense and the structure of your being has to change. The vibrational level has to change more to a light figure than a dense matter like we are. And I guess that's what happens. And that's truth, because people can do that even when they're on this plane. They can change the density of their bodies. And people do walk through walls and stuff. There are people that do that, real people. So I guess if you have a more highly evolved species or "being" is a better word they're able to assist what we already know, because you inherently know everything. And by raising that vibrational rate it wouldn't matter anyway, because even if the physical bodies did die, they would just move on someplace else anyway.

D: *But in this case they're taking the physical body with them.*

L: Yeah, but they're rearranging the particles to accommodate the transference.

D: *Are they taking all the survivors on the planet?*

L: (Sadly) No, I guess they're not. I would like to think they would. Lots of physical bodies were lost in the destruction. They're not taking everyone.

D: *Is there a reason why?*

L: The people who are more evolved are the ones who are being taken. I can't believe that either though, because it doesn't seem to fit. I guess it does. Who am I to judge?

D: *The ones that are more evolved are the ones that can make this transition.*

L: I guess. And I'm seeing a regression in the planet. The physical people going back to more primitive, more beastly state, like we used to be.

D: *You mean the ones that are left on the planet?*

L: Yeah. More back... before the caveman even.

D: *Is there a reason why they're regressing?*

L: After this happens the actual physical atmosphere on the planet changes. And to support the physical human life, the human species changes, because the planet becomes more dense. The air is more dense from all of these things that are happening. Things just start all over again. I can't believe we're starting again.

D: *Well, maybe this is one alternative. Maybe they're trying to show us the different things that could happen. But does this happen to all the people that are left on the Earth?*

L: I'd hate to say "all". Only because it would take so long if everything.... But no, just some, just some. That's what it is. The rational mind says it's like birth defects, because of whatever has happened. And the atmospheres have changed. But there have to be higher life forms, human forms.

D: *Then you think they're showing you what would happen to some of the people that are surviving?*

L: No, not the survivors. These are the offspring of the survivors, I guess.

D: *Let them show you the others that didn't evolve in that direction.*

L: (Pause) I can't see how such opposites exist. I don't think I'm on Earth anymore. The people are too light. Light in the physical structure, almost spirit of a spirit. It's not dense, to inhabit the Earth. But maybe with the change then the Earth will be heaven, right?

D: *These people you are seeing now are the ones that were taken away? And they're existing somewhere else.*

L: The people who are lighter are more evolved and are taken away. I don't know who can make that judgment. It's a very nice place. Calm. More gaseous. It's more like existence in a gas form, with blues and lavenders and purples. And you don't do things like you do on Earth, because you're not tied. You don't even have houses. And you have forms, but knowledge is acquired. It's just through thought. There are no tangible, solid books or whatever. There's nothing that has any density except the gaseous state. And it's a very free, very floating kind of place, where everyone is nice and everyone is happy.

D: *And there are no physical, solid structures?*

L: Yeah, there are some over there. Those crystalline things I was telling you about before. I don't think they're glass. So beautiful, rather ornate actually in structure. Crystal towers. There are some big things that structurally appear to be more like a Roman design, with columns. They're not made out of marble, like the Romans did. It's a bluish kind of glass, light blue glass. It's very pretty.

D: *What are those structures used for?*

L: I guess they're used for learning. That's just what popped in before you asked the question, because I knew you were going to ask it. But the learning occurs through sound, not books.

D: *Do you think all the people that were taken away by the crafts went to this place, or did they go to other places?*

L: Oh, no, they won't all go here. They'll all go to their homes. But not everyone's from here.

D: *You mean all these people are from other places? (Sure) They're not originally from Earth?*

L: Oh, I'm sure there are some people who are just from Earth. Everything's within that realm of possibility. But not everyone will go to this planet. Who knows where we originated from.

D: *They will go to an atmosphere that is familiar to them?*

L: Yes. Their home. Everyone will, because they travel in groups, be united again with mother in laws. (Chuckle) Family members. That's neverending.

D: *But this state is not what we call the "death" state.*

L: Oh, no, this is a physical state. Not dense physical like this body is dense physical.

D: I'm trying to understand this. All these people are taken aboard, are transcended some way, the molecules broken down, somehow taken onboard these craft. (Yes) But it was not everyone. All the ones who were taken on the craft are taken back to their home of origin?

L: Yes. They came to Earth to help in the evolution of the species, because as the species was progressing they forgot the godhead. And so they sent others to aid in that spiritual development, which was not there from the beginning. I guess that makes sense.

D: *And there were many of these?*

L: Oh, yeah, many, many. One side of me said these were the people who were picked up because their vibrational levels are higher. But I, personally can't see how anyone will be left behind. But then who is to judge? God in divine wisdom could take everyone along because we're all one.

D: *Yes. But do you see any of these people being returned to Earth, or do they all go somewhere else? I was thinking it was a temporary thing.*

L: People will be returned to Earth, people who choose to come back. Because what I'm seeing now is the very primitive kind of culture. And I guess the people that are returned are the people who will want to come back for their own development, who know that the planet has things to offer that they need to learn or remember. And the people who do come back, I think will be the leaders or the light beings for a while. To aid whom, I don't know, unless a different species is going to evolve.

D: *Are these people being brought back by the crafts in the physical body that they left in?*

L: No, I don't see them in the physical body that they left in. (She sighed.) No, they're not going to be in their same physical bodies. It's going to be one highly evolved species and one not so evolved species. It's almost like the angels will be looking after the new species that will be here. And if they are in tune then... I don't know. I think the planet will be very different. I don't know. I don't know. I don't know.

D: *You said you saw the survivors of them that turned into these animal like type people, regressed to the primitive state. Does the entire world become that way, or are there some that continue civilization.*

L: It would seem civilization starts over again.

D: *You don't see it as continuing in maybe isolated parts of the world?*

L: No. The world is back to the state where buildings and technology and cars and planes are no longer there. Back to a state where all the scrubs are just budding, and the trees are just beginning to grow. It's like almost at the beginning all over again. It's like if you go into the forest and find a tiny little chunk of forest that people haven't been walking in or disrupting, and everything is very new and very fresh. That's how the whole planet is.

D: *Do you think everything was destroyed?*

L: This is time down the way. Right after... what do I see? I see there's more water on the planet. Or more land masses covered by water.

I then asked her to describe what the world looked like as far as the parts of the continents that would be left above water. The amazing thing was that she described almost exactly the same thing that I reported in *Volume Two* of *Conversations With Nostradamus*.

She could not have gotten this information from the book, because it was not yet published when we were having this session in 1989.

D: *These could be possibilities. They don't have to be concrete truth. Well, do they have any advice?*
L: The advice is very simple, and has been taught through the centuries. Treat others as you would have them treat you.

This Golden Rule can be found in the seven basic religions on our planet:

BRAHMANISM: This is the sum of duty: do naught unto others which would cause you pain if done to you. (Mahabharata 5:1517)
BUDDHISM: Hurt not others in ways that you yourself would find hurtful. (Udana Varga 5:18)
CONFUCIANISM: Surely it is the maxim of loving kindness: Do not do unto others what you would not have them do unto you. (Analects 15:23)
TAOISM: Regard your neighbor's gain as your own gain and your neighbor's loss as your own loss. (T'ai Shang Kan Ying P'ien)
ZOROASTRIANISM: That nature alone is good which refrains from doing unto another whatsoever is not good for itself. (Dadistan I dinik 94:5)
JUDAISM: What is hateful to you, do not to your fellowman. That is the entire law; all the rest is commentary. (Talmud, Shabbat 31a)
CHRISTIANITY: All things whatsoever ye would that man should do to you, do ye even so to them; for this is the Law and the prophets. (Matthew 7:12)
ISLAM: No one of you is a believer until he desires for his brother that which he desires for himself. (Sunnah)

D: *Sometimes the simplest advice has the most wisdom.*
L: If the vibrational rate of the planet changes, by people becoming kinder, or people recognizing the God in everyone, the vibrational rate of the planet will change. And by bringing up that level, the planet Earth will be healed to some extent. And the cleansing that should be occurring, because of how we have battered the planet, won't necessarily have to occur. Thank the planet for her goodness, because there's no separation between us and our planet. Don't create the separation. We are all one together. The planet, us, the bird, the dog, there's no separation between anything. Just the

difference in manifestation of form. And if people realize that then we would have Heaven on the planet.

When LeeAnn awakened she discussed her perception of the place she found herself in immediately after falling asleep.

L: It looked like a Hall of Mirrors, but it wasn't glass, like when you look into a mirror you keep seeing the reflection again. This was more like a tunnel. Where you could keep seeing down, and it was divided into sections. The room was round or curved with the molded steps, and the hall went off in front of me.

Because she had earlier mentioned the concept of a hologram I wondered if this Hall of Mirrors had something to do with projecting the disaster images she saw. I explained the concept to her. She didn't even know what a hologram was.

D: *Apparently you were supposed to see this for whatever reason. Does it bother you?*
L: No. (Laugh) I made it up.

I laughed. This was the best way to integrate something that might be disturbing. If the subject does not take it too seriously it will not interfere with their life. Later when they are ready to explore it more deeply their mind will be able to handle it.

LeeAnn did not know I had been working with others on the maps of the Earth changes, and that we had been concentrating on the same shapes of the continents and conditions of the world that she had been describing. I later took her to meet one of the other participants in this project. When she talked with Beverly about these things she was amazed that some of the things she remembered matched what Beverly had received. (Beverly was the artist who drew the maps of the Earth changes in *Conversations With Nostradamus, Volume II.*)

Even though there are great similarities I still like to think of these catastrophic scenes as being alternate futures, probabilities and possibilities, instead of certainties. I don't want this to be our future, and we can take the advice of treating the Earth as a living being and being kinder to it and to each other. Maybe then we can avert this type of future.

Apparently the extraterrestrials aren't taking any chances. They are preparing for any worst case scenario. Maybe they understand human nature better than we do.

CHAPTER TEN
THE PLACE CALLED "HOME"

Several subjects have unexpectedly gone somewhere else instead of going into a past life while doing this type of therapy. It is definitely not Earth, but each of them emotionally consider it to be their "home". Often it seems like such a hostile environment that this description is hard to explain, but there is no denying the strong emotions the subject feels when they see it again. The first time this occurred was with Phil in *Keepers of the Garden* when he saw the Planet of the Three Spires. The emotional connection was overwhelming. It occurred again with Clara in Chapter 5 when she saw a similar planet with spire like structures. She also had a strong emotional reaction. If we deny the existence of reincarnation this would be difficult to explain. If the person lived only one life on the planet Earth, this would be considered the only home they have ever known. Why would they have such a powerful and emotional connection to a desolate alien, very unearth like planet? When they see it there is a strong home sickness and desire to remain there, instead of returning to their present Earth home.

I call these people "Star Children" although I realize this is a broad term. They consider *this* planet to be the alien environment. They do not want to be here. They are gentle people and do not understand how people can be so callous towards each other; how the world can have so much violence. They have a longing to go "home", even though they don't really know where "home" is. In most of these cases, when they are in trance they say they are experiencing their first Earth life, or have had only a few. Each of these Star Children say they volunteered to come here and experience life in the hope that their lifeforce that has not known violence will have a positive effect upon the Earth. They are called the infusion or transfusion of new blood. They volunteered, yet they do not know this consciously, and thus are very unhappy here. Many of them try to commit suicide in order to escape what they consider to be an unbearable situation.

Since my books have been translated into many languages, I now receive mail from people all over the world who are experiencing the same emotions. They thought they were the only ones in the world who had these feelings, and truly felt alone, because these feelings did not make any sense to their family and friends. It was a wonderful revelation to read my books and discover they were not alone and there were actually many others going through the same turmoil.

Since I worked with Phil in the late 1980s I have discovered many of these Star Children all over the world. Some are going through the same emotions as Phil. Others seem to have adjusted and are quite happy to be here. The latter are younger, so maybe the powers that be are getting better at helping them adjust. In each of these cases however their subconscious said the main reason they were here was to act as a conduit of energy that is needed at the present time in the evolution of Earth. Many, many have told me we are going through dramatic alterations as the Earth changes its vibration and prepares to raise the consciousness of the people of our planet to a higher dimension. The Star Children energy is needed to help stabilize this transition.

During one session a man said he had completed repaying all of his karma, and didn't have to be here, but was part of the collective sent by the Source. Others are collectors of information, although this is unknown to their conscious mind. An example of this was a prostitute client in London in 2000 who reported an extremely traumatic childhood and life. She definitely did not want to be in the physical and had attempted suicide in order to leave. Yet in trance she said she had been sent to gather information about human behavior. What better way to examine this side of humanity than as a prostitute? Another woman client was trying suicide in a more subtle way. Her body was slowly killing her as all of her organs developed serious problems. In trance she described that this was not home, and went to her perceived "home": a beautiful water world where she swam in contentment with no worries. When she was sent to this world to dwell in a heavy dense body, she rebelled against it, and was trying to destroy the body in the vain attempt to return home.

Much of this did not make sense to me in the early days of my work. Later as I received more complicated information about dimensions and other realities it began to have a strange type of logic. As I absorbed more and more information I encountered more of these types of souls, often under unusual circumstances.

I found two cases of subjects witnessing the destruction of a planet. In Singapore in 1999 I had a case of a Chinese woman who had an incredible sense of sadness all her life. Her parents remarked that she never smiled as a child. She also had a feeling of heaviness in her chest area that was almost pain. In the session she saw her home planet blowing up. The shock caused the pain in the chest area, and the sadness was caused by the overwhelming realization that she could never return "home", and that all the people she knew were gone.

This case had more validity because literature on UFOs and the paranormal are not readily available in Singapore. I was one of the first authors to lecture there at a newly opened metaphysical center

The government is very controlling about what type of material can be written or lectured about. 1999 was the first year that any type of talks of this nature were allowed. Even so, I was told by the owner of the center that I could lecture on all of my other books, but not about UFOs. I did however bring my UFO books with me, which all sold, so I did manage to get the information into the country. My woman client had not been exposed to such writings, and she was shocked by the session, because it was the strangest explanation she would ever have come up with.

In Memphis, in 2000, I encountered another case of similar drastic consequences. A woman relived a life as a male where she landed on a planet in a small craft. As she walked outside she was startled to find that the sand and dirt had been exposed to an incredible heat that had turned it into a glass like substance. She remarked that it must have taken an incredible heat source to do that. When she saw the ruins of a city she began to cry profusely. All that was left were horribly twisted and burned shells of buildings. There was no sign of life anywhere, and she knew everyone was burned so completely that not even their bones remained. Everyone had been completely incinerated. This was her (his) home and he was expecting to find family and friends, but there was no one.

She was overcome with emotion, and it took a while to release it so she could become objective. He went other places looking for life, but everywhere the destruction was complete. The only remaining vegetation were plants with sword pointed leaves. He then remembered that he had witnessed the cause of the destruction. From a larger craft he had seen an enormous explosion rising from the surface with huge billowing gray clouds. Apparently this was the cause, but he didn't know why it happened. He decided to go down and see, and discovered the horrible destruction of his home planet. In desperation all he wanted to do was get away from it, and return to the larger craft orbiting in the higher atmosphere.

He was completely distraught and crying as he docked with the larger craft. He had forgotten how to enter it (probably because of his emotional state). Finally when he relaxed he found himself inside. That was how he was supposed to enter, by using his mind. Completely drained and overcome with emotion, he went to his quarters and lay down on something that resembled a window seat. He just wanted to go to sleep and get away from the anxiety of the scene.

We could not follow the story any further, because he retreated into sleep and forgetfulness. We then pursued other topics relating to the client's problems. These cases show that the destruction of a home planet has occurred several times in the incredibly long history of the universe, and this can carry over into this life as extreme sadness, the feeling of not belonging, or longing to go "home", but not knowing where "home" is. The period of adjustment to a new world is often difficult, and is hidden within the records of the subconscious.

***

Dan was a young man from Australia who had been insistently emailing me from different countries, asking for my itinerary so he could find me in the U.S. He was trekking in South America and was coming to the U.S. in June 2000. I tried to discourage him from coming to the U.S. just to see me, but his emails were persistent. He planned to arrive in Los Angeles, and rent a car to drive to Chicago, being there at the time I would be speaking at a Dowser's Conference. He said that if he missed me he would follow me to Arkansas. So I agreed to work with him, and booked a session at the time he thought he would arrive. I discourage this type of behavior, but since he was so insistent I felt I should make an exception because he was traveling so far.

He was staying at a hostel near the Convention Center, and the next morning he was a little late arriving because of traffic, so we didn't get started on time. We didn't realize how significant this was until later. The organizer of the conference allowed me to use his room for private sessions, because we were staying (along with several others) at a private home quite a distance from the conference site. I had scheduled two sessions a day, and Dan was the only one on this day, because it was the last day of the conference.

During the discussion before the session he told me he was from Australia, but had accepted a wonderful job as a graphic designer for a large company in London. The job had started out fine, but after a while the pressure of schedules, life in the big city, etc. began to take its toll. It was affecting his health. Instead of returning to Australia he decided to quit his job and travel. Because he was a valuable employee his boss gave him a leave of absence, and told him he could come back to work whenever he got it all out of his system. This was why he went first to South America, and backpacked all over the country. His girlfriend accompanied him on part of the journey, but the rough living conditions were not exciting to her, and she finally left him in Argentina. He continued the rest of the adventure by himself, and finally arrived in the U.S. He had been watching his allotted money carefully, and had decided to return home to Australia after leaving the States. We had several things to explore during this session.

In my normal routine the person will descend from a cloud and find themselves in an appropriate past life that we can explore to find the cause of their problems. But instead of coming down into an Earth life Dan found himself going somewhere else.

Dan: I left the cloud, but I didn't go down. I see a big bright light with a silhouette. And the way those beams of light come through the silhouette, the light splinters, so I can't see any detail. I feel like I'm in space.

D: *But you can float through space too, if that's where you want to go.*

Dan: I'm sort of imagining this doorway in space. So maybe I should go over there. I feel like I'm swimming against a tide, to get to it. It's almost like my mind doesn't allow me to go over there. Or I don't know how.

I gave suggestions reinforcing that he was safe and protected and could explore anything he wanted to in safety.

Dan: I'm not sure if I've gone through it or not, but now I can see a massive, massive, very enormous green planet. It's mostly in eclipse, in shadow, so I can only see the edge of it. It's very far away. There are beautiful stars behind, and a bright Sun to the far left. And that's casting a shadow. I can see the edge of the planet, and it's a beautiful green, like emerald. I see a texture. It's not smooth; it looks bumpy like a science fiction moon. I am flying over a desert between some structures that are of no purpose other than to act as a gate, as a marker, if you like.

D: *Are they part of a wall?*

Dan: No. It's two pillars. Not unlike the Washington Monument, but sandy in color, and standing side by side. Like a doorway, but without a lintel or any door as such. It's just markers.

Here again was a planet with distinguishing spire like structures as its predominant feature.

D: *Flying through that door?*

Dan: Or above it, sort of like an eagle. As I look at it I feel a kind of longing, if you like. These two pillars are on a plain, like a desert. And an emerald sea is to the right, from my position. There's a cove further off in the distance. It's not a beach, as such. It's like the desert just stops. And then off a little further inland there are rocks, like a rock outcrop into the ocean. And it's very big.

D: *Do you have to go through the gate, the pillars, to get there?*

Dan: No, it's like a signpost. You're here. This is for want of a better word this is my home.

D: *You said there was a feeling of longing when you looked at the two pillars.*

Dan: Yeah. (Emotional) Seeing this place again brought up my earliest memory of feeling completely comfortable. I'm trying to explore further, but it's like I've taken a photo in my memory, and I hold on to it dearly.

This definitely gave me the feeling of deja vu, because this was the same emotional description given by Phil and Clara. Logically there was nothing about this place that would inspire that type of feeling. Yet I long ago learned that logic has nothing to do with it. Emotions displace logic.

Dan: And I know that in this place I do not have a body. I'm trying to look at myself, and I know that I'm just essence. I feel almost like I am the planet. I am this place, if you like. And here, the ocean is just like ours, but it's completely emerald green. And the deserts are like ours, but they're not familiar to this person. It's different, yet familiar. And I feel like an eagle, just looking at all things. I can see so far.

D: *Are there any cities, or is it just the land?*

Dan: If I looked into the desert, there just seems to be no one. No buildings, just desert. And if I had to speak honestly, what I feel is the pillars are almost like a tuning fork for energy. And my being knows this fork, this tone, this vibration. And it brings me back every time I need to be there, because it's like a focus, like a crystal. It's very comfortable here.

D: *That's good. But do you sense any other beings like yourself in this place?*

Dan: I feel like I'm not alone. I feel more stable, more comfortable. Like I'm so happy just to be there. I feel like I'm everything else. I can't help feeling that emotion inside me where I'm welcome. I'm just being. It's really hard to describe.

D: *But you feel like pure energy with no body?*

Dan: Yes, because I can't relate to anything. I'm all things, as it were. The stillness of the rocks, the heat of the desert, the rolling of the ocean. They're all comfortable and just nice.

D: *What do you do there?*

Dan: Just exist. But perhaps that's because I'm only focusing on one part, because it's so comfortable doing it. If I had to say I had a purpose, I couldn't tell you one, because it's just to be there. (Pause) One thing with these pillars is that I feel they help me travel. Say if I wanted to come here, I could use those pillars because I know them so well, to get me back there. That's just an example. I'm not saying that's what I've done.

D: *You mean to travel from wherever you were?*

Dan: To wherever I want to go. Anywhere. That's kind of like the front porch light. Those pillars are like the light we leave on for the pizza man. You know, this is where you are.

D: *To identify a place. But how can they help you to travel to other places?*

Dan: I don't think they actually help me travel as such. It's just a way to get back. Now I'm getting pictures of beautiful light. Just light. I'm having another image now, so I've left there. From a third party I can sort of see something happening, and I think it may just be an illusion of how it works. But it's sort of a jellyfish type because it's sort of orb in shape. There are these little pointy tendons or tentacles that keep me attached to that place. But not attached. Just like when the guys go in the potholes in the ocean or into the caves, and they leave a line of rope to guide them back to the surface. This is what this is.

D: *That's an illustration. You don't have a body, but you are connected to that place. But apparently you must have left that place at one time or another. Let's leave that scene, and I want you to go to the time that you did leave that place you consider home.*

Dan: Instinctively I just had need of a change. That's what first came. It was just time. I don't know why.

D: *It was not an incident or anything that happened?*

Dan: Have you ever sucked up a tissue with a vacuum cleaner? (Yeah) That's the sort of emotion I'm getting. Like watching it go 'swoosh'. Watching it disappear through a pipe, and feeling my energy just going 'swoosh' out. So I'm not sure if it was a conscious choice. Now I almost want to cry because it hurts. This whole thing just hurts. The separation.

D: *That's good, because when we get an emotion we know we're hitting something important. But you said it was like the energy was sucked up. You mean, away from that place?*

Dan: Yeah, if I had to describe what I am seeing, I would say that I was busy looking at my beautiful columns and my beautiful sea, and then all of a sudden I'm just not there. I cannot feel that choice being made. And I'm seeing things like galaxies, and wonderful scenes that I always stared at in books. And just stared and stared, and just wondered and wondered.

D: *They're so beautiful.*

Dan: Yeah, they are. They're too beautiful. When I try to think when I left my place, I'm seeing those things. And I know this to be a correct vision, because it's like a memory. It's as if I'm almost like an airplane coming in, or an eagle, because there's no sound. But I can see those columns, and am just feeling really good. And saying, "Here I am again." Excellent.

And then I'm just waiting until the next time I can come here
But when I spoke of the sucking? That doesn't feel comfortable.
I'm not sure where it's taking me. I can feel it now. It's a
realization that I'm not coming back.

D: *But we know it's there, and you can visit it any time you want
with your mind.*

Dan: Yeah, but it doesn't help. (Sniffling)

D: *You said it's the feeling of the energy, yourself, being sucked
up. And this time you know you're not going back. Let's
follow that feeling.*

Dan then tried to fight going on to something else. He truly did
not want to leave this place again after being separated from it for
so long. Finally after suggestions were applied he relaxed and found
himself in an unusual lifetime. He assumed it was Egypt because
there were pyramid shaped buildings that were part of a busy city. It
may have been a much older civilization. He lived in a huge pyramid
type building which had many huge rooms and underground ramps
and tunnels. He was very lonely and bored living in this large place
by himself, occasionally looking out of the window or doorway and
watching the activity of the people. Although he was not a prisoner
there, he felt separated and trapped in this existence. I moved him
forward to see what his job was. He worked as an advisor for only one
person, and he was bored because the person was not there often. The
rest of the time he had nothing to do. He felt he worked with universal
energies, and used gestures to focus his thought.

Dan: He's not here all the time. I'm seeing a big ball of light. I
see it moving through space. And I see us in direct
communication. I don't know what we're saying. I don't even
know why we're saying it. Except that maybe it's advice or
me telling him what's happening, like the news.

D: *Of Earth, or of this place where you are?*

Dan: This place. This isn't Earth. I'm pretty sure now. Things
here are too big. We have big things on Earth, but this place is
very much bigger. I'm telling him what's going on, and maybe
how we should deal with it. But I still get this overwhelming
feeling of just incompleteness. Honestly, it's like what I do
doesn't really matter, and it's so boring.

D: *But does this big ball of light sometimes come into that room?*

Dan: Yes, I think he has the ability. And now I'm getting pictures
of a very well set muscular individual. Large and strong. If
I looked at myself I would say I was average, and he's
enormous. I think he's much more important than I. I think he
governs this area.

D: *But when he comes there he looks like you?*

Dan: Yeah, but bigger. I don't think I'm very liked by anybody. I don't think he treats me with very much respect. Kind of like a servant. No politeness about it. I feel so lonely here. And I get the same sense that I have here on Earth. It's just that I want out. I want this to end. I feel really trapped, I think, but not imprisoned. I have to make that clear. I feel that I'm comfortable. My position is good. But I'm like a maitre'd for this big person. I tell him things, and if people want to see him they have to come through me. And I tell them if they can be seen. And it's just boring.

Unexpectedly someone was knocking at the door of the hotel room. I had put the "Do Not Disturb" sign on the door, and it was too late in the afternoon for the maid. But the knocking continued, so I gave Dan instructions to pause for a moment, and that any noises would not disturb him. And I went to see who it was. It was the conference director and his wife. They had brought a dolly and wanted to get their luggage. They had to check out or they would be charged for another day. I had not thought about that when I scheduled the session, so I was in a predicament. I asked them if they could come back in about fifteen minutes, allowing me to bring Dan out of trance. I really didn't like this, because we hadn't had a chance to work on any of his problems yet. However I had no choice but to bring him back to consciousness. They left but I knew they would return quickly.

I oriented Dan's personality back into his body and brought him up to the present day. I really didn't like having to work under rushed conditions, knowing I was not doing the best job. I felt it was better to bring him back to consciousness rather than try to rush and not do the work effectively, so I gave suggestions to his subconscious to help him, so he could learn to live with the human feelings. Yet I knew I needed more time to make the suggestions more effective, especially since I had not located the cause of his problems. I felt I was letting Dan down. If we had had the normal time I usually allotted I know we could have found the answer.

I woke him up just in time, because they came back knocking at the door. He was as unsatisfied as I was, because he also felt he had not found the answers, and had not completed the session. We went downstairs to the table at the conference where my daughter Nancy was selling my books. We knew there was no choice except to have another session to finish up the loose ends. I felt I owed it to him, and also knew I could not charge him for another session, because I felt responsible for the way this one turned out. So I agreed to let him come to Arkansas to my house, which I never allow strangers to do.

I told Dan to call me when he was in the vicinity, and we would meet him and bring him up on the mountain to my house. I am very cautious about letting any of my readers or fans know where I live, otherwise I would have no privacy at all. But I trusted my instincts that he was a nice young man, and he had come half way around the world to work with me. He had been staying at hostels that were very inexpensive compared to hotels, but there weren't any such places in Huntsville.

Dan stayed in Chicago for a few days to sightsee, then drove down to Arkansas. He arrived on the worst possible day. The night before we had one of our Ozark downpours that make the creeks rise and turn into raging rivers. He called from town and said he had spent the night on the banks of Beaver Lake in his tent. During the night the storm became so violent he woke up with several inches of water in his tent. He found out the hard way it apparently was not waterproof. He bought another tent and drove on to our small town of Huntsville.

When he called I had really forgotten that he would arrive that soon. We were more concerned with the weather. I told him the creek was up and the main road to our house was impassable. It would take a while before anyone could come down into town to lead him up the mountain on the back road. That is the only way to get to my house when the creek rises, and takes about an hour longer. He said he would wait in the little convenience store until someone came down. He at first asked for directions to come up our mountain, but I told him to forget about it. It is impossible to direct a stranger over the backroads if they don't know the area. He ended up waiting there for over two hours before we could get to him. On the way back to my house Nancy drove my car and I rode in his so I could point out the local sights along the way. The area is very isolated, natural and rustic, but I enjoy the privacy because I spend so much time traveling and lecturing in large cities constantly surrounded by crowds of people. When I am home I relish the isolation.

I had decided to let him stay in my spare bedroom for the night, but he insisted on pitching his tent in the yard. He actually hoped it would rain again during the night so he could see if it was waterproof. I fed him supper, and it was late at night before we were able to have the session. He was relaxed and it was easy to get him into a trance again. This time I knew we would have more time to explore his problems, and there was no chance of being disturbed. I hoped he would return to the same scene, and he went there immediately.

Dan: I'm looking at the entranceway to my chamber. There are no designs or anything on the wall. It's very plain. The walls are definitely stone. Again I can really feel it under my feet. It's cool, and it's nice. There are something like lanterns.

I think they're generated light, not fire. It's some sort of chemical process. It's just a lovely light. It's not offensive to my eyes.

D: *It's different, but it's not like a flame?*

Dan: No, it's definitely not fire. I'm looking right at it now. And it's sort of like... I want to say fluorescent light, but it's not. It's softened. It's a long gold tube with a glowing glass crystally type thing at the top. As far as I understand, they're sort of chemically producing light. I don't think there's much power involved, and no wiring is used. Yes, this is my place. The same window, and there's nothing obstructing my view, except when I look outside there's a pyramid to my right. There's a pyramid to my left, which is smaller. And a pyramid beside the one to my left that's smaller again.

D: *There are three then?*

Dan: There are four including mine. The one next to me is much bigger than mine. And mine is connected to the biggest one and to the other two. And I have to descend out of my chamber to get to them. They are connected by a series of tunnels with these lanterns along them, like corridors. I have to go down somehow. I'm trying to visualize how that happens. Shafts, I think, but I can't see any stairs.

D: *But it takes you underground.*

Dan: Yeah. The whole place feels sort of deliberate.

D: *Deliberate. What do you mean?*

Dan: They're not necessarily for living in. They're like strongholds focusing... a focus point for energy. And I'm remembering that this larger person we spoke of travels along energy, if you like. He has the ability to just become energy. I step out of my chamber onto a platform, and it's like an elevator. I can see flashing lights. This goes down below quickly.

D: *You said you were giving this person information.*

Dan: Yes, that's my job. It's clearer now. I would liaison between the people that treat him like a deity and I know he's not a deity. I know that he's just as much a part of the universe as any of us. Maybe it is that I've forgotten how to do what he does. I can see occasionally this big ball of light. And people I don't want to say "common" people but basically people that don't share the secrets, if you like. They worship him, a lot. They think he's a god. And I know he isn't. But there's nothing I can do about it, because I've forgotten some of the secrets. And he's not likely to tell me. It's this power thing going on. I can even see arguments now flashing in front of me. I say that it isn't right, and he doesn't care.

D: *It's not right that they worship him, you mean?*

Dan: Yeah, because all things in the universe are equal. But because he can do things they can't they naturally think he's some kind of a god. And I still have to keep him informed. I just know that I want out of this situation again. It's not a good feeling. I think about running away sometimes, but just lack of commitment, and fear. And lack of somewhere to go I think.

D: *Where would you go?*

Dan: That's it. I have no idea where I'd go. I'm pretty sure I'm the only one that knows that he shouldn't be worshipped the way he's worshipped. And the secrets that he has should be shared as an uplifting ideal, and not used as a point of "I am better than you." He's using people to draw energy from, I guess. I'm not sure if that's the right way to put it, but it's like an ego thing. "Look at this. Look what I can do. I am this. Therefore I am better." I'm trying to work with the idea that he comes from a different place. And I think it's more a different space than a different place. It's more that he's developed this idea of universal... it's hard to put into terms. Let's just say that there's a universal energy. And when you're in that river it can be done well, or it can be done poorly, or i can be not done at all. And he's done it poorly, because he's jumped into the river. It's given him these powers, that we might by looking at him say, "Oh, wow, that's pretty amazing You'd have to be a god to be doing those things." And then instead of using that power that has come about by self awareness. It's more than that. It's knowing and being. Instead of doing that and being humble with it, he's being completely egotistical with it. And here am I, knowing that I'm on this similar power, or at least have come from somewhere. A faint memory of another existence, or just understanding the powers that the universe holds, and the consciousnesses, if you like. And telling him that this isn't a good thing. And he's putting me down for it. He's loving it. It's like it's none of my business. "What are you going to do about it" kind of thing. This cockiness.

D: *But you said he's not there all the time. He comes and goes.*

Dan: He doesn't have to be there all the time. He can travel to wherever he likes. It's nothing. When you understand the principle of the universe, there's nothing actually to stop you being anywhere anytime. It's fundamental matter and energy And as we understand it, there is no difference between those things.

D: *Unless we put restrictions on it ourselves.*

Dan: Well, we can restrict matter into a form, but there is no difference between that matter and energy. When you understand that consciousness is the separating factor between any kind of form, then when that consciousness reaches a space where it is able to control that form, then what is the difference between anything in the form? There is none. It's just a collection of energy placed into physical matter.

D: *You said when you can control or when you can't control?*

Dan: When you can. When you understand.

D: *When you understand you can control the energy?*

Dan: (Sigh) Well, I'm saying "control", but it's not the word, because it's just what we understand. But it's more that you are the energy. You are it, so you can be it. The form of the physical matter is just physical energy. Time is energy. We are energy. Consciousness is energy. And we can direct that into a form. When you place this into its pure source, the source of consciousness, you can redirect it anywhere. It doesn't necessarily have to be in one spot at once. It can be anything you like it to be. If you wished you could exist for an eon without being missed from one part of time. What I'm seeing in front of my eyes is the idea of an elastic band being stretched. (Hand motions) And you hold one end with your fingers away up, so that part isn't being affected by the stretch, and it stays in its normal shape. Then you pull one end and it becomes thinner, but the other end that you've got your fingers on is not affected. So it looks like a rubber band. But the other side looks like a stretched long light bit of rubber. So what I'm trying to say is that we are continuous through consciousness. And we can "push? pull? manipulate?" But we can manipulate this by saying, "Well, I exist in this part of the band. I exist in that part of the band. I can stay in this part for an eon. I can live this part for a millisecond." But there's still no difference to that band, it's still part of the same physical matter. It's just deformed, separated, splintered.

D: *It's complicated. Does this mean that in that form it doesn't have to have a body?*

Dan: It comes back to the idea that I can exist as a blade of grass, and be a part of that energy, and be an energetic being of pure light simultaneously in different time spaces. What discerns those two energies is my conscious being.

D: *This goes back to the idea of there not being any time, and everything happening at once?*

Dan: Time is just an energy that spins. It's the pulsation of matter. As far as this body here understands it, this is what feels most correct, that it's the actual traveling of matter, physical matter. So therefore there isn't really time as such, but it exists on a causal plane I don't even know what that means but it exists causally. So if there is matter, there is time If there is energy, there is time. If there is consciousness, there is no time, because we are creating our physical worlds from consciousness.

D: *From consciousness. So if there is not consciousness, there is not time? Is that what you see?*

Dan: No. There is consciousness, there is no time. Time is material. What I'm seeing in front of my eyes is a big spinning ball of gas. I'm not sure entirely why that's relevant at the moment, but my whole body is shaking like a leaf.

This must have been internal, because his physical body was showing no signs of anything except relaxation.

Dan: The concept is hard to relay. We can only limit by our imaginations, because it just doesn't have any limits. So we can only imagine, therefore limit our conception of it, to try and grasp it. So we're in that. There is no time as such. So we can exist free the best word, the only word that's coming is: we can exist free. Now try and materialize a conscious thought just conscious. There are no other words. "Thought" is wrong, because thought is energy also. But conscious itself is like where the universe well, our universe anyway is defined before it happens.

D: *Before it happens.*

Dan: As thought to happen, is best. That's the freest words I can say. Consciousness defines it for to happen.

D: *For it to happen. But the consciousness is this energy you're talking about. Is that what you mean?*

Dan: Conscious defines energy, if you like.

D: *But this does not mean physical consciousness. It's like an energy consciousness?*

Dan: Thought is energy. But who has thought? I asked that question because I'm trying to illustrate a point. Where we have to say, "Well, thoughts are energy. But who thinks that thought?" And I am trying to suggest that this body believes or is feeling, that consciousness is that thinker. That consciousness itself is the driving force of all creation, as we know it. Whether it be metaphysical, spiritual, energetic, physical, material. All these things are derived by consciousness. It's through consciousness to learn or consciousness to exist, that these things exist. Like flipping a coin. You can't have one side of the coin without the other.

So now I'm being shown the ball of gas again, that spins to create a force. That force becomes denser, becomes what we understand, or at least what I understand because my conscious mind is shouting at me now, and I'm trying to ignore it, but it's harder. I can see it spinning. I can see creating. In order for there to be that matter it has to exist for a period. Period? It has to exist. So we grasp onto a concept of time, because we are limited? (He wasn't sure of that word.)

D: *That would make sense. We are limited in our physical bodies while we're on Earth, in this dimension or whatever it is.*

Dan: It not necessarily has to be though... but yes, I guess it does.

D: *We are limited, but in the other state we're not?*

Dan: Conscious state, no limits. It's almost like for want of a better shot for words a play group. This sounds trivial, I know, but we are always perfect. Yet we have lessons to learn. Consciousness derives growth? I think "growth" is the thing that's coming unless I want to say "manifestation" but I think somewhere between the two is correct. Consciousness derives somewhere between the idea of growth and manifestation, by being playful, creative, energetic. And for it to understand itself we create other things, other than what it is. I'm now being taken straight back to the planet where I was sucked off like a tissue. And I'm now having to create more things in order to grow. In order to become more creative I existed there for God knows how long it's just saying the word "eons" at me.

D: *You were existing there in the same form of energy that this other person is? Or would that make sense?*

Dan: I get a feeling of, with this being that we speak of, the one that's so egotistical that's where we're back to now he is near a state of total essence, but is still more an individual like you and I. Rather than existing wholly as I did in that existence on that planet with the tissue sucking effect. I could feel an individuality about myself, but more of an energy also. Much more, much more. But I'm trying to define this person for you.

D: *But he does form a body sometimes, doesn't he?*

Dan: Yes, he's fully able. It's like magic.

D: *But when you were on the other planet where you felt part of everything, were you the same kind of an energy he is now, or were you more advanced?*

Dan: I'm going to say: more simple. There was no intellect. There was no judgment on anything. It was like I was an infant. More uncomplicated. I didn't even understand the idea of physical realm, as such, as a material body.

D: *It was something you had never experienced?*

Dan: Never. But this one, I think he's progressed to this stage, from being humanoid, human, up to this idea of energetic sou levels. And he still has growth to go.

D: *So he wasn't at the point that you were.*

Dan: I think they're two different things. I think there is an ide of the simplest life form imaginable, which is so naive and whimsical, playful, gentle.

It sounded like he was describing an elemental energy. Was tha what he was on that planet? Just the most basic form of energy?

Dan: The first one exists and has only ever existed that way. It' there. And the other one, this being has progressed such a lon way in his physical evolutions that he started to really get los in the powers that the conscious universe has to offer. And he' becoming so aware that he can use them. There are other beings like that.

D: *This is why he became egotistical then.*

Dan: I think that's what happens.

D: *They have so much power and they enjoy using it, and they like being worshipped.*

Dan: Sure! I would too. I'd want to prance and sing and show off, if I could float or glow.

D: *Why did you have to leave that existence on the other planet i it was so simple and uncomplicated?*

Dan: I think it was to do with growth. We have an idea that is the goal, to exist in these forms, where pure energy is all tha we are. And we can be wondrous and glorious. But for consciousness to grow in a creative way we have to create. Let me illustrate it by asking, "What was I creating, except experience?" There was no love. There was no adventure. There was a little wonder, because I could sense that I would travel and see other places, and just experience their environment for a little while. But I had a longing to be back in my comfort zone, because that's what it was.

D: *That's why that place was like home.*

Dan: Always. I'm starting to sense now from a more objective point of view, rather than the emotion I felt last time. I'm starting to sense that I was there an extremely long time. I can't really put it into numbers. It was too long. That was the point, I think, it was too long. Maybe I was given opportunitie to leave on my own accord. And I was like, "Oh, I don't really want to go." Then all of a sudden, I think the decision was made for me. I'm being told that it was difficult for me to forget.

D: *That's why you had this feeling of not belonging, and wanting to go home, because you still had that memory. (Yes) And when you were with this other being you had a memory that you at one time could do more than he could.*

Dan: That's almost right. But I had no idea how to make the physical incarnation. He had every idea. He could come in like the wind, and form. Just one minute not be there, but the next second he could be. And I witnessed that. I can see shifts in light, and the body being composed out of that light. And him stepping forward from it. Not like a doorway. I don't think so anyway. Something kept saying: the pyramids just flashed straight up. Maybe the arrangements of those pyramids and the order they were in. It was: big, a little bit smaller, a little bit smaller, a little bit smaller, in a semi circle. Maybe that helped him get an idea of where he was to be. I don't really know. But I just got the flash.

D: *The way they were arranged?*

Dan: Yes, the pyramids helped.

D: *You said it was like a focus point of energy? So he was able to use that in some way?*

Dan: I think so. He would always materialize in his pyramid, never mine. Never the others either.

D: *Which one was his?*

Dan: The biggest one. And people would admire him, and that would make me sick.

D: *So whenever he would appear it was like the god had returned. (Yes) You were supposed to worship him like the rest of them did.*

Dan: Yes, he had an idea that I knew. And I think that's why I advised him, because I had some powers. And I guess when you get to a level that he was, you can see aura like you can see anything else. And you can read people, and therefore it's easier to have control over them as well. And it's easy to abuse that. Rather than honoring that person's individuality in their journey, you take advantage of it.

After a while the other entity stopped coming. There was no explanation and Dan was left sitting and waiting, bored and not knowing what to do next. The people started turning to him for advice, but he had none to give them.

Dan: I was confused. He'd left and they started looking to me for this deity. I said, "Well, run it yourselves." They didn't like that idea. So I hid basically. I'm in this big pyramid, and I'm hiding from all these people, knowing no one can get at me. Unless they're ushered into these complexes they don't know how to get into it. They needed a god. And I didn't want to be a hypocrite. After years of telling this guy he shouldn't be this way, I didn't want to become that guy, even though I didn't have his powers, and I was becoming older. But at the same time I can feel that I didn't do anything to help as well. And that sort of upset me. I'm in a cycle of just not knowing what to do. They want this deity. I'm in an energy focusing system of these pyramids. I imagine that might help, might amplify. The feeling I get is like shouting in my ears. "Where are you? When are you going to help us? Make the 'whatever' happen." I wanted to say "rain" then, but I'm not sure.

D: *They looked for him to help solve all their problems.*

Dan: Yeah. And perhaps he was at that stage where he could do that. I recall him standing there and creating miracles. Loneliness is the first word that came into my mind.

D: *What does it mean?*

Dan: Well, I was totally alone. After he left there was no one. (Big sigh) There is the idea that I'm not really making the most of this.

It was obvious that this was going nowhere. No new information was being added. So I had Dan go to the last day of his life in that lifetime.

D: *What are you doing now, and what do you see?*

Dan: I'm just in bed, dying alone. And the secrets are dying with me. There's no way for the people to use what I have in these pyramids, because I haven't shown them anything. Or I haven't taught anybody. It's just me alone. And that's it. I have my eyes closed.

D: *What's the matter with you when you die?*

Dan: I'm just old. I get a feeling of regret and loneliness, and just complete sorrow. I'm looking at my face right now, and there are a few tears in my eyes, and they just close. And I look like I don't know what's happening. I could have done better.

D: *What do you mean by complete sorrow?*

Dan: Like this whole thing was a waste. Like your whole being says, "You should have done that better," or "I wish that wasn't the way it was." And you have that sorrow well up inside you. And that's what I can see in my eyes as I look at them as they close.

I then took him to beyond the death experience and had him look back at the entire life, and see what the lesson was.

Dan: To do something. To make the most of any situation that you've created. People are going to be what they're going to be. And it's up to you to be what you're going to be. So you can take responsibility for yourself, or you can never do anything. And that gets you nowhere. Which is worse, not accomplishing anything when you know you can. I think that's pretty relevant in my life now. Everybody's got to do what they've got to do. And you can be defeated by it, and never do anything. If you're going to look at every single flaw that you have, you've still got that input to make, that help to give. And it's worse if you don't even do anything and don't try.

After this I worked with Dan and his subconscious to discover the source of his problems and how to solve them. The remainder of the session was very successful. I knew that all we needed was sufficient time to work on it, which was denied in Chicago by the abrupt ending of the session.

I then brought Dan forward to full consciousness. After talking for a while Dan went outside to his tent, where he slept like a rock until morning. After breakfast he left to do some more exploring and sight seeing in New Mexico and Arizona Indian country before returning to Los Angeles to turn in his rental car and return to Australia.

Weeks later he emailed me that the session had been a success and had made a significant change in his life. He was now not afraid of whatever the future might hold. Through our strange meeting he also supplied me with an interesting piece of information about the place that he considered "home".

***

While searching through my files to locate cases that should be in this book I found this one that was done in 1990. At the time I did not realize its relevance, but now I see it is another piece of the puzzle of Star Children. Much of my material must wait for years before it finds its niche.

Robert was a good looking young man appearing to be in his late thirties or early forties. He was a Viet Nam veteran who had been having many problems that he related to the war. Since his return he had been unable to hold a job, and was on disability. He spent a lot of time in the Veterans Administration Hospital where the doctors found that his physical problems (mostly stomach and intestinal, and nervousness) were caused by mental problems (or psychosomatic They had attempted to trace this to find out if any specific incident i Viet Nam caused it. They had been unsuccessful because he refused t talk about anything that happened during the war. They tried hypnos and were unsuccessful. Their only solution was to put him on drugs

His girl friend warned me that I would probably meet the sam obstacles because he steadfastly refused to approach the subject c Viet Nam. I told him that would be all right, because we didn't eve have to explore that area. We would look into his past lives and se if there was a clue there. I believe this helped him to relax, becaus he did not see me as a threat. The explanation that came out woul never have been understood by the doctors at the VA anyway. So hi subconscious was wisely protecting him by not allowing this stor to be revealed to the inappropriate people. He probably would hav ended up as a patient in a psychiatric hospital. Maybe this was wh his subconscious allowed him to tell it to me, because he was saf Whatever the reason, despite years of therapy and treatment by V doctors, this was the first time this explanation (or any explanatior was offered for his war related problems.

I went to the house where Robert was living with his girlfriend an her two boys. He had his own part of the house, like a small apartmen where he could be alone if he wished. This was where we conducte the session. After he was in a deep trance he entered a strange scen that did not sound Earthly. It took quite a bit of questioning to tr to determine where he was. Then it became obvious to me that h had not entered a past lifetime, which is the normal procedure for first regression. He apparently had skipped the past experiences an was in a place that sounded like the spirit realm where the soul goe between lives. It specifically sounded like the area where the school are located. Maybe his subconscious thought his answers would com more easily from this area rather than from exploring a specific pa; life.

He found himself in a large place with tall white walls, an different shades of light coming from an unknown source. He saw h was clothed in a white robe that seemed to be a part of him rather tha a garment.

R: My body doesn't need to be protected by clothing.
D: *Why is that?*
R: My body is one.
D: *Is it a physical body?*
R: No, not really. It works as a physical body, but it's not a physical body at all.
D: *Can you explain what you mean?*

320

R: I have energy inside of me. I can feel the warmth of my energy. I can see my arms. I feel I can pass through things. But not all the time. Only when I need to.

D: *Where do you think this structure is?*

R: It must be a housing of some sort. Or a communication. Or an auditorium.

D: *What do you mean by a communication?*

R: I'm waiting to go to a terminal. I'm supposed to get information there, before I go....

D: *Where are you going?*

R: That's not up to me to decide.

He had the feeling he had to wait for someone to come and tell him where to go, or to escort him. He saw that there were many hallways, and he wasn't sure which one to take without someone to give him directions. Although it didn't really matter, "Because I'll be here or I'll be there. It really doesn't matter where I be." There was the uncertainty that if he went off on his own he might be breaking some kind of rule. Finally he decided to go down one of the curving hallways. He then found himself in a large open area.

R: I'm standing in front of something. I see people, but they don't look like me. Maybe they look like me now. They're sitting up above, so they can see out around the whole place, all the corridors. They have auras. There are yellow auras, and blue auras, and green auras. And white auras. One person in the corner has a real white aura.

D: *Do they have clothes on?*

R: No. It is the same thing as with me. They don't need clothes. It's as if they have an information booth, and they're sitting up above everybody, so they can view out and see who's coming and who's going. And you can see them too. It's like a reception area. I'm asking what I have to do. (Pause) They said, "Don't be alarmed. You will go when the time is necessary for you to go. You will go back to school."

D: *Do you understand what they mean?*

R: I feel like everybody is being trained, going to school to learn more about what is love, what is life, what is God. But my concept of God is not their concept.

D: *What do you mean?*

R: God is everywhere.

D: *What is their concept?*

R: We are God. But we must worship God. We do not pray for God.

D: *Can you ask him some questions for me?*

321

R: I'll try.

D: *Ask him where this place is.*

R: It's in another dimension. Not necessarily where it is. It's in our solar system, but the solar system is not what we determine it is. Our galaxy has different solar systems. And this place is just a terminal, information area, for all the different worlds in our one particular universe.

D: *Are they physical?*

R: They're not really physical, just like I'm not physical.

D: *Can they tell you where you are going to go to school?*

R: They're finding out what my background is, and how I would benefit all of the universe. And how I can go forward. They wanted to know if my science background on Earth is what I truly want to have as my background. Or is it my spiritual nature that I really want to go forward with in my life. My background in biology and medicine is interesting to me, but it's more interesting to help people spiritually in recovering themselves.

D: *Have you had experience in biology and medicine in your work?*

R: On Earth I have degrees in nursing and biology, master's degrees. But the more I learned, the less I knew. There's so much to learn. We cannot conceive all the concepts that are open to us on Earth, because we are very limited and immature. I'm just standing here. I feel sort of foolish. It's like waiting to go to the bathroom.

D: *(Chuckle) Yes, but are they going to send you back to Earth once they find out what your background is?*

R: No, I'm going to go on. To another world. There are different worlds. There are hundreds and hundreds and thousands of worlds you can go to.

D: *How do you feel about that?*

R: Well, I'll make friends anywhere I go. It would be nice to know that I'm with some friends, but we're all on the same path anyway. And maybe I can just go on and make my own friends again.

D: *What about other lifetimes?*

R: I've lived other lifetimes. I've always been in the field of science and medicine and metaphysics.

D: *Then there's a lot of knowledge there to draw on, isn't there?*

R: Yeah. I feel like I'm very intelligent. And that's why they don't know where to put me. Because my intelligence doesn't match up with what I did on Earth. I've always been holding myself back.

D: *Do you mean you had a lot of potential that you didn't use? (Yes) And they want to put you somewhere where you can use that?*

R: Uh huh. So I can be happy.

D: *Do you think you'd be happy if you used all your potential? (Yeah) Can't you do it while you're alive on Earth?*

R: I don't know which direction to go, except just the way I'm going.

D: *If you do have a lot of potential, it would be shame to waste it, wouldn't it?*

R: It's never wasted. Knowledge is never wasted. That's one joy of knowledge and education. It's always there. It's the facts or the truth.

D: *You never lose it. You can always draw on it if you need it. Have you been to this place before?*

R: I might have been to a couple of places down the hall. I've never been in this one particular area.

D: *When do you go there?*

R: After you die.

D: *That was what I thought it sounded like. But they're not sure what they want you to do next time?*

R: I need to use the well rounded balance of knowledge that I have accumulated, to help other people who never have had opportunities like that. I've been very fortunate.

D: *Have you always lived on Earth in the physical lifetime?*

R: No. Earth is just a very small world. It's a challenge to live on Earth.

D: *Maybe that's why people are sent here.*

R: Everybody needs a challenge, and Earth is one of the challenges. It always seems like we can deal with this challenge. But after we're here we're so frustrated, because the challenges are greater than we actually felt they would be. Looking down at Earth... it's such a tiny planet, but it holds so much chaos that one man can't really change it.

D: *One man can sometimes do miracles. You never know until you try. Do you feel as though you have lived somewhere else more than you have lived on Earth?*

R: I've explored Earth quite a few times, but the next time I'm not going to come back to Earth. I'm going to go on to someplace else.

D: *What about the places you've lived before. Was there a favorite?*

R: I've always enjoyed the water. The water and the trees. On this other world there are different... it doesn't look like the same trees. These trees all look like the Douglas Fir trees.

And the water is blue because of the oxygen and the hydrogen.

D: *What are the people like that live there?*

R: They're like me now.

D: *You mean that energy type?*

R: Yes. There are physical things. Animals. But there's nothing to harm me, like on Earth.

D: *Why aren't you physical and more solid on that world?*

R: Because we don't have any waste, we don't have any food. We take energy in. This keeps the body from being denser.

D: *And that was one of your favorite places?*

R: Yes. Because you can just sit and smell the fragrance of the trees and the water. It's so peaceful.

D: *But did you accomplish anything while you were living there?*

R: Yes. Helping other people.

D: *Did that world have challenges?*

R: All worlds have challenges. Some challenges are not necessarily of evil nature, like on Earth. Other worlds have challenges where you need to know what is right and what is wrong. You have different paths to go down. But you have to make sure that the love of God is inside of you, and you choose that path. Because every time we choose that path it reinforces our goodness that we have inside.

D: *And that's very important. But you said these beings in that room are trying to help you.*

R: Yes. This is their assignment. It's their job to help place people. There are monitors up there inside the desks area. I'm not supposed to look at the monitors. I have a feeling that they're looking at something. It's like I'm being programmed. My memory of all that I've thought of, and what I am, they're running it through. They erase the bad parts and leave the good parts. I don't really need to remember the bad parts anymore, because that's on the physical nature.

D: *I guess they know what they're doing. Is it like a machine?*

R: The closest thing I can think of is like a computer. The man at the terminal was trying to say something, but he's not saying it very well. (Pause) It's not a computer. It's thought patterns vibrating at a certain wave length only known to them. It's like a fingerprint.

D: *So each person has their own individual thought pattern or vibration?*

R: It's built into like a terminal of a computer. It goes through to different worlds. It goes to that world which is the capital of our universe.

D: *It's kind of like a clearing house. And they're analyzing your talents and all of those things?*

R: Yes. This is what's coming through to me: I might be pretty good at being able to talk to people and comfort people. And to discuss philosophy of spiritual nature, which I can use through my science, my education, and my thirst for knowledge of the spiritual.

D: *Then what happens?*

R: They'll give me an assignment. I have some resting time. I've got to make my adjustments.

D: *Well, it's good to know that someone else is helping.*

R: There's always somebody helping. There are people helping me right now. They're different energies. They're right next to me. They're a different energy than I am. It's not really an energy, but it is energy. They feel very comforting. They've been with me on Earth.

D: *Are these energies like the other ones?*

R: No. The ones at the desks have more of a body shape form. Not white. They're kind of a mucky looking color. A teal color, maybe? Bluish greenish. They're sort of solid, but they're not solid. You can't really poke your arm through it. But the other energy that is with me is more of a light energy. That's what it is. It's light! Pure light. They're always with me. They're going to be a part of me.

D: *Do you think so?*

R: Yes. But I still don't talk their language. There's no talk between us. It's thought.

At this point I decided to take him ahead to a time when he had completed his resting, and was ready to accept his next assignment. He would be able to speed up the resting portion, but still get the benefits from it. I didn't need to count him there because he interrupted me before I had completed the instructions.

R: (Interrupted) Yeah, I'm right there, right on the edge, looking out into space. I'm with somebody. And I have to be right on their... I don't know what.... I'm engulfed with it. I'm supposed to get engulfed. Okay. I can go now. I can go. It's like angel wings. It's angels, but it's not angels. They're just different. It's kind of a pecking order. Everybody has their job. Everybody has different duties to help each other. And they always feel sorry for people who live on Earth. But they also feel sort of jealous, because they can't experience the emotions that we have experienced.

D: *These light energies?*

R: Yes. The light energy. They haven't experienced emotions, and crying and laughing, like we have experienced it. And the

325

pain. They don't know what pain is. Maybe it's me feeling tha I'm a little bit better than they are. But I don't have the powe they do. I'm supposed to be engulfed within this energy, anc be taken without being burnt, because we travel so fast. Ther has to be a little bit of friction. (Is this his own perception? Because a spirit would not be hurt.) And it keeps me safe. It keeps them safe.

D: *From our human perspective, you would think they were lucky not to have experienced emotions. It seems strange to think of them being jealous.*

R: Maybe they're more compassionate, and that's what I'm feeling.

D: *And you're traveling through space or what?*

R: I can go any time. I'm waiting on you.

D: *Waiting on me? Why?*

R: I don't know. I just thought I was. (I chuckled) Okay. We're ready. Are you going to go?

D: *I guess, if you're ready. I am just a guide to take you throug these many different things. That's all I am.*

R: Okay. Let's go!

D: *And they are keeping you safe. Tell me what it is like as you go.*

R: It feels like my head... Whoaaa! It felt like a big rush. We're on a beach now.

D: *Oh! That was quick, wasn't it?*

R: Yeah. They travel real fast. And we're on a beach. And I wil just be led to what I am supposed to be doing. (Pause) I'm not an infant. I have no age. I feel like an adult, yet there is n age. There's no time really. There's time for rest. It's not th time that we think of.

D: *Where is this beach?*

R: It's on a world. And there are different trees. I am by the wate because that's where I wanted to go. I need to walk... and there's a dwelling up above. It has a broad foundation, and it's... not pyramid shaped, but it has different levels getting smaller to the top. (Hand motions) And it has a little beacon thing up there, a little light house type thing. You don't feel like yourself walking, but you're walking. It just feels like I'n walking. But I don't really have a solid skin with hair on it. It's just.... (hard to explain.) You can grab hold of it.

D: *So it does have some substance. Tell me what the dwelling's like.*

R: There are stairs going up, steps. The building is blue, with a yellow trim. There are big picture windows. Big, big double doors, that are yellow. It's very large. Very beautiful. A lot o

light. Very comfortable looking. I would enjoy this place.
There are other people saying, "Hello!"

D: *Do they know you?*

R: Yes. They know me. They were waiting for me. Many of them
I know, but they don't have their names any more. I just know
that I've known them before. And it feels good to be with
people I used to know. They chose the same place I did.

D: *Is this a physical world?*

R: Fairly physical, yes.

D: *Are the people all like you?*

R: Yes. There are a couple of people over there that are taller.
They look wiser. They might be the superiors.

D: *Do they all have the same type of energy body, without any
features?*

R: They don't really need features. I don't really need features.
We have ears, but we don't really talk. We have eyes, and we
do see. We have smells. And it seems like I have so many
different senses. More than I have now on Earth. It's going to
be nice to experience. We're all there to be taught and to teach
each other.

D: *What type of senses do you have that you don't have on Earth?*

R: It is hard to explain. The smells... everybody, everything has
a different smell to it. And it's correlated with the light it looks
like. So I really don't need to go into it too much. Touch has
the same vibration level as the smell does. Everybody has an
aura, like they're encapsulated.

D: *What do you have to do there?*

R: I need to study and talk and learn. With these other people we
discuss our past lives. And we're supposed to be instructed
how to live on this planet.

D: *So you will stay on that planet for a while?*

R: Yeah, until we more or less pass our exams. Other people may
not pass them as fast as I might. And I might not pass them as
fast as some others.

D: *So there isn't any set time.*

R: No, there's no time.

D: *Do you know what you will do after you've passed your tests?*

R: No, that will be decided at that time. I enjoy the search for
knowledge.

I did not think we could learn anything further if he was going to
stay in that place for a while. The end of the session was drawing near,
and we still had not determined the cause of his physical problems
in this present lifetime. So I asked him to leave that scene so I could
speak to his subconscious, and perhaps get more explicit answers.

D: *I would like to ask your subconscious some questions relating to your life on Earth at the present time. Would that be all right?*

R: Let me get back to Earth.

I oriented him back to the present time and instructed his present consciousness to completely return to his body. At this point he began to move around, and I didn't want him to wake up yet.

D: *I want you to remain in this state, so I may speak to your subconscious and ask it questions.*

R: I still have memories of that.

D: *Oh, it was very beautiful. I want to speak to Robert's subconscious please. Why was Robert shown those scenes?*

R: Because he can tell people on Earth that life is forever. And that we're balanced and living life that we have here on Earth. We, in this physical body, don't have to be negative. We can be positive. And when we know love and give love, we experience what is beyond this world. We need to know we're spiritual, we're balanced. From science he knows why the sky is blue and the leaves are green. Why the worms go in and out. He knows every part of the body, every muscle, every bone. But he has never developed what he has thought of as his spiritual nature. Not religious faith, but spiritualism. He knew that there's always life after this world. Not necessarily on this world. If you come back to this Earth, you choose to come back. Or you're more or less told to come back, because you haven't fulfilled and learned the knowledge, the challenges of this disobedient world. It's going to school. That's all that we are. When we educate our young children, right from the start we are learning. We are always going to school. What we start off as an infant, and carry out through our adult life, we carry on in a different life after birth. We're always learning. And some people refuse to learn. It's like the old saying that you can take the donkey to the water trough. You can stick its nose and mouth right in the water, but you can't make him drink it. Until he finds out that the water quenches his thirst.

D: *Sometimes people just keep making the same mistakes.*

R: Yes. You can ram their head into the wall. In Robert's case, he has lived more lives on other worlds than on Earth. He just came to this world because it's a challenge, because he gets bored easily.

D: *Do you think this is part of his physical problems, because he's not used to a physical body.*

R: It's possible, I guess. Gosh durn, I didn't want to be here. (Chuckle) I kind of agree, because I don't want this body. But I'm stuck with it.

D: *Yes, for the time being, you are. And you have to learn to live with it. But it seems as though in other lifetimes, he didn't have this kind of a body to worry about.*

R: No, he didn't feel pain. Pain is hell.

D: *He didn't know what it was.*

R: No, there is no pain over there. You have to be physical to understand pain.

D: *Maybe this is something he came to learn.*

R: It is. And everybody else has to learn about Robert's pain too, because Robert can handle the pain. But he's having a hard time with his drugs. There's a physical dependency on drugs. When he gets clear with this Viet Nam stress that his body's going through, maybe he will ask the VA to be hospitalized for awhile. Because the poor guy has been on drugs for so many years, from trying to combat this pain. And this pain is never going to leave him until he dies.

D: *Do you think that, or do you have something to say about it?*

R: That's his destiny. He has to feel the pain, because he can handle the pain. And people have to learn from him.

D: *Doesn't that seem rather cruel?*

R: It's not cruel at all, because there's no time. When one person dies of cancer because he smoked too many cigarettes, the people around him learn an awfully harsh lesson. And so does he. But everybody goes on. It really doesn't matter, because it's just a flash of a few seconds of real time.

D: *If he had lifetimes where he didn't have a physical body, do you think that was why going to Viet Nam was so stressful?*

R: Yes. But it was something he wanted to do, and he was told to do. He knew he wasn't going to die, but he didn't know really. There was death all around him.

D: *And it brought fear.*

R: Yeah, but that was what kept him going. That's what made him do what he did. The challenge of the fear. There are not too many places in the universes that have war. Earth is one of the only places that you can experience war as man. It happened to man a long time ago, when the whole world defaulted.

D: *What do you mean, the whole world defaulted?*

R: There were other beings that came down to help us. And they tried to mate, and they tried to screw around and play God.

D: *And they were the ones that brought these situations?*

R: Yeah. They wanted to play army, cowboys and Indians. They set up a pattern. Humans are basically animals, and it's hard to break the pattern. It has to do with evolving out of the pattern. It's like a bad habit. Once you start biting your fingernails, like Robert does, it's hard to break it. Or saying certain swear word. It's hard to break it.

D: *So it's a habit of the human race, you mean.*

R: Yes. It's all of our problem.

D: *It was brought here by other beings?*

R: Yeah. They didn't know. It's not really their fault. I think it' just sort of ... happened.

D: *And now this is in the pattern of the Earth people.*

R: Yes. It's becoming better. Earth has had some success in its evolutionary patterns. The male likes to fight. And this is one of the places you can experience that. There are many experiences of Earth that you can go through, like starvation, war. There are other experiences. Being godlike in the politics Or you can experience just a pleasant, pleasant feeling of family life.

D: *Yes, you have many choices. So I get the feeling then that when he went to Viet Nam....*

R: That was my choice.

D: *But you were not prepared for the stress.*

R: No, no. Nobody told me about how bad it is.

D: *But apparently you learned a lesson from it. A lesson that will be valuable to you.*

R: Yeah, because I know what war is like. I know what fighting is like. So when I go on to another world, and if somebody became angry or started showing a you can call it a "recessive" trait I would know what it's like. And I could help those people get past that.

D: *That's very valuable. But do you really believe that Robert came into this life to experience the discomfort he is experiencing? (Yes) But wouldn't it be easier if we could help him to live with that?*

R: It will be easier as time goes on.

D: *Do you think if he understands where it's coming from, and the reason for it, it will make it easier for him to deal with?*

R: But he has a lot of physical problems.

D: *But can't you, as the subconscious, help him with these?*

R: Only if he can go to the subconscious, and ask for guidance, and ask for the natural endorphins in his body to help. He will get the pain so somebody else can experience helping him.

D: *But still it would be good if we could ease it. We don't want to make life miserable while he's learning these lessons.*

R: Robert's life's not miserable. He's got it made.

D: *Do you think so? I don't know if he would agree. But the important thing is, if he wants alleviation from the discomfort, he can go to the subconscious and ask for the natural endorphins to help him.*

R: Yes. Like right now, he doesn't have any pain.

D: *Yes. Those endorphins are very powerful. They're much more powerful than taking any kind of drugs. Because they are natural, and they are controlled by the subconscious.*

I then planted the suggestion that when he needed relief he could relax and ask the subconscious to release the natural endorphins. The subconscious tried to argue with me, "Yeah, but Robert's so sensitive to everybody else's pain."

I could understand why, because Robert was a very sensitive and compassionate person. After much discussion the subconscious agreed to do its part, if Robert would cooperate. The final outcome is always up to the person. If they do not truly want to cure themselves, for whatever reason, then nothing I can do will help.

I never worked with Robert again. I heard about him from time to time. He was still experiencing difficulties and was in and out of the VA hospital. It seemed as though he really did not want to release the lesson of pain, even though his subconscious was willing to work with him on the problem. I would like to think though that it did help by releasing the natural endorphins at times when he needed them, so he wouldn't be so addicted to the drugs. At least, he now knew some of the reasons why he was experiencing this part of his life. Maybe his subconscious was correct when it said the pain would never leave him until he died. If that is so, I hope he is learning his lesson, and also teaching others about pain and about living with someone who has chronic pain. If that is the reason, then it has merit because it teaches. That's really what it's all about, learning lessons, and progressing from here. If we learn a lesson well, then we don't have to repeat it.

Again, I can fully understand why Robert's subconscious would not allow this story to come out when he was working with the VA doctors. Maybe hearing this story might make them more understanding, and more open to looking for the cause of wartime stress in unusual places with unusual explanations.

***

RETURN TO THE TAPESTRY ROOM

I spent the month of March 2000 lecturing in all the main cities in Australia. I try to do some private sessions when I am traveling, because there is always a waiting list of people all over the world wanting therapy. Norma had written me after reading some of my books, and we made an appointment to have a session while I was in Gold Coast. She had many personal and physical problems she wanted to find explanations for. Also she had been fascinated by the description of the spirit world that we enter when we leave this life as reported in my book *Between Death and Life*. She wanted to see these places for herself, especially the Temple of Wisdom Complex with its wonderful Library and Tapestry Room. I told her this might be possible. I would have to take her through a past life first, and then see where she went after the death. This is the procedure I have found works best if we want to explore the spirit side.

She went into a deep state quickly and relived a past life in Victorian England that explained a lot of the personal karmic relationships she was involved with in this life. There were many details: dates, names and places in London, that could be checked and verified. I have done so many regressions now that this type of detail no longer surprises me. The important thing is the therapy that is derived from reliving the trauma and emotion of the lifetime. I normally leave it to the subject whether they want to investigate and verify it. I no longer need proof, and do not check these things out unless it is of value to include in a book. There will never be enough proof to convince a true skeptic, and a believer does not need proof. At this point in my work I am more fascinated by the unknown, which cannot be proven anyway.

When I took her to the end of that life she died peacefully as an old woman at her home surrounded by her family. As she drifted away from the physical body I asked her to describe what was happening.

> N: There's a light. Figures in robes and there's love and peace. They take her to a place that's very quiet and peaceful. There's no one around. It's just quiet and very misty.

This sounded like the place that others have described as the Resting Place, a type of sanctuary where souls can rest for a while before going on to another destination, either on that side or by returning to another body in a new lifetime.

> D: *A place where she can just rest for awhile?*
> N: (Softly) Yes. It's nice.
> D: *After that will she have to go somewhere else?*
> N: Yes, it's time. She has to go to the rooms of knowledge now.
> D: *I've heard of these places. Norma wanted to have the memory of what they looked like. What are you showing her?*
> N: There are pillars. And lots of books. And a dome... and people. And it's very... heavy, thick with knowledge. It's big. It goes

forever. It has many rooms beyond the stoned area. And there are walkways and books and tables and people.

D: *Who am I speaking to? Her subconscious or....?*

N: Norma's aware of Norma, but I am her higher self.

D: *I call it the subconscious. It's the part that has all of the information, isn't it? (Yes) That's what I like to speak to. I'm aware of some of the parts of this place. Is there a room called the "tapestry room"?*

N: Oh, yes.

This was described in *Between Death and Life* as a tapestry of life where every person's life is represented as a thread. The way it interweaves is a vivid description of how everyone's life influences everyone else. We are one and yet we are all interconnected.

D: *She wondered if she could see that room?*

N: She goes there all the time.

D: *Does she? (Yes) She doesn't know it, does she?*

N: She does, but she didn't believe it.

D: *Can you show her what the room looks like?*

N: It's a room full of light. It hasn't a ceiling, for the tapestry is very high. And it's very long. Goes a long way. There's no end. And it's moving. It's alive.

D: *What do you mean?*

N: It's alive with the light, and the threads are living things. They're not... material. They have feeling, and they have thought, and they have color, and they have life.

D: *The strands that make up the weaving of the tapestry?*

N: Yes. They're vibrant. Some of them are so bright. And they are all different thicknesses, and they have energy, entity. Their energy of their own. Each one is unique and beautiful. And they make up this movement and aliveness. Beautiful patterns. It changes like a movie on the screen.

D: *So it is like a living thing, rather than just a piece of cloth.*

N: Oh, it's not a cloth. A tapestry is even an understatement. It just doesn't describe it at all.

D: *It's something we can understand though with our limited knowledge. But if the threads, the strands, are alive, what do they represent?*

N: Oh, they are beautiful. They are people, their lives, their souls. They represent everything that we are.

D: *So it's an example of how it's all interwoven?*

N: Oh, yes. It's very, very intricate. Moreso than we ever imagined. For every life, every existence, every thought, every action, everything that we are, that we will be, what we have been, is represented in each strand. And we are all of those things as well.

D: *Does it represent only the present life, or is the strand the history of the soul?*

N: Yes, and the future and the... well, the soul. That it is.

D: *But if it is already interwoven, does this mean everything is set.*

N: Oh, no. In some areas of the strand it is set, depending on the last journey of the soul at that time, because some lives it chooses to lead do not have free will.

D: *They do not? Or they do not know they have?*

N: They do not have free will.

D: *So not every entity has free will?*

N: That's correct. It depends on the life it chooses. If it chooses a human life, it has free will. But if it chooses a different existence, in some instances it does not have free will. So therefore the strand changes in its texture and its illumination and its color and its thickness and its connection to other strands. It's very complex.

D: *So it all depends on the lesson the soul is learning at that time*

N: We would not call it a "lesson" as such. We would call it... remembrance. For the soul knows all. It knows all. It knows everything about all there is to know. It just does not always remember. And depending on the life it chooses to live, it remembers sometimes, and it remembers not sometimes.

D: *If it is a human life it would get confusing if we remember all those things.*

N: It is a life that the soul chooses when it is wanting to clear much. It would not choose a human life otherwise, for it is a difficult existence to choose, on many levels. It is also a very stimulating life to choose. For it is very full. Full of emotion and feeling and texture and vibrancy. In many other lives that a soul chooses there is not much variation. There is not much texture. For they sometimes do not have the third dimension to even relate to. They know not of the third dimension.

D: *Do they have to go through those type of lives before coming into an Earth life?*

N: Not necessarily. It depends on the soul's choosing. Then, of course, many souls have chosen many Earth lives, and get stuck on the third dimensional wheel. And they do not even know of other existences, therefore creating more karmic connection, and therefore having to return to Earth. For the soul it can be a frustrating thing, for they understand on the other side that there are other lives that can be lived. But they are so locked to the Earth plane they cannot leave it.

D: *They have to finish all that first.*

N: Not always all of the karma created by the karmic force. But much of the time there is so much to do, if they were not to have another Earth life they would lose the opportunity to get a body to come back to. And they would miss the connections they must make. They might miss the opportunity to contract with the next soul they must connect with. They tend to stay in similar circles. And those, like Norma, who know they do not need to be here very often, tend to move in circles of similar or like souls, and also journey out of them.

D: *But if they lose the opportunity to connect, it would take a great deal of time before they had the opportunity again. And that karma would have to be repaid eventually and cleared up. Is that what you mean?*

N: Yes. Norma is very aware of this. Those who are stuck in the third dimension are not truly aware. They know in their knowledge somewhere, especially inbetween lives, that there are other lives they can lead. But they know they must stay in the Earth dimension to fulfill the karmic debts. Or else they will miss out on the opportunity, and have to stay in spirit form for a long time. They can go to other alien lives, other dimensional lives. But they know that it limits them, for they miss to connect with those lives that are earthbound lives, that they must fulfill.

D: *But in the other lives, where they aren't even aware of the third dimension, do they also create karma?*

N: Oh, yes! (Emphatic) Oh, yes! It is part of the soul's journey to create karma.

D: *And work it out.*

N: It's to lift the vibration of that soul, to bring them back home to the God force.

D: *But in the other lives they do not create the intense karma that we do with the human body?*

N: It can be as intense, yes. And sometimes they can get stuck in an alien life.

D: *For the same reasons? (Oh, yes!) But as I'm aware of it, in some of the alien lives, they can live as long as they want. (Yes) So they would have plenty of time to work things out.*

N: We speak of lower alien lifeforms.

D: *Can you tell me about that?*

N: There are some who are like colonies of ants, in a sense. Who do not necessarily have bodies. They are energy, but are of one mind, so to speak.

D: *Like a group?*

N: Yes. And they move maybe like a flock of birds. And maybe move like ants. They connect with each other like a colony. They move as one, but as single entities. And they do not have the karmic intricacies that the human form does. It is more like a group karma, where they agree to do certain work together as a group. So if it is not fulfilled, it is not integrated and released.

D: *Are there others that are lower types of alien lifeforms?*

N: They can be workers for higher lifeforms. But the irony is that the souls of the higher lifeforms can sometimes choose to be a worker. Moving from different levels, so to speak. It is a fallacy that a soul moves upwards. It is not from one higher lifeform to the next higher lifeform. It's not like that.

D: *We tend to think that way.*

N: No, it jumps and twists. For all sorts of reasons a soul will choose a journey. Just sometimes for the fun of it, for the experience.

D: *To go back and experience something that's different at the time.*

N: Yes, it adds to the tapestry. It adds to the complexity of the soul.

D: *The variety.*

N: Yes, it adds. It gives. It fills. It makes the soul more complete. It's another piece of the puzzle.

D: *That makes sense to me. Norma was wondering if she had a galactic connection.*

N: Oh, yes! She is aware of the galactic lifeforms she has been, but she's not aware of the details on a conscious level. She knows much of herself. And she is learning much in this life. Unless she truly wants to return to third dimension, she will not need to come here again.

D: *So she is more or less completing her job here?*

N: There is never any completion as such, because you can come and go as you please. But she does enjoy the free will aspect of this journey.

D: *So at any time a soul could decide it doesn't want any more Earth lives, and go on and try something else.*

N: Only if it's cleared much of its karma. For, as we said, you can be locked to the Earth plane for many lifetimes. Because, of course, the more lifetimes you live, the more you are locked here, for the karma that you create.

D: *So it's better if you clear it all if you want to go on somewhere else.*

N: And many souls are aware of this. Not on a conscious level, of course; that's why they cram so much into one life. Many

souls that are here at this time of the Earth's evolution, have
had extraterrestrial lives. And many are not quite consciously
aware. More are now on this Earth plane than ever before, for
they are here for a reason: to help lift the vibration of Mother
Earth.

In *Keepers of the Garden* Phil said many souls that had never
known Earth lives had volunteered to come to help the Earth at this
time in its history. They were the infusion or transfusion of new blood,
the ones who have never known violence. Because they do not have
this in their soul's history they can help to change the vibration of the
Earth and raise it to a higher dimension where such things as violence
are impossible.

D: *This is what I have been told. That we are moving away from
the violence, and going into a different evolutionary period for
the Earth?*

N: Oh, yes, and Mother Earth has created this.

D: *Because she is also a living entity?*

N: Of course.

D: *Which many people don't realize.*

N: No, and she must interact with the other planets of this galaxy.
And then of course, beyond it as well. It's bigger than you
think.

D: *Yes. I have heard that not only is there the tapestry room which
represents the souls, but is it more complex than that.*

N: Oh, yes. The tapestry room represents only those souls who
are working in this universe, and the many universes beyond.
But there is more than that.

D: *Are there other tapestries, as an example, as an analogy?*

N: It is like that, but that is such a simplified explanation. Words
cannot describe. Imagine, or visualize, the universe, and
then send that to the infinite. And you will get an idea that each
star represents a life, a soul. And you will be just touching on
what it is all about.

D: *But the stars are physical objects, aren't they?*

N: Yes, but we are using the universe as an example of how many
and how complex soul journeys are. If you visualize or
imagine that each star represents a soul and its journey to the
infinite, you will understand how vast we really are.

D: *No limitations really, unless we place them upon ourselves. Is
that correct?*

N: Each life that is chosen by the soul represents a limitation for
a reason, a lesson, for clearing or bringing closer to the source,
because that is our soul purpose.

D: *To return to the source? (Yes) But we have much to do before we can return there, don't we?*

N: And isn't that the adventure?

D: *Yes. All the stumps and bumps along the way.*

N: Norma has been many lifeforms of all descriptions. And she is aware of this. She has already connected to those. What she does not understand is the vastness of her greatness. She believes that choosing this human form is belittling in some ways. She does not truly believe that she can be so great, knowing who she is in human form, with the foibles and the blockages of the human life she is living.

D: *Isn't that true of all of us?*

N: Oh, yes. But many souls do not even recognize their greatness, and have not even touched on the fact that they are great. For, of course, we all are.

D: *But in that respect, all of us are grander on the other planes, the other dimensions. When you say "greatness", how do you define that?*

N: All souls are great, of course, for they are part of the source. Many souls do not understand or know of their greatness, and therefore cannot feel the turmoil that Norma is feeling. For they do not have it in their consciousness. The turmoil she feels is that she is consciously aware of the greatness that she is. She cannot resolve the fact that she is in a human body, and that part of her journey is to integrate the greatness. The greatness that we speak of is her place in this plan. She is part of a bigger picture, the soul that is Norma.

This sounded familiar. The subconscious or higher self has said the same thing about many of my other subjects. Apparently we are all much greater than we give ourselves credit for. If we could only recognize this God spark in others, there would be no judgment, no prejudice. We would see that we are all souls on journeys working out different phases of karma. All attempting to return home to the God Source.

N: She has made many important decisions that affect many souls.

D: *In other lifetimes.*

N: It's beyond the many lifetimes when she is "Who we are". She understands that she does not need to be in life form to make decisions. She has made these decisions in soul form for many souls.

Apparently when we enter the Earth existence, the third dimensional reality, we exist with a facade as actors playing various roles. For some it is the adventure of the experience, the journey. For others it is entrapment in an illusion that takes on all the qualities of reality. No matter how we perceive it, we automatically create karma just by living in this dimension, and are trapped in this reality until we repay the debts. There is so much more going on behind the scenes that we can ever realize. But it has been said, "If we knew the answers, it wouldn't be a test." And so we long to return to that vague place we consider "home", unaware consciously that this cannot happen until we have completed our work here.

SECTION FIVE

Metaphysics or Quantum Physics?

CHAPTER ELEVEN
PARALLEL UNIVERSES

I was led into this strange and very deep discussion in the 1980s while exploring the lifetime of Tuin, the hunter, which is the basis for my book, *The Legend of Starcrash*. In that lifetime he killed and brought back to the village a very unusual animal. One which had never been seen before or since by the people. The Shaman of the tribe noted that it was a very strange occurrence and wanted to know all the details of the hunt. He was so impressed that he asked the butchers and skinners to take special care when preparing the meat. He wanted the skull to be preserved, and used it thereafter during the ceremonies honoring the winter solstice. All of the details as presented by Tuin suggested a paranormal experience of the highest degree. One which he had never experienced before, but which he readily accepted. The reality of it could not be denied by the people because the proof was visible through the preserved skull and skin. The description was so strange that I also knew it was not an animal that had ever lived on the planet Earth, at least not within known history. A zoologist also confirmed my suspicions. If the animal was not from Earth, then where did it come from?

After Tuin died and crossed over I was able to question him extensively about many of the curious events concerning his village. In this state he had access to knowledge that is denied the mortal. I questioned him about the finding of the strange animal. The answer that came forth was so complex that I knew it did not belong in that book. I summarized it in the barest, simplest details because I thought it would be so complicated that it would distract from the purpose of that book. It is offered here in its entirety. I cannot explain it further. Just listening to it confused me and left me dizzy. I felt very topsy turvy afterwards. The idea was so alien to my thinking that it disturbed me and completely muddled my reasoning mind. Although the concept may seem revolutionary to me, it may seem quite simple to someone else, someone who has no trouble grasping complex theories. Many people will probably say it is not a new theory at all, it is only new and startling to me. So be it. I asked the deceased Tuin's spirit if it could explain the mystery of the strange animal.

Beth: That was a rare occurrence. You must understand that our is not the only universe. Numerous parallel universes exist along side of ours, but because they vibrate at different speeds they are normally invisible to human eyes. The universes intersect with each other, but usually the points of intersection are not compatible. Thus inhabitants of the two different universes are not aware of the intersection. There may be some minor changes that one or two might notice, but it will be nothing major. At this one particular point, it was a rare occurrence of a compatible intersection. And when Tuin was out hunting he was in two universes simultaneously, but was not aware of it. The animal that he killed was an inhabitant of the other universe. But since it was a compatible intersection he was able to transport the animal into this universe without destroying its basic matrix.

D: *Do you mean the other universe was also a physical universe.*

Another subject had described universes composed of energy

B: Yes. It was a physical universe built along a different basic matrix. But since the intersection was compatible, the animal' matrix was not destroyed when it was brought across to this universe. That's what makes that occurrence so rare. If the intersection is not compatible, the basic matrix of anything from the other universe is destroyed and it no longer exists in this universe.

D: *How do you mean? It would just disappear or what?*

B: Yes. It would just dissolve into nothing and release the energy into the ether.

D: *Would somebody see it as a mirage or something similar?*

B: Perhaps. Under certain circumstances they would see it, then it would seem to shimmer and fade away into nothing.

D: *(I was trying to understand.) Are you saying that this other universe is existing side by side with this one?*

B: Yes, there are an infinite number of universes existing side by side with this one. And they're all interwoven like a cloth. (Sigh) The terms of this language are not sufficient.

D: *I've been told that before.*

B: (Searching for the words.) I'm going to have to misuse some terms to try to get this point across. These various universes universi?, universes, whichever are interwoven like a cloth into a gigantic cosmos, which contains the totality of all existence. But these universes are alive and so they are always moving and shifting, so it's like a living cloth. And as they are moving and shifting, their relationships with the other universes are always changing. And since there's an infinite number of them, the relationship is never the same twice. And for there to be a compatible intersection, like at this one incident with Tuin, there has to be a very unusual set of variables existing at the same time. Since it happens so rarely, it cannot be expressed with percentages, the number is too small. And so this universe is still side by side with this universe in relation to it, but it's a different relationship now because it has been shifting along with all the other universes through the eons, in this relationship of the gigantic cosmos. Do you understand?

I mumbled that I did, although I really didn't. This surprise barrage was so complicated, it was giving me a headache trying to keep up with it.

D: *But you said this does happen at times and people are not aware of it?*

B: Yes. This universe is intersecting with other universes all the time. It's just a matter of when and where. The when: every moment. This universe, at some point, is always intersecting with at least one other universe, if not more. And since there's an infinite number of universes and they're always intersecting, it's quite reasonable that several of these intersections take place on or near this planet where it can be observed by people. However, whether or not the intersection is compatible enough to be able to observe anything directly, is not as common. Usually it is a very small change that people with very ordinary perceptions would not notice. Only someone who is particularly observant would notice this very small difference. And it's usually nothing earth shaking or anything that would matter. It would just be a very small thing that maybe one or two people will notice, but they will not comment about it because it's such a small thing, and they feel that others would think they had mistaken what they had observed to start with.

D: *Could you give me an idea of what they might experience?*

B: Yes. For example, a person is walking one day and they notice this tree. It has a particular shape that is distinctive, and particularly beautiful. And they walk along the same place a week or so later, and they discover that the tree is no longer there. Or perhaps the shape is radically different, but it's nothing they could really prove one way or the other. It's just a small thing like that, but it's different from what was before. What happened is that at the point where the tree was, it had intersected with another universe and the effect either altered

the tree or destroyed its matrix to where it ceased to exist. C
perhaps it exists in altered form in the other universe now.

D: *Tuin did say that whenever he came across this animal, he
had a strange feeling with his senses. He knew something ou
of the ordinary was occurring.*

B: Yes, he was very highly developed psychically, and so he wa
aware of the fact that he was in two universes simultaneously
but he did not know how to state this verbally. He wasn't ver
sure of what he knew. He knew what he knew without really
knowing what he knew.

D: *Yes, he didn't know exactly what it was. But you mean this
was very unusual for him to be able to bring the animal back
to the people of the village?*

B: Yes. To be able to bring the animal back fully into his univers
without the animal dissolving into nothing is extremely
unusual. It rarely happens. It does happen, but just not very
often.

D: *Of course, the people were very hungry at that time, too. The
might have been part of it.*

B: Yes, their psychic abilities undoubtedly helped the animal to
make the transition.

D: *Then for many years afterward the animal's head and the ski
was used by the wise man, so it was definitely something
physical. Then when something like this happens, it very
rarely happens in the vicinity of people where they would
notice it?*

B: Well, it happens in the vicinity of people, but usually the
changes are so small or so minor that the majority of them do
not notice it. People have a tendency to see just what they
want to see. And if something different has happened, if they
don't want to see it, they won't. Or they are too busy to notice

D: *Or they think they imagined it. Is there ever any chance of a
human being crossing over into the other universe?*

B: That happens all the time. Many times human beings walking
down the street will cross over into another universe. Several
of the universes, particularly the ones that lie closest to this
one, are so similar as to be practically identical. So sometimes
whenever they are overlapping, people can cross over to the
other universe temporarily and then cross back without
destroying their matrix. It's the permanent transition that's so
very rare, as with the animal. And many times they will be i
another universe and they'll think, "Gee, I sure thought that
this and such had happened." And someone says, "Well, no,
that has never happened. You're just making that up." And
then a few days later they mention this again and someone

else says, "Well, yes, you're right, that did happen." Well, during that period of a few days when everyone was saying it had not happened, they were in another universe where it had not happened.

D: *This would be confusing to a human.*

B: Yes. It would make them think maybe they were imagining things. Hence they would soon dismiss it from their mind and forget the incident, so they would not be consciously aware they had been in another universe.

D: *But it sounds as though the universes are identical if they have the same people in both.*

B: Usually yes, and usually it will be just a few things that are slightly different.

D: *Then this would mean that we all have a counterpart, or more than one counterpart just like us?*

B: Yes. In most universes we have an identical counterpart whose basic experiences would be very similar. In some universes we would not have a counterpart, but it is rare for us to encounter these universes. When we do, it's a very shocking experience. When you go up to someone that you know you know, and you know who knows you. And you greet them and they stare at you as if to say, "Who are you? I don't know you. I've never seen you before."

D: *That would be very confusing. But then it is possible if you cross over, to cross right back again.*

B: Yes. Usually the crossover is only a very short period of time, maybe a few hours or perhaps even as long as a couple of days. But it's usually a very temporary crossing over. And generally the people who cross over just continue with their lives, their ordinary everyday activities. And they're not really aware of when they crossed over and crossed back. The moment of crossing is very ambiguous. But some people may remember something odd that happened while they were over there.

D: *Do they just notice they feel a little strange or what?*

B: Sometimes they don't even notice that. Sometimes they just notice something, for example, some particular building that exists in their universe. And they notice that one day they're walking and there is no building and has never been a building there. A few days later they notice there's a building there again. And by this way they would know they were temporarily in another universe where there had not been a building built where there had been in their universe.

D: *In other words, they're not absolutely identical.*

B: Right. They're never absolutely identical. There's always at least one thing different. And that one thing being different is enough to make a different universe. Sometimes it may be as small as a grain of sand being positioned differently on a beach, to be sufficient for it to be a different universe. And what makes it even more complex is that there are always new universes being created. For every action that is done, there is more than one possible outcome. In your universe one outcome is realized, but all the energy of the other outcomes have to go somewhere. And so these other different outcomes that were not realized in your universe, cause another universe to come into being that's practically identical to your universe except that this particular outcome is different. And from there the universe continues to develop in its own direction.

D: *You mean one person can cause this to happen? Or does it have to be many people?*

B: No, just one person. Anything. It happens all the time. The gigantic cosmos is continuously growing. And it's infinitely complex, to where one mind cannot grasp it. For example, in this universe, say your nose starts to itch. Now you can do several things. You can rub your nose or you can scratch it, or your body can decide to sneeze. All those three things will happen in this universe. Say you decide to sneeze, you do so. However the energy of the other two possible outcomes has to go somewhere. And so hence at that moment two other universes come into being, where in one you rubbed your nose and in the other one you scratched your nose. And that's the only difference at this point between those two universes and this one. And then they continue to develop. And they will be slightly different but they'll still be very similar to this one.

D: *This sounds like it could get very complicated.*

B: It is.

D: *I always believe that we come to crossroads many times in our lives. That we make a decision to do one thing and yet we could have several other decisions that would put us on another path. Does this mean that the other decision becomes a reality, too?*

B: Yes, the other decisions come to pass, too, but not in your universe. You come to a crossroads, as you put it, and you have a major decision. And you can do any one of several things. Depending on which thing you do, it could very well determine the general direction of the rest of your life. You make the decision to go one particular way. As soon as you make this decision to do one particular thing, the potential energy that was stored behind this causes other universes to come into being where all these other decisions also come to pass. To where now there are alternate yous who travel these different paths. And their lives will be different from yours because they made a different decision and they went into a different direction. And hence cause that universe to be different, and sometimes the effects can be very far reaching. To where in a short period of time, surprisingly enough, that universe is very different from yours.

D: *Yes, because your life could go in a totally different direction.*

B: And have a totally different effect on the people around you. It's a snowball effect which hence has a different effect on the people around them, et cetera, et cetera.

D: *But you're not really responsible for your decisions.*

B: No, no. You make the decision that you feel is best for you. Under your circumstances, it may be. And the other circumstances come into being to where the other sides of the decision are best for those circumstances that come into being, too. However, sometimes you make a decision, and you realize that you made the wrong decision, that you did not choose the best circumstance. When you realize this, what has happened is, this particular branch of your life split off from another universe, from your original universe. And the original "you" took the right decision and you acted out the alternate decision with the energy stored there. You lived with it and worked your life around it the best you could.

D: *Is it possible to get the other one back? (No) It's not possible to fuse the two together again?*

B: No. But it's not as fatalistic as it sounds. Because even though you made the wrong decision or you feel that you made the wrong decision, you can still make the best of it. Because you still have decisions to make every moment of your life, making these decisions wisely will help keep your life on the path you want it on.

D: *Then it's still possible to turn your life around and go the other way if you wanted to.*

B: Yes, you'll just be in a different universe than the alternate you who made the decision that you would have liked to have made.

D: *Well, it sounds as though your physical body is in many places at different times. (Yes) Is it an exact duplicate of this body? I'm trying to understand this in my limited earthling terms.*

I laughed nervously. This was becoming extremely complicated nd unsettling.

B: It starts out being an exact duplicate, but after a while differen changes take place. For example, in one universe you might receive an injury that you don't in this universe, which woul make a difference. It's very complicated. The hardest thing of all is trying to relate the different alternate yous in the alternate universes to your true self, to your soul. That's one thing that makes karma so complicated. Because of the pull o karma you must experience everything at least once to round out your experience, and to work out to your truest high self. Well, in each lifetime you are experiencing almost everythin, at once. But you still have to experience all these different things in their right proportions to round you out totally to where you will be a total person. Hence you have to go back several times through several lifetimes. And you end up existing in several universes each time. But that's the way it is. This language just isn't sufficient.

D: *But if all these various other counterparts are living separat lives, and yet they are all parts of us, why are we not aware o them? Why aren't we able to communicate, and know they exist?*

B: Because it would be too difficult and too complicated for you limited human minds to accept. It would be too overwhelming There are many, many concepts beyond what you accept as reality that you are not allowed to know about, because they would completely overload the human psyche. It is enough fo you to focus on the present life and circumstances you are living. But be advised, the true self, your soul, knows abou everything that your countless counterparts are doing, and keeps perfect track of it. You, as a human, don't have to be concerned with the complexity of it.

Thank goodness for small blessings! In the midst of all thi complicated information I was reminded of something another of m subjects said. He said I would never receive the answers to all of m questions, because some knowledge would be as poison rather tha medicine. It would harm rather than enlighten. So I suppose the huma will never be able to handle the full amount of information from th mind of God.

D: *It seems confusing to think that another counterpart of yourself, a physical counterpart, is doing things that you're not aware of.*

B: That's true. You may wonder when you cross over to anothe universe and you're interacting with an alternate set of people wouldn't the people you normally interact with miss you?

However, when you cross over, your counterpart has also crossed over and so you are not missed.

D: *I was wondering about that, if you could meet your own self.*

B: No. Because when you cross over it forms a vacuum that must be filled and so your counterpart automatically crosses over to fill the vacuum, until the tension comes to the point where you have to cross back over to the universe you belong in.

D: *Will the other people notice any difference?*

B: Perhaps. Some slight flaw, a subtle difference, usually in memories and such. They would say, "Do you remember when this and such happened?" And your counterpart might say, "Why, no, that never happened to me." And they'll just put it down to faulty memory or what have you.

D: *If your counterpart was pulled through the vacuum, would it also not know it was in an alternate universe?*

B: Not unless you and your counterpart were one of the few people who put two and two together, so to speak, and realized, "Gee, not everything is quite in place like it should be. Perhaps I'm in an alternate universe." And the thing that makes this interesting, and should help you understand your fellow companions, is that at any time you may be dealing with one of them from one of their alternate universes. To where if you say something and they don't remember it, instead of getting impatient with them, just remember, with this particular one, maybe it hasn't happened to them or hasn't happened to them yet. "Well, gee, I'm talking to one of their counterparts. In a few days...."

D: *Could the other one also have a totally different personality?*

B: No, the personality is generally the same. Sometimes different aspects of the personality will be developed a little differently due to a different set of experiences, but usually the personality is basically the same. Because the personality is one of the things that links your physical body to your true self.

D: *I was thinking that if they met somebody who looked like you but was totally different, then people would think something strange was going on.*

B: Right. But that never happens, because the personality is basically the same. Maybe some of the details might be different. For instance, in one universe someone might be friendly and outgoing and very talkative. Yet their alternate self might still be friendly but not as out going. They might be more shy and not as talkative. It would just be a minor alteration like that.

D: *Yes, and your family or people would just think, well, he's in a mood or something.*

B: Exactly.

D: *But is there ever a case where the two counterparts might meet each other?*

B: I don't think it's possible.

D: *I was thinking of stories or legends we've heard, like doppelgangers. Seeing your double.*

B: Yes. When you see your double like that, that's when the two universes are intersecting and you're still each in your separate universe. And you see them, but it's not very common

D: *That's probably why it's so rare when it has been reported.*

B: Yes. Usually what will happen is that someone else will see your double and tell you about it later.

D: *Oh. I've heard of cases like that. They'll say, "We saw you in such and such a place." And you say, "I wasn't there. I was home all day."*

B: Exactly. You were at home but you were in an alternate universe and your alternate was out wandering around.

D: *That would explain a lot of these strange cases we've heard of. But in the case of Tuin, the animal was totally different than any animal on Earth at that time.*

B: Yes. That was another reason why it was so rare for its matrix to survive and be permanently crossed over, because there was no counterpart in this universe. At least not on Earth. Now, there's a possibility that in that particular case, the animal does have a counterpart in this universe, but on another planet. At which point, when this animal crossed over and stayed crossed over, its counterpart either crossed over into another universe itself or it ceased to exist at that point.

D: *Another earthly animal wouldn't have crossed over in its place?*

B: No, because it was not the counterpart of this animal.

D: *It would have to be an exact counterpart then. But it did occur at a time when the village needed food and they did eat it. It didn't harm them in any way. It's very interesting, it's also very complicated.*

B: Yes. I feel I have perhaps left some mistaken impressions in your mind, due to the inadequacies of this language.

D: *Well, that's possible. Other people I've spoken to like this have also said that the language is inadequate to explain things. Sometimes they must draw analogies for me.*

B: True. Most inadequate, too. It leaves rather simplified notions in your mind.

D: *Yes, but sometimes that's the only way to explain things, even though it's not fully accurate.*

B: That is true. I don't want you to feel guilty or limit yourself on your actions simply because of the alternative things that also come to pass. Continue to live your life as you have always lived it, because it is the natural way of the gigantic cosmos. The fact is that when you were born in this universe, you were also born in several other universes, too. And so, actions and decisions that you make will cause another universe to come into existence or perhaps alter another universe that is similar enough. This is not to alarm you, because that happens all over all the time.

D: *This is a natural thing, in other words.*

B: Yes, and it's part of working out your karma. It's not like predestination either. You and all of your alternate yous have freedom of choice in the decisions that come up in your lives. And even though you make one decision, that doesn't automatically mean that an alternate you has to make the other decision. If another alternate you makes the other choice, then it's because they chose to. It is their free choice. And it usually ends up balancing that way. Occasionally you and your alternate yous choose one way and the other way was not chosen. Then another universe comes into being where that way was chosen, to keep the energy balanced. Do you understand?

D: *I'm trying to. This is going to take a bit of digesting and absorbing, trying to understand it. Any time I'm exposed to a new idea, this is what happens. I have to go over it before I really understand it.*

B: Feel free to ask me more questions when you have digested it. It's important that you understand.

D: *I feel I'm being led to give this information that I receive to many people.*

B: Yes, and it's important that you understand it as clearly as you can with the limitations of your language. So that when it is broadcast to other people they'll have a clear understanding and not a muddled understanding. For this particular concept could upset the religious institutions of your universe. And it could cause much, much unnecessary turmoil.

D: *You keep talking about these alternate people. Could one have one occupation and another a different occupation? Or would it be very similar?*

B: Oh, that depends. Many times it's not unusual for them to have similar occupations. For example, in this universe a person is good at working with their hands and so they do, say, electrical work. In another universe they may not be doing electrical work but may be doing something else where they're also working with their hands. They may be a craftsman or woodworker or something like that. Or if someone in this universe is an engineer, but they have a hobby, say, music. They're very passionate about music but it's just a hobby for them. Then in another universe they may be a musician instead of an engineer. So whatever your basic tendencies are in your personality, since the personality is basically the same across the universes. If it's a multi faceted personality to where the person is capable of doing many different things, in the other universes their counterpart may be doing something radically different than they are doing here, because the ability to do this is in their personality.

D: *For instance, now I am a writer. Would another part of me still be a housewife and not interested in writing?*

B: No, the interest to expand oneself would still be there. You may not necessarily take the direction of writing in another universe though. For example, in this universe instead of wanting to remain a housewife, you wanted to expand your mind and do something more fulfilling and you became a writer. In another universe you would have this same basic personality urge of not staying just a housewife. You would want to expand yourself, to do something else, so you might have started doing volunteer work. Or perhaps in another universe you might have gotten involved with crafts and such instead. Or, I perceive that you're interested in psychic things. Well, in another universe instead of getting involved with writing you may have gotten involved with psychic things, and not thought about writing about them, but just doing them.

D: *And when I thought of these different alternatives I could take then they became a reality somewhere else?*

B: Yes, if they weren't already a reality somewhere else.

D: *Ummm, this could get very complicated.*

B: It is very complex. And I feel strongly that you won't be able to absorb it this time. You will probably have to come back and ask me more questions, which is fine. It's important that you understand this and that it's clear. Any decision you make is right. There's no such thing as a wrong decision. You may feel later that you could have made a better decision. But at the time the decision you made was right for you. And so, do not feel guilty about so called mistakes that you have made in the past, because there's no such thing as a wrong decision.

D: *Because the other side of the decision exists somewhere.*

B: Yes, it is all balanced. And whenever a major decision comes up in your life, usually some form of that decision comes up in some of your alternate lives in the alternate universes. And so, usually most aspects of the decision will be represented in the final result. Occasionally, one of the aspects will not be represented and hence a new universe will come into being to represent that side of the decision, too. Whenever it happens you would not be aware of this because it's just a natural thing. And your life will continue along that line and you won't realize there's an additional alternate you. It's an automatic process and there's no physical phenomenon involved with it, so you don't know when it happens.

D: *Some of the questions I ask may seem very simple and very naive.*

B: That is to be expected so that you will understand. You have to start somewhere.

D: *Are these other alternate personalities all associated with the same family members? (Yes) It wouldn't be a different family or a different husband or children or anything like that.*

B: Occasionally. Usually it is a balanced representation. For example, if at one point in your life you had a choice between marrying one man or another man. And you decided on one man, in the other universes several alternate yous will decide on the same man. And usually several alternate yous will decide on the alternate man. Hence their universes will be different in that direction because an alternate you decided on the other man. And hence the family would be different that way. So, yes, there are yous that have different families, different ancestors and such as that because of these different decisions. But at the same time there are other universes where the same decisions were made and so the same family members would be involved.

D: *Then if you crossed over into a universe with a different husband and family, that would be very confusing.*

B: Yes, it would. But that doesn't happen very often, because since that universe is radically different it would be more difficult for you to be able to cross over successfully. It's usually with the universes where everything is very, very similar, almost identical, where the easiest accidental crossing over takes place.

D: *Would this have something to do with vibration levels?*

B: Yes, complimentary vibrations, complimentary energies. A universe where similar decisions have been made in the past. As in your universe where everything looks very close to being the same, with only a few minor, very subtle differences here and there, it's much easier to intersect with this universe. And intersect in such a way as to have an open portal for you to pass through. Now there may be incidents where this universe may intersect with another universe so that you may be able to observe things going on but it would not be an open portal, to where you would not be able to interact with things going on.

D: *You could see through but not go through?*

B: Right. For example, you may be walking one day and you may observe something that's different than you remembered it. But you don't go over to investigate, you just keep walking. You wonder about it and there's nobody around to ask about it. Hence you have interacted with that universe. You merely observed something different. Or if there are other people around, it would not occur to you to ask them about it. Or if you do, they will seem to not hear you because the portal is not open to where you can interact.

D: *Just like a window that you can see through, but not step through?*

B: Right. And you would not be able to tell the place where your universe ends and that universe begins. You'll just think you're looking across the street or what have you at something. And somewhere between you and there is where the two universes are intersecting.

D: *You said though that sometimes you see something and it begins to look shimmery and then it would just disappear?*

B: Yes, that's when the intersection is coming to an end and the universes are drawing apart. This would help explain many of the incidents of what you call ghosts and mirages, too. You have a phenomenon known as the Bermuda Triangle. That area, for some reason, keeps intersecting with this other particular universe. There's an unusual magnetism there, and it causes these planes to fly into the other universe. And most of the time their matrices dissolve.

D: *Then the people no longer exist when they go through there?*

B: Right. They pass over at that point.

D: *And the plane, the ships or whatever, the whole thing dissolves? It no longer exists on the other plane?*

B: After it passes out of this universe into the other universe, it's no longer existing in this universe for it has passed out. In the other universe it cannot exist because the vibrations do not coincide, and their counterparts are still over there. So one of them has to give. Usually it's the one that's most recently crossed over that dissolves. Sometimes it's the other one that dissolves, but this does not happen very often. This is the explanation for some of the accounts you have of someone walking across a field or something, then disappearing into thin air. Their counterpart had just crossed over into this universe and they had to go somewhere. And when they disappeared into thin air usually they have either crossed over into the other universe or their matrix has dissolved.

D: *But this is just the dissolving of the physical body. The soul cannot be harmed in any way, can it?*

B: No, no. This is just the physical body.

D: *Is the spiritual plane considered one of these parallel universes?*

B: There are infinite universes on the physical plane, but on the spiritual plane it's all basically one universe. We can interact with everything. On the physical plane some people work out their karma by leading several alternate lives in various parallel universes. Especially if they want to work out some particular details of one particular aspect of their karma. And the various decisions they make in the various universes have balanced out in such a way as to help their karma. Sometimes, since all these universes are on a physical plane, the protective barriers between them sometimes cancel out. And the person they talk to has already passed over from this one universe, but is still living in the other universe. It's difficult to explain.

D: *I thought when they died in one universe, all of their different alternates would also die.*

B: They do all die within the same general time, but not necessarily all at once. It depends on how long it takes them to work out that aspect of karma, of alternate solutions to this one aspect of karma in these various universes. It usually takes approximately the same amount of time, but it's not a clear cut ending because time doesn't have any meaning on this side. And so there's sometimes some discrepancies like that. But usually they'll appear because it's not often that these discrepancies coincide with the energy barriers nullifying themselves occasionally.

D: *Then if you see somebody and find out later they had died weeks before, you might be seeing an alternate?*

B: Yes. Another explanation is that sometimes when a spirit has died a few weeks before and they haven't adjusted yet to being on the spiritual plane, sometimes their spiritual echo can be particularly convincing, or particularly compatible with the physical vibration of things.

D: *Be physical enough to where someone could touch them and talk with them? (Yes) This would go along also with Jesus making Himself visible enough to where people could touch Him. When He was supposed to have come back after the Resurrection.*

B: Yes. When He first came back He was not fully adjusted to the spiritual level yet. And that's why He told the first peopl who were wanting to touch Him, to not touch Him, because He had not yet ascended to His Father. Yet later when Thoma wanted to touch Him, He had made some other adjustments t His spiritual echo to where He could be touched.

D: *That has always been confusing. If they were dead how coul' they be that physical. They also have the cases of the ghost hitchhikers, where they actually get in the car, and they're riding and talking to the people.*

B: Yes. And then disappear.

D: *Would that be along the same line? (Yes)*

This barrage of strange information left me mentally exhausted I felt as though my brain had been twisted and bent like a pretze Nothing had ever quite disturbed me as much as this avalanche. I knew it would take a long time, if ever, for me to absorb, sort it out an understand it. Maybe other readers will not have the same difficult and it will fit right in with their view of reality, or at least be plausibl enough to open their mind to radical thinking.

When Beth awakened the only thing she remembered about th session was a strange mental picture. She wanted to tell me about before it vanished.

B: Picture electronic models of the atom, where it shows the various electron shells and the paths of the electrons going, "Whirrrrr", around in all the directions. Now these paths of the electrons, instead of being electronic threads like they ar pictured, picture them as being silver bands instead. And picture this at the very electron levels, these silver bands about a fourth of an inch wide, I'd say. And the whole pictur being approximately about six inches around. (She made han motions to show the size.)

D: *It would be bigger than a baseball.*

B: About the size of a good sized grapefruit or cantaloupe. Anc these silver bands being about a fourth of an inch wide, goin around in all different directions. Roiling and undulating a little bit and moving and constantly shifting like it contained an explosion of silver bands. There's no way of counting then it's an infinite number of them. That's the picture in my min

D: *They're kind of entwined or what?*

B: Yeah, there'll be one going like this and another one overlapping and another one overlapping and another one overlapping. (Hand motions.) And they're all kind of intertwined and overlapping and crossing over. And the shif between them, and the relationships between them always altering and shifting and the angles changing and such as that.

D: *This may be another visualization picture they were trying to give me to show how the different universes operate. They talked about a cloth with all of the threads intertwining.*

B: Yes, I also saw the threads doing this.

D: *This must have been the picture in your mind, but they couldn't quite get that across, so they gave me the idea of a cloth because it was simpler to describe.*

B: Yes. Perhaps we need both concepts to help explain what it is like.

***

Information on the same subject from another source.

D: *If each one of us is living in different planes of existence at the same time, is this what is known as parallel lives?*

Phil: That is accurate. In the sense that each of you, at this point in your lives, are simply facets of your true entire self. You are pinpoints of awareness. Your total awareness is far beyond anything you could encompass or imagine at your level. Therefore, it is easy to see that as your awareness grows, as you broaden your reality of the spiritual ladder, you find that your awareness overlaps with that of other individuals. Such that at the ultimate level you are indeed on the God plane, where all is one. Your awareness on your level is simply a drawn out or focused pinpoint of that total spiritual awareness. And so it could be seen that at various levels your awareness would indeed overlap with others, such that ultimately all is one. Therefore, all lives ultimately are concurrent.

D: *You once said we were just the tips of our own icebergs.*

P: That is accurate.

D: *When the predicted Earth changes come about on our planet, how will that affect the parallel or interpenetrating universes?*

P: There will be experiences on this particular level which will be experienced on this plane. However, the experience as a whole will be shared on a much deeper level. On a race level as well as on a deeper level, the universal level. Even now experiences on other planets and in other areas of your universe are being shared by a deeper aspect of yourself. A farther up the ladder level of yourself. When and this is again on an individual level each of you experience that transition, which each must eventually experience, then you will see that there are others on other planes who have experienced

similar transitions. And they will be able to offer encouragemen
and energy, so that you will be assisted in whatever endeavor
you need.

***

More information came forth when Beth visited the Library o
the spirit plane during a session in 1986.

B: It has been a while since we have met in the library. The
knowledge is all here, sparkling and shiny and ready to be
learned. If the question happens to be located somewhere else
I will project myself there instead. It is no problem.

D: *One time I was asking you about UFOs and space ships from
outer space. And at that time you became quite upset with me
because I couldn't understand the concept of dimensions.
(Yes) You said these ships came from many dimensions, and
you said I was quite ignorant on the subject. (Laugh) Could
you enlighten me?*

B: (Exasperated) I will try. One difficulty is the planetary
influences under which you were born. It makes you hold very
solidly to what you perceive as reality, which occasionally
comes across on this level as being dense or stubborn. Which
is sometimes frustrating. I will try to explain to you about
dimensions. Where you are, on the road in the life you are
living at this point in your development, you perceive three
dimensions visually. That is height, width and depth. And
your scientists assume that the fourth dimension is time, to
take up the space of the rest of the object that you know is
there, but you cannot directly see, since light travels in a
straight line on your level of existence. Out of convenience
your wise men have labeled these dimensions: the first,
second, third and fourth dimensions, assuming that is all there
is. From their limited understanding of the nature of the
universe and their limited understanding of the mathematics
involved, this is sufficient to work out their equations.
However, there are many different ways of perceiving reality,
many different ways of experiencing "what is". And each of
these different ways contain and involve various dimensions.
These various dimensions are not necessarily length, width,
depth and time. These labels apply to but four dimensions
when there are really many dimensions. Do you understand
so far? (Yes) The various combinations of these different
dimensions contain various branches of the mega universe
that I have described to you before. Do you remember about

the universe and how it's always branching off and dividing and weaving together due to the nature of time?

D: *Yes. And then the parallel universes are all interweaving together?*

B: Exactly. These parallel universes not only involve the same dimensions with which you are familiar, but also other parallel universes that are involving with all the other dimensions that you have no way of perceiving. These other universes also contain intelligent life, higher life forms who are also working through the circle of karma. The beings in some of these universes are much more advanced than you are, spiritually, mentally and intellectually. Consequentially, many of them have discovered a way to travel from their universe to your universe by using certain wondrous devices, to alter the dimensions they are perceiving. And by altering the dimensions they perceive into the dimensions you perceive, it automatically puts them in your universe. It's hard to explain. Consequentially, that is why they are said to be from different dimensions. Because their universe occupies the same space, so to speak, as your universe, with a different set of dimensions so that nothing collides. To draw an analogy in your world: In an area on a foggy day, it's like having a piece of gauze hanging in the fog with some dew on the gauze and some mist in the fog. Now the gauze, the dew, the mist and the fog are all occupying the same space, but they're still separate from each other. This is the way it is with the different dimensions. Your set of dimensions might be the gauze, for example. One being's set of dimensions might be the fog, and the fog is all throughout the gauze and in the gauze, but it does not collide with the gauze. And all this being can perceive is the fog. Therefore, it is not aware of the gauze and does not collide with it. Whereas, all you're aware of is the gauze and the fibers that make up the gauze. You're not aware of the fog that's around and through the gauze and surrounding each of the fibers of the gauze. And you're not aware of the dew that has condensed on the gauze, for it is out of your perception. Do you understand?

D: *It's difficult. The scientists in our time think that these UFOs come from physical space as we know it.*

B: They come from physical space, but not as you know it. They alter their perception of reality to coincide with your perception of reality, which causes them to appear in space as you know it. One way they can obtain the fantastic speeds they use for traveling is by partially perceiving both universes, so they are able to condense the distance between the points. Which I know sounds totally confusing, but that's the only way it can be explained in your language. When I look at the so called "visual" representations of it in this library, the concepts involved are very elegant and simple like most large concepts that are the basic building blocks of the universe. But when I start trying to explain them in words, they sound much more complicated than they really are. Because I'm trying to explain what is not, as well as what is, so I will put across an accurate mental picture.

D: *I see. But the investigators think of UFOS coming from different planets. I don't know if they can understand this concept.*

B: They need to be very clear on this subject of the various dimensions. I've only used the labels of the four dimensions that you have. The three that you perceive visually are all that you can perceive with your five senses. You simply have no concepts anywhere in your brains or your language to deal with other dimensions. Therefore, I have not given them any labels. However, I will say this to help understanding. That which you consider to be part of the dimension called "time" actually encompasses several dimensions. Your world and universe does not contain just four dimensions. It is composed of many more dimensions than that, but the others are lumped under the label you call "time". That is why strange things often happen which are inexplicable, due to the nature of these various dimensions interacting with each other, which you perceive as one dimension. Therefore it's conflicting, nonsensical and confusing to you sometimes. The various natures of these various dimensions which you call "time" are these extra dimensions. You are capable of perceiving them, but your scientists try to rationalize them away. However your body is equipped to perceive them, and it is this perception of these other dimensions that gives rise to what you have labeled "psychic powers". These psychic powers are not anything extraordinary. They are along the same line of your being able to perceive depth, length, width. These psychic powers are your tuning in to these other dimensions that you have lumped under the concept of time.

D: *This is a subject that likely could go on for quite a while.*

B: It could. For several sessions. Several of your tapes.

D: *The main thing is that I can write it, and let those who can understand it, understand it, even if I can't grasp it all.*

B: Those who are higher educated may have a more difficult time understanding because they are more fixed in their ideas.

***

Information from Phil during a session in 1996 in Hollywood
where he was living at the time. I had been trying to meet with him for
quite a while, but my traveling schedule did not allow for it. My main
focus in this session was to tie up some loose ends and find missing
pieces that I could use in this book. It took many years of gathering bits
and pieces from various people all over the world to bring forth these
concepts and to clarify them, as best we can with our understanding.

Phil came to my hotel after he got off work. After catching up on
the last few months we started the session. As he relaxed on the bed
he began to speak before I gave him his keyword. I did not have to use
our normal procedure. He started before I even had the tape recorder
turned on. This only happened once before, in the early days of our
work when we were working on the story of the seeding of the Earth.

P: You are a record keeper, and there are now those who would
   facilitate this endeavor. You may ask that which you perceive
   to be your questions.
D: *I wanted those to be present who could provide information
   in analogies, if possible, to make it easier for the average
   person to understand.*
P: That is accurate. That has, as you yourself have noted
   previously, always been our trademark. To use your simplified
   symbolisms to convey the abstract concepts which we would
   impart to you. We find that it is perhaps easier for the human
   mind to visualize that which is familiar, as opposed to trying
   to conceptualize that which is abstract. It is necessary, due to
   the unique structure of your human mind and we would clarify
   here, not to say the brain, but rather the mind itself. The mental
   processes which are inherent in your human existence are not
   conventional. They are somewhat modified from the accepted
   norm of what we would call the "universal reality".
D: *I am involved in a project, and I am trying to understand many
   very complicated concepts. Can you explain the concept of
   simultaneous time?*
P: We see the reality being somewhat misrepresented in your
   conventional wisdom that your human mind seeks to define.
   This is both a hindrance and a help in your desire to understand.
   We would ask that you picture a disk lying on its flat face, so
   that the top of this disk is viewable to you.
D: *Looking down on it?*
P: That is correct. Then inscribe a point at some distance from
   the center of this disk, along a radius of a line from the center
   to the perimeter or outside edge of this disk. Then rotate this

disk, and notice that the path that is traveled by this inscribe point, seems to continue indefinitely in one direction. We would describe this as infinity. In that the perceived direction has never changed, and the end has never been met. You have never met yourself on this path. Therefore, to the observer who is positioned on this point, there is no end or no beginning There is simply motion or movement in a perceived forward direction. Then realize that this perception is due only to the fact that you are on the plane of your travel. Were you to remove yourself from that plane, or take the perspective of th one looking down on the disk, as opposed to the one who is on the disk, this perception would be apparent. The apparent discrepancy is that there is indeed a beginning and an end. Any position on that disk could be used as a reference, or beginning or end. It is simply not apparent from that position on the disk. When one removes oneself from the plane of apparent reality, then the true reality is manifest.

D: *Then the one who is on the disk, would that be the way we perceive it?*

P: That is how it is perceived, not that you perceive it.

D: Because we perceive it as proceeding in a linear fashion.

P: That is accurate. The perception is simply from a vantage point, and not from a reality. We find that many on your plan seek to define their reality by their vantage point. There are broader realities that go unnoticed, simply because people refuse to alter their vantage point. Which is something that i not possible to someone who defies the ability to do so.

D: *I think one of the complications we have with trying to understand simultaneous time, is the idea that instead of progressing in a linear fashion, everything is actually occurring at the same time. That is how we define simultaneou time.*

P: The concept itself is somewhat not accurate. Your definition of happening is, in itself, not quite able to comprehend the reality of existence. When we say "happening", the very idea of happening is defining. Happening is right now, as opposed to existing, which is undefined. The perception of happening is again somewhat limiting, in that by its definition, the word "happen" has to have both a beginning and an end. The very definition of "happening" indicates the beginning of some event, and the end of some event. Therefore, we would ask that you drop both these beginning and end points. And simply realize that there is that which is. Therefore, all is existing simultaneously, as opposed to all is happening simultaneously.

D: *One of the difficulties I have with this is, in our reality as we perceive it, you grow from a baby to a child to an adult. And that is linear. If it's all existing at the same time, how can that be defined?*

P: There exists many different scenarios in your lifetime, that you consciously perceive in a singular fashion. And here we refer to our other statement, that your mental processes are somewhat modified from the general accepted universal realities. Your mental processes in themselves define that which you perceive. They allow only a very small portion of reality at any given time. There are those who can see a much broader spectrum of existence, without these limiting factors, neither beginning nor end, but total existence. We speak here of many who are of much higher and advanced planes of awareness. However, it is possible for those on your plane to comprehend this and even experience this in some fashion or manner of degrees as they open their mind, so to say, to drop the barriers of beginning and end. The universe exists. It does not begin or end. It simply exists.

D: *But in our reality we see ourselves starting as a baby and the body grows and changes. Doesn't that contradict the idea of everything happening at once?*

P: The birth experience is very analogous to the mental concepts, or mental functions of your experience. There is a defined beginning and a defined end, a birth and death. And your life is defined by all of those points that fall in between the two boundaries. Were you to remove yourself from this defined set of perimeters and look at your total existence, you would see that the birth and death "bench marks" are simply definitions and not realities. Your soul is existing both in and out of the "bench marks" you describe as birth and death. You therefore take a higher or broader perspective, and see that you exist whether you are alive or not.

D: *Yes, these are things I can understand. I just can't put it into the perimeters of simultaneous time where everything would be occurring at once.*

P: The existence of terms such as "happening" or "beginning and end", are somewhat defining, in that they make you think in those terms. We would ask that you use different terms, such as "existence", which is not defining in beginning or end, but simply relates the existence of reality. Reality exists. It does not begin, and it does not end. Your definition of simultaneous time is simply an attempt to look at the whole picture in a two dimensional term, which is somewhat confusing, in that there is indeed this concept but not in your terms.

D: *We have to deal with the terms that our mind understands in the English language. All right. Let's go on to another one. I'm trying to understand the concept of parallel lifetimes, even parallel universes. Maybe that's two totally different things, but let's start with parallel lifetimes. They say these are lifetimes we are experiencing at the same time. And there again the concept of time comes up. But they are in different time periods, and may even overlap.*

P: This is indeed a similar concept, in that parallel time and parallel universes are indeed the simultaneous time and universes of which we spoke earlier. It is simply a matter of focusing your attention on one particular aspect of that which is the sum of all your experiences. We would refer again to the analogy of the circle, in which any one point defined on the circle can be either a beginning or an end. It is not defined by its character as one or the other. It is simply there. Then understand that all points on that circle exist simultaneously on that circle. And are neither beginning nor end, in and of themselves, but only by definition. They are not, in and of themselves, a point. They are simply a definition.

D: *We believe that we enter a body as a spirit and experience the life. But if we are also existing, living another lifetime that is parallel to it, how can that be defined? I'm thinking of one soul entering one body at one individual time.*

P: Your reality, you, your personal reality, could be defined as a circle. You, in your conscious state, can only comprehend the point or segment that your mind is capable of perceiving. Your awareness is only capable of perceiving that which is directly in front of you. Not to say that you cannot see beyond your own nose, but we would use that analogy in the sense of an overall picture. All that you are and all that you have been and all that you shall be, are on that circle. But your perception of that is simply that which is small enough for your conscious mind to perceive. You are, on higher planes, aware of the sum total of your existence. However, your conscious mind, on the plane from which you are speaking, is only capable of that which is most immediate to your conscious mind.

D: *I just had a thought. Whenever I am doing hypnosis and I take the person to other lifetimes, is that a way of changing the focus? Like switching channels on a television set.*

P: That is exactly right. It is indeed the same person or energy. The consciousness is simply directed forwards or backwards along this circle. This being exists. It does not begin, it does not end. It simply exists. You merely change your focus or perspective from one section of that existence to another.

There is no break in the existence. It is continuous and infinite in either direction. However, you may advance your perception to suit that which you seek. The knowledge you seek will be found on some other portion of that circle.

D: *Then it's as though the subconscious has the knowledge, the sum total of all of the lifetimes.*

P: The subconscious is the sum total of all those lifetimes. It is the circle itself. The conscious simply moves to that portion of the circle of which you seek information. And then relates that which is in that portion of the circle. We would clarify, as in your question, that in cases of mental aberrations or illness where the perception is distorted, then moving to another portion of the circle would cause a distortion in the perception. We speak here with the assumption that the realities are presented as they truly are, and not through a distorted lens of false impression. For that indeed is possible. The lens or conscious mind, need be clear and undistorted, so that the information from the different points on this circle, is both presented and.... We find here a difficulty in translating the word, to infer that the perception of that information is accurate.

D: *Then it sounds as though our concept of the subconscious is really in error. Is the subconscious most closely related to the soul or the spirit?*

P: There is actually no difference. The soul and spirit are identical. The subconscious, in your definition, is simply the intelligence or awareness of that soul. In your definition, the awareness of your soul is defined as the subconscious. The fact is that your soul is your awareness. That is one of the stumbling blocks in learning the realities of the universe. Is that your awareness is your reality. It is not that you perceive the universe through your awareness, the reality is your awareness. You are what you think. That is your true reality.

D: *We think that the subconscious is like the record keeper, the guardian of the systems of the body, and remains objective in that way. It is like a protector of the body. But I guess I have not correlated it with being the actual soul or spirit.*

P: The existence of your awareness validates the fact that you are. You think, therefore you are. And yet you are, and yet not know it. Therefore you think, therefore you are not.

D: *Oftentimes when I contact the subconscious directly and ask it for information about the body, it seems to be very objective and removed.*

P: The emotional aspects of living in an environment such as you find yourself in, require that there be some sort of interface, in order to function with the currents of realities that swirl around you. These emotions allow the intake of information from that which is being processed around you, to be assimilated into the existence of your soul. To translate the existences around you into a manner which can be perceived by your consciousness.

D: *I think that makes it a little easier. Another question along the same line. Can you give me a description or definition of other dimensions that are existing in close proximity to us, although they are invisible to us?*

P: There are many dimensions surrounding your defined area of reality. We would ask that you choose that which you perceive to be the most relevant, and define it in terms that you may understand. There are in fact many dimensions, both above and below your depth of perception. However, that is not to say that one or another is any greater or lesser than.

D: *They say there are many dimensions existing very close to us, but invisible to us, and yet they are very similar to ours. Does that make any sense?*

P: They are accessible to you, however, perhaps not apparent to you. There are many aspects of these other dimensions which overlap from one dimension to another. And yet there are many more aspects which are unique unto that particular dimension. There are times when your emotional states cause your mind to expand and broaden and enhance your perception of the world around you. For example, many people find that watching a particular sunset at a particular time in their life, or perhaps, time of day or year, will give them a feeling of awareness that is not common in their life. A oneness with nature that is uncommon. Or perhaps in the vernacular of those who seek these experiences, to become one with nature. They have attuned their consciousness to that particular thread which runs common to all of these universes. Therefore they feel the breath of their existence expand to the point that they feel they are in many other dimensions at once. And indeed they are. They are aware of it.

D: *Then it seems to bring up the same concept of where our focus is. The other dimensions are all there, but we can't perceive them because of our focus.*

P: That is accurate.

D: *Then it seems like those three topics go along together.*

P: That is accurate. The general scope of this conversation is more of perception as opposed to reality. The realities of the universe are there for all to perceive. However, the individual growth and understanding of the person who would be trying to understand it at any given point, would determine to what depth or breath or height they would be able to perceive these other realities.

D: *Then when they talk about raising our consciousness, does that mean we will become more aware of these other realities?*

P: That is accurate.

***

Discussion at one of the group meetings in the 1980s.

Q: *Sometimes we think of having various aspects of ourselves, that quite possibly might be living here on Earth at the same time that we do. How frequently is this true?*

Phil: My instant response was, very frequent. Much more frequent than we're aware of. In fact, the more thought projections we send out in those areas, the more "juice" we give that capability. However, our aspects have a life of their own. They exist, and most of the time are not conscious of their other aspects. Us and others.

***

During another session with Phil in 1999.

D: *I have been gathering information about different dimensions, and I wanted to expand on that. I do know, in my limited way, that the other dimensions that surround our planet are physical worlds, with physical human beings living on them. But they are vibrating at different speeds and are invisible to us. Can you give me any more information on that?*

Phil: There is a certain circular reality in that there is no sense of finiteness in the true reality. There are many shades of reality which are expressed in different ways. However, to say that a dimension is physical, as opposed to spiritual, is somewhat misleading. The concept seems to be understood as physical being different from spiritual. It is simply that that which you call "physical" has certain characteristics, which are somewhat separate or different from that which you call "spiritual". However, they are one and the same. It is simply a matter of there being certain differences which distinguish one from the other. If you were to define the true reality of green water as opposed to blue water, you could say that certainly green water is not the same as blue water. However, it's obvious that the true constituent of each, which is water, is entirely identical.

There is simply differences between the two, which distinguish them. So could you say that blue water is really different from green water?

D: *I have heard there are other beings living in these other dimensions. They are invisible to us, but they are living in what they consider a physical world.*

P: That is accurate. It is as the radio waves in your air are all existing at the same time, and all contain different information, different realities, but yet can exist in the same space at the same time. It is simply a matter of a difference in frequency. There is no interference until the frequencies attempt to share the same frequency at the same time.

D: *This causes what we call "static" or overlapping?*

P: Yes. Trouble.

D: *Does this happen with dimensions?*

P: Occasionally. But thankfully, in the scheme of things there are safeguards which prevent this. However, it is possible for an occasional overlap.

D: *What would happen if that occurred?*

P: Beings from different dimensions could interact and become aware of each other through their own sensory perceptions. The senses, which you call your "five senses", are instrument which are attuned to the frequencies on your level of existence. The beings which inhabit other levels of existence have sensory organs which are attuned to their own particular frequency of existence. If, for some reason, these levels of awareness were to overlap or to share the same frequency, then the sensory elements of each would be attuned to the same frequency. And the beings on each plane would be aware of each other.

D: *Would they know something unusual had happened?*

P: Perhaps, but not necessarily. There are between the dimension slight changes. Between successive dimensions the greater changes become more apparent. Such that the beings from several dimensions removed would, if they were able to comprehend that they were seeing, realize that there is indeed something very peculiar happening. However, because the changes are so subtle between the dimensions, each successive dimension is slightly different from the next. It could possibly be that one would not be, at least initially, aware that they had found themselves in another dimension.

D: *But it is possible to go back and forth.*

P: That is accurate.

D: *We have heard that sometimes there are windows that make it easier to go from one dimension to the other. Is this true?*

P: There are openings which are useful to allow beings, who have the knowledge and awareness, to be able to manifest this so called "window". However, there is not in your terminology, a certain place which can be defined as an existing phenomenon, in and of itself, which is static, that you can access at any time simply by walking up to it. The energies can be manipulated such that a window can be generated. However, it is not a naturally occurring phenomenon. There was, as you are aware, an experiment done by your Navy which is commonly referred to as the "Philadelphia Experiment". This is an example of an experiment with these "windows". There are those beings who are spiritually capable of passing from one dimension to the other. Your best example perhaps would be Jesus, who could access many different levels. After his ascension he could return to your plane consciously and appear. Even though he perhaps was not of your plane, he could come to your plane.

D: *You mean the government found a way to open the window to go back and forth, with the Philadelphia Experiment? Or they created a window?*

P: We would say that a window was opened. However, the ability to get back was not quite as finessed as the ability to open it. There were catastrophic results because of the inability to properly manipulate this phenomenon. It is a natural in the universal sense condition. These planes are simply natural and common. However, it is your level of understanding at this point which makes them or this concept somewhat supernatural. Nothing could be further from the truth. It is the basis of reality, in the universal sense.

D: *But the government found a way to do this.*

P: There are those who are working on manipulating these energies. There are some who have succeeded in more or less fashion. However, because of the lack of spiritual awareness, which is necessary, there is as yet perhaps a most crude fundamental understanding of this phenomenon.

D: *Are the experiments continuing?*

P: That is accurate. It is possible at this time to transport energy or matter through the dimensions. However, the spiritual realities which enable this phenomenon to occur are as yet not understood. The basis of understanding to this point has been technological. The spiritual component has not been understood. There have been experiments which have failed. And the participants were somewhat in worse shape afterwards than before. Their soul or spirit has the ability, or perhaps the resources, to heal these victims of these experiments when they have passed through the dimensional plane to that which you call the "spiritual" plane. There have been cases where individuals were completely lost to another dimension and were, in essence, trapped in another dimension.

D: *How could they be trapped if the soul can go anywhere it wants and do anything it wants.*

P: It is the physical components which we speak of. There are cases of the physical body being completely transported to another dimension with the soul intact.

D: *That's what you mean. The physical was trapped in another dimension, and couldn't get back.*

P: That is accurate. Your comprehension is adequate to allow us to see that which you are describing. And yes, it is true that they sometimes overlap. However, at this point it is not technologically feasible for someone on your plane to attempt this on a regular basis. It is in fact one of the manners in which those you call the "aliens" are able to maneuver through vast distances. It is simply a matter of going between the dimensions, and finding those portals which exist in their naturally occurring state. We wish here to define the difference between that which we were describing as a window as opposed to what we describe as a portal.

D: *Yes, I would like to know the difference.*

P: In the context in which we were speaking earlier, a window was a device which allowed one to simply pass from one plane of existence to another. This is not a naturally occurring device. A portal, however, is a naturally occurring phenomenon much like a tunnel, in which what you would call "distance" on a particular plane can be crossed. One would be able to travel great distances by going through these portals. However, these portals are on the same plane. They do not transcend the separate planes of reality. Once one has arrived at the destination on that particular plane, it is necessary to convert to the plane which one wishes to arrive at.

D: *That's the part I'm having confusion with. This is different from other dimensions, this is on the same plane.*

P: Portals are on the same plane. They don't transcend planes. There are portals within the planes themselves, however, the portals do not span the planes.

D: *And this is different than going between dimensions.*

P: That is accurate.

D: *I'm still a little confused on that. If we're thinking of the same plane of existence, would the aliens be coming from a physical star or part of the galaxy that is out there now. But rather than going by speed of light or whatever, they would just find a portal?*

P: That is accurate.

D: *So they're on this physical plane of reality, rather than in another dimension. They just found these doorways so they can go back and forth faster.*

P: That is accurate.

D: *All of this is confusing to me, but I just had an idea. Using the planet Venus as an example, in "our" dimension it appears that there is no life there. Could it be possible that in an "alternate" reality or a different dimension, there could be people living there?*

P: On the level in which you experience reality, there would not be. However, in higher dimensions there are in fact many lifeforms on many of the planets that are simply at a different level of expression. It would be simply that the expression, as it manifests on your level, does not convey or express the essence of what you would call "lifeforms". There is at the lower levels of that expression simply gas and rock. However, much as an iceberg is considered only partially visible, it's known that the entire expression of the iceberg is not visible. The level at which you are seeing the reality on Venus is simply a portion of that which is underwater, so to say. There are portions of the total expression which are invisible to you because your perceptions are not able to conceive the reality of the higher planes of existence.

D: *So on an alternate reality, another parallel world, so to speak, could there be a physical race living there?*

P: That is accurate. And in the sense of our iceberg analogy we would include the iceberg to transcend planes of existence.

When Phil awakened he discussed the portion of the session that e remembered.

P: The main thing I got was the fact that there's a difference between the dimensions. But that within a dimension there are levels of awareness even within a dimension. For example, there are things that we're not aware of on this dimension, much less the other dimensions. It's like the spectrum of light that is all one light in this dimension, and we may be only aware of certain portions of the spectrum. Our awareness is limited to a very small portion of this dimension. We're not completely aware of all the elements of this dimension, and much less the other dimensions. And so the concept of portals is within a dimension. You can travel great distances within this dimension, but there are not portals from this dimension to the next. But there are degrees of... it's almost like there are dimensions within dimensions. There are levels within this dimension that change enough that they would be different from the other levels within this dimension.

D: *Kind of like reading an octave. Each note would be a dimension, but it's still safe within an octave. (Yes) I really appreciated your explaining about the portals as opposed to the windows.*

P: The water seemed to be the easiest way to explain how we think of spiritual and physical. It's basically the same reality only in a different form.

We all agreed that we are growing and expanding to where we could handle and understand complicated information now that we never could have understood in the beginning of our work.

***

ARTICLE THAT APPEARED IN THE DAILY TELEGRAPH
London   Oct. 11, 1995

"WELCOME TO THE NEXT WORLD"
By Dr. Michio Kaku

Einstein's theory of gravity, which gives us the Big Bang theory and black holes, has been subjected to the most stringent test yet and passed with flying colors.

In the latest issue of Physics Today, astronomers from Harvard, MIT and the Haystack Observatory proudly announced that they had confirmed Einstein's theory to within an astonishing 0.04 percent accuracy by measuring the bending of radio waves from the quasar 3C279 near the edge of the visible universe. But there is some irony in this announcement. Each success only highlights a yawning gap. Even as scientists hail ever more accurate tests of Einstein's theory of warped space, Einstein himself knew that his theory broke down at the instance of the Big Bang. The theory had feet of clay.

Relativity was worthless, he realized, when it came to answering the most embarrassing cosmic question in all of science: What happened before the Big Bang? Ask any cosmologist this question, and they will throw up their hands, roll their eyes, and lament: "This may be forever beyond the reach of science. We just don't know."

Until now, that is. A remarkable consensus has been developing recently around what is called "quantum cosmology", in which scientists believe that a merger of quantum theory and Einstein's relativity may resolve these sticky theological questions. Theoretical physicists are rushing in where the angels fear to tread.

In particular, an appealing but startling new picture is emerging in quantum cosmology that may be able to synthesize some of the great mythologies of creation.

There are two dominant religious mythologies. According to Judaeo Christian belief, the universe had a definite beginning. This is the Genesis hypothesis, in which the universe was hatched from a Cosmic Egg. However, according to the Hindu Buddhist belief in Nirvana, the universe is timeless; it never had a beginning, nor will it have an end.

Quantum cosmology proposes a beautiful synthesis of these seemingly hostile viewpoints. In the beginning was Nothing. No space, no matter or energy. But according to the quantum principle, even Nothing was unstable. Nothing began to decay; that is, it began to "boil" with billions of tiny bubbles forming and expanding rapidly. Each bubble became an expanding universe.

If this is true, then our universe is actually part of a much larger "multiverse" of parallel universes, which is truly timeless, like Nirvana. As Steve Weinberg, the Nobel laureate physicist, has said: "An important implication is that there wasn't a beginning; that there were increasingly large Big Bangs, so that the (multiverse) goes on forever one doesn't have to grapple with the question of it before the Bang. The (multiverse) has just been here all along. I find that a very satisfying picture."

Universes can literally spring into existence as a quantum fluctuation of Nothing. This is because the positive energy found in matter is balanced against the negative energy of gravity, so the total energy of a bubble is zero. Thus, it takes no net energy to create a new universe.

Alan Guth, originator of the inflationary theory, once remarked: "It's often said there is no such thing as a free lunch. But the universe itself may be a free lunch."

And Andre Linde of Stanford has said: "If my colleagues and I are right, we may soon be saying goodbye to the idea that our universe was a single fireball created in the Big Bang."

Although this picture is appealing, it also raises more questions. Can life exist on these parallel universes? Cambridge cosmologist Stephen Hawking is doubtful: he believes that our universe may co exist with other universes, but our universe is special. The probability of forming these other bubbles is vanishingly small.

On the other hand, Weinberg believes most of these parallel universes are probably dead. To have stable DNA molecules, the proton must be stable for at least three billion years. In these dead universes, the protons might have decayed into a sea of electrons and neutrons.

Our universe may be one of the few compatible with life. This would, in fact, answer the age old question of why the physical constants of the universe fall in a narrow band compatible with the formation of life. If the charge of the electron, the gravitational constant, etc., were changed slightly, then life would have been impossible. This is called the Anthropic Principle. As Freeman Dyson of Princeton said: "It's as if the universe knew we were coming."

The strong version of this states that this proves the existence of God or an all powerful deity. But according to quantum cosmology, perhaps there are millions of dead universes. It was an accident, therefore, that our universe had conditions compatible with the formation of stable DNA molecules.

This leaves open the possibility, however, that there are parallel universes out there which are almost identical to ours, except for some fateful incident. Perhaps George III did not lose the Colonies in one such universe.

However, I can calculate the probability that one day you might be walking down the street, only to fall into a hole in space and enter a parallel universe. You would have to wait longer than the lifetime of the universe for such a cosmic event to happen.

As the biologist J.B.S. Haldane observed: "The universe is not only queerer than we suppose, it is queerer than we can suppose."

***

Dr. Michio Kaku is professor of theoretical physics at the City University of New York and author of Hyperspace: a Scientific Odyssey through the 10th Dimension (Oxford University Press).

It appears that the great scientific minds have part of the picture at least.

CHAPTER TWELVE
THE ENERGY AND THE ASSISTANTS

Much of the information included in this book was accumulated during the 1980s when I was a fledgling investigator. I was convinced that I had all the answers to life through my work as a past life therapist. All the evidence proved to me the existence of reincarnation, but I had placed the lives in a linear progression (or regression), because that was the only way most of our minds can conceive it. I had formed my opinions and theories based on the cases I had worked with. Then when I began to work with Phil my orderly belief system was disrupted. My work with him resulted in my book *Keepers of the Garden*, which exposed me to a radically different concept of the beginning of life on Earth. There was much more that was not included in that book. I was getting information and being exposed to concepts I had never heard of. They threatened to topple my secure world. At first I was so sure I had all the answers that I didn't want to explore any new theories that did not fit. I could have discarded them, but then I decided to keep an open mind and delve deeper. I realized that if I denied the information without examining it I would be no better than religious institutions that proclaim they have the "only" truth. Instead of throwing out the maverick material, I put it to the side to be looked at later. The time has now come to examine it and try to understand it, as best as our limited human minds can.

Instead of being isolated information from Phil, it began to emerge from many subjects all over the world, as though it was untapped truth and knowledge. I know I never could have understood it in the beginning of my work, and could have thrown it away. Now after over twenty years of research I realize I have been spoonfed small portions until I was ready to digest the more complicated information. Even if I don't understand it fully, and I am sure I only have a small portion of a much larger picture, I am now ready to present it to make others think.

In the early days of my experimenting in the 1980s we often had group meetings at Billie Cooper's house in Rogers, Arkansas. There I would put Phil in trance and anyone could ask questions. There would often be many people present, and naturally their questions centered around their personal problems (jobs and love lives). But occasionally more complex questions were asked, and I have isolated these to be

presented in this book, because I saw they followed a common thread
    The following would often happen when we asked the speaking
entity to identify itself.

P: We speak here as a collective energy. For there is no need for
personalization. There is no such thing as the "I" concept here
for all is "we".
D: *How many are you?*
P: To ascribe a physical number would be pointless. For in so
doing you would be attempting to define boundaries of
personality, that there would be x amount of personalities.
And from our perception this is not accurate. This is no
distinction. We simply coexist. There is no distinction between
one personality and another, or the beginning of one personality
and another. It is simply a shared and coexistent existence.
There is no distinction. Again we say, we are not linear in
time nor distance, and are somewhat unable to translate that
concept. We simply exist. We do not attempt to define our
existence. It is on your side that you must identify and separate
yourselves and isolate yourselves, so that you become "you".
We are we. We on this plane have no, what you would call,
identity, for there is at this level no need to identify. The
recognition of identity is instantaneous and complete. There
is no need to attach a label. For when one attaches labels,
one fixes on the label moreso than on the identity. This is done
on your plane because you do not have the awareness. Think
not of the label but of the energy. If you were as we, you now
sitting in this room could sit in total darkness and pass in
and out of each room, and each of you would recognize
instantly in total darkness, those who are sitting and who
is moving about. Please understand that what your awareness
encompasses is so vast, and is far more than your conscious
minds can comprehend. You are indeed one with the universe
And so you should not be surprised to find that there are many
aspects of yourselves that you have never been aware of.
D: *Would this include what we think of as past life experiences?*
P: These could be memories, nothing more than memories that
are shared, because of the fact that you are connected, each
and every one of you together, on your inner plane awareness
The memory of one of you is shared by each and every one of
you. You can remember each other's thoughts on a very deep
level. And so you may find that your past life is indeed quite
accurately called a memory of one who has lived that existence
We would say there is no such thing as past lives, for from our
point of view all has been, all is, and all shall be simultaneously

As we have no concept of time, each of you has already been each other and are being each other in your future. We know this is not very clear to you at this time. However, each of you will be given information in your near future, in which each of you will be challenged to examine this concept. That is: the past and present simultaneous with the future.

D: *That's what gets confusing. How is it that we are able to contact a certain past lifetime over and over again? Why wouldn't we go to different ones every time I regressed the person?*

P: You could also follow one single note throughout an entire symphony. If you could imagine hearing a single note played on a single instrument, and following this note throughout an entire symphony, you would see this note reappear, or more accurately, hear this note reappear throughout this symphony. And you could indeed identify this single note as a separate identity. In this same way you can recall these, what you would call, past lifetimes throughout your entire history, simply by narrowing your perspective to that one particular area you wish to choose. The conscious selection may seem random; however, it is in fact that you have preprogrammed yourself to return to that particular segment each and every time you return there.

D: *Can we use the word "vibration" or "energy"? That those who can review many past lives are simply able to review more of these energy levels than others?*

P: That is accurate. Each of you could follow many more lines than you could possibly comprehend. It is possible. However, there is the necessity for limiting one's experiences to only those areas which bring understanding and enlightenment. And so it would be wise to disregard those lifetimes which would bring disharmony, for that is not the intended purpose. Were you to instantly allow your awareness to take in all that is available to you, you would be overwhelmed. For there is far more occurring than you can possibly comprehend, even now as we speak, in each of your own separate personalities. For in the color white there are many, many separate colors, and you can easily pull out one separate color from that which is white. In this same way you yourself pulled out or isolated a particular energy which is a component of your Higher Self. And so this energy was brought down to your level, this aspect of personality, so to say. It was indeed a part and parcel of yourself given free rein on this level. You yourselves sitting in this room are simply the tips of an enormous iceberg. And were you more aware and consciously able, you could bring

more of that which is below the surface to your level, and vi
versa. That which you have isolated as your selves could g
to those higher levels in which your other aspects of energy
reside. Many of you do this at some point. It is not as if yo
are experiencing someone else. It is as if you are experiencin
a part of yourself that you have never seen before.

D: *Is it possible then to review a life that has not yet occurred?*

P: That is accurate. You can go anywhere you want to go: past
present, future, on the Earth or in space. It doesn't matter.
Anywhere. Going into the future may seem difficult at first,
simply because you are not used to thinking that way. So, ye
you could easily regress to a future life.

D: *Progress.*

P: It would be a matter of semantics. However, as has been state
all has already occurred and nothing has yet occurred,
simultaneously. Time is indeed a relative factor.

D: *Can you describe simultaneous time in a way that humans c*
this plane can understand it easily?

P: We shall try. If you would, please consider the difference
between a straight line and a circle. Were you to draw a lin
and connect two points on a straight line, you would find the
is no possibility for parallelism, in the sense that all are in t
same plane. However, were you to connect two points with
a circle there would indeed be the possibility of two points
being connected by a straight line. If you would consider tin
as a concept only, and in that context a circle, then it would
possible for two points in time to be connected. Suppose th
circle then were to become a spiral, such that the ends were
infinitely extended to the point that they were in fact the san
point. Then this spiral concept could be imagined to see tha
there is even within a circle, perhaps, a linear of sorts
progression, from one end to another. This time concept is on
which is particularly physical in nature, as all in the physica
world must obey certain fundamental concepts. A beginning
and an end. Life and death. Black and white. Plus and minu
It is necessary to segregate the realities from the spiritual
world, such that these realities are left in the physical, so tha
a polarizing process can be achieved. There is in this proce
a duality concept which is given. The plus and minus, and s
forth. There is therefore the free will, while in a circle there
no free will, because there is no beginning and no end, and r
black and no white. In physical you have one end or anothe
if you can follow this concept. The free will is not the end
which justifies the means. It is simply a byproduct of the
reality of polarizations. Free will simply evolved from the fa

that there are polarities in the physical world. Time is, however, not polarized. There is no plus time and no minus time. There is simply an idea of what is now and what is then. Which is, even as we speak, changing from that which is now to that which is then. So how could there be "now"? Time never stands still, so automatically the concept of now is simply thrown out the window. Now is instantly yesterday or past. The minute you realize that now is a thought, it has already become past. So there is no need to worry about now. You are always living in the future, if you so choose.

D: *But I've heard that we have many possible futures.*

P: That is accurate, but many times you can observe the ones most likely to happen to you from the direction your life has been heading up to that point. And there is also free will which dictates all that shall be.

D: *A question from the group: I have been concerned with energies, plus and minus, male and female, as we express them now. Are there ways we may balance those energies within us?*

P: First of all, one should be aware that many are polarized for a reason. There is, indeed, in nature as there is in the spirit world, those who are more of one than another. And then there are those who are equal. Perhaps we could use the yin and yang examples here. Is it any less noble to be all yin, than it is to be all yang? Or is it more noble to be a total balance between the two? It is not more right to be more of one than the other, nor is it even more right to be completely equal. There is only that which is most appropriate. For each particular lesson you should draw from that which is most appropriate, the yin or the yang. We see that your question speaks of harmonizing yourself. That is, to become more balanced in your energies. However, we would caution you in realizing that the middle of the road is not necessarily the most desirable place to be.

D: *Which brings up the question of homosexuality.*

P: This is simply a matter of energies, in that there are male and female energies. And in a male, when he is endowed with predominately female energies, he exerts this characteristic, which is predominately in females. This then is the reason for the attraction to males, for opposites do attract, whether they be in male or female bodies. And so this is delineated down to an energy level of female energy being in a male body, attracted to male energy in a male body.

D: *You said it's a female energy. What do you mean?*

P: The polarity or disposition of the soul is given as more predominately female energy.

D: *Would that mean the soul has had more female lives, or more female experience?*

P: This soul most likely would have, not that the predominance of lives would have programmed the soul to more female energy. There is, at creation of souls, a personality imprint which usually is more male or more female or somewhat more neutral.

D: *Then the past lives don't have anything to do with this?*

P: Yes, they have a lot to do with this, for they are experiences which are remembered, and so program somewhat the affectations of the individual in expressing the energies. The lives, however, do not determine whether the entity be male or female.

D: *I have found that if a soul had more lives of one sex than the other, it was more difficult for them to cope.*

P: That is correct, for there is more familiarity with the opposit sex. It could cause confusion for there is, in this society, much programming to be strictly either a man or a woman, and not simply one or the other with the genders crossed.

D: *Is this the main reason for homosexuality, or could there be other explanations?*

P: This is the most prevalent. However, there are cases where one chooses to incarnate in such a cross reality in order to learn lessons. Many lessons being: temperance, tolerance, patience, humility, etc. It may not simply be a matter of choic but of necessity.

Question: *There is a theory that the planet Earth is encircled with a band of energy. And recorded in this band is every action, every thought and everything that has ever occurred. And then anybody can receive information simply by tapping into that Is that accurate?*

P: That is an accurate statement. Yes, indeed, for there is what you might call an aura surrounding this planet, which is continuously built from the emotions and attitudes of those inhabitants who live on this planet. And so this aura reflects as a whole the race which populates the planet beneath it. Much as your aura as a whole reflects your personality. That is, the energy which resides in your aura.

D: *Our aura is influenced by the energies that our body creates*

P: That is accurate.

D: *How about the energies encircling the Earth?*

P: Are they future energies that have not been perhaps channele to a physical level? The answer is, yes. For your past, presen future progression is a processing type of process. An industrial process that is taking the energies from a higher plane and channeling them down to a lower plane, through your actions. And so your aura is a result of this processing. However, the energies always have been and always will be. They are from your point of view, however, rechanneled from one level to another. The Earth's aura is made up of those energies which have been processed from the higher to the lower energies. And so these are byproducts of the human experience. Much as the smoke from a smoke stack.

D: *Could you explain the difference between the higher energies and the lower energies?*

P: The higher energies are what you might call "God" or "truth consciousness" or "enlightenment". That which is. These are frequencies of the highest order, and are tapped through your mind and your consciousness. The lower energies are energies from the higher plane which have been brought down to a lower plane. They are a byproduct of the human experience. They are energies, however, they have been lowered to a level more closely attuned to your own. We speak here of energies in many different ways. Music, mathematics, amazement, wonder, love, hate. These are all energies.

D: *And I understand that all are recorded. That none are wasted, none are forgotten. Is that correct?*

P: None are ever lost. Many, however, are not used. For example, were the love energy surrounding your planet used more frequently than the hate energy or fear energy, we perceive that the aura surrounding your planet would be vastly different. And of a higher overall energy level. It is as if these byproducts, these auras given off are indicative of the energies which have been processed.

D: *If this planet were destroyed, what would become of these energies?*

P: They would simply be returned to the universe. And be reprocessed in another manner in another place in, as you might say, another time. Energy cannot be destroyed. It would be necessary however for the energies to be redirected. For they would drift aimlessly through the universe were they not rechanneled and reapplied to another area or plane, so they could be returned to a useful purpose.

D: *Then these energies are not lost, they are changed. They would not remain in the same form. Can you elaborate on what we call our "soul"? Would this be the same energy you have been talking about?*

P: There is a separateness here. We speak of energies in a ver free manner, which the soul processes. The soul here woul be the functioning machinery, if you might say that. The energies would be the fuels which feed the soul. The soul is spark, a fragment of the original One Soul. For all, at one time, were simply whole and together. And in what you cal the beginning of creation, this wholeness was splintered. And each of you were cast off to begin experiencing life as separate identities. This is what you have called the time of t Fall, where the knowledge was lost and the consciousness turned down towards the Earth. And these higher energy planes were disregarded and discarded. So you can see fror a strictly analogy standpoint there was a definite fall of consciousness, from the higher plane to the more base Earth plane. There was not, as has previously been felt, a surge o evil present when this fall occurred. It was simply that the attention of those inhabitants was shifted from the higher to the lower planes. That is what is meant by the Fall. This is n a right or wrong judgment. It is simply a fact which is in the realm of truth. And so you can see that when you lose your sight of who and what you are, then you would tend to wande as mankind has done on this planet for many millennia now. Thus the Fall is simply a forgetting of the true identity. A lowering of the consciousness, and forgetting that all are trul part of the whole.

D: *What caused the splintering, the breaking up, in the first place?*

P: This was an intentional act by the entire Soul, the One Who Soul, so that experience could be diverse. There was felt at that time the need for more diverse experience. It was recognized that to enable one to fully comprehend All That I then more experience would be necessary.

D: *This soul that splintered in the beginning came to have the Earth experience and took the form of a body. Then the body and the soul are separated at death. We know what happens to the body. What happens to the soul at that time?*

P: This is a highly individual basis. For many souls we would call them splinters find they have regressed beyond the point they found themselves originally. And so find themselves further from the truth than when they had originally incarnated And so there must be given those lessons which will erase the mistakes made. Others find that they have become more enlightened, and so are attuned to that level which is the One Soul.

D: *Do those that regress have to come and inhabit a body again*

P: No, for there is no have to. If it is most appropriate, yes, then that might be the best thing to do. However, there is no rule that says one has to incarnate.

D: *What eventually happens to the individual soul.*

P: The ultimate goal is for all souls to return to the One. And so bring with them all that has been experienced. It is as if each of you are out collecting experience and storing it away for some future date, when each and every one of you will return with your collection of experiences. And so share it with the whole once again. Then all that has been experienced from the beginning to the end of creation be shared. It is a symphony of experience.

D: *This original soul that splintered, would that be the same as our concept of God?*

P: That is accurate. It is the One, the All Being, the Truth, the Light. Many have their own particular label. You might say your identities are separate from this God. However, each of you are truly an individual piece or part of that which you call God. There is no God without each of you. For were each of you to simply discreate, then God Himself would discreate.

***

This session took place in 1987 after Phil had spent many months California working at various jobs, including the movies, and while was totally immersed in working on the Nostradamus information. e had moved back to our area and wanted to start working with me ain. We had no topic to focus on, so we decided to just see where is session led. I was always prepared for the unexpected. I used his yword and the elevator method. When the elevator door opened he w a brilliant white light.

P: It's totally white light. Total energy. This is an energy plane, or one realm of existence that we who might be called the "Assistants" dwell within. We are in essence pure energy form with no physical construction, but mere energy and composed of thought.

D: *What do you mean when you say you are assistants?*

P: We are those who come to assist in these endeavors which you have undertaken. That is, to seek knowledge that is available to those who would ask. We are fluid in nature, in that we may mold ourselves to the energies we find around us. We can conform to the energies which have called us. That is, yourselves. We are assistants. We bring that energy with us which is most conducive to the work which you are about to

participate in. We assist in balancing the energies and so bri
with us that which is most appropriate to whatever particula
situation we may find ourselves in. Again, we say "we", as
we are a collective consciousness and not singular identity.
We do not subscribe to the concept of singular identity, whi
in human terms would mean isolation, for we are definitely
not isolate. We are in communication and communion with
all other forms of energy at all times. There is no isolation
separation. We speak merely from the realm of existence in
which we occupy, to your realm of existence which you
occupy.

I was at a loss of how to ask questions. This was something th
I had not encountered before. I tried to relate it to something I w
familiar with in my work. I never knew what to expect next, since
was always being led into unfamiliar and uncharted territory.

D: *Do you have any connection with our guides or guardians?*
P: There is perhaps a differentiation here in that we are not
   yourselves or parts of yourself. We are, in fact, distinct from
   that aspect of yourself, and yet, in fact, are indeed part of
   yourselves, in that we are of the whole, one of the whole of
   creation. Therefore, we are in some facts part of yourselves
   and yet in others, not so. We are of and yet not of that whic
   you call "Earth" energies.
D: *Then you mean that our guides or guardians are aspects of*
   our own soul, our own self?
P: That is correct. For you are indeed your own guide, in that
   your higher self is always looking out for your lower self.
   You, who seek to identify yourself at one pinpoint of
   awareness, are merely a facet of your total self. You, by
   seeking to identify and isolate your awareness, segregate th
   particular aspect of yourself from your whole self. This is
   what we would call... we find the term nontranslateable her
   However, the concept would be isolation from the whole or
   personalization.
D: *As energies, did you ever have life on Earth or separation o*
   identity in that way?
P: We share in your isolation, in that we are, again, a part of yo
   existence. In that respect, yes, we have realized many
   incarnations. We are, however, not what you would call
   "inhabitants" of a particular plane. We are, in fact, multi
   dimensional and encompass many different levels of awarene
   simultaneously. Therefore we could not say that we have ev
   been, as you might say, personalized.

D: *I'm trying to differentiate. I thought you might have at one time had Earth identities and then evolved into a higher energy, as you are now. This is not correct?*

P: We could say, not that we have ever become fractionalized. We speak from a level which is multi dimensional and is not schismed or splintered into individual energy units. We are simply aware of many different levels simultaneously. Such that even now we speak on your level of existence, while being or existing on yet another level simultaneously. It is what you perhaps could call "trans awareness."

D: *Then this energy is the only existence you have ever had.*

P: We have evolved from a lesser breath of awareness to a more encompassing form of energy. However, we always have been a transawareal energy. Ours has always been one of an assistance mode of existence. In that we assist, we bring that which is needed to those who would ask for it. Ours is a service industry, as you might say.

D: *Of course, I am always bound by our conventional thinking. So please excuse my questions if they sound ignorant. But would you be the level that we consider "angels"? I know our concept is probably very limited.*

P: We feel that in your terminology, it would, in fact, be appropriate for some to say that we are indeed angels. For in your terminology, an angel is one who comes to assist in time of need. A messenger from God. A benefactor. There are, of course, many different ideas as to just what an angel is. However, for the purposes of illustration, we would allow ourselves to be classified as angels if it were appropriate.

D: *Of course, we have this mental picture of angels having human form.*

P: It is nothing more than pure energy which is attracted to another energy. It is a simple matter of attraction by like forces. It is perhaps possible to explain this by using the term "nuclear" level. In that the energies are indeed nuclear in essence. Nuclear being used here in the term of.... We find that perhaps this train of thought is inaccurate and we would wish to reverse ourselves here. And say that the concept we are trying to describe is of a more electrical nature. In that like charges repel and opposites attract. And in this manner one could see that when there is a difference in energy, then the surplus will naturally gravitate to the deficit. Which is basically where you get your polar opposites. One is of a surplus nature, the other being of a deficit nature. And so the two would naturally attract.

D: *Then when we use electricity, we are utilizing a part of what you represent? Would that be accurate?*

P: Better to say, a concept of what we are. For the principle is the same. Not necessarily using a portion of ourselves, in the concept of us being part of the electrical current flowing. However, in that all energy is of the whole, in that respect it is accurate to say that.

D: *Then the way we use electricity would be the way we could utilize your services?*

P: Perhaps to better explain, one might use the biology of your immune system. When there is a need in one part of the body for a particular defensive system, then the body as a whole mobilizes its metabolism to produce and send that required enzyme or protein to build the particular antibodies needed to repel an infection. Thus the body as a whole reacts to a pinpoint or a localization of infection, and so sends the particular needs of that defensive reaction to the area which has need. In the same way, the universe as a whole can mobilize and send any particular energy form to any particular place in the universe it is needed, to assist in the healing of, what we would call, "disharmony". We, in this analogy, could be compared to antibodies which are sent to heal disharmony.

D: *I'm always able to get a clearer picture through these analogies. I have been told about elementals? Have you any connection with that type of energy?*

P: As we said earlier, there is always a connection between all levels and forms of energy. There is merely a localization of one particular energy to one particular form of need. And so we are in contact and aware of that which you call "elemental" energies. We are not, however, what you would call "elemental" energy. For as you would perceive it, we are far above that yet encompassing it simultaneously.

D: *I wondered if you were of the same nature. I've heard that the elemental energy is very basic, and doesn't have the intelligence or understanding that you seem to have.*

P: Perhaps you would be looking at one end of a spectrum when you singularize or isolate what you would call "elemental" energy. You are merely looking at one particular aspect of a total energy and describing this as elemental. It is, however, part and parcel of a more complete picture.

D: *I've understood that the elemental energy is mostly associated with our Earth.*

P: It appears you would perceive it to be only lower life forms, such as your grasses and plants or particular forms of what you might perhaps call "low life" forms on your planet.

There is, of course, the energy which is associated with your higher life forms, that is, your cats and dogs. And also the energy which is associated with your highest life forms, that being yourselves. There is no distinction between the energies, in that they are again part and parcel of the whole. They are merely associated with one or more particular levels of awareness. For it would be a gross inaccuracy to say that grass is not aware, for it is indeed aware. The very ground that you walk on is indeed aware. To deny this would be to perhaps relegate yourselves to a position of God, all encompassing, all aware, and all else being below and unaware. This is not accurate. All of all creation is aware. Whether you perceive this or not, is entirely up to yourselves. For you have the capabilities to become aware of all of creation, from the lowest to highest forms of awareness. And not necessarily limited to your particular Earth. You could very possibly become aware of the whole of creation, simply by acknowledging the fact that all that is is aware.

D: *Of course, this would make living difficult in our physical life.*

P: We feel that perhaps it would make your life richer and fuller, because you would not feel so alone and cut off. For you would be in a brotherhood once again, as is your destiny. You have perhaps become isolated through many faults not your own, or perhaps through mischance. However, it ultimately is the responsibility of the individual as to how aware he or she becomes. If one chooses to deny the existence of others, then it is their prerogative. However, then they must be able to.... We would change this, in that we wish not to denote a meaning of punishment. We do not wish to express that concept. We are trying to imply that one creates one's own reality. And so one can see that when one creates one's own reality, one must live it.

D: *Yes, some people would look on it as a punishment. But if you created it yourself, you have to take the consequences.*

P: That is accurate.

D: *You keep speaking of the whole. Is that what we consider to be God?*

P: In a more enlightened approach, the whole is indeed what you would term "God", in that God would be all encompassing. However, we feel that your present or current concept of God is perhaps more generalized as to being an abstraction of human attributes elevated to a creator status.

D: *I was wondering if you would be considered of the creator status or co creators.*

P: There is, of course, some truth in what you say. However, w
feel it would be inappropriate to deem ourselves such.

D: *Then you have not evolved that far? I guess I'm trying to
physically place you somewhere.*

P: We have never been creators. We are not creators. We are i
fact possibly... however, we would wish to clarify this. Ther
is at this time a.... (Pause)

D: *What? A misunderstanding or what?*

A deep breath and then Phil abruptly opened his eyes. He wa
awake. This was unusual for him to do that. I asked him what happene

P: (He was wide awake now.) It shut off. It was like they wer
getting ready to say something, then there was a disruption i
the energy fields.

D: *Do you think it was something they shouldn't be talking
about?*

P: No, it was like there was interference. It happens sometime
you know, when different energies are coming and going. It
kind of delicate to get it balanced, and if an outside energy
comes in it breaks the connection.

D: *Like static or what?*

P: Well, it's not electrical energy. It's more like thought energy

D: *Something you thought?*

P: No, it's just outside energy. It's not bad, it was like the
connection was broken.

It was never clear what caused the interference, but Phil thoug
we should end the session for the day. That was all right with m
because the entire session had been a strain on me. We were discussin
a subject that was very complicated for me to comprehend, and I wa
having difficulty formulating questions. So I breathed a sigh of relie
as I left his house. I knew I would need time to digest and at lea
partially assimilate the information. Little did I know that I had n
seen the last of this strange energy.

We had scheduled a special meeting at Billie Cooper's house th
evening. They had also missed our sessions with Phil while he wa
living in California, so they were anxious to have him come agai
There were many present who had never seen this phenomenon, s
there was an air of curiosity in the room as we began. I again used h
keyword and the elevator method. When the door opened the brillia
light was back, almost as though it had never left. As I had not ha
time to formulate questions, my mind was racing trying to think ho
to begin.

D: *Is this the same light we saw this afternoon?*

P: That is accurate.

D: *Do you think this is the appropriate energy that can answer any questions that might be asked tonight?*

P: For this group at this time this would be as a liaison between that which you ask and that which you shall receive. For oftentimes one will ask that which is impractical to give, and so must receive that which is closest to that which has been asked for.

D: *When we contacted this energy this afternoon they said they were of an assistant nature. An assistant nature is the energy that is used when you want to create things in your life and make things happen. This is the energy that is brought forth and used, and it can be used in many ways. Am I correct in my definition?*

P: We would say that would be accurate.

D: *It is an energy that encompasses multi dimensions instead of being on one level. Therefore it had a great deal more knowledge than a single energy would. So maybe it is the appropriate one to come through tonight.*

P: We would say that perhaps a more defined explanation would be in order. We wish to explain that this energy is not of a storehouse nature. That is, a form of or receptacle for knowledge. It is simply a conduit through which that knowledge is passed. We bring that which is asked for. We do not hold or store this knowledge. Perhaps on your level this is an insignificant point. However in further conversations it may become quite apparent that there is indeed a profound difference between those who would channel this knowledge and those who would store or receive this knowledge.

The questions that were answered are incorporated into the various chapters of this book.

***

Many times at these meetings spirits, or whatever they were, would come forth that were curious about *us*. These would often amuse and startle us by asking us questions. Some of these questions were extremely difficult to answer, as they often involved concepts in our culture that we do not think too much about. When this happened we could readily appreciate the difficulty we were putting them through by some of the questions we often asked. But it is remarkable that they always were able to find the answers instantly, while we stumbled and conferred and often just shrugged our shoulders in resignation when they turned the tables on us.

P: There is no need to fear us as we speak through this man, he does this willingly and with no fear of ill consequence. Thus he brings this energy through him to share with you, for he ha found the truth in this energy, and so wishes to share it with others. In so giving he receives immeasurably. There is aga no need to fear us. We are simply some who have attained a level far above that which is in incarnate nature now on you planet. We are here to bring truth and enlightenment. And to assist in raising the consciousness on your planet, such that the ignorance and superstitions which seem to prevail would be dispelled and replaced with knowledge and truth. We come in peace and in harmony and in love. (The voice wa deeper and sounded different than Phil's. It sent chills throug me.) You are at this time being monitored by one who is far greater than anything ever experienced in this room. There i at this time a Watcher, a guardian now assigned to this room to protect those gathered here now who wish to learn. (The voice kept going lower and deeper. It was not anything like Phil's normal voice. This was also apparent to the others in the room.) We would now ask you, would we be able to ask you questions?

This was unexpected, but as I looked around the room the other were nodding their heads in agreement that we should try this differe angle.

A member of the group asked, "Are you the essence of lives tha have been lived on Earth?"

P: That would be an accurate statement, yes. If you could, imagine the collective consciousness of each of you in this room now, together without your physical bodies. Were you consciousness to be removed from your bodies, you would be joined together by a common interest, or a common goal. And so it is with us. For we find our energies are similar in vibration and very compatible, although not identical. We simply work very well together as one unit, sharing informatio and ideas and offering that which we are familiar with at any given time. There is no identity given nor necessary. We simply exist.

D: *And you wish to ask us some questions?*

P: At this time we would appreciate the opportunity. However, we will allow you to presage any commitments to this appointment tonight. In other words, you may go first.

D: *Either way you want to do it. There'll be time for all of us, I believe.*

P: There is one area we would wish to cover this evening, if it is in consensual agreement with your group. And that would be in the area of sexual awareness, or in other words, gender identity. For we here are not given sexual identity. We are simply etheric spiritual energy and find it somewhat amusing in no disrespectful terms that you see yourselves as one or another. You seem to have a very strong need to segregate yourselves according to gender identity. This we find most fascinating. As it would seem that there is some schism here in your own identity. We feel you have lost your true identity when you must relate to each other on these terms. That is simply an observation from our point of reference. And that is simply the item which we thought we would bring up for discussion, if you felt it appropriate.

D: *Hmmm, a rather strange subject. I don't suppose we have ever thought about it, have we?*

A member of the group volunteered, "Could I elaborate a little it, please?"

P: We would hope that you would. And so give us some insight into this apparition, so that we may possibly come to a better understanding of it from our level.

The member continued, "The way I understand it, you want to discuss the area of physical. And you being etheric energy, are not concerned with physical things, so you don't have to worry about sexual identity. But in a physical area this is very important, because represents our *very* identity. So you have come into an area for discussion that may be a little foreign to etheric energy. As long as we're confined to physical bodies, this is a very important part of our being, and we have to be concerned with it. Does this make sense to you?"

P: We are assimilating this response. And would reply thusly: We understand your concern. We understand your need to identify or to recognize your physical aspect. However, we feel and we are here not preaching, merely making an observation from our reference that there has become not so much a sense of custodial care given to these physical bodies, but more a sense of identity given to these physical bodies. It would seem as if the physical body itself has been given an identity.

D: *That's true. It has been given an identity because that's the way we recognize ourselves, being confined to time and material things. Could I ask a question? Have any of you energies ever been in a physical body?*

P: That is not accurate, for we have never been to a level where the physical could manifest itself. We are of an energy which is simply not conducive to formation of physical matter. It is an electro magnetic energy, and not of the structure or composition which would facilitate the formation of physical matter. There are none among us at this point who have ever experienced what you would call a "physical" incarnation, although that is not to say that we have not been on your plane before. We have, but not in a human form. There have been many forms other than human on your planet, which carried consciousness. However, you have no record of these forms for none have been given to be recorded.

Member: *What is your origin then?*

P: We speak from the essence of truth, of the One True God, as you would say in your vernacular. We hail from the givers of truth, the legion of light, or as you might say, the archangel. Ours is a message of information. We would define our role here as givers of truth. There are many other squadrons or legions whose responsibilities might include health matters, or perhaps rebuilding or reconstructing planets. There are those whose entire function is solely the construction of universes.

D: *The Creator level.*

P: That is correct. There are many different areas of expertise available to draw from. Since you seek information, you have contacted us, the givers of truth. And so here we are.

Member: *I think I understand that. We have responsibilities in our physical realm. What kind of responsibilities do you have. I know that you are not confined by time as we are. What do you occupy yourselves with? What does this energy do?*

P: There is on this plane much work and attention given to the formation and creation of subservient energies, or to paraphrase, making rings or circles in a pond. Our work, if we can grossly analogize this, is simply throwing stones in the water and causing the circles to radiate outward from where the stones or pebbles have landed. It is in these concentric circles which radiate outward, where we excel or are at our best. Of course, you understand this is a simple analogy. But the purpose is to create energy patterns which are useful to those lifeforms and energies which are at a level somewhat below ours. In other words, we make a very conducive atmosphere or environment in these energy circles. So that those who are working below us have a hospitable environment within which to work. It is a chain of hereditary environments much like your natural chain of hierarchies on your physical world. Does this make sense?

The members of the group responded that it did.

D: *It's a little complicated. But are these also energies that we ourselves can use to create things?*

P: Not directly. For these energies we deal with are at a level much higher than you could possibly manipulate directly. However, through situations such as this where there is a bridging effect, we can trade concepts and analogies and visualizations and rationalizations and so forth. So that our realities and truths may be bridged to your level of understanding and vice versa.

D: *This is why it seems so foreign to you to see our different concepts.*

P: That is accurate. We apologize here, for we truly do not wish to preach, but merely to observe. But we feel too much emphasis has been given on gender identity. And has been pulled from true identity, the consciousness or God self or Christ identity, or one of many hundred thousands of terms given to that which is. That which is your true identity, the energy that is energy like we ourselves are. Of course, you know your physical bodies are nothing more than an implement or a tool. It would be as if you, while riding in your car, assumed the identity of the car itself, and are not simply a passenger in the car. (Laughter) You would then feel that you are a Buick. You are big. You are red. You would feel your four tires beneath you. And you would feel every scratch and dent received on you. This, of course, is again a very simple analogy. However, we feel that it adequately at least from our point of view summarizes our perceptions of how physical reality seems to have transcended the spiritual reality.

D: *Yes, but whenever you enter the physical body, the subconscious forgets the other part and just concentrates on the physical. This is one of the hazards of entering the physical.*

P: That is an entirely accurate statement. It is indeed a hazard, one which is not exactly or necessarily a given but one which is truly prevalent.

Another member of the group interjected, "Are you saying th we have become so involved with the body which is carrying o spirit, to the point that we quote and feel every scratch, every bum and are proud of our color and et cetera, moreso than being involv with the true identity, the spirit?"

P: That is accurate, and a most enlightened insight into a very real problem on this planet. The true identity resides within the physical. And it is very unusual for an individual to recognize his true identity as that of the energy inside, and n of the vehicle around it.

D: *Then are we making too much of the division between the masculine and the feminine, instead of integrating both into our being?*

P: That is entirely accurate. For in this identity separation there given the social laws which dictate that energies encased in masculine energy, shall relate by social convention in a particular manner to those energies which are encased in a feminine vehicle. And we might use as an example, your customs of dating and body language and so forth. It is at this time, in this area of your planet, the accepted norm for t entire emphasis to be towards genders of opposite identity. And it is not accepted for genders of equal identity to be aware of each other, such as it is on our plane. We feel ther has been much misalignment due to this mistaken identificatio What we are saying here is not anything in terms of sexual relations, but simply of being friends. Many men are afraid be friends because they are both men. And many women ar afraid to be friends because they are both women. And yet many women and men are afraid to be friends, because they fear the motives are of an ulterior level. So you see there is much misunderstanding given because of this physical identification.

D: *Do you have the balance of the masculine and feminine energies in each of you?*

P: For all practical purposes there is no such thing as masculin and feminine energies at this level. There simply is energies There is no distinction.

Member: *I would think that to be able to recognize it you wou have had some experience with it. Then are you energies th were created by higher energies, or are you those that were created because of thought patterns from Earth?*

P: We were created by the Master, by the All One. The suprem God of all creation. We are not, as you might suspect, of Earth energies, for we come from a plane far above that whic could be approached by Earth energies. However, as you progress further from the male female level of existence, the distinction between male and female grows less and less. To the point such as we are here, so that there is no distinction whatsoever. It is simply for your purposes of procreation that there has been given this distinction. However, in spiritual there is no need for procreation. In spiritual there is no need for distinction, and so the further you recede from your physical plane, the less the distinction grows until the point where there is no distinction whatsoever.

D: *This is one of the lessons we chose to learn and experience, to come to this plane and into these physical bodies of different genders. Apparently you as an energy have not decided to experience those things, but it's all part of our learning.*

P: There is no choice in this matter. For were we to choose to incarnate, we simply could not. It is a matter of physics.

D: *You would not be allowed to, or not able to?*

P: It would not be possible for our energies to be contained in a physical body. It is a matter of vibration. The physical bodies which encompass your energies are vibrating at a level much too slowly to contain our energies. It would be as if trying to hold water in a bucket of screen. We are not making a judgment call here, for we understand your reasons for being incarnated in physical. There are many lessons to be learned here. However, we feel that and again we say this with as much loving care as we can possibly convey that there simply seems to be from our point of view, an over identification given to the physical vehicles. And less to the energy aspect of your identities. Perhaps we are prejudiced in our opinion because we are viewing it from a position that is removed from it.

D: *I thought maybe you were an evolving energy. That there might at some time come the point where you would incarnate in a body.*

P: Were it possible to bring a physical body up to a level which could contain us, then it would be possible. However, at this point, at least in our realm of experience and in the levels of physical matter we have experienced, it would not be possible.

D: *What is the difference between the spirit energy that we have dwelling in our bodies and your type of energy?*

P: Simply frequency of vibration. We find in your discussion much enlightenment. And we appreciate your honesty and frankness. We occasionally like to observe as well, so that we may learn from your discussions. We appreciate this, for there is not often those who would come to our level to share with us your truths, your concepts. Although they are not ours, we

appreciate sharing them with you, for they enlighten us also
There is apparently the idea that we are superior in some wa
because we are different. That is not the truth. We are at a
different vibration, possibly somewhat removed from your
own, however, this does not make us superior. In God's
kingdom there are no superiors and inferiors. There are simpl
those who exist in their appropriate form and space, and wh
are simply doing that which is to be done. There is no concep
of better than or less than. This is a particularly human concep

Member: *Are you a perfected being and do you have a path of
evolution on your level? Are you going back to the source o
all energy in the universe, or are you going to stay in this
level?*

P: First of all we would say that there are several suppositions
which we find to be not altogether accurate. We are not
perfected beings and far from it. We are learning beings also
We are ascendant beings. We are on an evolutionary path, as
you might choose to say. We do not have the ultimate answe
For were we to have already attained the final step, then ther
would be no way we could communicate through this vehicl
and allow him to live through it. It is an energy far beyond
anything that could accommodate a physical form. As the
physical form would simply vaporize, were this energy to
attempt to inhabit a body. It would simply raise the vibratio
of those physical molecules to a level far beyond that which
they could sustain, and would then become dissolute. We wis
not to frighten or to alarm you, but to give you a sense of the
power of that energy. For the energy would be so intense as
to cause everyone in this room surrounding him to simply
vaporize. You have no concept of the power of the whole Go
energy. It is far too powerful to be brought to this level. Th
energy runs the entire universe, all of creation. And as such
even in minuscule form, were it to be brought to this level, i
would do no good. At some point in your evolution and this
includes everyone in this room in the physical sense each
of you will, not only attain this level from which we speak,
but will surpass it, as we ourselves will. We, too, are an
evolutionary species. We are on an ascendant level and are
not perfected. However, we are more enlightened from the
point of view that our perspective is much broader than your
own. There are those things of which you have intimate
knowledge, of which we have no knowledge. And so it is by
communicating that we give and take of this knowledge. We
learn from this as you learn. We could just as easily group
ourselves together and contact one of you so that we could as

you questions. And oftentimes do.

D: *Then we will at some time attain that level?*

P: That is accurate. However, it is not given, it must be learned. For in increasing your knowledge and awareness, your frequency of vibration increases. And so the more you have become attuned to the absolute, to the one true God identity, the higher your vibration will increase. And so you will, through your process of spiritual evolution eventually attain that vibration at which we resonate now. But it is a presupposition that our level is where you wish to evolve to. Again there are many other areas and levels with which to evolve to. You might imagine yourself standing at the foot of an immense mountain, with many, many, many different paths to climb. You stand at the foot of one path that branches into a myriad of other paths. All eventually leading to the top, but yet not all in the same place even at the top. For perhaps there is at the highest level a plateau, so that you can be at many different places on this plateau. Then each of you is at some point below the plateau, perhaps near the bottom, for our analogy. And you can see that there is already some distance between yourself and the bottom. Because by reaching this level that we can communicate, you have already traveled some distance. Then you can see that with this mountainside being covered with different paths, there are many different ways to go in your ascendancy. We, perhaps are off to one side and at some level higher than you, if you choose to place us there. And we feel flattered that you would do so. Then you can see that perhaps you would want to follow the path or paths so you could reach our very same point on the side of this mountain. However, there are a multitude of choices, so that you would not need to or perhaps want to. Eventually you yourself would reach the plateau, perhaps in a much shorter time, or perhaps longer time, to use your terminology. Eventually we all would reach the plateau. However, we might not necessarily be at the same point even on the plateau. Does this make sense?

There was a lot of agreement from the group.

D: *But you didn't have to go through the evolution that we have to.*

P: It was not what you could call comparable. However, we ourselves have evolved from a lesser to a greater. There are energies more powerful than the level we have attained, that you cannot even imagine.

D: *Where do these energies come from? Where do they originate*

P: There is no space or time frame given to these energies. The are of a constructive type energy. They are somewhat of the building energies of the universe. They are constructive energies in that they assist and endeavor to construct universe That is, physical realities and the spiritual necessities attendate to that physical reality. They are builders of the universes.

D: *From the creator level? Co creator?*

P: Not so, for they are not of the creator. However, they are assimilators, perhaps that would be a more accurate term. Fe they in and of themselves do not create the materials which constitute a universe. However, they assemble those energie and realities to assemble a universe. Not to imply that they create out of nothing as would be on a creator level, but are more of the engineering status. They are the builders perhap not the creators.

D: *A while ago you said you would like to ask us some question*

P: Perhaps we should gather ourselves together here, for we are somewhat scattered about right now. We could perhaps poo our resources and see what is most relevant for us to ask abou as you yourselves did before this session. A very similar situation shall occur on our side, if you so choose. We woul prefer a short period of time so that we may gather our energie into one focus. (Pause) We would say that we have very littl understanding of your concept of fairness. For what is fair to one is oftentimes not fair to another. And yet perhaps tomorro it could be entirely reversed. How is it that your standards c justice can be so flexible?

That was a "biggie". There was much discussion about whethe anyone in our group even wanted to volunteer to touch it.

D: *That is a difficult question, but then we've been asking you difficult ones also. Now the tables are turned.*

Member: I have to admit there is very little fairness that is seer and recognized. I think our human nature enters into that. Because of human comforts we want everything to be fair as relates to us. And our inclination is to think of ourself befor we think of others. So until we reach a point where we accep other people, it's hard for us to be fair. And sometimes even when we try to be fair, it's not received by other people in th same way as was intended. So fairness becomes more of a concept than an actuality.

D: *You mean it's a selfish thing, in other words.*

Member: *That's what makes it seem selfish, yes. To be unfair.*

P: We would perhaps see then that your concept of fairness is quite dynamic. In that it changes, perhaps, by the hour, with the situations in which you find yourselves. Then could this also be said that fairness seems to be perhaps a very highly individual concept which has grossly been generalized by your society as given from God Himself? Then what is fair is good and therefore it is given by God.

Member: *I think that's true.*

D: *I think our upbringing influences a lot, too. The way you're raised.*

P: We feel perhaps that is why God is so misunderstood on your level. That perhaps His judgments and decrees seem to be in actuality simple human we search here for there is no quite accurate concept available to describe this.

D: *Maybe that's why it's so hard to explain. (Laughter)*

P: We would say that your concept of fairness is perhaps one of a litmus test which is used to allow yourselves the most comfortable passage through any particular time. To alleviate discomfort, in other words.

Another member: *Well, I have a different concept of fairness. If one thing or one privilege is fair for one person, then it should be the same advantage to every person involved. But our society doesn't let it be that way. It comes from, more or less, who you know to get more advantage. And that's not fair. And I'm not speaking for myself. I'm speaking for the entire United States or the entire world. This is my concept of fairness. Not, "Hey, I got cheated at the grocery store and that's not fair," because I'm not the only one that happens to. I'm probably talking in riddles.*

Member: *And also we're individuals and so we look at every separate thing because they are individuals and no two of us think alike.*

D: *Yes, that's what makes it difficult to say what's fair and what's not fair. We can't have a blanket description because we're all so different. I don't know if we answered that one very well.*

P: We feel perhaps we will go back to the drawing board. (Laughter from the group.)

D: *I'm sorry about that. We've probably got you more mixed up than ever. (Laughter)*

P: That is accurate. Again we are not here to argue moral issues. For from your point of view we have no morals. There is no need for morals, because morals are simply laws which are set up to govern behavior. And in our existence there is no such need for these outside governing influences. It is nonexistent. It is not necessary. And so we shall not choose to impose our artificial morals, which would be necessary to relate to your very real morals. For we have no such authority to do so. We have no real experience with which to have morals. Always when there are those who wish to learn we shall share that which we know to be true to us and to you. There are many things which are true to you which are not true to us. And again many things true to us which are not true to you. However, there are many things we can share which are true to us both.

D: *A common meeting ground.*

P: That is accurate. We would be most honored to come again, for always in these exchanges we learn as much if not more from you. We oftentimes do not understand your concepts until we can explain them from our point of view.

At this point a strange transition occurred. With a deep breath and a sigh Phil began speaking in his normal voice, which was higher pitched and livelier. It was evident to everyone that the other energy had gone and another one had taken its place. This one preferred to answer the mundane and ordinary questions concerning the Earth plane. The other energy had been present for over a half hour. When it left the change was immediate and complete. The questioning continued with each person asking personal questions regarding their daily lives.

The tape recorder had been left on and when Phil returned to the awake state he said one thing he remembered was that there was a lot more going on than he talked about. It was as though these energies did a lot of talking among themselves, either about what we were asking or what we were saying. However, it was not like speech. He just had the feeling of discussion. He probably wouldn't have been able to repeat it anyway.

Phil remembered that the group of entities asked us to define what fairness was. He had the impression of a group sometimes babbling so much he could not determine any one individual voice. It seemed that they said, "Why is it all right to kill a man on the battlefield and not a child in the womb?" This was the reason for the question about fairness. To help resolve their feeling of frustration about our apparent double standard.

***

During another meeting a member of the group had a question. "Many times when I wake up from a deep sleep I feel like I'm vibrating or my body is pulsating at a high rate. What causes this?"

P: Your soul, as you call it, is returning from a higher charged state, from being in the astral plane, which is a higher level of awareness. And you are returning to a lower level of awareness, so that your soul can return to your body. For your body vibrates at a certain frequency, and while your soul is in your body it is necessary that your soul be close to that vibrational frequency. For were your soul to be vibrating too fast, it would separate from your body. In your dream state oftentimes your dreams spur your soul on to a higher level of energy. And so you separate from your body and experience astral projection. Your soul and body must vibrate at, not necessarily, an equal frequency but similar or close frequency. Oftentimes when you are in depression your soul has lowered its vibration below that of your body, and so you feel quite blue or moody. Your moments of elevation are oftentimes when your soul is vibrating at a frequency higher than your body.

D: *Then by vibrating faster and separating from the body, these are the out of the body experiences that people have?*

P: That is accurate. For when you separate from your body, you are vibrating at a frequency which is higher than that which your body can maintain or withstand, and so there is the separation.

Returning from an OBE can also create temporary paralysis until ιe brain/body connection is reestablished.

***

MULTIPLE PERSONALITIES

Question: *I've always felt very uncomfortable on this plane, like I'm five different people.*

P: It is perhaps necessary for you to truly identify your selves. Does this concept surprise you? There are indeed separate entities or identities inside yourself, as many people have multiple personalities. This is not an alien concept. However, it seems that in this society it has become somewhat tainted with the idea that multiple personalities are automatically schizophrenic, or a symptom of mental illness, which is not the case at all. It is a simple aspect of nature which is very prevalent in all societies, and in all types of animals, human or otherwise. You, if you so choose can identify several identities within yourself. One who is shy and the introvert who likes to stay home and knit or crochet, or whatever it is that you like

403

to do. And then there are those times when you would prefe
to go out and kick up your heels, so to say, and just have a
good time. And this is not wrong. It is not any more wrong
than it is to stay home and be a homebody. Neither is wrong
Each speaks its own truths and its own appropriateness. Ther
are those aspects of yourself which choose to be studious an
cry for knowledge. The aspect of yourself that is very
maternal and very loving, and yet with the flip of a coin can b
as cold as blue steel. Does this ring a bell within you? Is it
unnatural to be very loving one minute and very cold the nex
If one finds oneself in the position that requires this, is it
unnatural, or is it not? It is not. Of course, it is not. There
is no need to fear multiple personalities, for that is simply a
aspect of yourself. We would encourage you to identify
these separate personalities or personality traits. They will
even assign themselves names if you so choose, and have
what you might call "separate" identities. These are simply
facets of your total personality. And it is this combination o
facets which make up the whole personality. When a
personality is not healthy, then these facets are out of sync,
or are not communicating with themselves. They are not
working together. A healthy personality has this makeup of
facets which are in harmony. There is no such thing as a
diamond with one facet, any more than there is a human wit
one personality. It is impossible. For the human personality b
its very existence requires multiple facets. The rainbow coul
be used as an analogy of harmony. This phenomenon gives
the appearance of the circular or perhaps semi circular aspec
with the different colors throughout. That is, harmony. The
sum of the color spectrum in a circular aspect, which is
representative of the whole. That is, the circle being infinite
and representing God. Therefore half is shown and half is no
apparent, which is again true of your own nature. Meaning
that you yourselves are physical and yet spiritual. Half is
shown and half is not. And yet in each and every one of you
you contain that which is not along with the complete spectrur
of all that is.

***

Another version of multiple personalities from another subject.

D: *Have you ever heard of what is called a "multiple personality"*
They seem to have many personalities in one body.

Brenda: Yes. Your psychologists are on the right track in tracking down the reasons why and the causes of. These multiple personalities are caused by spirits who have a particular heavy load of negative karma. And in the process of trying to deny this to themselves, they split themselves up into what appears to be separate entities, but actually it's different branches of the same entity. It's like having a flower with many petals. I'll use this unit's hand to demonstrate. (She raised her hand and pointed to the different fingers and the wrist as she gave her analogy.) You have a flower with many petals and the petals are connected at the base (the wrist). But the flower is positioned to where you only see the petals from half way up to the tips, and they look like separate objects. You can't see where they're joined together at the bottom. These multiple personality spirits appear to be separate entities because you're only seeing the part that appears separate. But at the base, at the core of the spirit they all connect together into one spirit. And, as I have mentioned, the spirit has a particularly heavy load of negative karma they have developed. And they're trying to deny this to themselves, and are wanting to escape from their current cycle of karma. So they keep striking out in all directions. And these different directions that the spirit strikes out, appears as different personalities within the body that the spirit is occupying.

D: *I have the theory that maybe these personalities were fragments or mirror images of personalities they had in past lives.*

B: Usually, yes. As the spirit strikes out in the different direction, it draws upon the recent past lives, of past personalities they used in other physical existences. But since the spirit is striking out wildly, it is usually distorted versions of these personalities or like you said, just a fragment of it, because the spirit is not being organized. The spirit is in a panic.

D: *They say sometimes the other personalities are male, female, adult or child. That was why I came up with that idea.*

B: Yes. It was a good idea. It's close to being the way it is. Because they draw upon their past memories, and the spirit does remember the past lives. And so they may draw upon various aspects or maybe just one particular aspect of one personality from a past life for one of these multiple personalities.

D: *And they bring them in to help them escape, so to speak, from their life, their karma.*

B: They think it helps them escape, but it doesn't. It's like having a fish flopping on your fishing line. It has about as much effect.

D: *The psychiatrist tries to unite them back into one personality. They say it's a very difficult thing to do.*

B: Yes. Psychiatrists are not really effective with that yet. They have the right idea in mind, but they're trying to apply glue to the tips of the separate pieces rather than trying to get down to the base where they're already united, and healing the rent on the base. But that's a very complex process, and they have not developed the ability to do that yet. But at least they are on the right track.

D: *One thing they have found in common is that there seems to be some kind of traumatic event in the person's life that caused this to happen in the first place.*

B: Yes. The traumatic event calls the attention of the spirit to the negative load of karma it's having to deal with. And that's why in these cases every time thereafter whenever a traumatic event happens the spirit strikes out in panic again, and another personality appears. The spirit doesn't realize they could turn this around and work it for good, for affirmative karma. They just panic again and strike out again, and hence another fragment appears.

D: *It sounds like they're not working out their karma.*

B: Yes, that is true. They're not coping with it.

D: *They keep fighting it.*

***

D: *Is there anything different about twins, either identical or not identical?*

B: No. Twins are usually like any other family member and siblings. They are two spirits that are closely related to each other karmically because they're working something out together, like husband and wife, other siblings or close relationships. However, in the case of identical twins, due to the resonance between the two bodies, they tend to have extra psychic abilities.

D: *I've heard one theory, that identical twins may be the same soul that has split into two parts to learn two different lessons.*

B: Not generally. Usually if a soul needs to learn two different lessons, they'll inhabit the same body but in two different universes. (Explained in Chapter 11.)

D: *They say some twins are so alike. They can be a whole continent apart and still do the same things.*

B: That's due to the resonance set up between their bodies and mental energies, because of the general pattern of the universe. When two things are very similar they're going to have a resonance between them. Their vibrations are so similar it's going to have similar effects and similar outcomes. And that's why twins separated at birth and raised a continent apart and not knowing each other, end up marrying people with the same names, having similar hobbies, similar jobs and such, because of the resonance.

D: *Sometimes they seem to have a mental connection, too.*

B: Oh, yes. Like I said, identical twins have an extra dose of psychic abilities between the two of them. Simply because their minds vibrate on the same level.

D: *Then they are just like anybody else. They're two spirits that came back so they could be together.*

B: Right. And being able to think alike and their psychic abilities, it's like plucking a string, then bringing a tuning fork near it and the tuning fork starts to vibrate.

D: *I thought one way I could prove or disprove it would be to regress twins and see if they went to the same personality in the same lifetime. You do not think this would happen?*

B: No, I do not believe so. They would probably overlap several times in past lifetimes and mention each other in other relationships. In a past life they may have been husband and wife or some other type of close relationship.

D: *They would be different characters, so to speak, in the same lifetime, but they wouldn't be the same person.*

***

THE RETURN OF CHRIST

During another session at Billie's the discussion turned to asking questions about Jesus.

Phil: It would be appropriate to say that He was in every sense a man. And yet in every sense He also was a woman. He was completely integrated, and had both the desires of a man and yet the intuition and feeling of a woman. We speak here not necessarily of sexual desires, but of human feelings. However, He was more than human. He was not, as you would say, an ordinary human. Could not the Master be here now?

D: *We think that He is among us in spirit.*

P: Could He not be in physical?

D: *On the Earth, you mean?*

P: That is accurate.

D: *Well, we've never thought about it.*

P: Perhaps He has come and you have not recognized Him. Is this possible?

D: *It could be. It was my understanding that His spirit should dwell in each of us.*

P: That is accurate.

D: *Then is that separate from dwelling in a body as a person?*

P: If the spirit is dwelling in a body, is He not incarnate?

D: *Well, if that would be a universal incarnation.*

P: That is accurate.

D: *Are you saying that He has come back to Earth?*

P: He is here. He is all around you.

D: *It's not just as one individual person?*

P: That is accurate.

D: *We thought maybe you meant that He had come back into physical form.*

P: He has come back in physical form. But He is not in, as you would say, one single individual body. He is working throug each and every one of you. This is in a very literal sense, th truth. It is not simply an eloquent figure of speech. The pow of Christ is within each and every one of you now incarnate i this room.

D: *I just had an idea. This might be what they mean by the secon coming of Christ.*

P: That is accurate. For in this influx of enlightenment, there is truly in every one here the spark of Christ. For each has a small piece of the Christ Spirit dwelling in them, and so throughout all of humanity. When all of humanity comes together in one mind, then there will literally as well as figuratively be the return of Christ.

D: *I think people are expecting Him to be one entity, one perso that returns again.*

P: This is an accurate perception, however, it is one which is n in this case true. You do perceive the situation accurately, however, the truth is that it is not the true situation. It is mor than that. It is that actually, and yet it is more.

D: *Then instead of one person returning, it has been returning several people.*

P: That is accurate. As within the entire planet.

D: *Actually then, Christ has already returned.*

P: That is accurate.

D: *It's just a different way of looking at it. That's why it would take a different concept to understand it. He has already returned in the spirit of several different people.*

P: In the spirit of many billions of people. For this spirit is tru over all the planet now, not in a given few.

D: *That way they can accomplish much more than one person.*

P: That is accurate. For the word is spread throughout the whole planet simultaneously. And is working its way from inward to outward.

D: *The Church wants us to think there would just be one person who would spread it whenever He returned again. There again, He would be worshipped though. That's the problem.*

P: That is an accurate assessment.

D: *This would be a different way of looking at it, that the Church would have trouble with.*

P: We would have trouble with the Church in this as well. For we try many times to reach those who are truly and honestly searching for the truth. However, they find they must turn outward instead of inward. They cannot seem to reach this concept to allow them to turn inward where the real truth lies.

D: *Yes, they must always have something or some person they can look to and worship. That's the only way they can interpret it. A statue, a picture or a concept of one person.*

P: That is accurate. A preacher or orator or statesman or doctor or one of many other forms of hero worship.

D: *That makes it much easier for some of them, I guess, if they get the word from that one source or ideology or whatever it is. And they don't have to rely on their own thinking, their own mind.*

P: That is accurate.

D: *It's an interesting concept.*

***

Q: *Is the Shroud of Turin the authentic burial shroud of Jesus?*

P: That is accurate. That relic which is called or ascribed as the Shroud of Turin is indeed that burial garment which the Master himself was wrapped in at the time of his physical death. It is imprinted with that energy radiated by the advance decomposition of his physical body, such that there would be no physical traces left of that body. This is indeed a purely natural phenomenon. It was somewhat advanced in its nature because it was not usual. However, it was not a miracle.

Q: *Can you tell us why some pictures and statues, especially of Christ or His mother, seem to produce tears or blood, and is there any significance to that?*

P: There is again this awareness we speak of, which permeates all that is. All of creation is a part and parcel of that God concept. Therefore the actual physical elements of which you speak are indeed a part and parcel of that God concept. They are indeed aware. However, in your definition they may not be alive. There is in these icons the awareness of that God concept. Awareness of not only their own awareness, but of those individuals and entities around them, yourselves, who are aware also. In your projections in viewing these icons there is transferred the awareness from one to the other. Or the awareness of the individuals viewing is oftentimes transferred to that icon. The phenomenon itself is a manifestation of that transfer of awareness. The tears are a manifestation of the awareness of the individuals who are viewing these icons. The sorrow is indeed genuine. The sham of humanity being the crucifixion of the one who had come save the very race which crucified Him.

Q: *I understand one produced tears that could be collected in a bottle. What would they show if they were analyzed?*

P: They would indeed be tears, or the content comparable to human tears.

D: *Even though they came from canvas and paint?*

P: That is accurate. You yourselves, again, are creators. This is indeed a purely physical and entirely natural phenomenon. is the transference of awareness. And in so doing, the formulation of a manifestation derived from the awareness, or that awareness which has been transferred. The individual themselves are transferring this awareness to the icons, not that the icons themselves are actually crying. But the awareness of the individuals, and the strength of their faith transferring this awareness to that icon.

D: *The human being is the catalyst then.*

P: The human being is the sender of this awareness. The icon being the catalyst.

D: *Even without them being consciously aware that they're actually doing this?*

P: That is accurate. Were there no one viewing these icons there would be no transference of awareness, and therefore there would be no miracles to be seen.

***

Member: *Then it's true if ten percent of all of us praying for the same thing....*

D: *It is magnified. It is not only multiplied, but squared.*

P: Right. Each of you carries within you a spark of this energy. A tiny time tablet, perhaps, to use the words in your vocabulary. A tiny fragment of this energy. And in so praying together, you are connecting these tiny sparks together and creating a much more potent and powerful level of this energy. So you can see how it is that when people pray together their energy increases. It is by joining this spark of the creator that this is done.

Member: *So we all have a spark of the creator in us. Part of us is God.*

P: That is accurate. That is what keeps you alive. We would like to elaborate on an opinionated aspect here. Many on the planet feel that in order to manifest something, they must become adamant to the point that there is no possibility for anything else to happen. The fault in this lies in the fact that what one says and what one thinks are often at odds with each other. What one truly believes is often not exactly what one says. And so when one says something, it is indeed setting off a reaction which could be quite opposite of what is said. And so in being so firm in this belief, there is given that manifestation which may seem to be entirely at odds with what is being said.

***

P: We would say that your doubting is somewhat more of a protective feature, in that you choose not to believe and so doubt. The information which oftentimes conflicts with that which you have agreed is reality, is uncomfortable to integrate. And you feel this is again, not unfounded, however, perhaps unnecessary. We would ask that you have more faith in yourself. Understand that you are not here to deceive yourself. You are in fact your own teacher. And you should listen and put more faith in that which you yourself are teaching yourself. You should understand yourself more as your own best friend and confidant than rival.

***

Q: *My questions have been answered as we went around the room. I feel like when my son was in the fifth grade and he said, "When I was in the third grade, I thought I knew everything." And I said, "Well, what about now?" And he said, "Now I know I know everything." (There was much laughter.)*

P: We would say that is most appropriate for human experience. For one catches sight of the next mountain and says, "Well, I must climb that," and so they do. And they say, "Oh, there's another one." And so each mountain below that is simply a mole hill. This is not quite the analogy which you were giving, but we are amused by both of them. And would like to enjoy them, for we are quite amused by human endeavors, of building mountains and becoming quite dissatisfied and so building another. Knowledge is the same way. A third grade builds a mountain of knowledge and looks and says, "Wow, now I know everything." And lo and behold, he looks and there is another mountain just to the east. And so he climbs that one and this third grade mountain is so small, and on and on and on. And so we are still building mountains here too. For there is never the tallest mountain reached until perfection. That is the ultimate mountain.

D: *I've come to that conclusion. The more you learn, the more you find you have to learn.*

CHAPTER THIRTEEN
THE USE AND MANIPULATION OF THE ENERGY FORCE

This session was conducted in 1989 with Beverly, an artist that had worked with many times. I used her keyword and counted her the inbetween lives spiritual state, where we could have access to formation.

D: *What are you doing? What do you see?*

Beverly: I don't see anything yet, but it's like I'm rocking on gentle waves. I am not in an ocean, but in the universe. I can look down and see the planet. It looks like all the pictures you see of the Earth. Blue and white.

D: *Is there anything different about it?*

B: No. It's just suspended in space, on a bed of grids, so to speak.

D: *What do you mean?*

B: It's like the universe is made up of grid lines throughout it. And they fluctuate, they move. They ebb and flow, like full bodied waves in the ocean. I don't mean crashing waves. I mean waves that move from very deep down in the water. They're gentle, but they're very deep, slow waving movements in space. And the Earth sits within this bed, as do all the other planets and stars and Suns.

D: *This shows that the universe is actually alive, if it is moving like that. Does that mean the Earth and the other planets are also moving? I'm thinking of the action of waves.*

B: They're not moving like space is. They're spinning and whatever within this undulating space. I have an example for you. Have you seen those glass boxes that have water in them, that flows back and forth, that businessmen sometimes buy to look at because it's relaxing.

D: *Yes, I've seen those.*

B: They move very slowly and evenly, and yet it goes up and down, and up and down. That's the bed of space.

D: *This doesn't disturb the planets that are within it?*

B: No. They spin and turn within this bed.

D: *The picture of a bed is as though they are lying on it.*

413

B: They're lying in it. As in an ocean there might be a fish swimming within it. Where there would be water above the fish and below the fish, and to the right and to the left. Perhap if I said it was more like the air in which we live, instead of bed, that would clarify it for you.

D: *All right. Because I had the picture of the Earth rocking ba and forth, like a ship being tossed on the sea.*

B: No. It's a very slow movement, but is full bodied. In other words, it moves throughout. It's not a surface wave.

D: *And this is what space is composed of? (Yes) I think we ha the idea of space being stagnant and empty.*

B: No, no. It is alive, and it is nourishing. It feeds everything within it. So it would have to be alive and moving.

D: *In what way does it feed?*

B: Nothing could grow in stagnation. Nothing could evolve or change. Its very essence feeds what's within it, just as the a allows us to breathe. If the air were not there to provide us with our breath happening, then we too would be dead.

D: *So the same thing is occurring on a larger scale, as though t Earth is a person. (Yes) There is something in space that contributes to the life. (Exactly) I can see what the air suppli us. What does space supply to the Earth, the worlds? An energy?*

B: Its presence is aliveness. Going back to the fish in the ocea if the fish were taken out of that place or if the water evaporate the fish would die. So it's not that the space feeds us some thing to nourish us. Its presence allows us to live, and there nourishes us, because without it we would not exist. There is life in it, and yes, it could be called an energy. But I'm afraid that would be misleading, because it's not an active energy. It is active, but on a subtle level.

D: *But it's not passive either.*

B: Right. As I said, it's active on a subtle level, while we think of energy as something with strong movement. There is energ with strong movement that passes through this space, and through us. But the space element itself that I've been talkin about is more of an inactive energy, yet not dead. Or a less active energy than we usually think of.

D: *What is this stronger energy you said that passes through a of it?*

B: The stronger energy is more like the life force, the creative thrust, that actually can be directed. While the space alivene isn't directed, it's just there. It just exists.

D: *It's very neutral?*

B: It's neutral, and yet it has a positiveness within it, because without it we wouldn't live. So you can't say it's totally neutral, as in "stagnant" or "dead". It does have life force in it and some movement.

D: *But it's not directed.*

B: Correct. It is like a constant, where more active energy can be directed and focused.

D: *This is the more active energy that you're talking about, that goes through everything.*

B: That is a separate kind of energy from the space aliveness or energy, yes.

D: *And this other energy that is stronger and directed, goes through everything on all levels?*

B: Yes, it does.

D: *Of course, I always wonder where something like that comes from. Everything has to come from somewhere, in our way of thinking.*

B: That's accurate in our way of thinking, and I don't know all the answers to that. But I don't think it has to come from somewhere. It is there, it is a given, it has always existed and always will. And so where could you say that it came from?

D: *But you did say it was directed.*

B: It is directable. Maybe that makes more sense or is more accurate. It can be directed, and it can be changed. The energy force could go into a flower and make it spring from the ground and grow and bloom. That same energy force could go into a runner that was running a marathon. It could go into a painter that was painting. It could go into childbirth, and recreate itself and continue and continue and continue. And instead of being a widespread energy when it's becoming a flower or a runner or a new child, it is directed or focused energy.

D: *That's what confused me when you said it was directed or directable. I always think that someone or something would have to direct it, to give it direction.*

B: Have you seen a top spinning? Once it begins to spin it recreates its own force, let's say. Now, of course, tops do topple. But there is such a thing, I believe called "centrifugal force", that once it begins spinning, it would continue. Such as the Earth itself. Once it begins spinning in its orbit, it just continues. No one has to keep pushing it like they would a child on a swing. It doesn't die down. And that would be somewhat the same with energy. It continues to recreate itself constantly. And where it originally came from if it did I do not know.

D: *Then it doesn't have to be directed by a superior force of son kind.*

B: That's beyond what I can talk about. To bring it down to a closer level, to something we could understand, is that the energy directs itself. It itself is consciousness and directs itself. And if there is something above and beyond that, I don't know what that is.

D: *You said it was something you couldn't talk about. Is it something you are not allowed to, or just something that yo don't know the answers to.*

B: No, it's just too big.

D: *Too big to bring down to our level of understanding?*

B: It's too big for me to understand.

D: *I guess it always goes back to our concept of God.*

B: I think our concept of God is very erroneous. We try to hav it be one person or one spirit or one energy that pushes the button to turn things on. And I don't think that's the way it works. But it is too vast for me to comprehend, and therefo too vast for me to relate to anyone.

D: *Then if this energy is directable, is it directable by human beings?*

B: The energy is the human being. The energy manifests as a human being. So the human being doesn't direct the energ the energy directs the human being.

D: *I was thinking if the energy was there, maybe it was there fo us to use in some way.*

B: We are ourselves using it. I know this is difficult. I don't knc how to clarify it.

D: *Unless you have another analogy.*

B: Perhaps. (Being an artist Beverly used what she was famili with to provide an analogy.) If you dropped I'll have to use thin paint, because thick paint wouldn't move. Let's say yo were dropping thin paint onto a piece of paper. Beautifully colored paint. And it dropped and spread in different directior and made a beautiful picture. The paint that has dropped or the paper is the result of the energy dropping. That energy controls the result that appeared on the paper. The painting the paper doesn't control the energy that dropped it. Do yo understand what I mean?

D: *Yes, I think so. When it dropped it just went by itself at random.*

B: Yes. But then the product, the finished painting I'm thinkii of an inkblot design, not a finished painting that you work c for many hours. But let's say that you dropped beautiful pai out from the sky onto this blotter paper, so that it ran in different directions, and formed a pattern of beauty. That completed pattern of beauty does not then rule the energy that dropped it. So energy manifests as a human form, and the energy itself has the control. The human form, that would then be the painting, doesn't control what dropped it.

D: *I guess I'm thinking of people who want to change their lives and create their own realities. Is this the type of energy they could use by direction of some type?*

B: Yes, but you can't do it from the wrong end, you see. The energy end is the end that has the energy and does the doing, not the blotter painting end, or the human end. Now the human end can affect a change in its results. But it stems not from the piece of paper, or the human body, it stems from the energy. The energy could drop another drop of paint, and change what existed the moment before.

D: *I'm trying to see if maybe we had more control in our life, that we would know how to direct this energy.*

B: We do. We have the control. But the control button is on the other end, it's not on the result end. It's on the energy end. I could be misreading what you're saying, but I think you're trying to say that you want the blotter paper to get up and direct the energy, the paint flow. And that isn't the way it works. If you use the human being as the blotter painting, and you use the dropping of the paint as the energy force, the dropping of the paint onto the blotter paper creates something that has what was within it, the paint, onto the blotter paper. And it's still there. But if there was no paint dropping any more, the blotter paper would be stagnant and permanent, just like it was. It would never change. And if the blotter paper tried to affect a change on the energy from where it came, that would be impossible. The energy, the paint, drops onto the blotter paper continuously to alter it. The blotter paper doesn't alter the energy.

D: *Then how can people effect changes, if it has to be on the other end? How can they use this and effect changes in their life?*

B: That's how they do it, with this energy force that's dropping the paint. You see, we're both connected. But that's where the change comes from, the energy force, not from the blotter paper or the human form that's flat.

D: *Then how can they create a change? I'm trying to think of a way people can use this energy to help themselves.*

B: They do, but... maybe I've given you a bad analogy. The paper without the paint continually dropping on it would be dead paper. Now the interaction of the energy dropping the paint onto the paper is a continuous back and forth energy exchange.

But the way to push the button is not on the surface end, the dead body end or the paper end. The button gets pushed from where it drops from.

D: *But how can we make this button be pushed?*

B: We are that button. We are not the piece of paper. So we push it every time we drop the paint.

D: *Then we do have control by our own minds?*

B: It's more than the mind. Yes, the mind is a part of it, but there is an energy that is even greater than the mind, that encompasses it. That the mind is within. And that is greater than the mind.

D: *But the idea, the desire, has to start with the human mind. As to what they want to change, and what they want to create.*

B: Going back, because we've used the example already of the paint dropping, let's say it's from an eye dropper, because it doesn't even have a hand. Or from a faucet handle. The eye dropper maybe won't work. But it's dropping liquid paint on a piece of paper. If it quits dropping, that piece of paper would just be dead debris. But it doesn't quit dropping. It continues to drop, and therefore the paper that it falls upon is ever changing. And they feed back on each other. Because the energy, in the way of paint, that's dropped on the paper gives energy to the paper. An energy begets itself, so it spreads out and feeds back to the source, the eye dropper. So there is a continual revolution there. The paper on its own could not direct the energy, because it is nothing on its own. It was created out of the drop to begin with. Do you understand a little more clearly?

D: *I think so. I'm just trying to find some workable way that we, as humans, could use this. I know that's the bottom end of the scale.*

B: No, it's not the bottom end of the scale. It is simply the way humans are using the energy in this level. It is not the bottom. The very word "bottom" designates a higher or top, or something to elevate to. And that's not an accurate description. There are just many forms and many ways that energy can be directed. And one is not necessarily any better or worse than the other.

D: *I wanted to find some practical way that a human being could direct this energy. Would there be a procedure they could follow to create an objective and bring it into reality?*

B: Yes. They could direct that energy.

D: *How do they do this?*

B: In our physical bodies it would be mental. It's more than that, though. The mental feedback from the paper to its energy source is minute compared to the energy source. It's a part the way we could this piece of paper could activate what it wants. That, I think is what you're asking.

D: *Yes. In life.*

B: The energy itself is life. It is also light. If we try to separate it from the blotter paper, we're making a big mistake. That would be the blotter paper trying to have control over the energy. So it must work in cooperation. There must be a flow. And the way it could be directed, would be to tune in on the original energy. It's more a matter of attention and focus, and tuning in to where that flow is constant and smooth. If the blotter paper wanted to work on its own and go off on a tangent, it could. Because it has energy of its own, that would then start another cycle. But it would be very small and probably misdirected, compared to if it fed back into its own source. And that would keep the force working constantly. And as long as the blotter paper over here on my right fed into the energy source on my left (hand motions), as long as this worked or the energy was directed back and forth, feeding into its manifestation and back to its source, into its manifestation and back to its source, even if it were a flower. Feeding into the flower and letting it grow, dropping its seed, feeding back to the source, coming up again, growing, dropping its seed, feeding back into the source while it was in that non plant stage. So it would be constantly. You can understand how it wouldn't be physically manifested during the winter, for instance, but that it would come up again in the spring. But human beings don't hibernate, although they do go in and out of degrees of aliveness. They're subtle. Perhaps the dream state, perhaps an in and out that we're not real consciously aware of. And as long as that kept feeding back into the source from which it came, there would be an ongoing energy that would not become less. It would maintain its level of energy. Now if this blotter paper over here decided to go off on a tangent and create something, it could. And it would create something that would feed back into it over and over. But it would be of lesser strength than if it was feeding back into its original source. It's like rays that would go out. Do you see what I mean?

D: *Yes. But in the example of the flower, all that is automatic. It happens anyway. It's a constant feeding back to the source. This is what the life force is.*

B: Yes. And it is the same with people.

D: *But it's an automatic thing that they don't really think about.*

B: It would happen whether they thought about it or not. But you could direct it. And that direction would come from a higher level than our own consciousness, as a rule. Almost like it were guided. And if it were not guided sufficiently, this wou be the time, the area in which our energies would be misdirected, and things would happen that we probably did not intend.

D: *Because we sent the wrong energy waves out?*

B: No, we sent the right energy waves out, but we didn't know how to direct them or we didn't have enough strength to dire them to effect what we wanted, and so they sort of went haywire. Like static on a radio when it's not tuned in right. you're tuned in then it would come out very clear. But if y sent it out without any direction, there could be static, which could look like just a lot of mess. Because it wasn't focuse right or directed properly.

D: *Then we have to know how to direct this and focus it?*

B: Yes. But more than just the human knowing how. The energ flow that created us knows how, and we would need to tune back into that. Then we wouldn't have to figure it out for ourself alone. We would be figuring it out for ourself, becau that is ourself. But we would be tuning into an even strong frequency, higher level of consciousness, that would help direct this, rather than trying to take all the power for oursel and direct it erroneously.

D: *But you said we must have more contact. How can we do th consciously?*

B: I think it's a matter of... if I say "repairing the damage", I'm afraid it will be misleading. But I know of nothing else to sa right now. If we did not interfere with the workings it woul work okay by itself. Now when we send out energy that's misdirected or is static, let's say, left alone it will dissipate a go back into the original energy. But if one person sends ou misdirected energy, and a dozen other people happen to sen it out at the same time and in the same place, then it gains power. A misdirected energy power, you see. And it makes i more difficult, because it is now starting to form and solidif into a power of its own. And it makes it harder for it to natural dissipate and fall back into the natural flow.

D: *It's taken on a life of its own then.*

B: Yes. And once it's done that then we must consciously work at dissipating it. Before that we would not have had to. It would have gone back into the flow automatically. But whe there are enough misdirected energies sent out at the same time or in the same place and it gains some force, then it wi continue spinning off of itself. Doing the same thing that it knows to do, which is misdirected energy. Unless we break that up and let it dissipate back into the normal flow, which happens unconsciously, by the way. I think that was part of your initial question, "How can we consciously do it?" We don't have to consciously do it. It just does. The only time we need to consciously do it, is when it's gone astray.

D: *How do we break up this misguided energy? You would have to break it up in order to let it go back to the source.*

B: By seeding, this would be one way. I don't know that it's all of the ways. But let's say you have this flow going from giant energy source into its manifestation, of which we're only one, a human body. There are many, many things that that energy is going out and manifesting as. But if we're interested in this one right now, the human being, and that human sends out because it now has energy, it now has life too. And energy just recreates itself. So then it sends out its own, and let's say it's misdirected. How do we break that up, is your question. By coming back to the initial energy source, allowing positive or natural energy flow to go into this, and having it seeded into the misdirected one, to the point that it dilutes it enough that it can then fall back into the normal unconscious to humans routine. There is consciousness here, so I want to clarify that. There is, in this big energy source, its consciousness, which it spreads into us as the energy goes back and forth.

D: *That was the consciousness you said was beyond our understanding.*

B: Yes, yes.

D: *But then we have to send out good thoughts and positive thoughts, or could we do it by asking the original source to send positive thoughts.*

B: It's more like tuning into it. Let's say that the original source has everything. It can create any and everything, not only in this world but in all of the worlds. And it is always sending out this energy to us. If we want one thing instead of another, we just tune in on that band.

D: *But we have to do this with a conscious effort. In our physical body, we have to be told to do certain things in order to be able to do it.*

B: With their own consciousness they can direct it. Theirs is going to go all out too, and it's going to create other things. But what they want to take in from the big source, they tune into. Open up that channel to let that come in instead of something else. And so that becomes a more prominent and predominant part of their makeup. And then the same thing gets spun out into what they manifest.

D: *People are always asking me how they can create what they want. They want a formula, a step by step method.*

B: Yes, I know, and that's very hard. And I wish there were a more helpful answer, but I think there is not. I think that when we learn to walk the straight line, so to speak and I don't mean morally I mean that when we wobble our energies dissipate along the way. If we're walking a fence line, the more we walk it straight the more power we have to create what we want. But you see, right now we wobble. So sometimes we create it and sometimes we wobble off and undo it, and then get back on and recreate it. Perhaps it's just to practice walking it, to where we don't wobble so much and lose some of the things that we want.

D: *It also has a lot to do with belief systems.*

B: Oh, yes, that would involve what you want. If you didn't have a belief system, you wouldn't want one thing over another. You see, it's all there.

D: *You would just take whatever came your way.*

B: Exactly. And our belief system is what makes us have a preference for one thing over another, whether it's rain, let's say, or sunshine. They're all manifestations, all the rain and the sunshine. If we didn't have a belief system one would be just as good to us as the other; in fact, they are. It's our belief system that says sunshine is preferable to rain. And if we get to that point of realization we're already there; we just don't know we are. In fact, we are always at it; we don't have an awareness of it. When we have an awareness that everything is as good as everything else, we won't even try to focus on getting what we want. We have it all.

D: *There are people who just go with the flow, so to speak, and take whatever comes. They don't know they can choose something over something else.*

B: But unfortunately we suffer with that. We obviously suffer we have severe pain rather than bodily comfort. I sense that what you're saying. They go with the flow whether it hurts not. But I'm saying there is a higher level than that, to where hurt feels just as good as good does. Where we are not affected by hurt being hurt. All of what we have been talking about of course, so, but it's all leading up to an ultimate in which won't make any difference. We will go through the process learning perhaps, as human beings. Let's talk from that level Of how to direct back into this energy and get what we want We are in that process, and it may or may not be a lengthy one. Since we don't know anything about time anyhow, it's hard to judge that. But you see, over here, this big energy source (hand motions) doesn't care what it sends out because all of it's just as good as anything else. We, over here on Earth, with our belief systems, decide that one's better than the other. And what you're asking is how do we train ourselves to only pick the good.

D: *Or what we want.*

B: Or what we want, yes, out of what's being shot out, so to speak. And so we will go through this process of learning how to do that. And at that point we will realize that all of that was not necessary, because all of it is what we want anyhow. If we realize that, we wouldn't have to learn how to get what we want.

D: *Then we actually can use any of it. What we consider positive, negative or whatever.*

B: Absolutely. All of it is just energy with no good, no bad, no hurt, no feel good, no right, no wrong, no anything. But mainly because of our belief system, we want to separate it into parts that are right and wrong, and good and bad. And as a result we want to choose just what we want out of that. When we reach a level where we understand that all of that was unnecessary there was no right, no wrong, no good, no bad, no hurt, no feel good then we won't need to have even learned how to get what we want.

D: *But being human beings, that's where our focus is.*

B: That's where it is right now, yes. Before we can pull into our lives what we want, we have to arrive at the awareness that it doesn't make any difference. Because as long as it does make a difference, we make it harder on ourselves to get it. Only when it no longer makes a difference, does the flow become so even, that we can tune in so easily that we can have anything we want. It's sort of like, it takes money to make money. As long as you've got it, you can keep making it. When you don't have it, is when you're in trouble, in this life. And so when we end up raising our level of awareness, then we realize we can have all the money, help, whatever we want. But by then, since we know we can do it, it's just thought, it no longer matters. We're not so attached to it. Until we realize that, we're very attached to it, because we think we can't get it.

D: *That does make a lot of sense.*

B: I will give an example. As you are climbing a ladder, stairway to Heaven, so to speak, every step that you continue to go up, the ones beneath it dissolve. It's like you project the stairway in front of you, because you think you need it to climb to the next star. And it dissolves underneath you as you go, because you no longer need it. You're coming from this star going to that one. (Hand motions) And you're building your ladder, which as you climb is dissolving. And then you get up here this star. Now what was true all along was, when you were at this star, you could have been at this other star any time you wanted to without using the ladder. But the only way we know that is to get there on this ladder, which then is no good and not worth anything. I don't mean it's no good. I mean it no longer serves a purpose. And if we think we're building that ladder so others can follow us, we are in error, because each person has to build their own ladder. You can't travel on someone else's brain or energy. That's not what it is, but maybe in these terms it will be explainable. You can't live someone else's life.

D: *Yes, but wouldn't the ladder serve its purpose to show them the way?*

B: It only shows the person who is living that life the way. Another person would have to build their own ladder to get there.

D: *I thought if you learned something, you could pass it on as knowledge to help other people.*

B: Yes, that could be. But the ladder is more like the livingness of it, than it is knowledge. And each person must do their own livingness. We can't ride to Heaven on someone else's coat tails.

D: *But we can give them examples and show them?*

B: Yes. Each entity, doing what it does, gives examples whether it wants to or not. It just does it. Another entity, with a level of awareness, can see that. In actuality they wouldn't need to borrow or utilize what another one has learned. But they think they do, and so they do.

D: *They don't want to start from scratch and figure it all out for themselves. That's why we have examples, we have books.*

B: Yes. And so if that is helpful and we use that and it guides us that's fine. There is nothing wrong with that. But in truth, if there were only one human being on the face of the Earth ever and he saw nothing of anyone else's examples that had preceded him, he would still get to that star. And would probably do it just as quickly, if time existed anywhere.

D: *By figuring it out himself.*

B: It's not a matter of figuring it out, it is a natural evolution. You plant a seed in the ground, it grows up. It becomes whatever the seed was. If you plant an acorn, what grows out is an oak tree. It's not a birch or a rabbit. And we have within us all of this. And if we are left completely alone, we will still wind up at the same place. But because of this static energy around us that interferes with that natural flow, we want to grab straws for help. And because the static is there, and we think we need to grab straws for help, we do. But underlying all of that, we wouldn't really need to and will get there anyhow. It just eases our human minds to have help out there, or what we think of as help.

D: *Yes, that's the human part of it. Well, all this energy you're talking about, I'm wondering how our human soul fits in.*

B: That is probably what you would call a "soul". The spirit, the life force, would be the closest way I could explain it. That is what we generally label as a "soul" here.

D: *That's the part that remains after the physical body dies.*

B: Yes, because, it would continue on and on. Energy cannot go away.

D: *But it appears that it remains individualized as a personality.*

B: It can if it wants to. It can do whatever it wants to do. It can individualize as a flower, or it can individualize as a human being. Either with the same exact awareness as it did the moment before, or with a different awareness. It can do anything it wants to do. It is creation.

D: *The energy or the soul?*

B: It's all one and the same. And it can divide itself, or it can sort of coagulate as one big entity. Picture that you are spraying water out of a hose nozzle. By turning that nozzle, you can either make it come out as separate drops, or you can change the nozzle and make it come out as one flow. Or you can spread it even wider, and have it just little bitty drops like a spray. Or however you want to do it. It's all the same.

D: *It's all so complicated. That's why I'm trying to put it into terms I can understand. Because if I can't understand it it's hard for me to pass it on to someone else.*

B: There's a difference between logically understanding and being aware of. And I think we can be aware of things and know them, that we don't logically understand. It's sort of like putting a square peg in a round hole. They don't quite fit.

D: *So it would be very difficult for us to even hope to try to understand much of this. We're limited by our human brains. We just have to realize and feel that it's true.*

B: Yes. As long as we're limited within our belief systems, it's difficult if not impossible to understand it logically. Because our belief systems are so limited in size, and what we're trying to understand and become aware of is so big, that it won't all fit into our little box of belief systems. Until we dispense with that box, we can't let all of it come in. It's going to happen whether you understand it all or not, because that is the nature of it.

D: *But I try to write about these things, so that people can be aware of them.*

B: Yes. And that is very helpful, because it does expand people boxes of belief. And that is where seeing others that have gone before us does help. It would happen anyhow. But seeir those that have gone before us, allows us to expand our box little bit with our awareness of that. And what you do in writing about these things helps people see that there's something on the other side of that box. They can push it op a little bit and include it. And they will keep doing that and doing that and doing that, until their box gets big enough to handle all of this. Well, not all of it, but it would be a continuir process.

D: *In other words, they can't handle it until they're ready for it anyway.*

B: That's true. You can write all the books you want to, but un someone is willing to read it, it's not going to do that persor any good. It may do you good, and it may do others good. B it's not going to help the person that's not ready to look ove the edge of his box. And when they are ready to look over t edge, anything will help.

D: *Then they'll be looking for things that will supply the information. It seems very clear to you, but it's complicated to me.*

B: It is not so clear to me either, except that I know that it's so.

***

D: *We have read about universal mind, universal consciousnes Is it true that we are all connected in some way, that we can get information from universal mind once we become more enlightened?*

Phil: That is accurate, for all are eventually one, the God conce encompasses all of creation. All, period. Therefore, since eac of you is indeed a part of the whole, then each of you is inde an aspect of the other. You are indeed part of each other.

D: *Is that the way metaphysical healing takes place? Where yo can manipulate the energy that is available and the energies we are all interconnected with?*

P: It would be somewhat more complicated than that. Howeve the concept is indeed accurate in that the energies you speak of are part of yourselves, and you are part of the energies. It as if you are swimming in energies and you yourselves are a part and parcel of the very waters you swim in. By manipulatir the waters around you, you can cause currents to push or pull from you to someone, or from someone to you. These currents, as you can well imagine, are the energies of which we speak. You need only direct these energies with your mind to form these currents. There can be storehouses of these currents available to those who would need them. And in this manipulation, you find these storehouses are available to you yourself. It is creating and discreating energies. You yourselves on your plane are, in every truest sense of the word, gods, in that you can and do create your creations in your own plane and dimensions of awareness. However, you are not as equal to or as great as the overall, total encompassing aspect of the God concept which you have. None of you on this plane could ever hope to attain that level. However, it is sufficient to say that each of you has a part of that total, overall consciousness within you. And you are indeed capable of creating and discreating. Therefore, you are by your own definition of God, the Creator, a god in and of yourself. You, yourselves are god creators. Perhaps not on a level which you ascribe to the all encompassing God. However, it is important here to note that you, yourselves are indeed creators.

***

Phil: There is a physical energy spectrum. There are those energies which constitute and in proper proportion make that which you perceive as physical. In proper combination of different energies there is manifested physical form. The physical form you see about you is a combination of many different physical energies manifested to produce those forms that you see. Your eyes perceive those energies and so you perceive physical form.

***

Brenda: I am within a nexus that is an intersection point of several universes in continuance. I am observing how they interact. And I'm looking at the patterns that they cause in their structure of existence.

D: *That sounds complicated. Is it beautiful to watch?*

B: Yes, it is. Really complex and beautiful. It's difficult to describe. It depends on what level you look at it. On one level it looks like do you know what sheet lightning looks like? (Yes) Imagine sheet lightning of every conceivable color and see it all interacting with each other. The various sheets of energy of the various colors flowing and flickering around. And you look at it at another level and you can see the grid of time warping around and interacting and changing It just depends on what level you look at it. There are other levels. It's very complex and it's very beautiful.

***

Brenda: I am observing the network of basic energy particles that make up the universe and hold it together. You could describe it several different ways, depending on your perceptions and what level of organization you look at it. On the one hand it looks like a loosely woven blanket with each individual thread representing particular types of energy, weaving in and out and interacting with the other energies, keeping everything together and in order. And on the other hand if you look at it another way, it looks like an energy fog since everything is energy and it will spread all over. It's as if you were in a fog and you could see each individual particle that makes up the fog, to use an analogy. Where you are on your Earth plane, fog is composed of tiny particles of moisture. It's as if you could see each individual particle unique and complete in itself. Yet in this case each individual particle is a particle of energy, and each individual particle is alive in its own way. It's excited. It vibrates and moves around with its tiny sphere of influence. And this is everywhere with the countless multitudes of particles.

D: *Would this be like atoms?*

B: Smaller than atoms. Atoms are clusters of energy particles. These are like the sub atomic physical properties that your scientists are trying to study. (Pause) I can't make the connection with your language. They have such strange names that your scientists use. Quarks? Things like small tiny neutrinos of energy. The energies and particles involved with what is labeled in your language as the new physics. This is the first glimmering of an idea of how things are. Since this is a new field you are studying, you have no knowledge of it yet. You just barely suspect that this aspect of things exists. Your scientists are trying to understand it and to qualify it. To give it rules to explain things that they observe, but what they are observing is a very incomplete picture. To use an analogy, it's as if a lengthy film is being shown in your theater. And all you see is one single frame of the film, of the entire picture. And trying to explain what the film is about and the plot of the story.

D: *Just from one frame?*

B: Right. And that's what your scientists are trying to do about this energy. What they have observed is the equivalent of having seen maybe one small detail in that one frame. Maybe the color of the hair of one of the actors in this one frame. And from that information they try to build what the film was about. The plot of the story, who wrote it, what the music was about and all that. And it's impossible. They need to learn more and observe more before they can figure out what is truly going on. They have already made the correct connection between this new physics and the ancient science of mysticism. But the ancient science of mysticism is partially left over from the former civilization, and partially from millennia of observation. Observation collected of these things that are caused by this fog of energy, that people have observed and tried to explain.

D: *But how can they get the whole picture? They can't see these things.*

B: No, but they can observe effects of these things, which would help them to understand what these are. The main thing they need to do is keep their minds open to anything, no matter how preposterous sounding or how improbable it may seem at first. Because all improbabilities and all things that seem preposterous are part of the universe too. Things called "chance" and "coincidence" are general labels of things that have been observed that are caused by this.

D: *You said this was based on the science of mysticism. Many people think of that as witchcraft and the occult. Is that what you mean?*

B: Yes, partially. In the age you are presently in, people have cut themselves off from their roots. And in the process of doing this they have denied mysticism, saying they are a modern and educated people; that science explains everything. When science finally advances to its ultimate peak, everybody will be mystics. By mysticism I refer to anything that deals with the higher levels of things, including witchcraft, occult, the different mystic religions from the East: Buddhism or Hinduism and such as that.

D: *Many people just lump it all together as being on the dark side.*

B: Yes. The power can be perverted and used for the wrong reasons, as can anything. But it is to mankind's benefit to become familiar and comfortable with this power and use it for solving his problems. There are still cultures that are more open to this than others. In your culture, it has closed this. But there are many individuals that practice this and use it in their lives and help keep their traditions alive, which is important. That seems to be a characteristic of mankind. Things that they don't understand they lump together in categories and shut them up in a closet and forget about them or try to. And everything that exists can be learned from and you can benefit from everything that exists some things more than others, 'tis true but in general. For example, in your science of medicine they have developed vaccine. And so now vaccines are used by everybody to help prevent disease and prevent a imbalance of the body. In former civilizations the sciences developed what is now called mysticism, and everyone used it to help prevent imbalance of the harmonious whole. By its very nature it accomplished what all of your individual sciences are trying to accomplish now. Their sciences started out as similar individual sciences and then united as they became far advanced in the fields of knowledge And they realized that everything is one, is a harmonious whole. They united and the people learned and applied the knowledge that developed. It is what is known as mysticism because they had aspired to the ultimate and found that this underlying energy organizes everything. And if one is aware of this and knows how this can be altered or manipulated to achieve what you wish while staying in harmony with it, then all that needs to be done is done.

D: *You mean they found they didn't need it for medicine?*

B: When they got to this level where they could be in harmony with the whole, medicine was no longer needed. It was superfluous, because it was rare if someone became ill. They knew where they were out of balance. And they altered their energies to put everything back in balance. Then they would no longer be ill.

D: *Can you tell me what civilizations developed this to such a high degree?*

B: It was several civilizations but they were in contact with each other. It was a worldwide type of knowledge, but different parts of the world had subtly different ways of looking at things, due to their culture. There was the civilization of Atlantis, and there was a civilization in South America. And there were several civilizations in the East: one in India, one in the mountains in what is now called "Tibet" and "Sri Lanka". And two different civilizations sprang up in the place called "China", but they were living in harmony with each other. They were considered as one civilization with a dual type of culture. And these civilizations all contributed to the development of the science from their various viewpoints to help make it a complete whole.

D: *Were these other civilizations in existence at the same time as Atlantis?*

B: Yes. Atlantis predated most of them, but they were all old civilizations. The civilization in Tibet and South America started about the same time as Atlantis, and the other civilizations came a little later. But they existed long enough that they all advanced to a high degree.

D: *I think many people have the idea that those civilizations came along after the destruction.*

B: A new set of civilizations did come after the destruction of Atlantis. When Atlantis was destroyed it shook the whole world, in so far as human interaction was concerned, sciences, art, etc. The whole world felt its effects. Atlantis was the major civilization, the center of civilization in general. And when it was destroyed, it seemed to have sapped the vital energy from the other civilizations, so that they went into decline. But these other civilizations gave rise to the present day world.

***

Brenda: I'm looking at the entire structure of time. It's very intricate. It's almost like a hollow globe made of fine silver wire. And all of these wires are going around and intersecting with each other, rather like a three dimensional model of the atom and how you see the electrons going around. There's a series of silver wires going around like that. And there is another series of silver wires going around at right angles to intersect with all of these. And it forms this hollow globe. It's hard to describe, it's very intricate.

D: *It sounds complicated.*

B: And one thing to give you hope, with it being structured like this, that means anything can happen. Because all the possible combinations are present here.

D: *You mean it's not set, or predestined, to where it has to be.*

B: No. This is the reason why magic and such works. Because if you want something to happen, and you meditate on it and project mental energy towards this happening, it will cause your life to be directed into that time stream.

***

Brenda: It may be rehashing what you have heard before, but it cannot be emphasized too much. First of all you must reali that anything that generates energy puts out vibrations. Thin that generate light, which is a form of energy, put out light vibrations and you see them as radiating, such as a light bul Or something that generates sound, you see it vibrating and you hear the sound, but it's still vibration and it's still energ Your brain also generates energy. Anything that happens in your brain generates energy, and hence generates vibrations Which means, any of your bodily processes or any of your thoughts or any emotion, puts out vibrations. And these vibrations affect the ether that surrounds you. You're surrounded by and filled with and shot through with vibratio from billions of different sources. These vibrations are of a levels and strengths. And the energy put out by your brain i sufficient to affect some of these levels of vibrations. Consequently, one can affect future outcomes by what one thinks. I know you have heard this before, but I'm explainir it to you again, so you will not be discouraged when things seem not to work out at first. You just keep thinking about what you want to come to pass and it comes to pass. Sometimes in unexpected ways, because sometimes the vibrations have to go through many channels to affect what needs to be affected. I can see this very plainly. I don't kno if I'm explaining it so it will be convincing to you.

D: *You're doing a very good job. If I get confused I'll ask you.*

B: Your brain is the vibrational center of your body. And there is a focus of these vibrations, called the solar plexus. And that's like a lens focusing light. The solar plexus focuses the vibrations and then sends them out again to all parts of the body, and out into your aura to keep things balanced. That i why when you meditate and open yourself up to absorb vibrations to replenish your vibrations, you should picture them entering through the top of your head and then going down to your solar plexus. So that the solar plexus can sprea these vibrations out to your body where they are needed so that all will be in balance.

D: *I was taught to go through the body energizing each chakra and then passing off the excess through the feet down into t ground. Would that be incorrect?*

B: Not incorrect. It is a way of doing it. When you're going through each chakra, make sure you also charge the solar plexus. That way it revitalizes your body, but you also need to be sure that you revitalize your aura as well, which exten way beyond your body. And so, make sure you send an extr.

jolt of energy to the solar plexus, to make sure that your aura is being revitalized to its very limits to help protect you from any harm that may come in your direction. And then, any excess energy, yes, should be sent out through the soles of your feet into the Earth mother. It's recharging your aura, and helps protect you when your defenses are down, like when you're asleep. It is wise to do extra things to protect yourself during the day. Either by picturing your aura as being brilliantly white or golden, or by picturing a pyramid of energy around you. By whatever method you are comfortable with, because when you are interacting with other people you need extra protection. But at night, in the privacy of your home when you're going to sleep, the protection of your aura should be sufficient. You may want to picture a pyramid of energy around you just before going to sleep, but you won't need to worry about it. You'll be protected during the night while you're asleep, because the subconscious does a very good job of it. And if you're in a reclining position when you're projecting the pyramid, picture yourself as being approximately one third up from the bottom of the pyramid, because that is the focus of the strength and energy of the pyramid.

D: *You mean as though the body was levitated about that far above the bottom of the pyramid.*

B: Yes, but you'll still be totally surrounded by the pyramid, even the underside of your body. It is a very powerful figure. It is a focus. It is hard to explain everything the pyramid can do.

D: *Many people have told me there is nothing to worry about. You don't have to be protected against anything.*

B: It's like lightning. Lightning is a neutral force. It's not good or bad, it's just there. It's very powerful. On the one hand it can be used to generate electricity. On the other hand it can kill people. These forces are basically neutral and one can use them for one's own ends if one is careful. But at the same time, when one is opening oneself up for exploration and new experiences, one must make sure one is protected, because these neutral forces have no morality. They just act in the way their energy flows in a particular situation. And you must make sure that you are protected against any negative flows. It is good that you follow our advise. It helps you to advance and it makes it easier for us to communicate with you.

D: *But anyway, you were saying that you send these vibrations out for what you want to accomplish. (Yes) Once you send it out then it must happen?*

B: There are things that can influence it. Like for example, you send out thoughts that you want something to happen. And they'll go out and start causing things to fall into place for it to happen. But if, later on, you get discouraged or depress and you send out thoughts of, "Gee, it'll never happen", it w weaken its impetus. And when you get over your depressio you must send out strong thoughts again, positive thoughts help it regain its impetus so that it will come to pass.

D: *To reemphasize the first thoughts?*

B: Right. And this works with anything. Any change in your li be it business or personal. A relationship between you and another, or something you want to do, or personal dreams, anything.

D: *I've been taught that thoughts are very powerful and they ca accomplish what you want.*

B: Yes, they can. And that's why you must be careful about negative thoughts because they are powerful, too. And they can help neutralize your positive thoughts. So if you want your positive thoughts to come to pass, keep thinking positively about them. Meditate intensely on them. Do true visualization. Are you familiar with that concept?

D: *Where you visualize it as already happened?*

B: Yes. Or perhaps even picture it happening as if you were floating above and watching it. And then afterwards picture all the positive changes that have come to pass as a result of it happening. And how the world and your life would be aft it has happened.

D: *I was taught to visualize it as already happening and to fill with as much detail as possible.*

B: Yes, exactly. Add dialogue, feelings and everything, as if yo were observing real life. Remember the bigger the project i sometimes the longer it will take because there are more channels that your thoughts must go through in order to hav more pieces fall into place for it.

***

At a group meeting we were asking about healing energy. member of the group asked, "I have an interest in helping others heal. Where does the energy come from that is used in the act helping others?"

Phil: The cosmic energies of which we spoke earlier, are those energies of which you ask. You need merely to open your mind in order to focus these energies. Open and accept, and your mind will work as truly as a crystal.

D: *Can anybody use these energies or are they special gifts for healing?*

P: These energies are for virtually everyone in the universe to use for their benefit and others if they so choose. They are not exclusive to any one. You may use these energies as you see fit.

D: *Can these energies be harmful to the person who is helping or the person they are healing?*

P: There is such a thing as over loading, but this is not so harmful. It is merely an imbalance. You would not kill anyone by using these energies. Fear not, for these are God's gifts, as surely as the sunlight and air on your planet. Cherish them and use them in good faith and they will in time cherish you.

The member: *Several people receive what we call a "healing", yet within a short period of time, six months or a year they develop another problem or go back to the same problem.*

P: You are saying the healing does not stay or take?

The member: *Well, it seems that way to us. They are healed for a period of time and then they go back to the same illness.*

P: Yes, this is natural. The effects are not always permanent. If the illness is to such a degree, a periodic rehealing, a booster, if you will, would be necessary and appropriate. This does not discount the effects of the healing nor does it exaggerate the illness. It's simply a fact that a booster may oftentimes be necessary. You will become familiar with these actions the more often that you use these energies. Some illnesses may require one short healing session, others may require an extended, sometimes lifetime, commitment to effect a cure. The first question as far as healing is concerned, can be best visualized as a leaky bucket. If the bucket has holes in it, you would need to continually fill it with water. The bucket will leak water until the holes are plugged. Healing is merely, in this instance of illustration, filling the bucket with water, which will cover the symptoms temporarily. The holes in the bucket need to be plugged and the healing will be complete.

The member: *Is it possible that we have been preprogrammed for a time to die. Is it possible that this is in our DNA or is hereditary. For example, a person is born and they are to live to be thirty five. They could die earlier by an accident or they could extent that. Is that possible?*

P: It could be because of many different reasons. It could be preprogrammed in order to live the life a prearranged time period, or it could be from improper diet or life style. It could be from accident. There are many things which could cause a hole in the bucket, so to say. As to a time on life, death is necessary in order to progress. Stagnation would occur if there were no death to move one to the spirit side. This is an ongoing process which is best suited for the learning of much information. All is as it should be in this respect.

The member: *I was just curious whether we could lengthen it or shorten it with free will. I wondered if my DNA had some kind of preprogramming.*

P: There is a maximum programed in the DNA. The actual time allotted is almost certainly dependent on the individual.

The talk gravitated toward using energy for helping in financial situations.

P: This energy, you might be surprised to find, is an almost identical energy, manifested in different ways, however. The energy which brings finances is indeed the same energy which brings health or disease. Are you surprised to learn this? To stimulate an increase in financial energy would be using the same technique of visualizations and affirmations that are used in healing energy. This is simply as if you were passing the same ray of white light through two separate prisms. One which had a tendency to bring out more of a blue color, and one which would tend to bring out more of a green color. It is indeed the same energy, however, it is translated differently. The energy is basically neutral, it is simply how it is used. This energy can bring poverty or wealth, or it can bring health or disease. It can bring many things. It can bring happiness and sadness, or it can bring sanity or insanity. Always, it is how it is used, and in the intent is how it is manifested.

D: *Most people think it's either good or bad.*

P: Many would choose to decide that someone else had done them wrong and caused it to happen. And in so doing are defeating their very purpose for living. And that is, to learn to focus these energies in the most constructive way possible. That truly is the underlying reason for being born incarnate, physical, is to learn to become manipulators of this energy.

D: *Maybe that's one of the lessons we're trying to learn.*

P: That is the lesson we are all trying to learn. That is the lesson to be learned on this planet. For everything can be traced back to this. The lessons of healing, the lessons of love, the lessons of understanding, the lessons of patience. All have their roots in this basic foundation: the use of the energies. So it reflects in the physical plane most closely what is the true plan, which is God's plan. Those who manipulate this energy unwisely or unknowingly find they create situations around them which are not productive, or true to the plan. The entire purpose for incarnating and learning, is to learn to become adept manipulators of this energy. And in all your doings you are learning to manipulate this one way or another, be it financial or political or healthwise or one of many, many different ways.

D: *Most people don't realize they draw to them what they want, even if it's bad.*

P: Not so much that they draw it to them, but that they manifest it. Each of you manifest what you find. It is not that it is out there and it comes to you. Of course, you know we are having a semantic discussion, but it is a fine point which needs to be understood. That you actually do manifest what you find. It's not that it's floating around and somehow attaches to you, and then you find yourself in the pits and the woes of agony and despair. No, no. It's that this situation which one finds so unpleasant has been manifested, has been brought on by a misuse or misunderstanding of the energies. It is not brought to one, it is brought by one.

D: *The way people say, "Everything always goes wrong. Everything I do, nothing works out."*

P: Yes, and that reinforces the whole concept of "everything happens to me". And so one goes through life thinking about how wrong life is to them, and how miserable everything is. And their very thoughts are channeling the energy into that very type of situation. You get what you ask for.

D: *Of course, they'd be the last ones to admit they are actually causing this to happen to themself. They say, "I don't want to be unhappy. I don't want to be sick."*

P: That is accurate. And the hardest person to listen to is yourself. There is at this time on this planet a lack of understanding of the relationship between emotions and health. For were you to integrate all of these understandings the recuperation would be much quicker and more affective. So it can be said from an emotional point of view, that by bringing disharmony into harmony, then this disharmony is spread throughout, assuming that the body is in harmony to begin with. So you can look at it as a matter of disharmony or dis ease. And being brought into one who is not at peace with oneself, you can see that this disease is brought into the body system and spread throughout. So one feels ill at ease and out of harmony simply from an emotional point of view. It can be looked at in a mathematical point of view, if you would care to pursue it to that level. For instance, if you have what you might call a perfect equation, one which works out perfectly, with no remainders and no divisors. We will be careful here because this vehicle does not have a higher level of understanding of mathematics, but we will use his level to explain this. If you can see that there is a given equation which satisfies a certain set of calculations, and this comes out to a perfectly balanced answer, then that is harmony. However, if one enter into this equation one variable or one number, perhaps whi tends to cause the remainders to appear, or the equation to n come to a perfect settlement, then there will be, as you mig relate, disharmony or disease. There is in fact a remainder, mathematical terms.

D: *It doesn't come out even.*

P: That is correct. It can be related through music as a discord through any one of a number of different methods of what you might call "analogies". These are all true and concurrer and all happen simultaneously. It is simply that you choose this happening in one or more levels of awareness.

D: *Then what can these people do to realign or to come back in harmony with themselves?*

P: They should see themselves always surrounded by that whi is the most perfect possible. And so they should use their judgment always in light of this fact, to maintain this level c perfect quality living. Always keep in mind this harmony factor, that that which is perceived will be the most appropria for that purpose. That is true for all aspects of human awareness. Always keep in mind that one will receive and o will do that which is most appropriate for oneself, or for whatever the undertaking is. For in so doing, you naturally attract to yourself, if you wish to relate to that level of speec the very thing which you are asking for. You are, in effect, manifesting the reality of the most harmonious situation. Many on the planet feel that in order to manifest something they must become adamant to the point that there is no possibility for anything else to happen. The fault in this lies the fact that what one says and what one thinks are often at odds with each other. What one truly believes is often not exactly what one says. And so when one says something, it is indeed setting off a reaction which could be quite opposit of that which is said. And so in being so firm in this belief, there is given the manifestation which may seem to be entire at odds with that which is being said. One manifests that which one fears the most, because one is saying that they w not see it, or it will not happen. But yet by continually thinki about that, whatever that may be, one creates that. And just surely has to meet or face that very thing which one so strong

438

says they do not want to meet.

D: *That is a paradox of being human.*

P: That is accurate. It is a paradox of being a manipulator of the energies. It is a pitfall of becoming or being less enlightened. And so it would behoove everyone who is, as they are on this planet now, a manipulator of the energies, to become more enlightened. And to know more about how to manifest that which is truly desired.

D: *It would make life a lot easier if people could only realize that they do have a great deal of control over situations and events.*

P: That is accurate. They could have in their lives the true harmony that everyone seeks. Some are more proficient and adept at this than others. We would say to you now gathered in this room, that each of you in your own way can now see a journey which lies ahead of you. Actually in very simple terms, everyone on this planet has this same journey. However, many are more aware of it than others.

D: *We're all on the same path, just going different directions.*

P: That is accurate. However, all paths will eventually converge and meet in one single place.

D: *It just takes many more twists and turns along the way.*

P: That is accurate.

CHAPTER FOURTEEN
THE TRANSFORMATION OF THE HUMAN BODY

In 1999 I had my first exposure to the mention of DNA changes the human body when I had a session with Luigi at our UFO Conferenc in Eureka Springs. I met his mother in Florida at a conference a fe months before, and there wasn't time to have a private session. Whe I told her about the UFO conference in Eureka Springs she decided come with her daughter. She phoned her son, Luigi, in Italy and to him about it, so he traveled all the way from Europe to attend. Whe he arrived she decided that he needed the session more than she di because he had had some disturbing UFO experiences (presumably and he wanted to explore them. Harriet sat in on the session, as d his mother. She thought I might have trouble with his accent, and th he might have trouble translating to English while under hypnosi It turned out that we didn't have any problems. In the discussic beforehand he told me what he remembered, so we planned to retu to that day and get more details. He had been to school at night for acting class in Pavia, Italy, and was driving home when the incide occurred. In his recollection he and his girlfriend saw a light in the sl and pulled off the highway to watch it. That was all that happened, y it disturbed him.

During the session I was not surprised when we discovered th much more actually occurred than just seeing the light. When Lui entered the deep trance state he relived the incident. They thoug perhaps the light was a plane crashing, and pulled off the highw to watch. When they got out of the car they saw it was a huge cra that moved slowly until it stopped overhead. Then a door opened fro underneath and a beam of light came down towards them. The ne thing he saw was that he was lying on a table in a room that resemble an operating room with a large light overhead. When he sat up he sa a being approaching him that seemed to be composed entirely of ligh To my surprise the being embraced him. Luigi then became emotion as he said, "I feel safe there. I feel happy." He had difficulty findir the correct words in English to describe what the being felt like as h touched it. "Like if somebody gives you energy, and you can feel i When it embraced me it felt like physical. But if you touch it... it is r solid."

I then wanted to ask the being questions, and it agreed. It said he as onboard a craft, and this was not the first time he had been there. asked why he didn't remember and Luigi said, "Better for me. I will ow later on. Now it's too early." He said this had been going on for long time, and they had met before in other lifetimes. The being had ed for six hundred years in our reckoning of time.

I had heard this before when working on these type of cases. any times the beings have followed souls through several lifetimes, d had interactions with them, because they can live as long as they ant. Sometimes the alien becomes frustrated because the person does t remember, and they have to be reminded again of their agreement d commitment to the project.

In broken English Luigi repeated what the being was telling him. will know at the right moment. I will have an important role in hat's going to happen. And they have been already telling us. Big anges. Very big changes on the Earth. Continents will move. And e water... and they're coming back. We won't recognize anything. nd they will be very sad for us. Humans have been doing all those rty things, stupid things. But it's not the end of the world. It will : the end of an era." The entities could not do anything to stop these ings, but they were trying to slow it down. His role was to save :ople, and they would teach him how to do this.

Of course, I am always looking for a time frame. They said it ould be very soon. I knew that did not tell me much, because their nse of time is different from ours. He said, "Maximum twenty years." uigi was then shown a big explosion, and a toxic cloud that would read over the land, and people running and trying to hide.

Then he was told the same thing I have already mentioned in is book, that they would be able to save certain selected ones by king them onboard crafts. There would be many, many crafts and the :ople would have to live onboard for a long time. Then they would : brought back, "And with their help we keep on growing. We start ;ain. Everything is changed. It will be very hard for us. It has already appened in the past."

I asked who these people were. "They are from different planets, fferent galaxies. Like a union? To save the planet. First of all they :lp us, because we are different. And this is a planet that has to be ived, because we change, and we won't have the mask anymore. hey go around galaxies. Mostly with ours, because we are more in fficulties. And we can't come out from that on our own, because we ow always deeper. And we won't be physical as we are now. He owed me how we will be. We look like... sort of like a ghost, but ith a figure."

D: *A ghost. You mean like you can see through?*

L: Not exactly. It's hard to describe that. I don't know how to describe that. Not solid anymore.

D: *More like a spirit?*

L: Yes, but not a spirit. He's showing it to me, but I don't know how to explain it. Not as they are. But almost. He just showed me. He just became a pig. To show me he can become how he wants to become.

D: *Yes. Tell him I understand what he's saying. He's an energy being, isn't he? (Yes) He can become what he wants to become. But he said we will not be like that.*

L: Almost, but not quite.

D: *But the body will still be physical to a certain extent? (Yes, yes.) Will it still need food?*

L: Not as much as now. Different.

D: *Will it still need sleep? Things that a body needs?*

L: A few. Not with this.

D: *Will it still have to create other beings like... I'm thinking of reproduction?*

L: He says sex will be different. Not physical anymore. It will be like a union of energy, but he says it feels nice. It feels good anyway. He's showing me. Like two balls coming together and creating something. It's hard to explain.

This type of reproduction was described in *The Custodians*.

D: *I think I know what you mean. But I'm trying to find out if it was almost physical, how it would be alike and how it would be different. Will we need to have houses and buildings like we do now? (Yes) And cities.*

L: Cities? Because we won't be as they are. That's too much. And too early.

D: *If we're not really solid, will we still use our bodies to build things?*

L: With the head. The mind will be very strong. We won't need to talk anymore. And we will be able to live much more.

D: *Can he answer some questions about you? Because I know Luigi has been wondering what has been happening lately when he said he woke up and was shaking and vibrating. Can this being tell you what is happening during those times?*

L: Yes. Working on the system. Working on the DNA. Putting it up... in spirant (Phonetic. Did he mean spirals?).

D: *Can you explain what you mean?*

L: Yes. Because we have humans two spirals of DNA. We will have twelve.

D: *Why do we have to have twelve?*

L: That's a higher level we can get.

D: *But how will that help the body?*

L: Because we used to have twelve. Many millions of years ago.

D: *Then what happened?*

L: Genetical experimentations. Could bring us back to twelve. They reduced to two.

D: *What was the experimentation that was done?*

L: For to see how... what happening. And I guess to make... what we do on rats. On animals. They have done it on us.

D: *You mean they have done it?*

L: No, no, no, not them. Other beings.

D: *Why would they want to do that?*

L: To see. Just curiosity.

D: *To see what would happen if they changed the DNA to two, you mean?*

L: Yes. That's why we are like that now. And we have that big mask. That's why humans are so limited. And that's why there are people who don't believe in UFOs and all sort of things.

D: *Are we all being experimented on, to increase the DNA?*

L: A part of us will have six, and another part twelve.

D: *And they are doing this now on certain people in the population, you mean.*

L: Yes, on many people. To change the DNA. To prepare us.

D: *He said they're doing it now to Luigi's body. Will this hurt the body in any way?*

L: No, no, not at all. We won't have the diseases we have now anymore. It's a very slow process, and it takes years.

D: *But those whose bodies have been prepared are the ones that will be taken onboard the craft when the changes occur?*

L: Yes, but they say, many, many, many, many, many, will have that.

I had a thought while typing this. It was mentioned in my book *The Custodians* that the human body cannot survive space travel aboard their crafts in its present state. The body cannot handle the acceleration, and the change in the vibrations of a different dimension. This was one thing that would prevent mankind from traveling in space as they do, because we cannot handle the speeding up of the vibrations to cross dimensions. Will the change in DNA enable the body to adjust to these changes? Is that one of the reasons for it? He said it was preparation.

D: *So they're working on many people. (Yes) Is this why more and more people are seeing UFOs, and having experiences with extraterrestrials?*

L: Because it has to become normal for us to see them.

D: *They're letting themselves be seen more now, because they want people to get used to them? (Yes) Then when these thin, are happening to Luigi's body, he shouldn't worry about them (No) They are natural.*

L: Yes. Some feel them more, and some feel them less. But he quite sensitive. And very soon I will go on the ship physicall And I will remember. And they will give me many informatio

He then remembered leaving the ship to return to his car. He w crying, "And everything happiness, because I feel good." This w quite a contrast to what he felt when he was reporting the sightin Then there was a great fear of the unknown, and wonder about wha if anything, had occurred.

Because of the difficulty with the broken English I have great condensed this tape and decided to put most of it into narration.

The following cases came from other parts of the United Stat and provide more information of the changing of the human body.

***

I met John, an older man, on a tour with a group on the beautif island of Bali in the summer of 2000. In addition to visiting t temples and taking part in the various ceremonies, he wished to ha a private session with me. He had been involved with metaphysi for many years, and had already learned details about many of h past lives through personal meditation. He was more interested discovering any alien associations. He had no conscious memori of any involvement with them, but because of many unusual even throughout his life he suspected there might be a connection. I to him that when I am doing a regression I do not lead the person or try influence them, thus he would go where he was supposed to go.

The session was held in a beautiful luxurious hotel on the beac The perfume of flowers and the lilting singing of birds filled the air, ar filtered in through the open windows as we began. I used the techniqu designed to put the subject into an appropriate past life. Because I had no conscious memories of extraterrestrial interactions, it seeme best to begin in my normal fashion by taking him to a past life firs But that did not happen.

When John entered the scene he saw himself standing in h backyard dressed in his pajamas staring at a strange looking objec It was a shiny silver convex shaped disk supported on legs. H exclaimed, "It's maybe twenty, thirty feet long. I'm surprised, becau: it's so narrow, so slim. I think somebody would have to lie down in order to fit. It's not what I thought it should look like."

Trying to find a time reference, I asked what he looked like. He id he had his beard, but it was dark (it is now gray). He has had a ard for about fifteen years, and his body felt younger. That gave us appropriate time frame. He stood watching the shining disk until noticed another source of light to his left. It was a much larger ip with multiple layers. "It has a general luminescent quality that ems to be lighting up the area. It's metallic, but unlike the silver disk iich is thin. It's so big I can't see all of it at one time. They're very ferent from each other."

When I asked him why he was standing in the yard he related a ory that has become very familiar in my investigations of this type phenomenon. "Somebody brought me so I could see it. I was just ing to bed when I saw something flitting around the corner of the om. They took me up through the ceiling. I can't remember that rt. Everything blacked out when I got up to the ceiling. On the tside, this being had one arm under my butt and one arm behind my ck. We were floating up to a... it appears to be a beam of light. Up o a bay of some sort, and coming into an area that is white, sparkly an, and very modern looking."

There he was greeted by several beings who seemed to know him. ley escorted him into a room. "There is a medical examining table th some type of metal like stirrups at the end for the feet. The table similar to what's at a doctor's office on Earth, except for these metal tensions. It's a padded surface, very light gray color. I'm asked to down on this. I don't seem to be frightened. I'm sort of used to eir what I call funny faces. It's like I've done it before, and here I am ain for my annual checkup or something similar."

The figures were standing beside the table leaning over him. "I'm t conscious of them doing anything other than just looking at me. I ess maybe scanning me with their minds, their eyes or something." ere wasn't any kind of equipment or instruments. The beings were her small, but there was one taller being that projected a feminite eling of kindliness toward him. It was not participating, but stood hind the others merely observing.

He then got up from the table and walked with the others into other part of the ship. They went through an opening into a large und domed area with stepped up layers around the sides. A bright tht was emanating from a large glowing crystal in the center of the om. John thought this might be the power source for the ship. They ilked around the perimeter of the domed room and turned down a rrow hallway into another room. There he was put into a strange vice that stood against a wall.

J: I'm standing up in this... I'm being strapped in... It's sort of glass... all transparent. It's a little deeper than I am. It's not a tube, it's an oblong thing with a flat back. I'm standing in this transparent thing, and now there's light coming down from above. I guess I'm being infused with light energy of some sort. It's like I'm standing outside watching myself.

I reassured him that he was safe. This sounded similar to P (*Keepers of the Garden*) watching what was being done to him because his personality was removed and separated from his body. I also became the observer.

J: It's just this light coming from the top. It's illuminating my head, and I guess the light is going down through my body. feels like an infusion of energy, altering my molecular structure. I guess it's transforming it more and more into a light body or something, even though I still feel very heavy inside. But I guess that's what it's about. It seems to be jus tinkling sensation. I'm getting now something about alterir the DNA strands, increasing the DNA strands.

D: *What do you mean?*

J: That the light energy coming into the body is altering and increasing the... you know the DNA strands are really like strands of light in a sense. And they're being altered and expanded, increased. That means it increases their capacity hold more and more light, with each infusion. That doesn't last very long; they're opening the door and I'm stepping o

D: *And the light process is changing the DNA in some way?*

J: That's the understanding I have.

D: *What is the purpose of changing the DNA?*

J: To hold more and more light, and to transform the body into more and more of a light body. Less dense. Being able to ho more and more celestial light. And the purpose is to reach state of Christ consciousness.

D: *Do you know how the DNA is being changed? Can you ask anyone there? Maybe they can explain it to you.*

This has worked in the past. When we have a question that t subject does not know the answer to, I have them ask one of the bein to supply the information.

J: Yes, I'll ask how the DNA is being changed. (Pause) Well, they show me... I see a visualization of these strands, coils being all sort of lit up or sparkly with light or something. A apparently they give birth to... split off and make other strand through this fusion of light.

D: *How many strands are they splitting off into?*

J: I'm hearing "six", but I don't see six.

D: *And this has to be done every so often?*

J: I guess it's an ongoing procedure more and more frequently at this time. Sometimes more than once during a twenty four hour period. When I take a nap and then during the sleep state at night. That's why I'm being encouraged to take frequent meditation breaks. Every hour at least, to maintain this certain level of vibration.

D: *Why does it have to be repeated? Doesn't the DNA remain like that whenever it's expanded?*

J: It stays like that, but in order to maintain itself at a high level of light course it depends also on the inbetween infusions, and on my mental ability to access my own God force, the light within, so to speak. It keeps those strands activated, so they can become more and more permanent. And that's preparing for the next step. But it has to be sort of consolidated or solidified.

D: *Before they go on to the next step?*

J: The next, yes. And a lot of that depends on my willingness and my ability to constantly tune into the Christ consciousness, my higher self.

D: *Is this something that's been going on for many years?*

J: Yes, but it's accelerating now that I've proven to them that I'm dedicated to fulfilling my divine purpose, so to speak, and caring to stay on the spiritual path. I have proven that I truly want to be of service to humankind. And so I have reached a certain point of passing tests and challenges, and staying the course. Then this acceleration process is being stepped up.

D: *But it has to be done at an increasing rate to make it a permanent change in the body?*

J: Continue to increase it to the eventual twelve strands. That is the eventual goal of reaching the exalted fifth dimensional state of being.

D: *But it would not become solid if this was not repeated on a regular basis?*

J: It's like it could ossify or become stagnant or... I'm seeing this... exactly like muscles in the body. If they're not used they become....

D: *Atrophied?*

J: It's the same thing. And so I have to do my part with meditation and tuning in and affirming my intentions. Then they will aid in their technological process, going in and accelerating the whole thing. It would take many, many years to accomplish through strictly meditation.

D: *But if this process was stopped at any time, then it would atrophy. It wouldn't continue?*

J: It would be higher than my state used to be, but would fall short of what it is intended and can be. The Ultimate Goal: t fifth dimensional state of vibration and consciousness.

D: *Ask them, when they do this, are they activating something with the light, or are they creating something in the body, n DNA, that was not there before?*

J: Oh, no. They have started with the two strands, and as I sa somehow through this process they kept giving birth to oth strands, increasing the number of cells or whatever.

D: *Almost the way cells divide?*

J: Hmmm, I guess that's what they're trying to say.

D: *Is this being done to everyone?*

J: It's being done primarily to those who incarnated specifical to help humankind during this evolved greater state of consciousness. It will happen to a lesser degree to those wh are not presently conscious of their spiritual selves, who do not know they are spiritual. So primarily they are still mire in the density of consciousness.

D: *The others who are having it done, do they all have to go onboard crafts like this to have it activated?*

J: The answer is yes.

D: *It is? You said awhile ago that they could do it when you're meditating or sleeping?*

J: I guess I'm taken during those times for another process tha is less intense, but let's see. (Pause) There is something that can be conducted when I am out of body. There are technological surgeons, they are saying, who are able to remove your etheric body and fuse it with the greater light quotient. (Confused) As I understand it. And then return it to my physical body without going all the way up to the moth ship. They have smaller laboratory ships where this is done

D: *So it doesn't always have to be done with the machine then.*

J: I'm trying to see if it's a technological device, or whether th technological surgeons are doing it with their mind. I think that's what it is. Their mind power also can aid and abet thi process, but not to the same degree as the mind and the technology device on the larger ship. But both are effective and both are being done on a regular basis now.

D: *How does this process affect the body?*

J: The body becomes lighter, and the cellular structure, the membranes become thinner and thinner, and lighter and lighter. We desire lighter and lighter foods. The body has mo and more difficulty digesting and processing the heavy dense foods. That's why I guess I've had a desire for more and more liquids. And I very seldom, when I am at home, eat anything other than a fruit smoothie. I dump it all in and make a thick liquid breakfast and lunch. And several times a week I have a liquid lunch of just carrots and tomato juice and celery and fresh vegetables.

D: *So it makes you not want the heavier foods?*

J: Right. More and more I have been feeling that for quite a while now.

D: *How do these changes affect the health of the body?*

J: It would be a healthier body as it changes more and more into a light body.

D: *The body becomes healthier to where there is no illness, you mean?*

J: No, there will be continued illness, but after the process is complete, the body will be much more immune to most diseases, but not completely free. It has increased my mental powers, and when the transformation is complete I will have much more control over my body than I do now. And I will be able to correct it and rebalance it much at will, so to speak.

D: *So even the changing of just a few strands can make a difference in the body, before it gets to the completed state?*

J: It makes some differences, but in the transition process there is a tendency for more imbalances to take place, because the old is being replaced by the new. And the old wants to hang on to itself to maintain a status quo, until a certain point where the new is solid and the new strands are the majority. It's almost like a democratic process, then the new will be dominant. And the acceleration process will again speed up, as more and more of the old is replaced with the new.

D: *So during that time that the body is undergoing changes, it is still more resistant to disease and illness?*

J: Not necessarily.

D: *I was wondering how the body was affected, and how it felt.*

Up to this point John's voice was soft, sleepy and often difficult transcribe as the words slurred together. Now the voice became ıder and more distinct, easier to understand and transcribe. This was sure clue to me that the other entity had finally begun to answer for hn instead of him hearing the answers. It also could indicate that ᴇ subconscious had entered into the conversation. Either way the swers were flowing much easier, which I always like. Then I know I ı in touch with the true information, and I can obtain more accurate swers without the interference of the skeptical and critical conscious mind.

D: *Will doing this increase the life span of the individual?*

J: Greatly.

D: *By the time it is completed, or while the entire process is go[ing] on?*

J: The human being during this transition process is still susceptible to many adverse affects that exist on the planet this particular time. However, there are other factors of a protective nature that are aiding and abetting human beings who are going through this process, plus as much added protection as possible. And during the shipboard visitation scanning devices are utilized that can often reduce any intrusive bacteria or infectious particles. But it is not a perf[ect] procedure at this point in time. There is a great deal of experimentation and scientific observation as to the most dramatic transformation of the human body into a considerab[ly] different body, a light body.

D: *So you're not really sure how it's going to end up, because you're still experimenting?*

J: We certainly will receive the final tactile product, so to spea[k] but the process of the transition still consists of many mysteri[es].

D: *But when you're giving this protection to make someone mo[re] resistant to bacteria and such, is this done with machines? [Or] how is that process done?*

J: When one is in the glass chamber and being infused with th[e] light, it destroys a number of the interesting things that can permeate the human body.

D: *What was the purpose of the scanning in the beginning, on t[he] table?*

J: In general just to determine his general physical, mental, emotional welfare. To see to what degree he is balanced, to see to what degree his various bodies: physical, mental, emotional, etheric and astral bodies, are in or out of alignmer[t]. And just a visual examination of physical conditions and so forth, that should be observed and recorded and compared t[o] previous visits and examinations and....

D: *It's just like a checkup to see if everything is going the way [it] should? (Yes) And if it was not, would you make adjustment[s]?*

J: Yes. Adjustments would partly be technological and partly increased instructions through the meditation process, as to what the using the term "chosen beingness" can do in terms [of] overcoming current issues, judgmental behavior, or feelings of lack. The feeling of not trusting in the universe to alway[s] provide everything that is needed at any given time, no matt[er] what the circumstances are. To eventually let go of all feelings of the material world as a source of security. And counting on the spiritual and metaphysical world, so to speak, as the source of security.

D: *That's difficult. But you said, if adjustments were to be made that was done with technological devices. Would that be these machines with the light?*

J: Probably, but the human person must do his or her part. We cannot superimpose our technological expertise beyond what the human person is willing to do on their own on the physical plane. It must be a perfect harmony between the willingness to progress spiritually, so as to work in tandem together. If one takes the steps necessary on the mental plane, those steps will be rewarded by our increased participation to help that individual. If the individual stops, unwilling to go ahead on its preselected chosen path which each person chooses before incarnation then the process will come to a standstill. Free will is very important for everyone of the Earth. They must see through and transcend the illusion that exists in present mass consciousness. And trust in the higher spiritual laws and processes.

D: *Is this being done on several people who are spiritually at the right point?*

J: Tens of thousands of people at this time. It's when humankind reaches the critical mass, those who have increased their vibration rates and their ability to hold ever increasing amounts of light celestial light, we must say then the "Hundredth Monkey Syndrome" will become a reality and this Earth will have achieved a state of higher consciousness, and it will affect others on the planet. And this higher consciousness welfare will spread from the relatively few into greater and greater numbers, simply because of the oneness of all creation. Simply because everyone exists within the one line, the one love of God.

D: *What will happen to those who don't participate? Those that are still in the denser mindset, in the physical sense.*

J: Every soul will make its own choice, to participate or not to participate in this process. And many will not participate. Many will hang onto their old value systems. Many will hold onto the illusion of what they have come to believe in during their incarnation on Earth, and will not see beyond this illusion. And therefore they will leave their bodies and be reassigned to another planet whose lessons are a continuation of those on the planet Earth at this particular time. The planet Earth will become another school, a higher school on which the fifth dimensional vibration will determine the new curriculum, the new lessons available for those souls to participate in on a higher level than that which is now availab in the three dimensional consciousness.

D: *I have been told that those people would be left behind. Tha what it means?*

J: They will be left behind in terms of their own growth. They will not move with and continue to step and grow with the others who are dedicated, and have practiced the mental anc physical disciplines necessary to involve themselves spiritually.

D: *So when they leave their bodies, they will not come back her This will be in an entirely different place then. (Yes) And th is happening with tens of thousands of people, and they don know it consciously, do they? Just as John didn't know it consciously.*

J: John knows a lot because of his direct teachings. And there are many on Earth today who are in direct contact with their guides from many planetary systems, who are here to assist humankind to move up to the higher levels of vibration and consciousness. And more and more are being awakened ever day because of their particular preselected time table when they came into the body on Earth. Your soul comes in with a preselected agenda which includes a time table for awakening so to speak. That awakening will be triggered by certain events that happen on the planet. These events can be simpl contact with other people, spiritual teachers who will tell ther something that will awaken and start their process. Some wil be awakened by geophysical calamities, so to speak, that wil happen in their vicinity, be it a hurricane or a tornado or an earthquake. So there are many different devices or processe for triggering the awakening of souls coming onto the planet at this particular time. Some will be suddenly and dramaticall awakened, as John was, by their preselected, preappointed guides. While others will come to the self realization proces more gradually, through different experiences and so forth. There are catalysts as this process is being "rolled out", so to speak.

D: *All over the world then.*

J: Yes. Although America is, at this time, the primary area for receiving and disseminating information, by people in the books they write, movies they make. And other forms of communication that will be disseminated throughout the world. That is not to say other people in other countries are not receiving information too, but the U.S. of A. is the publishing center, so to speak, of spiritual information at this particular time.

D: *It spreads outward from America and affects a lot more people that way. (Yes) Is this another reason why the lifespan is being increased?*

J: As the new Earth unfolds the state of being will be dramatically different from the current reality, because when one reaches the higher state of consciousness, fifth dimensional consciousness, there is no longer ignorance of the cosmic process. There is no longer an ignorance of God permeating all life everywhere. Therefore one is free of the limitations of birth and maturation and death in a relatively short period of time. One in the fifth dimensional consciousness realizes that they can have a much greater control over not only how long they live, which can be hundreds of years but the whole process of creation. Because the creation of realities will occur very, very quickly when one reaches that state of fifth dimensional consciousness. So control over the body or multiple bodies, and the ability to travel freely out of the body throughout the universe will be commonplace.

D: *I was told that I would be around to see all these things, because age would not be the same. Is that what you mean?*

J: Yes. The old paradigm that exists on Earth now of a relatively short lifespan will be a distant memory.

D: *But only for those who are preparing for this.*

J: Those who achieve the state of fifth dimensional consciousness will move ahead and participate in the new Earth, and will be able to do these things.

D: *I have also been told that the extraterrestrials have been checking human bodies trying to find cures for diseases so the body can live longer. Is that correct?*

J: That is correct.

D: *That one of the purposes for the physical examinations was to try to stop some of these progressive diseases that are in the world.*

J: As the physical body goes through its transformation process it will become more immune. The humans or the new humans, or the hybrids coming that will participate in the new Earth, will bring greater awareness, greater knowledge to cure the old diseases, so to speak. So it's not only a current ongoing process, but one that will continue into the higher states of consciousness. And in the higher states of consciousness the elimination of these things will be accelerated, because of the vastly increased intelligence, utilization of the mind, greater access to very advanced technology. Many things that do not exist on the planet at this particular time or if they do exist, are being suppressed or not utilized or held in secret for one motivation or another.

D: *I was told that the people who are onboard these crafts have already mastered this. They can live as long as they want, are free of disease, and they don't die until they are ready to die.*

J: That is correct.

D: *And that they're trying to get the humans to the similar state.*

J: Yes, or at least a state that is considerably beyond where current humankind is.

D: *We probably always will have some limitations then.*

J: Yes. Always a work in progress, so to speak, is a constantly evolving series of challenges, or overcoming those challenges.

D: *Because this is a planet of learning lessons, as well as having free will.*

J: All planets have their lessons, so to speak. Even those lessons that are beyond your wildest imagination on Earth in the current state of three dimensional limitations. But the universe is, and always will be, a process of growth and expansion, and challenges. No matter how high the vibration rate, no matter what level civilizations and beings have attained, with each level of spiraling upward, new challenges are encountered for continued growth.

D: *So the Earth can never become a truly perfect place, because of free will, and the lessons here. (Yes) I have one more question. These things you were talking about, about the changing of the DNA. Does the United States government know these things? Have you shared these concepts with them?*

J: There are several scientists within the USA and other countries who are aware of the mutation process, so to speak. They are somewhat puzzled and amazed at the process now unfolding on the planet. And they look at it as a rather sudden and dramatic mutational process. But many are aware.

D: *You mean they can scientifically see these changes that are occurring?*

J: Many are aware. Many are also afraid to disclose this information for fear of ridicule by their scientific peers, who have not had direct experience and observation of this process.

D: *So they can, with their scientific instruments, see that these changes are taking place in the human body.*

J: That is correct.

Other investigators and writers have discovered information about the activation and progress to twelve strand DNA, but they assume

ll happen spontaneously. It appears that it will be a gradual process
activate the DNA to produce (or give birth to) more strands. If these
w strands can solidify and become permanent then they will produce
re strands. Thus it will not happen quickly, but is definitely being
ggered within the bodies of tens of thousands of people worldwide.
s all part of a divine plan that we only have a faint glimpse of at the
esent time.

Before the session I had listed questions that John wanted to find
answers to. One involved an unusual dream that had remained in
memory.

D: *John said he had a very, very real dream one night of seeing a
spaceship out the window. He felt the need to scream, but he
couldn't. Was that just a dream, or was it an experience, or
what?*

J: That was more than a dream. That was an encounter in another
dimension. And the presence of our ship brought back some
traumatic memories stemming primarily from his childhood
experiences when the current soul was not developed to the
current maturity that exists within John at this particular time.
When he was a child our strange, non human appearance
unfortunately frightened him, and left certain traumatic scars,
so to speak, emotional scars.

D: *Because children often don't understand.*

J: Yes. And we deeply regret that this happened, and that the
scars still remain. So for John the appearance of the ship was
two fold. It did trigger that memory, and sense of terror. Also
it served the purpose however of making John aware that he
had inner work to do to overcome this past experience. And
he has made much progress in that respect since that time.

D: *Is this one of the reasons why these memories are clouded
over or removed, because it's harder for a child to understand
what's happening? Would that be a reason for not allowing
the person to remember?*

J: Very definitely. Also as one evolves spiritually and raises their
vibration rate to a point of truly feeling one with all creation,
and maintaining a state of loving consciousness, then there is
nothing to fear. Because the universal fact of life, so to speak,
of being one with all life, becomes not only accepted
intellectually, but a deep felt knowing. Therefore the oneness
of all creation is accepted, no matter what the appearance of
the lifeforms are. Each lifeform, no matter how bizarre the
form may be compared to current Earthly awareness, when
one reaches that state of universal oneness and unconditional
love for all, then the fear dissipates. It is no longer a reality for

that particular person.

I have been told by the extraterrestrials that fear is the strong[e]
emotion that humans have. If they cannot understand someth[i]
they color it with fear to make it fit into their mind's framewo[r]
With understanding of the experience fear vanishes. This has be[en]
the platform of my work with people who think they have had
called "unpleasant" experiences. When they can understand what h[as]
occurred they can integrate it into their present life and live with
rather than fear and retreat from it.

I think it is quite remarkable that two men a world apart cou[ld]
come up with an identical scenario without knowing the informati[on]
I had been accumulating from all over the world. I think this ad[ds]
validity.

***

A session that was expected to be a normal one for therapy, w[as]
conducted while I was speaking at the Laughlin UFO Conference
Nevada in 2000. During my initial interview I always make a list
questions that the subject wants to find the answers to. This way I c[an]
give them as much help as possible and they can get the most benefit o[ut]
of the session. In many of these cases the answers are not what I wou[ld]
normally expect. When working with the subconscious I have learn[ed]
to keep an open mind and continue to ask questions as the objecti[ve]
reporter, even though the session goes in an unexpected directio[n]
With my insatiable curiosity I am open to any new information, [no]
matter how strange.

Lee was a young woman in her early forties, and we had just go[ne]
through a past life and were making the connections with her prese[nt]
life with the help of her subconscious.

D: *Is there a connection between that lifetime and the present o[ne]*
   Lee is living?
L: Yes, but it's gradual. Nothing happens in one lifetime. I don[']t
   like the slowness. That life was showing her it's all right to
   stand up for what you think is right. It's all right to be alon[e]
   It doesn't really matter that we're alone. We just think we ar[e]
   We're never alone really.
D: *She has some questions she would like to ask. In her prese[nt]*
   life as Lee she never married, and has refrained from sex. S[he]
   wanted to know the reason for that.
L: Part of me didn't come from this reality. A part of me that's
   here now is not from this time, and is not from this space. I[t]
   doesn't understand sex as sex is understood on this planet.

It doesn't understand time as time is understood on this planet. This planet is extremely slow, and very, very difficult to be in. And that part of me has come here on its own, and I don't have help here for this.

D: *What part are you talking about?*

L: We're all parts. We're never just one part. It came here as light. The light already knows. The light comes here completely pure, and it's a very strange experience to be here, but it's okay. It can be adjusted to.

D: *But Lee has had many physical lives on Earth, hasn't she?*

L: Yes, but that's only part of her. She's never been just Lee. That's just a belief system. It's more than that. It's not male, it's not female. It's light. It's understanding of a different type. There are no words in the vocabulary for this. It's new.

D: Her soul is the same soul that's gone through all these lifetimes and learning the experiences. Isn't that true? (Yes) Are you talking about something else that has come in?

I was thinking of the little glowing light beings that Bartholomew ɔke with, who were volunteering to come and help. (Section One)

L: (She had difficulty trying to express it.) Time doesn't exist at all. Time is not. Time is only in your dimension, in this dimension here. It doesn't exist the same anywhere else. It's very slow. It's very hard to express in this. It needs clarification.

D: *But we are trapped in this system of time in this reality. (Yes) This part that is different, that doesn't understand these things, where did that part come from?*

L: It comes from... not from stars. Not from your solar system. It doesn't come from your belief in a solar system, because that's what all the dimensions here are. It's just what you need for your learning.

D: *For our reality.*

L: Yes. You create masters. You create teachers. Those are only creations.

D: *But they help us learn.*

L: Yes. They're here for that purpose.

D: *Where does the other part come from?*

L: The other part is beyond... it's not out somewhere. It's not here, it's not there. It is. It's a vibratory rate, but it's not a vibratory rate. It's so far beyond that, that there are not words to express it. It has to be felt. It is beginning to be felt on this planet, but it's taken so long.

D: *This part, how does it become a part of her?*

L: Releasing old concepts, old ideas. Being able to reunite wi
it. It's been there. It's always been there. But we tie ourselv
up when we're on this planet. And when we tie ourselves u
we can't see it.

D: *I'm trying to understand. Does this part take over?*

L: It has nothing to take over. It is. It just is. There is no taki
over. We think we're being controlled. That's what's wron
on this planet. We're always afraid of being controlled by
something or somebody, but we're never controlled. This i
the illusion of it. We have never been controlled. We only
think we are.

D: *But if it's always been here, why aren't other people aware
it?*

L: It doesn't have words. It doesn't have location. It doesn't ha
sound. It doesn't have anything that can be recognized. It'
totally silent, and yet it's totally powerful. And it's just... ve
slow. (Sigh) It's been taking so many lives. Time on this plar
is not even correct. The history books don't have it correct
Time is just not what we have been led to think it is.

D: *You said it didn't take over. How does this part attach itself
the physical person? (Pause) Or is that the right word?*

I was still thinking that the part she was describing was somethi
separate from her soul or personality as we perceive it. The m
logical conclusion would be a type of possession by some enti
Other investigators have reported cases of this, but in all my years
work I have never found anything of this type.

L: The physical is only here. Here it is not even in the time frar
that you think it is. The life span is not even in the time frar
that you think it is. It's all. All, but we have planned to go
through it. People go through this, but it's not all of who we
are.

D: *You said this is a part of her. Is this another part of everyon
(Yes) All humans have this other part?*

L: There's gradations of it. Everyone has it, but not everyone
will see it.

D: *They won't know it's there? (Yes) What about masters or
spiritual teachers? Are they aware to a greater degree than
others?*

L: Some of them.

D: *But this part in Lee is more predominant in this lifetime and
that's why she never married? (Yes) In other lifetimes it wo
not as predominant? (No) I was thinking that if it is more
predominant in this lifetime, when did this part enter or*

become attached to her body, but you mean it's been there all along.

L: It doesn't happen in a sequence of events. It's there. It's not in this linear time frame. And that's why it seems that it attaches itself, but it doesn't. There is just so much. There are worlds and worlds of information. And none of it is limited to birth and death. Birth to death is a very small part of this. And it really doesn't matter. We think it matters. It does and yet it doesn't. It's just a little tiny, tiny flicker. And the other part is the most important, but it's not limited. This is the hardest part to describe. You can't describe something that is unlimited.

D: *That's true. Would this part be the equivalent of God, as we know it?*

L: We don't know God. We think we do, but we don't. God is so vast. God is a name we've given for ultimate power that goes beyond the galaxies. It goes beyond anything that minds can conceive of.

D: *Is this other part connected with that, or is it separate?*

L: No, it's connected with it.

I was really trying hard to understand this foreign concept, so it was difficult to think of questions that would extract more information.

D: *So it's like an all encompassing energy or power. (Yes) And it is in everyone, or there?*

L: It's there.

D: *But not everyone is aware of it.*

L: Yes. Bodies are more loosely put together than can be imagined. We look at them as solid, but they aren't, from other standpoints. From other realities they are not. Sometimes people are frightened of this, but it's not something to be frightened of. The universe is right in its way of doing things.

D: *Why are people afraid of it?*

L: Because they don't see far enough. It has nothing to do with seeing with the eyes. You can't reach it. You can't reach the end of the universe. You can't reach the end of anything, because there is no end. And words, the language... the genetic structure of the body doesn't contain it yet. It has hints of it, but it doesn't contain it. We're not separate from it. It's there for us, but we have separated ourselves into individuals to experience this. There's no experience that's wrong.

D: *Everything has a purpose or a lesson. (Yes) But we all have individual souls, don't we?*

L: A soul is a much larger concept that we can envision by calling it "individual". We can be individual at one moment, and we

can be a vast soul at another moment. And there's no divisi
of time in that. That goes from one to the other.

D: *I like to think of an individual spirit having experiences and
learning lessons.*

L: Spirit goes out and learns lessons through individual sparks
and it returns with all the knowledge of those experiences.

D: *It does this and becomes part of this larger soul? (Yes) An
that larger soul is equivalent to God?*

L: It's equivalent to what we think of as God, because we have
not understood God. It's too vast. We have to put perimete
We make our own hierarchies in order to understand.

D: *We conceive of God as the Creator of everything that we
know. Is that correct?*

L: We are also that creator. We are not separate from God. W
are all part of the same creation. There is no division.

D: *With that understanding, I've told people they can create
anything they want in the physical, can't they?*

L: No, because there are bindings here. There are ways of
learning here that we are experiencing. Yes, in one way we
could, and in another way we have chosen not to. It's choic
to go this way.

D: *We put limitations on ourselves.*

L: We've put limitations on for this experience.

D: *But this other part does not manifest in most people's lives t
cause their lives to be different. Is that true?*

L: This is what they are, but they can't touch it with their five
senses. There is not the capacity yet, even in the brain, to
begin to understand this properly. What's happening is that
it's changing. There is not the circuitry in the brain to hand
this. There never will be in the human brain as it now exist
This is changing.

D: *How is it changing?*

L: There is ahead of us a leap. It is not gradual. There is a lea
but not every one will make that leap. Some will, some will
not. But that does not mean they are left behind. They are ju
on a different route. It's an upgrading of ability that it's tim
for. Many things are changing right now on the planet. The
are many problems brewing under the surface of the ocean
and the ground. We've created it for the experience. And it
not something to fear. It can cause fear, but....

D: *Everything happens for a reason.*

L: Yes, it does.

D: *But you said the circuitry in our minds, our brains, is
changing?*

L: We will be able to handle more. We will never know it all. There is no ending.

D: *How is this happening?*

L: For a long time the human brain was stagnant. It did not and could not go any further. There have been upgradings done. Just as computers are upgraded, human brains are upgraded too. It is taking place. It's a new bridging of circuitry.

D: *Is this on a genetic level?*

L: The cells are changing. The genetics are changing. (As though watching something.) Oh, I don't know what those are! The cells are changing. The genetics are changing. There is more capacity. People think their brains have to grow larger in order to have more capacity. They don't. They just have to be... it's a different wiring. It's a different configuration.

D: *They always say we don't use all of our brains anyway.*

L: We don't.

D: *Is this something that was automatically programmed into our circuitry, or is it something that is occurring from outside?*

L: It was placed there originally to see how it would develop. It could only take place when certain changes have happened in the atmosphere on the planet. You have to watch the young children for this. Some of them. Not all of them, but some of them, very much. Young children have something new that has not been seen before. They won't see it on x rays, on any type of equipment like that. It's a new development. We all have the capacity for it. Not everyone yet, but it's there.

D: *So it's turning up gradually in the adults too? (Yes) But it was something that was put in our bodies when we were created?*

L: There was hope for it to develop, but twice it's failed. Then it was restarted, and it seems to at last have taken hold.

D: *I have been told that extraterrestrials are the ones who created our physical body. Are they the ones who programmed this into our system? (Yes) You said it has failed twice. (Yes) Can you tell me about that? Is that in our history?*

L: It was before written history, to begin with. There isn't a written history for this in the beginning. Then again your whole history's wrong. So much of it's wrong. It's been rewritten. It's been falsely written. It's not correct.

You don't say something like that to me without peaking y interest. I am always looking for "lost" knowledge, especially owledge that has incorrectly come down to us. I am always searching r the "true" version.

L: It feels it was a failing in planning. Something wasn't allow for.

D: *You mean something unexpected occurred? (Yes.) Was mankind developing too fast?*

L: They were developing in the wrong direction. Man would have developed too quickly for the planet that was housing him. There were mistakes made. It would have caused an imbalance too early in the system.

D: *Too much too soon? (Yes) And that was before the time of recorded history?*

L: Yes. They had to make changes.

I wondered whether she was talking about Atlantis. I have be told that mankind developed his mind potential to a very high degre but then he misused it so the ability was taken away. This was at t time of the destruction of Atlantis. It was said that the abilities wou return in our time period if we were at the stage when we could u them wisely.

D: *What happened at the second time?*

L: There was a split off. The Bible doesn't have it right about races going in different directions. That's not correct information. (She seemed frustrated, apparently having difficulty about how to word it.) The history of this planet will never be known through the writings that are on this planet now. Those writings have not been correct. There a hints, but they've not been correct.

D: *That's what I'm trying to do in my work, restore lost knowledge.*

L: Some of it was taken away. Some of it was deliberately lost. Some of it was buried. And there is a return of it now, but it's fragmented. And it's the fragments that you have to look for. And the fragments come bit by bit. They don't con all in one piece. And the fragments will be hidden in the brai of some of the people that you work with in the future.

D: *And I have to put these together? (Yes) But you said it spli at the second time when it didn't work? Can you explain tha*

L: There was a genetic experiment done that did not work properly. And it made confusion. The Bible wrote about tha in the story of the Tower of Babel. That was a genetic experiment that was not completely accurate.

D: *So the mind at that time was trying to expand?*

L: Yes. It couldn't do it. It fragmented. It lost its ability to comprehend properly, and divided itself.

D: *And then everything had to start again? (Yes) Although not all the way back to the beginning.*

L: No. In another form.

D: *And now we are reaching the point again? (Yes) And they think it will work this time?*

L: Yes. It's coming together. But it's in such a different way, that people are not looking for it in the right direction. We're becoming overbalanced in our technology, and that's where the largest problem lies. The spiritual has not been emphasized enough. Religion is nothing, but spirituality is everything. And there's an overbalance, and the planet loses its balance when the balance is off. The mind, the body, the spirit goes out of balance. So does the planet. We are responsible for that.

D: *So at this time the extraterrestrials have triggered it again to work in the right direction?*

L: Yes, it's been triggered. But they can only do so much, because we have our lessons to learn.

D: *Yes, that's true. When it is triggered, is it done through these sightings and interaction with them?*

L: Yes, it's in many different ways that it comes about.

D: *But this is something that we need for this time period?*

L: Yes. It's always been there to be used.

D: *And they think now we're coming to the time when we can open up more capacity.*

L: Yes. But if it happens too fast there is not the circuitry to take care of it. Circuitry is not even the best use of language for that. There are things in the brain that a doctor cannot see. An x ray cannot tell you. None of these things.

D: *But circuitry is a word we understand. (Yes) So we have to use analogies and words that we can comprehend, otherwise it's too hard to explain to people.*

L: Yes. It has no words. It has no understanding. When you look into the darkness of the ocean, you can't throw light down there. You just cannot. You will disturb what's already settled there. There are those that need it. And those that need to swim in the dark. And their whole lifeform would be destroyed and totally ruined, if that was done. It cannot be done quickly, although jumps do take place. Leaps can take place, but only when the circuitry is there and in place, and when the balance is there. The planet is in a desperate state right now. The planet is not stable at all. There are people walking around with no conception of what is happening to them, or happening to their brains, to their bodies under the increased heaviness of the vibrations and the plasma. Plasma? Something about a plasma vortex. I don't understand. There's a plasma vortex of some sort that's influencing this. There is no good or bad here. There's just experience. But we have that ability with us to be balanced. There's a combination of an electrical magnetic stimulation on different portions of the brain which could not be discovered until this time in history. In the time that can bring it out. Before this it would not have been ready. It can reopen circuitry that has been closed. If you look at your pyramids you will find an image of what is now happening on the planet. But you have to look deeply at the history of the pyramids to find that corroboration. It's there but it's not written on the walls. What is now happening at this time is a reordering of the circuitry of the brain. Egypt knew this. They had a different system of bringing it out. Their system was rudimentary to what can now occur on the planet. Although their system was aided by extraterrestrial life. If anyone says it was not true, it was true. As it was, they had an upgrading. There have been similar upgradings throughout the planet in different areas.

D: *But sometimes it was too soon. Is that what you mean?*

L: Most of the time it happened when it should happen. But again we're on the edge of imbalance. But the imbalance is not just planetary. It's surrounding the planet. It's the thinking, it's the misuse of environmental balance. We have all that knowledge, but we've destroyed it. We've subjugated it. We've lost a lot of it.

D: *We have to start all over again.*

L: Something's being done on the East coast of the United States. It won't be immediate, but it's in some laboratories now. It's in Virginia.

D: *New technology or what?*

L: Yes. It's the beginnings. Still there's a new technology.

D: *One thing I've been told. Our physical age doesn't matter, does it?*

L: It has nothing to do with it. Our age is about to be expanded anyway. Not by many years as yet. We have a lot of work to do yet before that can happen.

In this case I learned that not only was the genetic makeup of the human body being changed to withstand disease and age, but the brain was also undergoing developments and expansion. The mention of children showing this amazing development at a young age has already been documented. There are several books on the subject, and testing is being done in some parts of the country. Children are being born with the advanced circuitry already in place. The adults are the ones that will have to catch up.

This strange concept of a part speaking to me that was separate om the client, yet an integral part of them was difficult for my human ind to comprehend. Yet I have since found other cases, and one is ported in the last chapter.

***

More information of this type came through Phil in 1999. I had t had a session with Phil for a few years. After working for a while California he was living back in Arkansas at this time and came to e UFO Conference in Eureka Springs. Harriet was present during is session. She was also delighted to see him after such a long time.

I used the office building method that Phil was accustomed to and hen the elevator door opened he saw the familiar brilliant white light at was often present during our sessions. There was someone ready d waiting to take us where we needed to go for information.

P: He says the information is being given at this time, because it's time for the human race to understand the ignorance that has caused them to be so fearful for many, many, many years. Knowledge, awareness, and understanding can allow people to express themselves more fully and completely, and to not close off portions of their reality due to fear and ignorance. He's saying you're being given a key which will allow you to access these areas of information which have been inaccessible for many eons. The understanding of who we are and where we came from had so completely changed, that there was no basis for this knowledge to be comprehended. But in these times of spiritual awakening and uplift the true history and genetic reality of the human race can be once again more completely and fully understood in its entirety.

D: *You said they were going to give me the key?*

P: There are those who are your counterparts on the spiritual plane who are working with you. As well as in you, to further this endeavor which you have undertaken. Not just this particular episode in which we are speaking now, but the entire effort to bring the knowledge and awareness to the masses. This key will allow you access to certain areas of information which have as yet been unavailable to those who would endeavor to research the history and reality of the human species.

D: *We have several things we are interested in right now. We've been getting information concerning the DNA of the human body, that something is happening to it, and changing. Can you tell us anything about that?*

P: Certain changes are being made which are allowing certain functions of the body to become enhanced. The human mod is being somewhat manipulated in order to enhance its survivability and ability to resist and withstand certain environmental challenges. This is necessary in order for the human body to be able to tolerate certain atmospheric conditions on other planets, and in other conditions. The bod prototype which you are wearing can be used in many other places throughout the universe. And so this physical body i being adapted to be able to survive certain planetary condition which are different from your own.

D: *Does this mean that these human bodies will go to other planets?*

P: That is accurate. There will be the use of these genetically engineered bodies on other planets, which will be inhabited l souls who have chosen that sphere to allow them to participa in their spiritual duties.

D: *I've been hearing that something is definitely occurring wit. the DNA of the bodies that are living now.*

P: There are many changes which have been introduced throug environmental conditions on your planet, not genetically manipulated. There have been many changes in your environment which have caused changes in your physiologic expression. The reaction to these chemicals and energies in your atmosphere and environment have mandated these changes in your body. The body is simply reacting to these stimuli.

D: *You mean as though the immune system is adapting or reacti in some way?*

P: That is accurate. The adaptability to meet its environment and to make changes automatically was programmed into th human expression at its creation. There are those lifeforms which do not have this automatic adaptability built in, and a therefore dependent on outside manipulation in order to change. The human body however has been given an ability automatically adapt to its environment such that close manipulation is not necessary. The bodies are simply reactir to these changes in your environment.

D: *If the bodies did not adapt, would the body die?*

P: There would be less tolerance as the environment changed, and became perhaps more challenging to the body. The bod would become less and less able to tolerate it. And so as the conditions further changed there would be less resistance to the environmental challenges. And yes, the bodies would at some point not be able to sustain in the environment.

D: *So what is happening to our environment is poisoning the body and forcing it to adapt?*

P: That is accurate.

D: *So if it didn't change then it wouldn't survive.*

P: Assuming that the environment did not change to a more harmonious state. For with the removal of the challenges the body would have learned and patterned its defenses in order to be able to withstand. If these challenges were removed the body would change back again to adapt to the environment in which it found itself.

D: *I've been told there are some extraterrestrials that look human but are not really human because their internal organs have learned to adapt to many different environments.*

P: That is accurate.

D: *So we are going along that path?*

P: That is accurate.

D: *I have been told that was one of the reasons we would have difficulty traveling and living in space is because our bodies can't adapt at this time.*

P: We would say that "at this time" is the key. We're aware that these changes do indeed take time. However the manipulation can be done through successive generations in order to allow a quite capable tolerance to many different kinds of environment.

D: *Or can it occur quickly in one body in one generation?*

P: Depending on the particular change needed, it could be accomplished in fact in one generation. However, more radically different changes would require a much longer time frame, in order to allow these changes to occur naturally.

D: *Like a form of evolution, although speeded up.*

P: That is accurate.

D: *Is everyone changing? Or is it just certain groups, certain people?*

P: All humans living at this time on this planet are experiencing environmentally caused changes to their immune systems. The other changes we speak of are not environmental, but are intentional genetic manipulations. However, the genetic manipulation is being controlled within a certain population that has been selected, because of previous generational... (had difficulty finding the correct word)... harvesting, perhaps would be one way to phrase it. However, we are sensitive of your moral conditioning toward "harvesting" in a conventional sense.

D: *Our use of words.*

P: That is accurate.

D: *So if certain groups or certain people have been selected, t
genetic manipulation is not occurring to everyone?*

P: That is accurate. Manipulation is caused from within the
womb at the period of conception. And so as this being grow
and becomes a producing, or breeding, or perhaps breeding
capable, each successive generation is then slightly altered
propagate the desired change. This is a generational endeav
in that each succeeding generation is slightly different from
the previous.

D: *Would these selected people be different in some way that th
average people would notice?*

P: The breeding and manipulation that is being done on your
planet is not what you would call "noticeable" from one
generation to the next. However, if you could compare
perhaps ten generations side by side, or the numbers of ten
generations removed, there would be a more noticeable chan
in physiological, emotional and spiritual components.

D: *Of course, most people would say that was because of the
difference in the food, and the advances our medical scienc
have made.*

P: And there would be changes based on those stimuli. Howev
the changes which we speak of here are much more subtle
than you would notice due to environmental or social change

***

This session occurred while I was speaking at a UFO Conferen
in Clearwater, Florida in November 1999. Marie talked to me aft
arriving at the conference, and showed me some strange writing s
had done while I was lecturing. She said she does this strange writi
all the time, and has no idea what it means or why she is writing it.
thought it would be a good idea to put her together with a woma
met the previous year at a UFO conference in Wisconsin. The writi
looked strangely similar. Another woman had given me sampl
of what she called alien writing, but it looked more like scrawl
automatic writing, because it was in English.

Marie wanted to have a session, and one of the things she want
to explore was why she was compelled to do the strange writing. S
had also had an unusual experience the year before while attending t
Gateway course at the Monroe Institute in Virginia. This is an intensi
course for those who want to learn how to consciously accomplish O
of the Body travel, remote viewing, and how to use their minds
remarkable ways.

The session was held in my hotel room at the conference.
started normally enough. When she entered the deep trance state

468

turned her to the time of the incident. She was standing outside of
e Institute and then was entering the building, but it soon became
vious that she was describing something else besides the normal
rroundings that should have been there.

M: I'm entering the building... I see all of the wood, and the
fabrics around. I'm checking out the atmosphere. Possibly
seeing if I'm not sure what I'm looking for seeing... I'm seeing
through the air. I'm seeing more than I normally see.
D: *What do you think of that place?*
M: That it's not what I thought. It's bigger, and there's more going
on. I am almost overwhelmed by the vastness of the space
contained in there.
D: *You thought it was only going to be a small group with your*
program.
M: I guess so.
D: *And there are other things going on?*

I thought she meant there were other programs with other
rticipants occurring at the same time. It soon became apparent that
e was not describing the physical entrance to this building. She was
eing something in this trance state that had not been visible to her
ysical eyes, but which was not hidden from her subconscious. Was
e able to see into another dimension?

M: There's a hole as I'm seeing it now. It's like a canyon or a
portal.
D: *What do you mean?*
M: That's all I can sense when I look. I'm walking in and suddenly
the physical space disappears and a different kind of space is
in its place. And it's vast. And it's clear.
D: *You mean instead of the walls and the rooms, there's something*
else there?
M: Right. Like that was a false structure. There's a stage for
physical understanding, for some comfort for the physical
being.
D: *Are there other people there also?*

I was wondering if the other people who were arriving to take the
urse were seeing the same thing.

M: I don't see any people in this room now. And they're supposed
to be there. I'm getting a sense of incredibly highly charged
"stuff" in this vast space. I don't see beings. Once I walked
in, what I thought was the physical reality that I was about to

experience, now that I can see it from here, it's an illusion o
what it really is. And there is an opportunity to shift from
knowing and relating in three dimensions to existing in mo
than the third dimension.

D: *But at the time you didn't sense this consciously, is that wh
you mean?*

M: Right. I did not know that until just now. And it is very rea
and very physical in its own sense, but not as we know it.

D: *What kind of a program are you going to be studying there?*

M: About light.

My next sentence was completely blanked out. It shifted so f
away I could barely hear some words. With the following senten
the sound returned to normal. This sometimes happens when doi
this type of work, and the tape recorder almost seems to be affecte
by bursts of energy. She was breathing heavily, and seemed to b
experiencing some type of discomfort. Was she also picking up tl
same energy that affected my recorder? I gave her suggestions for we
being, and asked her what was affecting her.

M: I don't know. (Heavy breathing.) It's being most totally, ar
it's a shock.

D: *Why do you think it would affect you that way?*

M: Because it's so different. So much about the other energies
that we house.

D: *In our bodies, you mean?*

M: Partly in our bodies, but it's beyond our bodies. Our bodies
are like little grounding devices, because of this dimensiona
thing.

D: *What does this place look like?*

M: It doesn't look like I thought. It doesn't look like the wood
and the fabric.

D: *I mean, does it look like a building?*

M: The real institute does that you walk into.

D: *But what you're seeing now.*

M: No. I'm on a balcony, a very tall balcony. And there is a
balcony there in the physical. But this is much broader, and
it's like crystal. There's lots of crystal. I'm looking down in
the center of the room. And it's quite illuminating and brea
taking and shocking. It's an overlay. There's something
existing as well as the physical.

D: *That's a good word for it, an overlay.*

Could it be possible that the Monroe Institute is actually locate
over some type of interdimensional doorway or portal that is invisib

our conscious senses? This may partially explain some of the
remarkable events that occur there.

D: *Are you alone?*
M:(A whisper.) I'm alone. There's my physical body that feels
very standing up and isolated and... like it hasn't shifted over
yet. And now that I'm moving ahead in this, I see that I'm
being asked to let go and shift from my physical. It's very
beautiful.

She became emotional and started crying.

D: *What's the matter?*
M:(Emotionally) It's so pretty. (Crying)

Marie was an artist. One of the things she wanted to find out about
was why she was unable to paint anymore. She had no inspiration.
So I suggested that she would be able to remember the scene she
was looking at and be able to recreate it in a painting.

M:(Emotional and in awe.) I could try. Yeah.
D: *Most people would never realize there was something that*
beautiful there, would they?
M:No, they couldn't see it. I couldn't see it. I couldn't know it
before now.
D: *Let's allow you to keep the memory of the picture in your*
mind so you can paint it. And we can get it as exact as we can.
M:(Tearfully) I want to. I want to.

I gave the subconscious suggestions so she would be able to retain
the memory and use it later. Seeing such a beautiful scene was affecting
her emotionally. Although this was an unexpected development I
wanted to move forward and explore the unusual event that occurred
at the Institute. She remembered seeing a beautiful light while sitting
in a dark isolation booth with earphones on her head.

D: *I know it's hard to leave that place because it is so beautiful,*
but we want to explore some other things. Let's leave that
scene, and let's move to the time when you had the strange
experience with the light. And you were listening to some
tapes?
M:(The emotion and the crying stopped.) In a small box.
D: *Are the tapes music?*
M:They're vibrations.
D: *You're listening through earphones?*

M:Right. You're by yourself with earphones.

D: *In a room by yourself?*

M:A tiny box. You sleep and listen to tapes and ....

D: *You sleep in there?*

M:Yes, it's an isolation booth that you sleep in.

D: *Does it bother you being closed in like that?*

M:No, I like it. It's where I can meet them.

D: *Meet who?*

M:I don't know. These very smart beings.

D: *All right. As you were listening to the sound vibrations through the earphones something happened, didn't it? (Yes) We can go through that again and see it in more detail. Wh happened first?*

M:I got scared.

D: *Why?*

M:Because I'd never felt anything like this. God!! It feels like this incredibly benevolent pure love. It comes to you, and yo can't believe it. (Emotional) You can't believe it's with you And you can see it.

D: *This is caused by listening to the earphones?*

M:It opens up an opportunity to be so open, and to meet with th right frequency.

D: *You have to be open to doing this, with no blocks, or what?*

M:You have to long for it on some level.

D: *Then what happens?*

M:Then it gained my trust. The white light. And stabilized me It hooked with me, so I wouldn't be afraid.

D: *Just the white light?*

M:At first. And then when I was stable I felt more vibration nex to my left side. It startled me because it was so different fror the white light. And somehow I was directed to turn my hea and look. It was all dark in this space, but I could look, I coul see and feel. Shimmering. It's a space being. I didn't know that. You can almost see into it, but it's the clearest blue. Deer clear blue. You can more feel it than see it.

D: *Why do you say it's a space being?*

M:I don't know. That just came out.

D: *Could you see any features or anything that might make you think that?*

M:Just deep blue. I don't know where this comes from. It's jus a sense that it comes from a star. It feels right in my heart when I say that.

D: *What was the first white light you saw?*

M:It was a direct of God. It wasn't God, but it pretended to feel like the love of God. But it was an intelligence that was guiding this connection between me and this being. It knew about human emotions so much that it could intensify the best and safest emotions that we know. And provide that, in order for the linkup to happen.

D: *And the other blue light, or whatever it is, came at that time and came next to you?*

M: Into me.

D: *Into you. Did you have to allow it to come into you?*

M: Yes. It waited for me to acknowledge it. And then in the gentlest, slowest, most easy manner, it just glided, like an overlay. It vibrated, and I feel like that now. It was just vibrating. And I think it was changing me. It was reforming my system.

D: *Why was it doing that?*

M: For higher work. So I wouldn't be hurt and burned.

D: *How could you be hurt or burned?*

M: There's something that can burn us. This is protection. Radiation. Some kind of radiation experiments.

D: *And this is giving you a protection? Changing you, you said?*

M: Yes, at my cellular level. Starting on the physical cellular level, but it's also adjusting something to house more new systems for the future.

D: *New systems. What do you mean?*

M: New star seeds. For this planet. Systems that reside in the body, but they're not of the body.

D: *It is creating new systems in the body that weren't there before?*

M: It's seeding the system.

D: *This won't harm the body in any way, will it?*

M: No. Genetically I'm geared to help this transition. (She seemed elated.) It's complete. And it's alive. And it's safe.

D: *Where is this radiation coming from that might hurt people?*

M: From beneath the Earth. Now I see the core of the Earth. I just see a ball. It may even be some kind of radiation that gets injected into us, or put into us for some bad reason. And this blue system can alter you enough so this I want to say "core" material will be deactivated.

D: *Into our bodies, you mean?*

M: It can be, or it can be put in the core of the Earth. You could swallow it. (Emotional) That was painful to think about that.

D: *How could we get it into our bodies?*

M: You could swallow it. (Almost crying.) You could be forced. Like some kind of war. You can survive. (She was emotional.)

D: *Are there other ways it can get into the body?*

M: You could be bombarded, beamed with it. This blue light system would protect you, and you would not be hurt.

D: *Who would bombard the people with something like that?*

M: There's another race that would like the genetic material. A they could take it in this way. But this blue energy would render it impossible.

D: *Is this blue energy being used with other people also?*

M: Yes. Lots of people now. When it arrives, and when it's tim you'll be given a choice to accept it or not.

D: *Because not everyone can go to the Monroe Institute.*

M: No, it can happen other places.

D: *Is it something that happens and they don't realize it?*

M: They don't know what it's for. They think all this love that coming to them, and it's so good, it's so seductive, that of course you want this. And it's the only way it can fuse with your system, because you have to say "yes" with your heart

D: *Does it always happen on a conscious level where people remember it happening?*

M: Yes. And you know about the conscious exchange.

D: *But it sounds good because it's a way of protecting people.*

M: It's part of the bigger plan. There's going to be a big war.

D: *On Earth?*

M: It's going to involve people on Earth. There's red energy wi this other group. And it's very hot. And they won't win, bu they're going to try very hard to take what they want and nee

D: *But this will cause the radiation?*

M: Yeah, this group. It's their method.

D: *But everyone won't be open to this love energy, will they?*

M: No. They have to learn how to connect with their heart first before the opening and the infusion can happen.

D: *Because there are many people in this world that are very bitter, very negative.*

M: Right. And that will get in the way.

D: *What will happen to the people that don't have this protectio*

M: They'll wither. They'll fry. They won't be protected.

D: *So this protective energy is coming to more and more peopl on the Earth? (Yes) This is the plan, to have more people survive?*

M: Yes. The plan is.

D: *And why were you given this protection?*

M: Because I can speak. Because I'll be working with many people. And I tell them the right words at the right time. I w act as a key for them to open to receiving.

D: *Does this blue light have any connection with you doing yo healing work?*

She had recently begun doing this service.

M: (A revelation.) Oh, yes! You see, when I'm doing the healing work I am the blue light being. And I do to others what the blue light being did to me. I can transfer that to people. That's why they come to me.

D: *A while ago you called it a "seeding". They get the energy into people and they can transfer it to others.*

M: Yes, that's right. It's so one on one though. That's the hard part, but that's what I have to do for a while. It takes so much time to just do one at a time. This is my purpose. I think now that I've seen all of this, that I've been in contact more than I realized. I couldn't put it all together. I couldn't see the big picture.

A remark here. When she was talking about something being done the physical body to prevent radiation from harming it, it reminded of Karen's regression that was reported in *The Custodians*. In her ion that she was shown by the aliens, she was trying to help people o were dying all around her, yet she could not get sick herself. It med to be some type of radiation poisoning and nothing she could would help. It was heart breaking, and she was very uncomfortable ile watching the scene. Just before it she had seen a cloud over land and the water that did something, and poisoned the fish etc. ondered whether Marie's story of having something done to the ysical body to prepare them for just such a scenario, could have ne bearing on Karen's.

D: *We have another question. This strange writing that Marie has been receiving. Do you know anything about that?*

M: It's like rain. It's like light. It rains down through these channels around the world, the Earth. And if you look at it, it will change you.

D: *Is it a language?*

M: It is information. It's coming from a higher source that's caring for us, and watching our evolution.

D: *Why are they putting it into symbols?*

M: Because the symbols activate new patterns within the energy field itself.

D: *Just seeing the symbols?*

M: Right. The person can actually follow the pattern and identify the movement.

D: *Is this a language that someone somewhere speaks or writes?*

M: It has been spoken.

D: *So it is a language that someone somewhere understands?*

M: It's more like a mathematical type language, if you could imagine that.

D: *I've been told that some of the space beings use symbols. A this is how they transfer blocks of information, in symbols.*

M: It's not quite like the language that you know here, or even ancient scripts. It's not like that. It's a pattern. It appears wh it's two dimensional, as a language. But if you could see ea piece as a movement that activates a different part of the bei then you'd understand it better.

D: *Then when Marie is writing this, it doesn't say something l a page in a book? (No) So if I asked her to look at this pa she has written she wouldn't be able to tell me what it says. that correct?*

M: (Hesitant) You could try.

D: *All right. Let's let Marie open her eyes and look at the pap (I held the paper she had written in front of her.) Can you s the paper? Is it saying something in words?*

M: (As she studied the paper) Yes, it is, actually.

D: *How is it read? From which direction?*

M: (She motioned from the paper towards her eyes.) It comes t way.

D: *What do you mean?*

M: It's not this way, this way, this way. (Motions)

D: *Not up and down, nor does it go in succession.*

M: It's this way. It comes from the paper at you. It's giving information. It's almost like you put it here. (She put her ha over her heart.) And you feel it. And the best you can do sometimes is just look at it, and take it in here.

D: *But what information is it giving you?*

M: It's encouragement. And it's a way of knowing the straight course of your heart, knowing about the greatness.

D: *So when she writes this, is this another way of getting it int her body? (Yes) The same way that the blue light did?*

M: It's different, but in a way, yes, it's changing things there. E it's almost as if you can imagine light coming from each symbol, and changing you by its own radiation.

The example drawn by Marie looks more like fast handwriting shorthand. Since working with her I have received samples of stran writing from all over the world. This writing appears more structur (like printing). In all of the cases the people feel compelled to write t symbols. There appears to be no logic in their behavior. In Book Tv I will include these samples, and computer analysis to find similariti

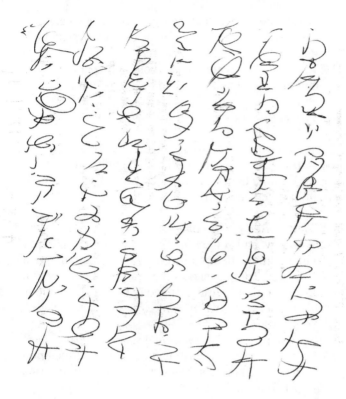

I took the paper away, and had her close her eyes again.

D: *Otherwise we would think of it like our writing, and we would expect it to say words. So it's okay if Marie continues to write these things.*

M: Yes. They're cleansing.

D: *They are supplying information in ways we could not imagine. (Right) We have one more question. She has had dreams in the past about operations. Can you tell her anything about that? Were they just dreams or what?*

Marie had vivid childhood memories of physical operations that ⸱re performed on her body, and going to see doctors. She could not derstand why her family denied that they had occurred. They said thing had ever been done to her.

M: I think that she knows. It was so clear, that it was all by agreement. And she had asked years ago, years ago to work with us.

D: *So they were not dreams? They were memories of things that happened?*

M: When she had reached the right age. They were adjustmen~ that were made, but it was done on the physical body.

D: *What were the adjustments for?*

M: To remove old patterns that would prevent her from movin~ into the work that she would be doing later. They had to be removed surgically.

D: *Surgically! All right.*

There was another unusual occurrence while Marie was at t~ Monroe Institute. She experienced a high pitched tone that seemed~ pierce right through her head. It lasted several seconds and was ve~ unpleasant. I asked about that.

D: *What caused the discomfort?*

M: She knew, and at the time she didn't want to accept it. It w~ a high tuning attempt to adjust the receptors in the templar lobes, to be able to access more information, and it had to b~ done in a group setting. It had to be done with the others.

D: *Were other people also being affected the same way?*

M: Yes, it was a plan.

D: *Were they giving information or taking information?*

M: No, it was just the adjustment of the part of the brain, but it's not the brain. The being that receives all information, a~ higher frequencies can now be accessed.

D: *It was so she could receive more information. (Yes) They were not taking anything away then. (No)*

If I was able to access this many cases within a year that spoke~ the manipulation of the human body, how many others are out there th~ have not been accessed? They said these changes were being done ~ tens of thousands of people all over the Earth. It may truly be simi~ to the Hundredth Monkey Syndrome, and will go unnoticed until t~ critical mass has been reached, and the reality of this phenomen~ cannot be denied.

I was still receiving more information about the changing~ the DNA structure of the human body as this book was going to t~ printers. This will be expanded upon in Book Two of *The Convolut~ Universe.* I originally thought I should hold this entire chapter so t~ material could be added, but I think this would delay the preparati~ of people's minds. They must be ready to understand the dramatic a~ dynamic changes that are coming.

CHAPTER FIFTEEN
THE MECHANICAL PERSON

This session was conducted in my hotel room in London in ptember 2000 while I was on a lecture tour in England. Johanna s a young woman who had only lived in England for two years. She s from Germany, but I thought her accent was perfect. She said she d a natural talent for languages and caught on very fast. She did not ve very many complaints, mostly curiosity. Some of her requests med trivial to me, but every person's problem seems important to m. She was even worried about having had some teeth pulled as hild. I thought it was the feeling of having to be perfect, but she d not see it quite that way. I had no idea of what to expect (as with eryone that comes for a session), but I certainly did not expect the st life that came forth. At the end I asked if she would allow me use the tape, because it was certainly a first. And at this point in research I thought I could not be surprised any more. Every time nake that assumption something new comes to me to once again allenge my thinking. She made a copy of the tape and sent it to my tel later.

I used the cloud method which normally takes the person to an propriate past life when they descend from the cloud. Once again I is to be surprised.

D: *Tell me the first thing that you see as you drift down to the Earth.*

J: Actually I'm not drifting to the Earth. I'm drifting somewhere else. I'm drifting down on a sort of grayish planet. It looks strange, metallic. It gives me a strange feeling. Very odd. Not so nice.

D: *Why does it bother you?*

J: It feels very cool. And it's not soft like the cloud. It's hard.

D: *What does it look like beneath your feet?*

J: It's sort of stony. Stone, it's dust as well. And there is no grass at all, nor anything like plants. At least where I am at the moment. It's gray and metallic as well. There seem to be buildings of some sort on the surface of the planet. They're in the distance, but I could walk over there if I wanted to.

D: *What do the buildings look like?*

J: Asymmetric. It's like half a roof sort of thing. You know, you take a house and it has a very steep roof, and you cut t[...] in half, then you get the sort of building I mean. It has a v[...] straight front, and little windows, if that's what they are. Th[...] may be air holes or something, I don't know.

D: *Do all the buildings look alike?*

J: I can see only a few at the moment, and these look like tha[...] Everything else is stone, and mountains, small mountains.

D: *In the background?*

J: Yeah, and where I am as well.

D: *Is it bright out?*

J: No, it's not bright.

D: *I was wondering if there was a Sun.*

J: No, I can't see a Sun. It's more darkish. You can see everythin[...] but it's not bright.

I then asked her to look down at her feet so I could find out wh[...] she looked like. She gasped, and seemed to be totally surprised [...] what she saw. It was totally unexpected to her.

J: It's troublesome for me to say, but I guess I'll have to say i[...] They're metallic. They're sort of horrible things like... if y[...] imagine the hooves of a horse, but pointed and very technic[...] That's my feet. (This made her very uncomfortable.)

I was also surprised, but I have learned to go with whatever t[...] subject sees, and try to think of questions, no matter how strange t[...] situation. There is always a reason for the subconscious choosing t[...] life they go into.

D: *That is strange, as though they are made out of some kind o[...] metal?*

J: Yeah. It feels like I'm sort of metallic myself. And the han[...] are a bit like that... they're sort of like claws, but there are on[...] two bits. You know, like the feet. It's like two pointed thin[...] like a hoof. And the hands are similar.

D: *Instead of having fingers or digits of any kind?*

J: Yeah. It doesn't feel human at all. I feel odd.

D: *Do you have any idea what your face is like? (Pause) I imagi[...] you can't see yourself, can you?*

J: I want to go to the lake and see myself in the water.

D: *Is there a lake near there?*

J: Yeah, I can go. (Pause) I walk in a funny way as if, like a [...] machine almost. It's different from how I am now in my bo[...]

in this life. I can see my arm which is a bit funny too, which affirms my shock. Actually it's like a metallic thing, the whole thing. And I walk over to this lake, and I make movements that are not smooth. I stagger over there and I look in the water.

D: *Stiff movements?*

J: Stiff, yes, and I feel sort of like a robot when they walk. Just move one side forward and the other side forward. Not very elegant actually. Even though the body is not too ugly, but I'll have a look at my face in a minute.

I gave instructions that it would not bother her to look at herself, matter how unusual it might be.

J: I have something like eyes, and they have the look like eyes, but... how they're setting in my face, it's more like a triangle. They're setting in a triangle.

D: *Instead of an oval?*

J: Yeah. The flat is on top, and the point is downward. They're quite nice eyes, that's a relief. They're strange, those dark eyes, and they seem to have a jelly like quality. But the rest of the face is metallic.

D: *Do you have a mouth or a nose?*

J: I have some sort of mouth, yeah, but it's more like an opening. Like a round little thing. And the nose... I'm not sure about a nose. There's sort of slits, slots. Very strange.

D: *Can you get any sense about what it's like on the inside of you?*

J: There's a lot of machinery going on there. Machinery.

D: *I was wondering if you had organs like humans.*

J: I seem to have things inside of me, yes. I don't know if they're organs or what they are. A lot of machinery. Actually there seems to be more machinery than anything else. I don't know if I have blood or anything like that. I'm... grayish, darkish ... a dark gray sort of metal.

D: *That's like the color of the whole planet, isn't it? Dark gray?*

J: Yeah. Even though there are variations on the planet. When you get closer there is white as well, white stone and also darker gray stone. And the buildings are very dark. They're sort of shiny gray. What do you call this metal which is so dark and gray? The house is shiny, reflecting. It's like the stuff they have on Earth, not like silver, but dark.

D: *Aluminum is bright, not dark. But no trees or grass or anything?*

J: No, no trees or grass, no.

D: *Do you think you live over there in that city where those buildings are?*

J: Yeah, I belong there somehow. That's where I've been ma

D: *Do you want to go over and see that place closer?*

J: Hmm, it is quite a distance.

D: *You don't have to walk. You can move very quickly.*

J: Yeah, I can go there. It's a huge city of these houses.

D: *It's bigger than you thought it was?*

J: No, that's a different place. The one where I saw the one two, that's just that. But I've moved to the other place wh I've been made. That's all sorts of shapes of houses, but al very shiny and gray and dark. And we can go underneath. can go into the planet. There are many things happening under the surface. The main thing is happening sort of in secret. It's underneath.

D: *Is that the part you're most familiar with?*

J: That's where I come from. That's where I've been made.

D: *How do you go down there?*

J: I just know how to go down. There are openings, but you just go through. It's not like doors. It's just because you w to go through, you go through. And you sort of not float do but glide down. There are many paths, and you just go dov like if you had a modern tube system where you just push through the air or something in a tube.

D: *Like paths or sidewalks?*

J: Yeah, but you don't really walk. You fall into it. You deci where you want to go, and that's where it pushes you.

D: *And you said you were made down in that area?*

J: Yeah. There's a lot of fire. And there are tables where they make things.

D: *Fire? You mean like welding or machines or....?*

J: Yeah, maybe welding. There are fireplaces where they deal with metal. And they make shapes. And there are other pla in another room where they do the interior.

D: *The different parts and everything?*

J: Yeah, the insides of it. It all works together.

D: *Can you see the people who are making these machines?*

J: Yeah. They are more fleshy in the face. And the rest of it I can't see because they're in a sort of plasticy protection clothing. They wear this clothing all over the body.

D: *Is this because of where they're working?*

J: Yes, it has to be very clean.

D: *What do they look like?*

J: (She appeared to be studying them.) Not like me. They ha softer faces, and they're quite pale. They look quite huma what we call "human". Pale and slightly pinkish. They have eyebrows, which I don't.

D: *Do they have hair?*

J: They have hair, yeah, and they have very extreme hair. Very light blond or completely black. I can't see any other color. Quite short. It's sort of slick, slickened back. I can see men, and they're quite good looking.

D: *Do you see any women or is it all men?*

J: I can't see any women at the moment, no.

D: *And these men are making these machines?*

J: Yeah, they're making us.

D: *Do you see others that look like you?*

J: No. I only see half ones. I mean, parts of that process.

D: *So they're in the process of being made. Why are they creating people... things like you? I don't know if I should call you a person or not. Why are they creating you?*

J: They want to experiment, and see if they can do it. They also use us for things which they don't want to do. Or they can't do, because it's too dangerous or something.

D: *Like servants or workers?*

J: Yeah, more like workers. Workers who have to do a certain task.

D: *It sounds like they have been experimenting for a while, because it worked real well, didn't it?*

J: Yeah. There's a great big space. And they're making new ones. I don't know why. I suppose we're wearing out after a while. We can't go on forever, so they need to make new ones. It's very strange.

D: *But is it all machines?*

J: It's all machines. There is something like a soul. That's what is so strange, because I have feelings as well. I'm not just a machine, you know.

D: *Are they able to put a soul, a spirit into these machines?*

J: I think they put part of theirs into it.

D: *What do you mean?*

J: They divide up theirs. They give us a little bit of theirs. So we're not them, but we're sort of functioning in their way.

D: *Otherwise you would be like a robot, a machine?*

J: Yeah. They want us to do the things right. Or to rely on our emotions as well as the task we have to do. We wouldn't be sophisticated enough to do it if we didn't have that piece. We'd just be programmed. But, as well as being very well equipped for the task with a metal body, we also need to do things where we need soulfulness somehow. And that was why they give us a little bit of theirs, because that's the only

way they... I mean they don't create souls. They don't have
that ability. Maybe God does it or somebody. But they don't
have a soul to give us. They can only do it by sacrificing a
little bit of theirs. And that's what they put into us.

This was the part I was having difficulty understanding. If she
went to a lifetime where she was a mechanical person, a machine
robot, how could she communicate with me? How could she have
feelings? A mechanical creation would not have a soul assigned to it
and a soul would not normally choose to enter it. This was a totally
new idea, that someone could give a machine a piece of their own soul
so it would be able to function more effectively in this alien world.

D: *Can you see how that's being done?*
J: I can see they do a ceremony. They get together and they sort
of "spit" it out, and put it into the machine when it's finished.
D: *What do you mean by "spit it out"?*
J: They seem to decide that they want to give a bit, and they spit
it from their mouth into the machine person.
D: *What does it look like when they spit it out?*
J: (Pause) I can't really see it. They put it into the machine
directly.
D: *You mean it's invisible?*
J: Yeah. Or like when you breathe out you don't really see
anything unless it's cold. That sort of thing.
D: *This... activates it?*
J: That just lets it go there. And that's what gives the feeling to
the machine. Without it it would be just a machine, and they
have to put in computer chips or things to make it do very
menial tasks. But they want more than that.
D: *Does it take anything away from them when they give it a*
piece of themself?
J: Yes, it takes away that piece of themself. They have to be
content with less. They have to give up a little bit of their
power to make things happen, which they want to happen.
Otherwise they wouldn't be able to do it.
D: *Do you think there would be any other way they could activate*
the machines?
J: No, they couldn't, no. They need a soul.
D: *Many times things are activated by the mind.*
J: Oh, no, it's not like that. They don't have this power of the
mind. They don't have that yet.
D: *But they're able to give it a little bit of themself, divide it off*
to activate the machine.

J: Yeah. That's what they can do. I mean, the machine will work with just the electricity or what they've got to stimulate the parts and everything. Because it's programmed, it would work. But it wouldn't work in this sophisticated way. So they decided they would make a little sacrifice, and put ten or twenty percent in. And they can still have their soul parts, which I guess they think is quite enough. So they give a little bit to the machine so it can act more accordingly.

D: *Does the machine think on its own and have an intellect?*

J: The machine has thinking power, yes. But of course it's programmed. It's only thinking because it's been programmed. It's been given all that by them.

D: *It can't go off on its own as an individual?*

J: No, no. It's only when it has the soul bit, it can react in a different way. That's the difference. It will still only do what it's supposed to do, but it has more variety in reacting.

D: *So it is not like a complete being that can function and think on its own like a human? (No, no.) But it gives it more abilities than a machine.*

J: Yes, that's right.

D: *More of a personality, I guess. (Yes) Well, as a machine can you talk? Can you communicate with them?*

J: No. We can talk, yes. It doesn't sound very nice. It's like it's language, but it doesn't sound pretty.

D: *Is that the way they communicate?*

J: No, they have nice voices, but we have only machine voices.

D: *So they do communicate verbally, in words.*

J: Yes, they can. They give us commands in words, as well as with the insides, the machinery. They can't simply think and we do it. They have to tell us.

D: *And you're able to communicate with them.*

J: All we say is "yes" or "understood" or something.

D: *So even though you do have a certain amount of intellect you can't communicate like a thinking human being.*

J: We're not supposed to. We could, but we're not supposed to. We're programmed to understand the task, and say "understood", and do it.

D: *Well, the individual who gave you a piece of its soul, of itself, does that individual feel any attraction to you, or connection?*

J: I think the only connection we have is that I know which one it is. I can see the face.

D: *I was thinking if it gave you a portion of itself it might feel connected to you in some way.*

J: It might, but I don't know that. I can't feel that. I know which one it was, and maybe I feel something for it, or with it or.... I can't say.

D: *Well, it's a different way of existing, isn't it?*

J: Yes, it's a strange way of existing.

D: *Do you have to consume anything? I am thinking of sustenance. How do you stay alive? As a machine, I think that's probably a strange question.*

J: We don't really eat anything. Also we don't go to toilet. W get something like a substance, like an oil, but that's only f the machinery. We don't get anything for the soul.

D: *How do they put the oil in you?*

J: They just put it where it's needed, little levers and holes wh you need regular oil. You know, it's like a car or something

D: *But at least they didn't want to just have machines. They wanted them to have more personality. (Yeah) But like yo said, it does wear out. And that's why they have to keep making more?*

J: Yeah, they really want to explore everything, and they nee many workers. Because of where they're going, they don't know the environment and what it's going to be like. And have to be stable against heat. Because if we have to go to a different planet where it's very hot, we have to be able to survive that, and not dry out. So the oil is sort of heat proo And our hands are heat proof actually. I realize now the fe are heat proof as well. Everything is heat proof.

D: *I would think metal would conduct heat, but I guess it's a different kind.*

J: It's a different kind. We don't have it on Earth. It just look on the outside like something we have.

D: *So they take you on their exploring of other planets.*

J: Yeah, they send us off for tasks, so we can see which planet conducive for whatever the purpose is.

D: *When they take you there, what do they take you in?*

J: Those round things which we travel in. And they put in the destination. We know they give it a little card, and insert th and that's the destination. So it transports us there.

D: *Do they go with you?*

J: No, no. They would never go with us. No, no. We have to do it. Because they have a skin, and they're pinkish. They wouldn't have any protection from light, because it's very intense light where we're going. That's why we have dark eyes. We also have special sunglasses. They are sunglasse which are... (confused, difficult to describe)... how do you s that? Like a thin, plasticy thing. But it has little holes in it, only a certain amount of light gets through. And all the rest dark. That's how we give ourselves extra protection.

D: *Is that a part of your eye?*

J: No, that's like something extra which we put on top. We put it over the eyes, like sunglasses almost.

D: *When you go to these places, they could also be very cold, couldn't they?*

J: They could be, yes.

D: *Can you function in any kind of temperature, any kind of environment?*

J: Yes, but we're especially made for the heat places.

D: *Well, see yourself being sent to one of these places. You said they put the card in the machine?*

J: Yeah. And we enter that and the capsule is closed, and the capsule goes where we're supposed to go. And it has to be rather heat proof as well, even more than we are somehow. Because otherwise it's not going to bring us back.

D: *They have to bring you back with information?*

J: Right. We have an automatic registration of information. It goes through the eyes.

D: *Does that record information in some way, like data or something? (Yeah.) What do you do when you get to the place?*

J: It lands there. We have to go through the heat. And travel around in the heat, and see what's underneath. And if there are people, or not, what there is.

D: *Like a heat barrier, you mean? (Yeah, yeah.) And you land there to see if there's life?*

J: And if there's life, and what kind. So they can be prepared in case they manage to go through the heat. So they can either possess the planet or explore it. And if not, they better not do it. So they get this kind of information.

D: *If it's the kind of place they could go to and survive.*

J: Yeah. And that's why we need the soul as well, because we can feel as well if it's pleasant, or if the people are good or bad.

D: *A machine wouldn't be able to do that. (No) A machine could record information, but it couldn't give them things that they need to know.*

J: Yeah. But there's also a disadvantage about it. Because we have soul okay, maybe it is only ten or twenty percent but we have it. Which means we have all the emotions which go with that. Which means we feel things like attraction amongst each other.

D: *You mean each other as a machine?*

J: Yeah. And maybe even with other creatures from other planets. There could be other ones which are similar enough

to create an attraction. And of course, we're not supposed
live or feel that. We don't have any reproduction organs.
They've blocked that. They made us, but we feel all the
feelings. That's very strange.

D: *That's one of the disadvantages?*

J: Yes, because we suffer from that. And also for them it's
something they don't understand. They have to deal with i
when we come back. And we don't want to do our task,
because we've met somebody. It is very difficult.

D: *Because that part of the soul has an attraction, a feeling.*

J: (Sadly) They actually are very cruel to us, because they pro
to us that there is no hope. And they do things with our bodi
funny things. Because we think there might be a chance if th
give us something inside. If they make it proper, we could
actually do this. We could have connections like they have.
We could be in love, and have a family and stuff, but they
are not prepared to do that. On the contrary, they laugh. Th
do things with me. You know, they put something through,
like a screw driver, and they say, "Look, there's nothing in
It's ridiculous. It's just metallic. You don't have anything.
There can't be any feeling." But it's like a phantom pain. \
have it, because we think we have something that is fruitfu
there, because of the soul part. They probably don't quite
realize what it must be like. And they think, "Oh, they're j
machines." But we aren't. We have all the needs. It's only
to a minor degree maybe, a lesser degree, but in our own w
we have these needs. And they don't allow us to live it.

D: *So they didn't realize they were also handicapping you by
giving you these feelings.*

J: I think they had no idea.

D: *But like you said, they're still experimenting.*

J: That's true, they're experimenting, and they didn't really
realize what could happen.

This made me think of references to recent movies and TV shov
In "Bicentennial Man" Robin Williams was a robot that evolved to t
point he was indistinguishable from a human, with all the feelings a
emotions. Also in a "Star Trek, Next Generation" episode when D<
was to be disassembled, and had to prove that he was really almo
human. In both cases "normal" human beings could not believe th
machines could develop the capacity to feel and experience emotio
and exhibit characteristics that we categorize as belonging strictly
the human race.

D: *When you go to these places, do you gather information by just watching everything?*

J: Yeah. And basically by going there. By standing it measuring the temperature, and seeing how dense the girdle is around this planet. And how cold or warm it is underneath, if there is population, or if not. And if there is population, it's like taking a photograph through your eyes. Just looking at them puts the information in to some degree. And they can get that out at the other end, and reproduce the data.

D: *What about the people, the beings that live on these planets? How do they react when they see you?*

J: Oh, we truly have to try to not be seen, because they're rather shocked when they see us.

D: *That's what I was thinking. You wouldn't look like them.*

J: Oh, not at all. They'd be horrified. We can only do that when they're... like in trance. Sometimes we have to do something to make them not aware that we're there. Sort of blocking out the conscious part of the conscious mind then we take the photograph and go away. And they relax and are normal again. They don't remember it.

D: *Maybe that's why you have to have that little human part, because a machine wouldn't know how to do these things.*

J: No, it wouldn't be sensitive to realize the other person is concentrating, or it's asleep, or it's day dreaming, or whatever they are.

D: *And if it were seen, it wouldn't know how to hide.*

J: No. It wouldn't understand the shock at all that it's causing. Whereas we can know, we can see that there are different kinds of people, and they react. And we prefer the machine people. I mean, I'd rather be with a machine person in love rather than somebody else. It's very difficult.

This description of the purpose and the duties of the robots unded very similar to the little gray beings seen in UFO cases. In e Custodians I was told that these little beings had been created to rform tasks and to enter physical environments that would be harmful the beings on the larger craft. When I suggested that they sounded e robots, I was told that they were not mechanical, but biologically :ated beings that were used strictly as workers. They also seem to ve a certain amount of intelligence, in that they can do the tasks, t do not seem to be emotionally involved. It is this cold attitude it most frightens those humans who have had contact with them. I ' to explain in my therapy that this is because they are not a fully nking, functioning being. Could they be a more updated version of : mechanical robot workers? Could the scientific technology have

progressed from machinery to bionics over time? Could they also
activated by a spark given to them by their creators? I am not sayi
these were created by the same race of beings, but their purposes ;
remarkably similar.

D: *Well, do you feel happiness or joy with your work? Do you*
   have those kind of emotions?
J: I have a sense of duty. I don't really have joy with the wor
   I'm doing it because I'm supposed to be doing it.
D: *You're programmed to do it.*
J: Yes, and it's what I'm supposed to be doing, so that's right.
   feels right to be doing it, but it's not something that gives n
   anything in particular.
D: *So you can't say you like your work. You're just doing it.*
J: Yeah. I also don't dislike it. You just do it.
D: *So what do you do whenever you finish exploring the plane*
J: We come back, and they take the information out. And
   sometimes they give us a bit of a rest, and oil us and stuff.
   Sometimes we immediately go back to somewhere else.
D: *Because you don't get tired like they would.*
J: No, we just get emotionally tired inside, if that's what you c
   it. But they don't know anyway.
D: *You don't have any way to communicate and tell them abou*
   your feelings.
J: Yes, we can, but we're not supposed to. They make fun if
   we'd say we want such and such. They laugh, because we a
   only about ten percent human. You know if you want to sa
   that, and we're not supposed to. They don't realize what
   they've given us. It's a much broader thing, a gift or whatev
   than they realize.
D: *I wonder if they knew if it would make a difference.*
J: No, because they would want to control us. They have us or
   because of what they want.
D: *I thought it might make a difference if they really knew.*
J: The only thing I could think that could happen is, instead
   of poking around in our lower parts of the body, they'd simp
   fill it up with some sort of impenetrable metallic thing. An
   they would laugh again, and say, "Look, now it's in there.
   That's what you've got. You've got nothing."
D: *I thought because they can't really know what you're feelin*
   that might be one of the reasons they can't do anything abo
   it.
J: No, they don't want to. Whenever we say something, whatev
   it's about, if it's not to do with the task, they just laugh.

D: *You said if one wears out they have to create another one. What happens to that human part? Is that transferred to the new one?*

J: I think so. It's going into the other one.

D: *So they don't have to do it again?*

J: No, everybody only gives a donation once.

D: *And then whenever the body rusts out or wears out....*

J: Yeah, or whatever it is. They just put it into the next one.

D: *How can they do that? How would it be transferred from one machine to another?*

J: (Whisper) How can they do that? (Pause) I think it's the same thing like in the ceremony. They let it be sucked in by the other one, by the new one. The new one seems to suck it in from the old one.

D: *Then the other one is probably used for parts, I guess.*

J: Yeah, or they just put it into the fire and make something new out of it.

D: *So this part that is like a soul....*

J: It's sort of recycled.

D: *Just going from machine to machine. So they only have to do it one time. But you don't really have any choice about the whole thing, do you? (No) Well, let's leave that scene, and move ahead to an important day, when something is happening that you consider to be important as this machine. What are you doing now? What do you see?*

J: I'm with somebody. With a machine person. And we really want to live in a different way. And she's actually more how shall I say it? she longs for this. She opened my eyes a little bit. She seems to have more soul or something. And she says it's not enough to be just like a machine. We also have this other bit. And we want to do other things as well, not just going into the heat and exploring. We want to have you might call it a private life.

D: *How do you know it's a "she"? Do you feel yourself as having a sex or a gender?*

J: I feel like I'm a "he", because I got the soul from a he. And she's from a different area. And she's a she. I know that. I can feel that. I can always feel when I'm working if I'm surrounded by a he or by a she.

D: *She came from a different area?*

J: Yes. And she's doing tasks like me, but maybe she has a bit too much soul or something. She's thought a lot about this, and she wants us to escape or to do something else.

D: *What do you feel about it? Is there a way to escape?*

J: I don't know. I trust her. I think there might be if she says

D: *Is there anywhere you could go?*

J: She thinks there are many places we could go, because they wouldn't know if we went somewhere different. Like after the task, before they give us the new information. If we planned out where we could go, they wouldn't know.

D: *In the capsule, you mean?*

J: No, just on the planet. If we just walk out to the task, but instead we walk somewhere else. And we just don't come back.

D: *Wouldn't they be able to track you some way?*

J: I don't know. Perhaps they would.

D: *Is that her plan?*

J: It's just a hope. It's just a little, little hope. It's not a really thought through plan, because that's all she can come up wi

D: *But it's an idea.*

J: It's a nice idea, and it would be worth trying, wouldn't it?

D: *Yes. Is that what she wants to do after the next task?*

J: She doesn't want to do it on her own, because obviously th reason why we want to do it is because of that private bit. sort of soul exchange. And we don't have very much of it, b we think it might grow when we use it more or something.

D: *Yes, and if you were by yourself you would be lonely. You can feel loneliness. Is that right?*

J: Yeah, we can feel that. And we have longings for indescribal closeness, which we have never experienced.

D: *You have longings for others of your own kind, so you could just go off by yourself and exist alone. (No, no.) What do y decide to do?*

J: I think it sounds all very alluring what she says. And I thin it would be worth trying. And that gives her courage to say "Perhaps we should try it soon." Rather sooner than later. So we decide to find ways to go to these distant places whe there is a grotto or something. In the mountains there's a litt hole, and perhaps we could hide there for awhile. Because we need is oil or something like that, so it's not a problem.

D: *So you think you could do it and they wouldn't know the difference. (Yes) What do you decide to do?*

J: We decide to do that after the next task. When the next opportunity arises.

D: *Tell me what's happening.*

J: She has come back, and she's in a different capsule, but she on the same mission. Which is strange, because she hasn't been before. I don't know how that worked out. Maybe sh swapped with somebody or something. But she was on the same mission. And yes, we do escape. We do escape. We just walk away to this place. But of course we haven't realized that they have more means than one to find us. And of course they find us the next morning. They find us very quickly. They realize the next day that we've gone. And they just use their machinery to find us where we are located. They find us quicker than I thought.

D: *Then what happened?*

J: First of all they gave us nasty laughter to make fun of us. And then they sort of poke our lower parts of the body. They poke it, and make funny jokes about our nonexistent sex, and how silly we think we are. How clever we think we are, and really that they are the masters. One comes in who is really upset, like he's personally offended, because of what we've allowed ourselves to do. (Sigh) And that's the one who gives the order that we get smashed in the lower part of the body. We get smashed while we have the soul still in us.

D: *They don't realize it's nothing to do with sex. It's just companionship, isn't it?*

J: They think that's what we think we want to do. And they make fun of it.

D: *So that's what he has decreed, that you will be smashed?*

J: Yeah, we will be smashed in that part of the body. "We will show you how ridiculous you are." And to both of us it would happen, like a humiliation and a punishment. And of course it is like a death penalty, isn't it? (Yes) Because it means we're going to be melted again. (Sadly) And what happens to the soul bit?

D: *Yes, that's what I was wondering. What happens?*

J: They do that to us, yes. We can sense the humiliation. Although we can't feel the body or anything, we can feel the humiliation.

D: *You can't really feel pain in a metal body.*

J: No, no. But we feel all the rest. And we feel the power they have, and basically that they can simply treat us like nothing. So they smash the body, and then throw us into the fire.

D: *With the soul still inside? They don't usually do that, do they?*

J: No, the soul must have been ... I don't know what they do with the soul.

D: *Let's see what happens after they threw you into the fire. Move to where it's over with. What happened to you, the real you?*

J: It's just circling. It's left the fire, and it's circling around. And it's able to communicate with the other soul as well, so that's quite nice. But then again our existence has not been possible in the way we wanted.

D: *What do you decide to do?*
J: We decide to float away, very far away.
D: *They can't catch you now, can they?*
J: No, they don't even notice us. They've actually completely forgotten about it.
D: *Normally they would have put you into another body.*
J: Yes, that's true. They'd thought about it too late or something, I don't know.
D: *Maybe they thought you were not the kind they wanted, so it would be better to get rid of you.*
J: That's a possibility, yeah. I don't know.
D: *But that's good. You escaped, didn't you?*
J: Actually, after all we did, yeah. That's true.
D: *You escaped in a different way than you thought. (Yeah) You don't have to live in that kind of existence any more. You can go anywhere you want.*
J: Yeah, that's true.

I then asked to speak to Johanna's subconscious. That is how I can get the answers and apply the therapy by speaking directly to the part that keeps the records of the personality, and it can be influenced to make positive changes. I have never been refused access, because it realizes that I have the person's welfare foremost in my work. I believe it knows my motives very clearly, and if I did not have the proper motives I would be denied access. It is always easy to tell when the subconscious is speaking, because it is objective and speaks about the client in the third person, treating them as a separate personality.

D: *Why did the subconscious show Johanna that unusual lifetime?*
J: To show her that the humiliation part is still very strong with her. She has a fear of being humiliated. There's a strong link.

In this present life one of the problems Johanna has is that she easily feels humiliation, even when it is not intentional. This has kept her from developing her full potential, and pursuing many goals.

D: *That body was not human. Has Johanna had many lives in a fully human body?*
J: Yes, she has had many other human lives as well. But that one is still influencing her. It was also to help her understand why her need for freedom is so strong. To be independent.
D: *But I thought it was strange that she was created in that unusual way, and given a portion of a soul.*
J: That's not surprising, because before that she had a life where she didn't appreciate the soul part of herself enough. People

say, "Oh, it's just your soul. Oh, that emotional little bit is not important." And she was shown what it is like when the soul cannot find expression. Or how restricting it is to only have ten or twenty percent, instead of the full amount.

D: *To me that's confusing. Can you answer? She thought that the person who created her gave her part of its soul. Is that what happened?*

J: Yes. But none the less she was in herself in the machine life. She was a complete well, as complete can be person. So she had to experience the restrictedness of having more machine life than soul life.

D: *But whenever the other person gave her part of his soul, it would be his, wouldn't it, instead of hers?*

J: It was a part of her, wasn't it? I mean, she was both.

D: *That just occurred to me. You mean she was also the person who gave her life?*

J: Yes, but she didn't know that at all. Because otherwise she wouldn't have had this experience, if they had told her that. If she'd been told we're more than one person. We have soul bits all over the place.

D: *Because essentially they couldn't create life. They were just able to transfer a part of themselves?*

J: That's right.

D: *So she would actually know in the machine she was lesser. (Yes) So part of her went on with the man and it has made karma also. (Yes) And the other part exists in Johanna now.*

J: And also it will explain to her why in this life she takes her soul more important than anything.

D: *At this point she realizes the value of it, because there was a time when she had just a very small part of it. (Right) She had some more questions. Does this also explain the problems in her physical female organs?*

Before the session she discussed problems with irregular menstrual periods with lots of cramping.

J: Yes, it does. The fear of being humiliated by a male person, because the one who decided about the smashing was a man. And the whole feeling was about humiliation as well. Also the probing and the poking they did with the tools when they laughed about them was part of her soul memory as well. So it was not feeling safe in a female role.

D: *So she didn't want to be a full female and have children.*

She has never married and never wanted children. She presen
has a platonic relationship with a man.

J: Yes. The danger of being smashed like that by somebody w
    is more powerful seems a very real danger.

I continued to ask the questions she had requested, and ma
of the present day problems stemmed from being easily humiliate
even though unintentionally. The major part of my therapy work
putting the pieces together and persuading the subconscious to relea
the physical discomforts, because they are not needed in the prese
lifetime. They have their roots in another lifetime. Once the connecti
is made and understanding comes, then the problem is released a
physical and emotional benefits are immediate. The symptoms ha
served their purpose of getting the conscious mind's attention, so th
are no longer needed. Many cases of female problems and infertili
etc. can be traced back to events from past lives. However, this w
the strangest explanation I have ever had for these type of physic
problems.

The therapy connection was important, but to me the mo
interesting aspect of this case was that a soul can inhabit a machi
body. Also that the soul could divide itself, and a splinter could ve
off and become another personality learning different lessons than t
host or original soul. The two would have never even been awa
of each other, or that there was a separation. So how many piec
of us have splintered and become soul bits without our conscio
awareness? We will probably never know, and it goes back to the id
that we are essentially all part of everyone, and all is one.

***

In my early days of doing regression therapy I had a case th
bears some similarity, and at the time I had no idea what I had foun
It did not fit the mold that I was trying to put my cases into at th
time, mostly linear reincarnation. A woman went to a past life whe
she was a highly trained priestess who was dedicated to working at
temple and as an advisor to the people. She was to remain celiba
closed up in the temple, and led a very lonely life.

Until one day a stranger sailed into the harbor, and they ended
falling in love. She was faced with a difficult choice: to leave with h
lover, or stay with her sworn vows in the temple. She finally decid
to sail away, and that was where the confusion (on my part) came i
She was reporting the scene from two separate viewpoints: as she w
happily sailing away, and as she was standing on the shore bitter
sobbing because a piece of her was leaving. Apparently the part

r that was on the ship was not aware of the part that was left behind. most as though the decision had split her into two people. I could ver understand this concept.

Yet it also goes along with the concept reported in Chapter 11 out parallel lives and dimensions. When we make a decision the ergy of the one we did not choose has to go somewhere. And so splits off and becomes another "you" living out the other decision. aybe in this case the priestess was aware of what happened because her training, where normally she should not have known anything d occurred. She would have watched the man sail away, and felt rrow for herself in that way, not because a piece of herself was aving. If nothing else, these cases have taught me to think and plore complicated concepts with an open mind.

CHAPTER SIXTEEN
THE GOD SOURCE?

I was speaking at a UFO Conference in Berkeley in Novemb[
2000, and staying at the nearby Y.M.C.A. This session was one
several that I conducted in my room at the Y. Shirley was a woman
her forties that had wanted a session for a long time, but every tim
came to this part of California there was a long waiting list. Final
we had a chance to get together. There was heavy construction goi
on across the street where a five story building was being complete
All of my sessions at this location had the same problem. The noi
disturbed me, but didn't seem to bother the subject once they we
under. They are oblivious to any disturbance when they are in th
state of trance. Once in Memphis a tornado alert siren went off on t
of the building next to the motel I was in. It continued for a half ho
and was very noticeable on the tape, but the subject had no memo
of it at all.

Shirley went into the deep trance quickly, and I proceeded to ta
her into a past life to locate the answers to her problems. She regress
to a rural life where farmers were working in a field. She saw hers
in a male body, but she did not seem to be a participant, only a
observer. Often when this happens they are not from the area ai
might be traveling through, and have stopped to watch the scene.
these cases I can usually take them back to where they were traveli
from, or take them ahead to their destination. This did not work wi
Shirley. She was not involved in any of the scenes she went to. Ev
though they were filled with vivid detail, she was only an observer.

She said, "I recognize these places, but I'm not comfortab
there. I feel out of place, like I'm not who I am. Nothing really seer
familiar to me. It's like I'm struggling."

Since she felt out of place I asked her to move to where she f
comfortable, where she felt like she belonged. To go to a place th
was familiar.

She took me completely off guard with her quick and unexpect
answer, "The Sun!" I asked her to explain what she meant.

S: We can go into the Sun. That's where I feel comfortable an
   familiar.

D: *In the Sun?*

S: In the Sun. With the light. I'm a part of it. It's just one big light. And it's hot.

D: *Our Sun, or is it... something similar?*

S: It's the Sun.

D: *It is the Sun? (Yes) Well, what's it like to be a part of that?*

S: (Big breath) Normal! It feels home. I don't have a body. I do have consciousness. I'm a part of the whole thing, and not separate.

Since she was so positive and satisfied I decided to go along with I have had subjects describe some very strange experiences that ːre unexpected. The subconscious always takes them to whatever ːy are supposed to see, and it's usually for an important reason. It ll benefit the subject, even if I don't understand it.

D: *A part of the whole light? Well, what is it like to be in the Sun? Many people wonder about that.*

S: As you approach it, it's extremely bright and hot. But as you go into it, it is not hot anymore. Once you become it, it's just a ball of light. With consciousness.

D: *The Sun has consciousness too?*

S: Yes. It's a larger consciousness. It goes on and on forever.

D: *But aren't there many Suns in many places?*

S: Not like this. There's just this one.

D: *This is different than a star that is a Sun? Is that what you mean?*

S: Yes. It's pure energy.

D: *Because there are many Suns, aren't there, with many planets orbiting around them?*

S: I don't know. All I know is that I went towards this ball of light I recognized. As soon as I knew it was my home, and when I went into it I didn't have a form. I just had total consciousness and energy.

D: *You feel like that is your home? (Yes) And that's where you're comfortable? (Yes) Well, that's very good. Does it feel strange to not have a body?*

S: No. It feels normal.

D: *Had you been there a long time, or do you know?*

S: I don't know, but I recognize it. It's who I am.

D: *Are there other beings, other entities with you?*

S: Yes, but once you're there you're not different. It's like you are the entity. As I pull out of the Sun, or pull out of this ball of energy and light, then I become different. And there are other entities. As they pull out they become separate. As they go into, it is just one.

D: *So that is a comfortable feeling to be all part of one thing? (Yes) And then you are able to pull back out again.*

S: Yes, if I wanted to, I could pull back out.

D: *Do you have a name for this place?*

S: I don't have a name for it.

D: *We like to put names and labels on things. But are you ther for a long time?*

It was difficult to think of questions for something so unfamili

S: I can be here for a long time. If I'm there it's not likely tha would want to go out again. But I can.

D: *But you can't always stay in one place, can you?*

S: I can. I don't know why I would go out, but sometimes we out.

I was trying to think how to move her, because this seemed to going nowhere. She could be content to stay there indefinitely.

D: *And you can go out and come back in again? (Yes) And wh you go out then you separate into different individual entitie (Yes) All right. Let's see where you go when you go out. T me what happens when you go out and become an individu entity.*

S: It's not comfortable. It's very upsetting. It's... that physica the feeling is unpleasant.

D: *When you leave the light, you mean you become physical a an entity?*

S: Physically as an entity. It's much more different. Not to be part of the whole thing is very, very disturbing. And it's ve cold. And it's very heavy. And it's very alone.

D: *You are separate then, and in the other you are part of everything? Would that be right?*

S: You're not a part of it. You're just it.

D: *You are it.*

S: It's not like you are a whole bunch of, going into one. You j are it. There's no separation. No difference. There's only a difference when you go out. That's when you pull apart, a you become "us" and "them" or many, or... a boundary.

D: *What do you mean by a boundary?*

S: Because you have a form, so there's a boundary around you And because of that form, it keeps you from being separatele

D: *I'm trying to understand. Why would you take a form then*

S: I think it's to serve who you choose. I think it's some form of serving and sacrifice that we go... to help....

D: *To help who?*

S: To help the others who may not know how to get back.

D: *Does everyone come from the same place?*

S: I think so. If I'm approaching it, I can answer better. If I'm going into it, yes. But when I come out of it, and am outside of it, there's too much difference to know everything.

D: *You mean you lose some of the information or knowledge?*

S: Yes, I think so. It's like when I'm approaching, I know, I'm sure, I am. But when I go away from it, I lose some of that. And yet I choose to go away.

D: *But do you think all of these individual entities come from the one place?*

S: It's the only place I know.

D: *The only one you're familiar with. (Yes) I was curious if there were other places like that.*

S: My sense is that there is only one place.

D: *And then people go out and come back as individuals. (Yes) Do they come back in cycles, at intervals or what?*

S: Yes. It's not all at once. It's random, when something's completed, or when you need to become energized.

D: *You mean you have to go back periodically to be energized? (Yes) If you don't, what would happen?*

S: It's not that we wouldn't. We have to go home. You go back. You get energized so that you can continue to go out. And you never will not go back.

D: *So you go back and forth then.*

S: Yes. Sometimes you'll stay longer. And sometimes you'll stay less.

D: *But it's always a place you will eventually go back to? (Yes) Well, where do you go when you're journeying away from this light?*

S: I guess I go to planets. Earth, other places too.

D: *Can you describe what you mean? What other kind of places would you go to?*

The construction, riveting, and noise of heavy equipment across the street was becoming very loud and was distracting me. It however did not seem to bother Shirley at all.

S: Places that are different. That have not as much color as Earth. Have different forms not of the material.

D: *What do you mean?*

S: No vegetation. Nothing with color. No flowers, no birds. Drab. Red colors. Gross red colors. Mounds, clays.

D: *Do they have physical surroundings, like mountains or dirt anything?*

S: There are mountains, but they're different there. They're pointy, and very lined and sharp.

D: *How do you know where to go when you go out to these different places?*

S: When I move there's something in me that... I'm sent. I'm se to help the host.

D: *How do you know where you have to go?*

S: The consciousness sends us. We just know.

D: *You mean, the big light that you left? The consciousness? that what you call it? (Yes) It sends you, tells you where to go?*

S: Yes. It's more like mental telepathy. It's like I just know. I' a part of the whole thing, so I know where to go. And wher leave it I become more of an individual light being.

D: *You're separate at that time. And you seem to instinctively know where you're supposed to go? (Yes) And then when y get there, what happens?*

S: I'll become, I think, a form like the forms wherever I go. A I help as I am needed.

D: *So the forms can be different any place you go. (Yes) How c you become these forms?*

S: I think I just think them.

D: *I guess I'm thinking of souls and spirits and how they woul enter a form. Is it different than that?*

S: I think the form, and I'm there.

D: *I'm thinking in Earth terms.*

S: You mean like if I'm born. (Yes) I don't see myself being born. On Earth... let me think, if I went to Earth.

D: *Because Earth is what I'm familiar with. I know that others are probably different.*

S: I was heading somewhere else.

D: *We can go back to that in a minute. I wanted to clarify this part, if possible. If you were coming to Earth, how would it happen?*

S: I think coming to Earth, I sometimes can be born. But I don have to be.

D: *I'm thinking of the soul or spirit, whatever you call yourself entering a baby as it is born.*

S: I don't have to do it that way.

D: *How would you do it if you did it a different way?*

S: I would just go into something.

D: *But wouldn't there already be a spirit inside?*

S: Not if I went in. Not when I would go in. But very seldom, on Earth, do we do that.

D: *Because I've been told one is assigned to each form?*

S: Sometimes you vacate. Sometimes a soul   it's an agreement sometimes they leave. And I can come in.

This sounded somewhat like a "walk in". These are described in *etween Death and Life.* Normally another soul trades places with the ul currently occupying the body if that soul has taken on more than can handle. It is an acceptable alternative to suicide.

D: *Do you call yourself a soul or a spirit?*

S: I am not a spirit. I'm a soul.

D: *How would you define yourself, as a soul? I know sometimes the language is not sufficient.*

S: Yes, because I don't use language. Think. You just think. It's consciousness. And I'm consciousness, things can happen very fast.

D: *So would you consider yourself a soul as a piece of consciousness?*

S: I am consciousness.

D: *You are consciousness, but you're also an individual.*

S: On Earth, on other places, but when I go home I'm just the one.

D: *When you come to Earth you enter a form when it's being born as a baby?*

S: When we go to Earth, and I go into a baby, I don't go into just any baby. I go in where I'm needed. I can see a soul in the baby that I go to. And I think I join that soul.

D: *So it's different than the other souls or spirits do? Is that what you mean? (Yes) Where they are assigned to one, you do it in a different way?*

S: I think so, because I don't see me being born. I see me making a choice. And it's an agreement.

D: *With the soul that's already there?*

S: Yes. Such a situation maybe.

D: *And you can do this at any time during the life of the form?*

S: I do it and stay with it the whole time. And then I leave. But I can do it in any stage.

D: *That's what I meant. It doesn't have to be a baby? You can enter it at any stage? (Yes) As long as it's in agreement with the soul that's already there? (Yes) And the consciousness is the one that instinctively tells you where you're supposed to go next? (Yes) And you said when you go to other places, other planets or other realms, it's done differently?*

S: I think I go in as an adult form. I see the form and I just becor
it. But there's already a form.

D: *So there are no smaller versions of it, like babies. They're (*
mature, adult forms?

S: When I go in at that stage. At least in this place.

D: *I keep thinking of the physical, but it may not be that way.*

S: It's a physical entry. When I say I'm an individual when I
leave the mass of energy consciousness, I am a form of
something outside of that energy consciousness. I may not I
a form as what yet is going to happen. So I still am energy
consciousness, but I have a form that's undescribable.

D: *And you have a consciousness, a personality that thinks, do,*
you?

S: I am told, yes, as consciousness.

D: *So in that way you do have an individuality, even though*
you're energy. Is that what you mean?

S: Yes. And I am of service.

D: *These places you go where you think a body, is that how the*
other entities at that place create bodies also? (Yes)

Now in addition to the construction noises some kids started
pep rally on the street below with shouting, singing, and drummir
because we were in the vicinity of several schools. Again it did n
seem to bother Shirley.

D: *I'm asking so many questions because I'm trying to understa,*
difficult concepts. So in those places people or entities don
have to go through a growth process. They just create the for
they want to be in by thinking it. Is that correct? (Yes) So
there are many other ways of doing things besides what we
know on Earth. (Yes) That's why it's a little hard for me to
comprehend. But if you brought the body into existence by
thinking it, then it wouldn't die, would it?

S: I never die. The body of whoever I go to will die, and then \
separate. And their soul goes their own way. And I go bacl

D: *So every time you do this you're always with another soul i,*
the body?

S: Yes, I think so.

D: *You never are in the body by yourself. That sounds differen*
It's not the way we normally think of spirits and souls.

S: I am consciousness.

D: *But you mean there is another soul in these bodies, the*
physical form, even when you think it into existence? (Yes)
And then you combine with that.

S: I don't combine.

D: *How do you do it? Join with it? That would be combining.*

S: I don't become one with it. I serve it. And then I go home.

D: *Doesn't that make you more like an observer? I'm probably not using the right terminology.*

S: I'm not an observer.

D: *You said you serve the soul, but you're a consciousness. Can you help me understand it?*

S: This person who is lying here is having a hard time understanding this too.

D: *Just let the information flow through, and we can sort it out later. This way we can both understand it. You said you're not the observer. If you serve the soul that is in the body, you are not the soul that is having the experience.*

S: It may be that I join the soul, and that I am pure consciousness. I have a soul, but I am not my soul. I am now pure consciousness. An energy. I have been there long enough that that's my home. I help planets. I go to certain places that I'm needed, and I help the beings on the planet. And when I go into them it's where I'm needed at the time I'm needed. When I go into the soul, a baby, my consciousness predominates. I override that consciousness until I'm not needed.

D: *Can this happen before the body actually dies, that you're not needed?*

S: Yes. But usually not.

D: *Well, if there is another soul assigned to that body, and you're more or less helping that soul, does that mean you do not create karma for yourself?*

S: I can create karma. I don't have to. But sometimes I can forget too much and can create karma. And then I lose track somewhat of my home, until I remember. Those are the times I spend longer times away. Then I can be born in a different way. But when I remember, I go home. I never, never forget. But sometimes if I have a buildup of some serious karma, I have to work it out before I will remember.

D: *At that time are you the predominant soul in the body, instead of the helper? (Yes) You can switch back and forth? (Yes) You can help the soul or if you create karma then you become the soul that has to experience it. Does that make sense? (Yes) I guess we always think of possession, but it doesn't sound like that.*

S: No. No, it's always by choice, and it's only when I'm needed.

D: *But sometimes you do get trapped, so to speak, and have to be the predominant one in the body till you work it out. (Yes) And then you can either go home, or switch back and forth again?*

S: I go home. It's not ... sometimes I will forget.

D: *Then the majority of what you have done has been as a help* *rather than living a physical life. Is that what you mean? (Ye* *So even on other planets, other dimensions, you have tried* *help. (Yes) But at this time when you're in the body of Shirl* *are you the helper or are you the predominant soul?*

S: I'm going in to see. (Pause) I am the predominant soul.

D: *In this lifetime then. (Yes) Is this why in her conscious mi* *she has felt disconnected in this life? (Yes) She keeps sayir* *she wants to go home. She knows she doesn't belong here.* *(Yes) Because she is more connected with you than the averag* *person? (Yes) That makes sense, doesn't it?*

This bears a resemblance to the other cases in this book whe people longed to go home, yet did not know where "home" was. most of these cases when they returned home it was a strange physic planet. This case with Shirley seemed to indicate an even deep longing for home that went beyond the physical or original host plane These other subjects often felt they were a part of the place the found themselves in, and they also had a great hesitancy to leave. Y Shirley's sounded even more basic and essential. Maybe a memo from a part of our primordial mind that existed before the creation physical worlds, that has been a part of us forever.

D: *Why did you get trapped, so to speak, in this body, and becom* *the predominant soul? (Pause) You created karma, I guess* *or you wouldn't be the predominant soul, would you?*

S: Ego. I misused some power.

D: *Tell me about it.*

S: I created false things.

D: *You said you can think things into existence?*

S: No. When I come from my center I can think into existence But I can't think things into existence.

D: *But you said, at another time, you created false things?*

S: I experimented on animals. I made them into different form

D: *Was this in a lifetime you were living at that time? (Yes) W* *did you do that?*

S: Because I wanted to create something. And I had the ability

D: *As a physical entity you were doing these things? (Yes) I* *guess I'm thinking of a scientist or something? (Yes) Did y* *just do it out of curiosity or what?*

S: It was to see if it worked.

D: *Were others doing the same thing?*

S: Yes. But I was one of the heads. It was morally not right.

D: *But you said, creating false things.*

S: Humans and animals. Experimenting on different animals. Creating with body parts. Surgically and genetically.

D: *Would these strange creatures live? (Yes) This place where you were doing this, did it have a name?*

S: Atlantis. It wasn't right in, it was somewhere near there.

D: *Just out of curiosity to see if it could be done.*

S: Yes, it came from ego.

D: *What did you do with these creatures after they were created?*

S: Let them go.

D: *Could they recreate themselves? Could they reproduce?*

S: Some could. Some couldn't. I had come in to another soul. The soul was a scientist. The soul had ego. A lot of ego. And I got lost in the ego.

D: *You got too involved then, and so it became your karma. (Yes) But weren't people doing many things that weren't right in those days, because they were just curious?*

S: Yes. But because I got caught up into ego, my conscious ego was used wrongly. I had power.

D: *And then you were, more or less, caught up in the cycle of having to return and repay the karma. (Yes) And that caused you to be trapped into the physical on the human Earth plane? (Yes) So have you been repaying these things?*

S: I have repaid.

D: *That's a big debt, but do you think you have almost completed that karma? (Yes) So maybe it won't be much longer, and you can go home. But at this point you have to stay with Shirley, with this body? (Yes) This means that Shirley has a great deal of untapped knowledge and information she doesn't even know is there. (Yes) If she wants to use it in this lifetime, would she be able to tap into that power and that information?*

S: Somewhat.

I then proceeded to ask this part of her (I didn't know if I was ~~sp~~eaking to her subconscious or not) the questions she had written ~~do~~wn before the session. This part was so closely aligned with her, it ~~w~~as able to give her important advice to help her understand events in ~~he~~r life. One thing in particular she had asked about was her deep and ~~clo~~se affinity to animals. She can mentally communicate with them. I ~~su~~spected the answer would be tied in with the life in Atlantis where ~~sh~~e had abused animals to a great degree. I was correct, because it ~~sa~~id that she had now evolved to the point she had become one with ~~an~~imals in a positive way.

Shirley had had a strange experience a few years ago that she ~~wa~~nted me to ask about. During a rebirthing session she saw herself

living a life as an extraterrestrial in a reptilian body. Sometimes wh
relaxing during the rebirthing process the subject will have drama
experiences, often going beyond reliving the birth experience, a
bringing in past life scenes. She wanted to find more information abc
this.

> D: *Once when she was doing rebirthing she went to an experien*
>   *where she was in a reptilian form. She wanted to know, is th*
>   *a true memory, or what was happening?*
> S: Yes, that was a true memory. It wasn't who she was. It wa
>   who I am. And actually I am not separate from her, but I a

I was confused again. This whole session was presenti
information I had never encountered before.

> D: *You said you're the predominant soul now as Shirley. (Yes)*
>   *Have you been together always, as souls? (Yes) Every lifetin*
>   *you have lived, she has lived? (Yes) And sometimes she wa*
>   *the predominant one, and sometimes you are?*
> S: She's been the predominant soul, but I am starting to be the
>   predominant soul.
> D: *But you've always been together, and you've been helping h*
>   *the whole time. (Yes) But that was a lifetime she lived*
>   *somewhere else in a reptilian form?*
> S: That was a memory that I had. Since I have been in her soul a
>   a part of her, and yet not separate, yet not the same   there a
>   no words I came with my memory. And when she was rebirthe
>   she saw herself as that.
> D: *That's the hard part, trying to separate these two things,*
>   *because we are so used to thinking in our physical terms.*
> S: Those are the boundaries.

After asking more questions pertaining to Shirley's physic:
condition I asked that unusual part of her to recede, and brought h
back to full consciousness. Needless to say I was confused by this nev
information, and knew it would take time to digest. I also wondere
how difficult it would be for Shirley to comprehend after she had
chance to listen to the tape.

Since this session I had a similar experience with a man in 200I
He also regressed to a bright light that was so comfortable he wanted t
stay there. He expressed the feeling of great loneliness and separatio
when he had to leave it and individualize in order to journey on thes
soul explorations.

What did we contact? The Source? Universal consciousness
Fragmented soul part? God source?

The more questions we ask the more questions are brought . It seems to be never ending. We will probably never be able to derstand it all, and there will always be more complicated concepts t beyond our reach. Yet for me and my insatiable curiosity that's the citement of the search and the adventure of probing the unknown. I ill continue the journey.

ABOUT THE AUTHOR

Dolores Cannon is recognized as a pioneer in the field of past-life
ression. She is a hypnotherapist who specializes in the recovery
l cataloging of "Lost Knowledge". Her roots in hypnosis go back
the 1960s, and she has been specializing in past-life therapy since
: 1970s. She has developed her own technique and has founded the
antum Healing Hypnosis Academy. Traveling all over the world
ching this unique healing method she has trained over 4000 students
ce 2002. This is her main focus now. However, she has been active
UFO and Crop Circle investigations for over 27 years since Lou
rish got her involved in the subject. She has been involved with the
ark Mountain UFO Conference since its inception 27 years ago by
u Farish and Ed Mazur. After Lou died she inherited the conference
l has been putting it on the past two years.

Dolores has written 17 books about her research in hypnosis and
O cases. These books are translated into over 20 languages. She
nded her publishing company, Ozark Mountain Publishing, 22 years
o in 1992, and currently has over 50 authors that she publishes. In
dition to the UFO conference she also puts on another conference,
: Transformation Conference, which is a showcase for her authors.

She has appeared on numerous TV shows and documentaries
all the major networks, and also throughout the world. She has

spoken on over 1000 radio shows, including Art Bell's Dreamla
George Noory's Coast to Coast, and Shirley MacLaine, plus speak
at innumerable conferences worldwide. In addition she has had
own weekly radio show, the Metaphysical Hour, on BBS Radio
nine years. She has received numerous awards from organizati
and hypnosis schools, including Outstanding Service and Lifeti
Achievement awards. She was the first foreigner to receive
Orpheus Award in Bulgaria for the highest achievement in the field
psychic research.

Dolores made her transition on October 18, 2014. She touc
many and will be deeply missed.

Other Books By Ozark Mountain Publishing, Inc.

Other Books By Ozark Mountain Publishing, Inc.

Guy Needler
Avoiding Karma
Beyond the Source – Book 1, Book 2
The Anne Dialogues
The History of God
The Origin Speaks
James Nussbaumer
The Master of Everything
Mastering Your own Spiritual Freedom
Sherry O'Brian
Peaks and Valleys
Riet Okken
The Liberating Power of Emotions
John Panella
The Gnostic Papers
Victor Parachin
Sit a Bit
Nikki Pattillo
A Spiritual Evolution
Children of the Stars
Rev. Grant H. Pealer
A Funny Thing Happened on the
    Way to Heaven
Worlds Beyond Death
Karen Peebles
The Other Side of Suicide
Victoria Pendragon
Born Healers
Feng Shui from the Inside, Out
Sleep Magic
Michael Perlin
Fantastic Adventures in Metaphysics
Walter Pullen
Evolution of the Spirit
Christine Ramos, RN
A Journey Into Being
Debra Rayburn
Let's Get Natural With Herbs
Charmian Redwood
A New Earth Rising
Coming Home to Lemuria
David Rivinus
Always Dreaming

Briceida Ryan
The Ultimate Dictionary of Dream
    Language
M. Don Schorn
Elder Gods of Antiquity
Legacy of the Elder Gods
Gardens of the Elder Gods
Reincarnation...Stepping Stones o
Garnet Schulhauser
Dance of Heavenly Bliss
Dancing Forever with Spirit
Dancing on a Stamp
Annie Stillwater Gray
Education of a Guardian Angel
The Dawn Book
Work of a Guardian Angel
Blair Styra
Don't Change the Channel
Natalie Sudman
Application of Impossible Things
L.R. Sumpter
We Are the Creators
Dee Wallace/Jarrad Hewett
The Big E
Dee Wallace
Conscious Creation
James Wawro
Ask Your Inner Voice
Janie Wells
Embracing the Human Journey
Payment for Passage
Dennis Wheatley/ Maria Wheat
The Essential Dowsing Guide
Jacquelyn Wiersma
The Zodiac Recipe
Sherry Wilde
The Forgotten Promise
Stuart Wilson & Joanna Prentis
Atlantis and the New Consciousne
Beyond Limitations
The Essenes -Children of the Ligh
The Magdalene Version
Power of the Magdalene
Robert Winterhalter
The Healing Christ

For more information about any of the above titles, soon to be released titles,
or other items in our catalog, write, phone or visit our website:
PO Box 754, Huntsville, AR 72740
479-738-2348/800-935-0045
www.ozarkmt.com